CONTENTS

Let us now examine the following kind of language-game: when A gives an order B has to write down series of signs according to a certain formation rule.

The first of these series is meant to be that of the natural numbers in decimal notation.—How does he get to understand this notation?—First of all series of numbers will be written down for him and he will be required to copy them. . . . And here already there is a normal and an abnormal learner's reaction.—At first perhaps we guide his hand in writing out the series 0 to 9; but then the *possibility of getting him to understand* will depend on his going on to write it down independently . . . but not in the right order: he writes sometimes one sometimes another at random. And then communication stops at *that* point.—Or again, he makes "*mistakes*" in the order.—The difference between this and the first case will of course be one of frequency.—Or he makes a *systematic* mistake; for example, he copies every other number, or he copies the series 0, 1, 2, 3, 4, 5, . . . like this: 1, 0, 3, 2, 5, 4, . . . Here we shall almost be tempted to say that he has understood *wrong*.

Notice, however, that there is no sharp distinction between a random mistake and a systematic one. That is, between what you are inclined to call "random" and what "systematic."

Perhaps it is possible to wean him from the systematic mistake (as from a bad habit). Or perhaps one accepts his way of copying and tries to teach him ours as an offshoot, a variant of his.—And here too our pupil's capacity to learn may come to an end.

LUDWIG WITTGENSTEIN, *Philosophical Investigations* (§143)

It is the central commonplace of Renaissance literary theory that the purpose of poetry is to please and instruct. Criticism's stewardship of poetic pleasure is not my subject here, at least not directly; what I am concerned with is teaching, toward which our attitude is often confused. Modern critics are intellectual citizens of a long, post-Romantic epoch in which didactic poetry has enjoyed a diminished reputation. We have come to favor other purposes for poems, other ways of reading them, and where a didactic design is palpable we do not feel bound to its lesson—we may indeed feel more obliged to upend it. At the same time, we still speak reflexively not only of what we learn from the writing of the period, but about what this or that book "teaches" us, and versions of the phrase "the education of the reader" are in wide currency. As a matter of critical idiom it is possible to move easily and without much self-consciousness between talking about what a book means and what it has to teach, as though they were effectively the same thing. When this happens, the notion of teaching becomes as broad as meaning itself.

Among the consequences of this confusion is that we can lose sight of just how formidably complicated the relation once was between the enterprises of fiction-making and instruction. For us moderns, poetry and school are on the most familiar, if not the easiest, terms. In the English-speaking world we have had almost five hundred years to get used to the idea that what we now call literature should have a place at the center of the curriculum. In the later decades of the sixteenth century, however, that place was

A note on texts: I have made an effort to cite the most widely available editions, which means that quotations from earlier periods are sometimes modernized, sometimes not. In the case of unedited texts, and also of works by Edmund Spenser (whose poetry is customarily printed in original spelling), I have tacitly modernized u to v, v to u, and i to j where appropriate.

new, and it was consolidated in the midst of what has been described as an educational revolution—when schools were being founded at an unprecedented rate, and Elizabeth's government was taking an unprecedented interest in what was taught there, and how. The culture of teaching that was English humanism moved poetry and pedagogy to new prominence in intellectual life and pressed them closer together than ever before. Any poet of the age knew that he should be writing to teach: Horace, and Sir Philip Sidney, said as much. But the question of *how* to teach had a new complexion. Should that poet, trained at St. Paul's or Winchester or Merchant Taylors' and perhaps at one of the universities too, teach the way he was taught? Should he write for the reader educated in the new humanist schools; should the design of his work anticipate and flatter that reader's training? Where would such choices place him among his countrymen, at a moment when this intellectual and pedagogical program had an increasingly complicated place in national life?

Questions about how to make good the obligation to instruct are fundamental to the literature of the period, and any number of books could be written on the subject, probing the didactic accommodations and evasions of lyric poetry, or the drama, or epic. The present study offers a framework for thinking about literary didacticism across all these cases: it asks what such a forceful "culture of teaching"—I borrow the phrase from Rebecca Bushnell—might mean to a teaching poem, and it aims to clarify what counted as teaching for the humanists, and as learning.[1] But it assays this project by way of a handful of works from a dissident and defiantly extracurricular genre, the romances written by John Lyly (*Euphues*), Philip Sidney (*Arcadia*), and Edmund Spenser (*The Faerie Queene*). No fictions of the time were more preoccupied with teaching. The men who wrote them were all trained in the humanist grammar schools, trained there to read poems, even to write them. Taking up this particular literary kind provided them with a uniquely powerful language and laboratory for thinking about what Spenser called the fashioning of a gentleman.[2]

Yet for all that they are not didactic poets—notwithstanding their profound investment in pedagogy, and notwithstanding more than four hundred years of reading them as sage and serious teachers. Over the following

---

1. Bushnell's book is called *A Culture of Teaching: Early Modern Humanism in Theory and Practice*.

2. In his letter to Raleigh, Spenser writes that the purpose of his poem is "to fashion a gentleman or noble person in vertuous and gentle discipline" (*The Faerie Queene*, ed. Hamilton, 714). Subsequent citations to the poem are by Book, canto, and stanza number in parentheses in the text.

chapters I want to diagnose a counterimpulse, not a different kind of teaching but a skepticism or even despair about the very possibility of teaching. More than any generation before them school had defined for these writers the prestige and the good of poetry, and it had given them the tools to write, even taught them how to think. But they also had reasons, like many of their generation, to feel that they had been betrayed by that training and the promises it had made them. When they rejected the protocols of instruction bequeathed by their teachers, they turned against instruction itself as a literary project; because, for all that they were still fashioned in those schools, they also turned against themselves. Their skepticism and self-doubt smolder at the historical roots of English humanism.

——————

Two scenes of instruction will set the stage: scenes that both represent teaching (among their characters) and aspire to do it (in teaching the reader), a doubleness typical of much that follows.

> Faire Lady, then said that victorious knight,
> The things, that grievous were to doe, or beare,
> Them to renew, I wote, breeds no delight;
> Best musicke breeds delight in loathing eare:
> But th'only good, that growes of passed feare,
> Is to be wise, and ware of like agein.
> This daies ensample hath this lesson deare
> Deepe written in my heart with yron pen,
> That blisse may not abide in state of mortal men.[3] (1.8.44)

These words are spoken by Spenser's Prince Arthur two-thirds of the way through the first book of *The Faerie Queene*; they are a study in lesson-making, but they look back on a grim sequence of events. Redcrosse, the knight who set off with such millennial promise in canto i, has been seduced by the enchantress Duessa, and has come to grief in the dungeon of the giant Orgoglio. Rescuing him takes Arthur through chambers washed with the blood of guiltless babes, and when the prisoner is brought back up to daylight he is enfeebled and emaciated, his flesh "shronk up like withered flowres" (1.8.41). The governing tone is horror. Now, however, the giant is dead, Duessa is bound, and Redcrosse's destined bride Una is standing by:

---

3. I have discussed this episode and the structure of the Spenserian stanza in more detail in my article, "The Method of Spenser's Stanza."

it falls to Arthur to make sense of what has happened. The stanza offers its characteristic shape to the lesson he draws, a nine-line sermon that broods its way through the eccentric, double-take rhyme scheme to wind up at the wise hexameter, self-balanced on its medial caesura. "That blisse may not abide in state of mortall men." The long line is the nub of the lesson, and its sententious authority squares the teaching inside the poem with the address to its reader outside.

The way to the *sententia*, however, is troubled by an anxiety, a peculiarly pedagogical anxiety, that pervades the whole poem. What Arthur is trying to do is to take an experience of suffering and make it useful; what Spenser is trying to do (at least, one of the things he is trying to do) is to distill several stanzas of narration into a portable moral. Both might be said to be teaching, a teaching that here is something like an act of translation, or representation, or even generic modulation. The prince begins by parsing "grievous things" into those done and those suffered, a distinction reassuring in its conventionality. Next, a modest *concessio*, allowing that there is no pleasure to be had in recalling past pains. The way is being prepared for the assertion of a moral. But the difficulty of the task already begins to make itself felt in that word "renew," which is *topos* enough to call up another scene of bitter memory: Dido's hall at the beginning of *Aeneid* II, where Aeneas is pressed to tell the fall of Troy and hesitates for fear that he will only renew (*renovare*) his grief.[4] Such renewing is the first risk Arthur's pedagogy encounters, the risk that the act of instruction will merely repeat the pain it is meant to transmute.

"Best musicke breeds delight in loathing eare," says the prince, pressing on: for those who fear the pain of memory, music—perhaps the music of a comforting rhetoric, such as Una has supplied in the preceding stanzas— offers solace.[5] Now he raises an opposite risk, the temptation to displace painful experience altogether by a sweet senselessness. Fixed momentarily on the horns of this dilemma, he turns with the stanza's middle line toward an answer: the only good that can come of past suffering is to learn not to repeat it, to be "ware of like again." Here we come to momentary rest at a

---

4. Virgil, *Aeneid*, 2:3. "Renew" is Surrey's word in his translation: "O Quene, it is thy wil, / I shold renew a woe can not be told" (*The Aeneid of Henry Howard, Earl of Surrey*, ed. Ridley, 49).

5. A. C. Hamilton surveys the confusions prompted by the line in his edition, noting eighteenth-century emendations of "delight" to "dislike" or "no delight"; he goes on, "If the text is kept, possible paraphrases are: 'music best breeds delight, not a recital of grievous matters'; or 'only the best music, not a recital etc., may breed delight'" (*The Faerie Queene*, ed. Hamilton, 111n).

proper lesson, one that in its ease of statement and practical difficulty may be as close as we will get to a motto for *The Faerie Queene*. But Arthur is not finished, and it is in the next three lines that the didactic project becomes most urgent and compacted. He reflects on "This daies ensample," giving a kind of boundedness and point to what has happened, drawing the line of an example around its edges. Just as quickly, he moves to the "lesson deare" of that example, and then comes the iron pen, the stylus that writes this lesson on the tender parchment of the heart. There is a lot of didactic technology in play, and the final violence of the image—it startles awake a sleeping metaphor from Jeremiah—chastens the lines' swift movement from ensample to lesson to the alexandrine.[6] It is as though at the next-to-last minute the teacher fears that the comfort of the lesson might displace too much of the pain that called for it; as though the act of inscription, the act of teaching itself must be made painful for the lesson to stay. All the same comes the lesson in the last line: "That blisse may not abide in state of mortal men."

Just what kind of a lesson a maxim makes will be much to the point in what follows. For now, there are three things to observe. First, instruction here might be said to be a matter of representation, of somehow transmuting raw experience (or narrative) to lesson—giving it an intelligible shape, making it into useful knowledge. Second, the instructive movement from day to example to lesson is jerky, self-conscious, and uncertain. And third, it is very hard to say how this lesson is received. Arthur speaks these words primarily to Una, but she does not respond, at least not right away, and when he turns to Redcrosse the knight is obdurately silent. How do we know they understand?

Now, the second scene of instruction:

> Take a sentence or two in the beginning of that little booke, called *Sententiae pueriles*: . . .
>   *Amicis opitulare* . . .
> If you will, you may aske them by a question of the contrary, Must you not helpe your friends? The childe answereth, Yes. Then bid him give you a sentence to prove it; hee answereth, *Amicis opitulare*.

6. "The sinne of Judah is writen with a penne of yron, & with the point of a diamonde, & graven upon the table of their heart" (*Geneva Bible*, ed. Berry, Jer. 17:1).

Or aske by distribution thus; Whether must you helpe or forsake your friends?
The childe answereth, I must helpe them. Then bid him to give you a sentence;
he answereth, *Amicis opitulare.*
Or thus by Comparison; Whether ought you to helpe your friends, or others
first? or friends or enemies, &c. When the childe hath answered, ever bid him
give his sentence. So on in the rest.[7]

It would be hard to imagine a more different pedagogical occasion. The first
was out of doors, ad hoc, precariously near to tragedy, and full of anxious
triple-thinking; here we have a systematic procedure that sounds native
to the schoolroom. There are, however, at least two important similarities
between the schoolmaster's script (from John Brinsley's manual, *Ludus
Literarius*) and Arthur's pedagogical excruciations. The first is the importance of the *sententia* as the stuff and the proof of learning. Brinsley's pithy
formula—*amicis opitulare*, aid your friends—is precisely what the student is
supposed to know, in just that minimal order of words. Each of the little
exchanges finds its satisfaction and closure there. Spenser's Arthur may not
call for an echo of his own hard-won maxim, but he too brings his lesson
to an end by offering up such a formula. In both cases, the *sententia* is the
genre in which knowledge is consolidated: in the speaking of it, learning is
made recognizable. The work of teaching is to give knowing this shape.

The second similarity between these scenes is the restless energy devoted
to the problem of whether or not the student *understands*. Arthur anticipates
several ways that the day's example could be misconstrued. Brinsley, for his
part, replays his little scene of instruction three times, varying the approach
in each. Compared to Arthur, he may seem confident and systematic, taking
the question through the "places" of distribution and comparison in order
to disrupt the dead repetition of catechism.[8] But doubt haunts his method.
All of the pedagogical ingenuity on display in *Ludus Literarius* is unfolded,
in dialogue form, as the good schoolmaster Philoponus's response to the
failed schoolmaster Spoudaeus, whose laments are a catalog of everything
that can go wrong in the humanist classroom. "I my selfe have so long
laboured in this moyling and drudging life," Spoudaeus complains at the
outset, "without any fruite to speake of, and with so many discouragements
and vexations insteede of any true comfort, that I waxe utterly wearie of my

7. Brinsley, *Ludus Literarius*, T4r–T4v. Peter Mack discusses this passage in "Renaissance
Habits of Reading," where he takes a dim view of Brinsley's pedagogy: "What is troubling is
the degree of simplification and the drilling" (4).

8. On the places see chapter 1.

place, and my life is a continuall burden unto me."[9] The specter of such fruitless labor—labor for which no result can be shown—is renewed by Spoudaeus in question after question, and it drives the manual's preoccupation with proving that students have understood something. Brinsley's reforming ambition is a refrain: "to teach schollars to understand whatsoever they learn, & to be able to give a reason of every thing why it is so. . . . *Legere & non intelligere negligere est* [to read and not to understand is not to read]."[10]

This preoccupation with *understanding*—understanding as something uncommonly hard and elusive—is a special mark of the later sixteenth century. Historians of humanist education often compensate for a patchy record by emphasizing the continuity of schoolroom practices throughout the English Renaissance, drawing on later writing to illuminate earlier decades. I will avail myself of the same strategy more than once. But it is only possible because the school manuals themselves were changing, becoming over time, like Brinsley's, far more specific both in their critiques and in their remedies.[11] Such doubts as Spoudeus's are the engine of that explicitness. From Elyot to Ascham to Brinsley and beyond, English writing about education offers more and more examples, more and more specific exercises, more and more classroom detail; it has recourse to an ever-growing repertoire of textbooks, and is more and more explicit about how to use them.[12] There is a parallel development in the era's printed catechisms, which, according to Ian Green, devised increasingly sophisticated means to distinguish "between, on the one hand, the mechanical parroting of words and, on the other, a real understanding of their meaning and commitment to their implementation."[13] (The pressure of England's long

---

9. Brinsley, *Ludus Literarius*, B1v–B2r.

10. Ibid., G1r–G1v. *Negligere* literally means "neglect" but puns on *non legere*, not read.

11. T. W. Baldwin writes in 1944 of the "continuity and cohesion of the tradition" represented by Brinsley (*William Shakspere's Small Latine & Lesse Greeke*, 1:450). In 2002, Peter Mack echoes this defense in justifying his own use of *Ludus Literarius* to describe the sixteenth century: "Although Brinsley's work was first published in 1612, his assumptions are so close to those of the humanist educational theorists and his observations add so much practical detail (which may well have been based on his experiences as a pupil and teacher within Elizabeth's reign) that to exclude him would impoverish our understanding of Elizabethan education" (*Elizabethan Rhetoric*, 12–13).

12. Baldwin observes this but does not interpret it: "the later authors happen to be more definitely systematic" (*Small Latine*, 2:290).

13. Green, *The Christian's ABC*, 232. Green describes the emphasis on "shorter questions" (246) among many catechists, questions intended to combat mere memorization of long passages of doctrine; Brinsley thinks along the same lines: "The principall meanes for their understanding, is, by asking short questions of the matter" (*Ludus*, G3r). Compare Socrates'

wrestle with Reformation theology—with its problems of inward assurance and outward evidence—is felt in both contexts.) One might assume that urgency about ordinary understanding as the fruit of classroom labor would be a historically constant preoccupation. What else do teachers ever care about? But over this period it is the subject of increasingly obvious and intense concern—harder and harder, it would seem, to be sure of.

That gathering doubt is the subject of this book. As early as the 1560s, the great success of humanism as a reform movement is accompanied by a gradually rising tide of dissatisfaction with its methods, dissatisfaction particularly with the ways its students were trained to read. Such restlessness stems at least partly from testing its program in an ever-wider field, and giving its students time to age into disillusionment. The consequence is a loss of faith in the forms of understanding that had been cultivated day to day in institutions where an increasing proportion of privileged Englishmen spent their formative years, and where they learned not only to read but (to the extent that these can be separated) also to write, and to think. Brinsley's *Ludus Literarius*, printed in 1612 after a career of schoolmastering that began in the previous century, is an attempt to breathe new life into those forms. *Sententia* remains his all-purpose answer, but he integrates his maxim into a more flexible regime of questioning. Spenser's wilderness displacement of the scene of instruction, by contrast, depends at least as heavily on the same final form—it encourages us to read for the same *kind* of lesson, even if that lesson sounds more Calvinist than humanist—while leaving us far less easy with its authority.

Much of what follows is an attempt to fit scenes like these together: to show first how both might emerge out of a growing crisis of confidence in the humanist program, and second, how romance could offer a literary landscape within which to critique that program and experiment with alternatives. The idea that romance in particular would register this discontent might seem counterintuitive, and for some good reasons. Romance is the literary kind most tendentiously foreign to school. It went unrecognized among the classical hierarchies of genre that structured the humanist curriculum, and it was not until the next century that the label became at all familiar in English criticism. Its boundaries are notoriously blurry: the canonical works we might now be inclined to regard as its cornerstones—the

---

"short-answer method" for doing philosophy with speechifying rhetoricians in the *Gorgias*, 449c.

Odyssey, or the first six books of the *Aeneid*—were read under other auspices. Above all, the schoolmasters hated it. There will be occasion in what follows to linger over the rich scorn of men like Ascham and Francis Clement for Italian tales and Arthurian matter.[14]

At the same time, this very distance from the classroom makes romance a promising vantage for thinking twice about instruction, in the way pastoral is good for thinking about cities. As with country and city, the distance is not as great as the schoolmasters often proclaimed. Romances tend, for example, to be stories of younger people with something to learn, and they tend to put those young people in the way of some kind of real-world lesson—the tantalizing promise, so important to what follows, of learning by experience. To that extent they are narratives of education in a polemically extracurricular sense of the word, and hence rivals of the schoolroom's own account of how to grow up and grow wise. Moreover, like any poet in an age that defended poetry for its instructive power, these romancers were obliged to *teach*, or at least to reckon with that imperative. All this made their works a uniquely sensitive register of the changing relations between literature and school in the decades of humanism's first triumph, when secular poetry was first assuming its new (and now so familiar) position at the center of the curriculum.

This network of problems, particularly the connection between the romance and the humanist schoolroom, is not new to modern criticism. There is no want of studies of the impact of grammar-school training on writers like Marlowe, Shakespeare, or Milton. The rhetorical discipline and virtuosity cultivated in the classrooms where they labored over Lily's *Grammar* and Aphthonius's exercises make an unmistakable contribution to their literary art. (Milton excepted, these studies have tended to focus on the drama: soliloquies are obvious descendants of the declamation, schoolboys cut their teeth on Terence, and at some schools, including Spenser's and Sidney's, the boys performed Latin plays at holidays.[15]) There are accounts too of the relation of romance to the intellectual and institutional context of

---

14. The most complete account of what I mean by "romance" I defer until chapter 2, where I allow Roger Ascham's polemic to gather some representative texts. The terms of the Italian debate over *romanzo*—the multiple plot, the appeal to a popular audience, the recalcitrance to rules generally—are all significant to the works I consider here. The most important aspect of this mostly unregulated literary kind for my purposes is its extravagant narratives, with their tolerance for accident and error.

15. See for example, Altman, *The Tudor Play of Mind*, and Bate, *Shakespeare and Ovid*, especially pp. 1–48 and 101–17; Mulder, *The Temple of the Mind*, treats the influence of rhetorical training on other genres, including lyric and epic. On Milton see Clark, *John Milton at St. Paul's School*, and DuRocher, *Milton among the Romans*.

late-century humanism; it has long been recognized that the fictions of those two decades are almost exclusively the work of young men trained in the grammar schools and universities.[16] Finally, many critics have worried the problem of what these romances have to teach on their own terms, working in modes descended sometimes from the reader response criticism Stanley Fish made famous with *Surprised by Sin* (a book that gave the phrase "education of the reader" to any number of subsequent studies), sometimes from the tutorials in indeterminacy offered by critics of a deconstructive bent.[17]

But while the present book owes a debt to all this work, its project is quite different. It is about humanist reading practices, insofar as the fictions I will consider turn out to be preoccupied with the ways they will be encountered, understood, and remembered by their audience. But I take such problems of reading to be inseparable from teaching, and bound to the ur-scene of instruction for the writers I consider, the Elizabethan grammar school. School will be a heuristic—the first, best window onto humanism as a culture of teaching—but also the shaping origin of a range of compositional and interpretive habits, and a scene to which the imagination of these writers (especially Lyly and Sidney) returns with surprising frequency and intensity. The very act of reading will emerge as much harder to separate from teaching—teaching with all of its problems of knowledge and authority—than is at all intuitive for us today. A particular crucible for such problems will be scenes like Arthur's, where a poem is bound to the double business of staging a scene of instruction and instructing its reader. This study will dwell on such scenes in order to ask, what does teaching look like? What lesson is at stake? What would it mean to get it? Does the teaching here succeed, or fail? Each of these encounters, by the overdetermined accident of its historical moment, is set near the beginning of the long-running success of the humanities in the West. We still have a great deal to learn from what these reluctant teachers first saw there.

A final word, or nearly final word, on the perversity of my central claim. I take the very possibility of literary didacticism in these poems to be emptied out: their writers lose faith in the idea that literature can teach, because they

---

16. Richard Helgerson's *The Elizabethan Prodigals* has been the most generative such account; Kinney's *Humanist Poetics* and Maslen's *Elizabethan Fictions* make more recent contributions.

17. Many such accounts will be cited in what follows. See for example Parker's *Inescapable Romance*, or Astell's "Sidney's Didactic Method in *The Old Arcadia*." Ascoli's *Ariosto's Bitter Harmony* is a particularly idiosyncratic and resourceful treatment of the educative powers of romance.

cannot free their books—their teaching books—from a culture of teaching that they take to be compromised, even bankrupt. Such an argument flies in the face of hundreds of years of reading *Arcadia* and *The Faerie Queene* as though they were written to instruct us. How could it be true to say they are not? A full answer can only be given in what follows, but let me suggest three ideas worth keeping in mind along the way. First, the fact that a book will not teach—and though teaching is a protean thing, I will try to be exacting about the forms it can take, and particularly the forms in which it would have been recognized in the period—does not mean we cannot learn from it. In the course of our lives we learn a great deal, perhaps most of what we know, in situations that do not have a particularly didactic structure. Learning does not entail teaching any more than teaching does learning. (Another way of putting it: I do not want to mistake a *resistance* to teaching for just another *kind* of teaching.) Second: our own endless disagreement over exactly what these books *do* teach might just give us some pause; the particular interpretive recalcitrance that makes them so interesting may have something to do with a stance toward instruction per se.

And third: our confidence in instruction generally may just be on less certain footing than we often allow ourselves to recognize. What *do* our own students really learn? What are the instruments that we use to test them intended to show; how well do they work; what do they protect them, and us, from recognizing? One might say, of course students learn something in our classes. But do they learn what we teach? Do they really understand? Questions like these can precipitate us into a skepticism that makes the sheer diversity and unaccountability of experience in any classroom seem impossibly inconsistent with the aims we frame for the enterprise. To profit by this book, the reader will have to give him- or herself at least partly over to such worries; I hope it will be tonic to explore them, if not to dwell there. What happens to the mind that does will be amply documented in what follows.

———

Chapter 1 will be occupied almost entirely with the schoolroom, so before venturing there, one more glance at *The Faerie Queene*. Throughout the book I will treat instruction as a representational problem with two aspects: the representation of knowledge, and of knowing; what the stuff being taught looks like, and what it looks like to learn it. One-half of that double problem is worked out in Arthur's lesson-making. The other half waits on the knight to speak. Since Redcrosse will not break his silence, Una leaps in to answer the question he cannot, the question of what to do with Duessa: "To doe her die (quoth *Una*) were despight, / And shame t'avenge so weake an enimy; / But spoile her of her scarlot robe, and let her fly" (1.8.45). What follows over the next three stanzas is the canto's infamous blazon of Duessa's nakedness, the animal menagerie of her "neather parts" (48). Fascination and disgust charge the description in equal measure. When it is over, the role of teacher—pointing, naming, explaining—seems to have passed to Una herself:

> Such then (said *Una*) as she seemeth here,
> Such is the face of falshood, such the sight
> Of fowle *Duessa*, when her borrowed light
> Is laid away, and counterfesaunce knowne. (1.8.49)

Here is another lesson, by way not of a maxim but a new emblem, made by stripping away a veil to reveal the seductress's nature. *This* is what falshood looks like when it can no longer borrow other lights or other clothes, says Una. It has always been Duessa's beautiful face that has given trouble, as her ally Night, half-deceived herself, reminds us: "In that fayre face / The false resemblaunce of Deceipt, I wist / Did closely lurke" (1.5.27). Now that we can see her face clearly, how can we but turn away in disgust? How could we ever be deceived again?

This lesson seems to be a comfort: Duessa flees into the woods in shame, and the three travelers retire to a nearby castle "To rest them selves, and weary powres repaire, / Where store they fownd of al, that dainty was and rare" (1.8.50). It is a great power of allegory to define, judge, and move all at once, and in her act of unveiling Una has fashioned an image of falshood that will forever banish its power to seduce. The result is a potent act of pedagogical representation, and a kind of allegory-making-as-teaching that goes on all the time in the poem. But at a minimum the lesson is lost on Redcrosse: not only will he not speak, but the next canto has him falling victim to Despaire. Nor is it clear what use this particular lesson—however gratefully received—could ever have been to him, or to any of us. Una wants to point to what falshood *really* looks like, but it is the *face* of falshood she claims to have revealed. And is it not the point about falshood that its face is always beguiling, always different from its nature? Perhaps the role of the teacher is to make the truth obvious, but here that impulse betrays its aims. Una has made an emblem of falshood that abstracts it—in that act of pointing, "Such is the face"—from the narrative within which its operations have been made so painstakingly intelligible. *Falshood never looks like that.*

The claim that it does has a comforting music to it, but will not help when the next Duessa comes along.

If this kind of poetic teaching is a mistake, or prone to mistake, that mistake goes to the heart of *The Faerie Queene*'s didactic procedures as an allegorical poem. Mistakes more generally—malfunctions and abuses of teaching, dogged failures to learn—go to the heart of my own story. There is a kinship between the failed schoolmaster Spoudaeus and Edmund Spenser, and the most reliable fact about teaching and learning in romance is that they will go wrong. That observation more than any other gave this book its first impetus: why, in these supposedly didactic fictions, do we encounter such a relentless parade of failed instruction? Why does no one ever learn anything in romance? And what are we to learn from that?

CHAPTER ONE

Telling Learning

How do I know you understand? Well: I may be satisfied to hear you repeat my words back, just as I spoke them or in some more-or-less elegant variation. Or it may suffice merely that you profess agreement: "Yes, I understand!" But I might also press the matter, asking you questions: what follows? Can you give an example? What about this or that objection? I may, when I ask, be waiting on a particular response, or perhaps I will accept only answers that I could not have predicted. Sometimes it will not be words I am looking for at all; I will be most persuaded by a particular look in your eyes, or a timely nod, or an attitude of your body, relaxed and confident or stiffened with outrage. Perhaps nothing will count but your laughing or bursting into tears—*that* is when I know you *really* understand, no matter what you say. And perhaps I still won't be sure, not until I see what you *do* about it. And how long, in that case, will I have to wait? And how will I know when I have waited long enough? We sometimes imagine understanding as a singular experience, the dawning of an inner light that lets us see clearly what was once obscure. "Ah, *now* I understand." But the forms by which it is expressed and recognized are as various as its occasions. There are many understandings.

Of course, there are circumstances under which it is necessary to constrain this field of possibility, and chief among them—paradigmatic, in fact—is school. It won't do to allow students to demonstrate their command of Book II of the *Aeneid* merely by a well-timed tear for Hecuba. The scene of instruction that is the classroom is set up to specify more narrowly what counts as knowledge and what learning it looks like: it is the schoolmaster's job to prove that the students learn, and he has to prove it to several audiences, not only to himself and his charges but also to parents, neighbors, an interested state. The daily routines that provide the proof, the classroom's exercises, must be constructed in such a way that both the matter to be learned and the condition of knowing it take specific, agreed-upon forms. Such exercises will need to have beginnings and endings, so it will be obvious where and when to look for learning, and they will need to provide criteria for success and failure, to tell whether it has actually happened or not.

Take, for example, an exercise described in the statutes of the Friar's School at Bangor in 1569, one that is as universal in English schools as it is rudimentary:

> The said Scholars shall daily use to commit to their memory and care without the book by the Schoolmaster's or Usher's appointment all petty sentences within their ordinary lectures which the Schoolmaster or Husher shall require and hear without the Book at the time appointed for the rendering of their said ordinary Lectures.[1]

The rules of this little game are simple and familiar: the students commit to memory maxims ("petty sentences") from texts read to them by the schoolmaster or his assistant, the usher, and at the appointed time (typically first thing in the morning) they render or recite those maxims back. The exercise begins with the master's solicitation—"*Da mihi sententia*"—and ends with the student's response. Success consists in accurate repetition, failure in anything short of it. The point of playing this game is to produce a representation of the schoolboy's knowledge, in the form of the sentence he repeats. How do I know the student knows that love conquers all? That he can conjugate *vinco*? That he respects my authority? Because he says, "*amor vincit omnia*."[2] Saying those words, at least within the parameters of the game, is what it means to know, to have learned, to understand.

It will pay to pause and reflect—for if you are reading this book, chances are you are a teacher—on some of the pedagogical transactions that structure your own daily work. They are invariably built around and shaped by the need to produce some proof of their success, whether that proof is a repeated word or an expository essay. Much of the most important recent thinking about institutional education has been about *habitus*, the often unremarked forms of behavior, like raising your hand or queuing for lunch, by which students are made part of the school's society and of the

---

1. T. W. Baldwin, *Small Latine*, 1:307.
2. Brinsley uses this sentence as an example for a series of exercises in *Ludus Literarius*, U4r-v.

society the school serves. About such routines there will be more to say. But my focus is on the behaviors and artifacts that are made to count *as representations*, that are taken for signs of learning and that give closure to particular instructional routines. When the question arises, what is learning? or even, what is knowledge? they are what we are apt to point to.

———

In this introduction I will take circumscribed scenes like the repetition game above very seriously: they will be the building blocks of everything that follows. Such ordinary, daily routines are the origins of the techniques that school-trained readers bring to any text they take up in later life, and their authority extends well beyond the classroom. A routine like the game of repetition I have just described might be said to imply an account, at least a provisional account, of what knowledge is per se. If to know is to repeat, knowledge is the text held in memory, word for word. If that is what knowledge is, then knowing, understanding, must in turn be the kind of memory that can retain and reproduce such texts. Such a routine may entail no very specific picture of thinking, but it is amenable to such commonplace metaphors of mind as a wax tablet or a bottle for the wine of new knowledge. Out of a daily obligation, then, an exercise performed in the chill earliest hours of the school day in a long, drafty hall, it is possible to read an account both of knowledge and of knowing.

This last claim may seem exaggerated, but what follows is dedicated to showing the world-shaping power that such scenes of instruction possess, and just how wide are the consequences of recognizing English humanism as a culture of teaching. For the moment let me suggest why these matters might be so important to poets, and particularly to the sort of poets who tell stories. The first reason is simply that poets *were* teachers, or thought they had to be. Instruction was the better half, the justifying half, of what Sidney called his "unelected vocation."[3] This means that a poet had to decide, on some level, whether his work would "fashion a gentleman" (in Spenser's phrase) as he himself had been fashioned.[4] The second reason is that a poet who chose to write in the vein of romance took on the challenge of representing learning *within* his fiction, insofar as the stories he gave himself to work with were filled with hermits admonishing young men, allegorical houses of strict discipline, and other exhibits of instruction. Such a poet had to make learning visible, as the schoolmaster has to make

3. Sidney, *Miscellaneous Prose*, 73.
4. Spenser, *The Faerie Queene*, ed. Hamilton, 714.

it visible in the classroom. Could the conventions of school suffice? What would learning look like without them? Finally, these poets could expect that their fictions would be read according to the techniques taught in school, and their didactic ambitions understood in school terms. Should they write to accommodate those expectations? To be read as if in school? It is this complex predicament that I set out to describe: the poet-as-teacher in a culture of teaching, a culture that made him and that, in the cases I will study, he finds he cannot endorse.

For all these reasons, this introduction must begin in school—a common place, in fact, for the period's romances themselves to begin. And it will begin there with four premises: (1) that the scene of instruction is shaped by an epistemological problem, the question *how do I know you understand?*; (2) that particular pedagogical practices are constructed to answer that question by providing specific representations of what the student knows; (3) that those same practices, or exercises, simultaneously make larger representations of knowledge, knowing, learning, and thinking, representations that (as we will see) vary and need not be mutually consistent; and (4) that those exercises and the representations they make are foundational for (a) how poets understood their vocation and (b) how trained readers would approach their works. Much of this introduction will be devoted to a patient anatomy of these exercises, understood as modes both of teaching and of understanding (where the two will turn out—an important point, but one that will take some developing—to be difficult to separate). I will use them to construct a *poetics of pedagogy*, a repertory of representational conventions that both structure and constrain fictions that themselves profess to teach. The story I ultimately want to tell is about how the resources of a particular literary kind were exploited to critique those conventions, and to challenge how a period imagined the very nature of teaching and learning. Again and again one finds the oblong box of the Tudor classroom superimposed on the labyrinth of romance. The fit is never easy.

William Kempe's Schoolroom

I remarked that romances often start in school. Euphues sets out for Naples from the university at Athens, and Sidney's princes wash up in Arcadia after years of instruction in Thessaly. They and many heroes like them follow the career path marked out by the biblical parable of the prodigal son, a template for Elizabethan fiction well described by Richard Helgerson: stories that start in rectitude and good learning, veer into romance wandering, and finally return to the safety of home.[5] That model will be important here for its implication of a sharp divide between phases of instruction and self-loss. I will ask, in due course: do characters learn anything from that middle phase of vagrancy, and do readers? Or does it function simply to burn away rebellious energies, leaving us with lessons that look at the end just as they were in the beginning? Does the *experience* of the middle—a term on which the next chapter will place special weight—make a difference? In order to address those questions of the middle, it will be necessary first to study the discipline instituted on either side. That will involve, as I have said, picking out particular school exercises and scrutinizing them for the shape they give to knowledge—assembling a poetics of pedagogy. In preparation I will sketch their context, the schoolboy career that Lyly would have known at St. Paul's, Sidney at Shrewsbury, Spenser at Merchant Taylors'.

William Kempe, schoolmaster at Plymouth for the last twenty years of the sixteenth century, will serve as guide. Kempe took his BA degree from Cambridge in 1581, and he returned the same year to his home town, where he taught until his death. In many ways he was typical of his profession: he likely presided over somewhere between fifty and eighty boys ages five to sixteen, the average for grammar schools in the period, and he had the daily help of an usher who worked primarily with the lower forms. His school-room at Plymouth was the chapel of an old almshouse, a room probably about twenty to thirty feet wide and sixty to eighty feet long, furnished with benches along two walls and a lectern in front. He was paid twenty pounds a year for his pains.[6] He was less typical in his relatively early embrace of the reforms of Petrus Ramus, and in order to give a fair picture of what the likes of Philip Sidney lived through as schoolboys, and lived to see as adults, I will sometimes compare his curriculum to the more Erasmian program of

5. Helgerson's *The Elizabethan Prodigals* describes not only how this narrative pattern structured many fictions of the period, but also how it provided their authors with a frame for their own dalliance with romance as a form. I will return to Helgerson's argument in chapter 2.

6. Kempe's biography is supplied in Robert David Pepper's dissertation, "*The Education of Children in Learning* (1588) by William Kempe of Plymouth: A Critical Edition," 23–108. We do not know the enrollments at the Plymouth school during Kempe's tenure, though we know that at the time of its founding in 1561 some thirty benches were installed: see Bracken, "The Plymouth Grammar School," 144. The dimensions given are a rough average for the period. The most prominent schools were generally larger: Merchant Taylors' had exceeded its statutory limit of 250 students by 1569, and Shrewsbury, with 360 in 1581, fit all its students in a schoolroom of twenty-one by seventy-eight feet. For these figures see Alexander, *The Growth of English Education, 1348–1648*, 198, and Draper, *Four Centuries of Merchant Taylors' School*; see also Brown, *Elizabethan Schooldays*, 8, 16.

the earlier century. But Kempe was unusual above all for setting down so much detailed information about his job. *The Education of Children in Learning*, which was printed in 1588, is the most detailed English pedagogical manual of its century.

An important problem is lodged right at the roots of his curriculum. He begins by describing what should happen in petty school, the scene of first formal instruction in reading and writing English, where he wants boys at the age of five (assuming that "naturall use" will have already given them a practical command of vernacular grammar).[7] The ladder of formal instruction begins with learning "to knowe the letters by their figures" and "to sound them aright by their proper names" (223), pointing to the letters in a primer or a hornbook—a kind of degree zero of pedagogy. Next comes making letters. Erasmus, in his *De Recta Pronuntiatione*, recommends teaching by *imitation*, having students trace them with the aid of translucent paper or ivory letter-forms.[8] Kempe's advice is subtly, vitally different. Speaking and writing, he claims, are parallel ways of rendering written signs ("with the mouth" and "with the hand"), and the letters themselves are "the artificiall *precepts* in this facultie" (223, italics mine). Letters are not objects of imitation to which the student conforms his hand and himself; they are already, even at the alphabetical bottom of the curriculum, rules for following.

Kempe's consciousness of this distinction between instruction by imitation and by precept—and his particular, tacitly polemical version of it—emerges when he takes a long view of his method:

> all knowledge is taught generally both by precepts of arte, and also by practise of the same precepts. They are practised partly by observing examples of them in other mens workes, and partly by making somewhat of our owne; and that first by imitation, and at length without imitation. (223)

Aristotle had bequeathed to the Renaissance the idea that "imitation is natural to man from childhood," the irreducible inclination to make yourself after what you see. Erasmus usually puts his thinking about education on the same foundation: "we observe even in the newly born a sort of innate, parrot-like desire, or rather delight, in copying and repeating [*aemulandi*

---

7. Kempe, *The Education of Children in Learning*, in *Four Tudor Books on Education*, ed. Pepper, 223. Subsequent citations in this chapter will be given in parentheses in the text.

8. Erasmus, *De Recta Pronuntiatione*, in *Works*, 26:397–98. For more on techniques of teaching handwriting, especially as a disciplinary practice, see Goldberg, *Writing Matter: From the Hands of the English Renaissance*.

reddendique] what they have heard."[9] Learning begins with an instinct man shares with the apes and the parrots, an instinct sustained by a bodily, prerational pleasure. Kempe, by contrast, starts school with precepts. His idea of imitation teaches students to see through texts to the skeleton of principles by which they were constructed. This commitment is to method, to a rule-bound account of the mind's work in learning—from the inside out, one might say, rather than the outside in.

———————

That contest between imitation and precept plays out up and down the curriculum, and it is one thread to follow both through the forms and through the following chapters. The next step for Kempe's students was grammar school proper, divided into two phases that ordinary usage would call lower and upper grammar and that Kempe calls the second and third "degrees." Here the main business was learning Latin and its literature: the classical trivium, grammar in the lower school from ages seven to twelve, and rhetoric and logic in the upper school up to age sixteen (with a smattering of Greek and mathematics). We should picture the boys arranged by age in the benches along the long walls, Kempe up at his lectern and the usher moving among them, sometimes exercising the individual forms, sometimes the whole school. The youngest scholars, the seven-year-olds of the first form, begin with the so-called accidence from Lily's *Grammar*, written in the English they had learned to read in petty school. They were supposed to get "by hart the parts of speach with their properties . . . whereof [they] shall rehearse afterwards some part ordinarily every day, illustrating the same with examples of divers Nounes and Verbes" (226–27). This routine follows the rules of *repetition* above: the boys memorize the texts of grammar precepts, and recite them in response to the master's cues. The illustrations Kempe mentions could have been declensions or conjugations performed on the fly, or, more likely at this stage, the reproduction of memorized examples, of which Lily provides many. (From his description, there is no way to tell the difference.)

That first year is devoted largely to memorizing and repeating precepts: "tossing all the rules," as Roger Ascham, author of the influential *Schoolmaster* (1570), had said disparagingly.[10] The boys would likely have begun

9. Aristotle, *Poetics*, 1448b5; Erasmus, *De Recta Pronuntiatione*, in *Works*, 26:369–70. For another side of Erasmus, see his sententious *Institutio Principis Christiani*, discussed in chapter 3.

10. Ascham, *Schoolmaster*, 86. The influence of Ascham on Kempe is apparent in his "copied imitation," the use of specific models to guide composition. But he has little of Ascham's antipathy toward rules: his concern with method reflects the Ramist side of his inheritance.

mastering Saturday *catechisms* too, a common English school practice, though not one Kempe mentions. In the second form, at the age of eight, they begin "to practise the precepts of Grammar, in expounding and unfolding the works of Latin Authors" (227). This is the first entry into the classroom of Latin literature, primarily in the form of dialogues written for the purpose, and Kempe's expounding and unfolding inaugurate another durable routine:

> The Maister shall first reade sensibly a competent Lecture, then declare the argument and scope of the Author, afterward english it either word for word, or phrase for phrase.... Last of all teach ... the divers sorts of the words, their properties and syntaxes of speach. And about three or foure houres after, the Schollar shall be diligently in every point examined, and tryed how he can referre the examples of his Lecture to the rules of Art. (227)

Declaring the argument and scope of the author means providing some framing information (historical, generic, philological) and perhaps offering a *sententia* or prudential maxim under which the sense of the whole might be gathered. This introduction is followed by what most educators called "construing," giving English equivalents of the words; then "parsing," explaining the syntax of each word by reference to Lily's rules. Three new operations have been added to mere repetition: *analysis*, breaking the text into its proper parts; *epitome*, summarizing its essence; and a sorting of cases according to their precepts that I will call *classification*. I understand because I can isolate its parts, because I know its motto or moral or essence, because I recognize its kind.

The second form also sees the first grammar *drills*, exercises in which the student performs systematic, formal manipulations of model sentences. Students take a short "lecture," *pater bonus diligit filium probum*, through a series of grammatical transformations: "Ma. a father. Sch. *pater*. M. fathers. S. *patres*. M. a good father. S. *pater bonus*.... M. good fathers love honest sonnes. S. *patres boni diligunt filios probos*" (228). Here the rules are different again: the boys prove their understanding not by repeating, nor by sorting elements, but by generating novel forms according to the precepts of grammar. (Modern linguists would call such precepts "productive rules."[11]) Again however it is worth noting that the master begins by "propound[ing] the like sentence with diversitie, first of Nombers, then of Genders" (227) and so on: there is room to wonder whether the boys were not actually

---

11. See for example Pinker, *Words and Rules*, 6.

making new forms but just repeating transformations he had already shown them.

———————

With the third form, Kempe's young scholars turn to their first exercises in *composition* and to imitation per se, the discipline of cultivating the graces of Roman (and particularly Ciceronian) style that the humanists called *imitatio*. Initially the task is close to *translation*: they take an epistle and "translat[e] . . . the same speach into another [of] like sentence, but altered with many varieties at once, and chiefly with the last varietie of the words" (229). A speech on ambition becomes a speech on avarice; structures of argument are conserved, while a commonplace book—stocked with "principall phrases" (229) from the boys' reading—supplies variety in local expression. The original is never out of sight. After some more practice the boys progress to an exercise "without imitation," taking the master's English translation of an unfamiliar piece of Cicero and rendering it in Latin. This time, Cicero's text is withheld, but only until they finish their own versions: each boy's translation is still ultimately set beside the Latin original, "wherewith he shall conferre his owne, and correct it" (230). Whatever is inchoate about imitation is rendered concrete in the last gesture. Conferring and correcting may well mean simply conforming the original to its model, making the whole thing a test first of memory, then of diligence in collation.

A brief contrast with the instructions that Erasmus gives in his influential *De Copia* will be particularly useful here. His account of the ideal of abundant, varied style does not depend on immediate models. Cicero is digested into students' commonplace books along with the rest of their reading, making examples of his phrasing available for copious treatment of set themes like "happiness does not consist in riches" or "one should or should not travel abroad."[12] Erasmus cares most of all, in *De Copia* at least, for variety, and understanding is represented by an act of amplification or dilation. (I understand it because I can make more of it.) Such exercises would naturally be more difficult to judge than what T. W. Baldwin calls Kempe's "copied imitation": they are not quite as clean in their proof. Kempe's version became more and more common in English schools during the late century.[13]

The fourth and fifth forms continue exercises in copied imitation with readings of increasing difficulty, including not only Cicero but also Terence

12. Erasmus, *Works*, 24:680.   13. T. W. Baldwin, *Small Latine*, 2:181.

and Ovid, and the sixth form begins "the third degree for Logike and
Rhetorike" (232). (In most schools the boys would also begin formal *disputations*, though like catechisms Kempe does not mention them.) To the
precepts of grammar are added the laws of two new arts. Logic is the first of
them, and it begins with *inventio*, the technique of marshalling arguments
and evidence, followed by *iudicium* (or *dispositio*), putting those elements
into order. Kempe also introduces the rhetorical discipline of *elocutio*, which
ornaments arguments with the tropes and figures, and the niceties of *pronuntiatio*, or delivery. (His division here between logic and rhetoric is the
most direct reflection of his embrace of Ramus's reforms.[14]) This sequence
comprises the elements, minus *memoria*, of the fivefold Ciceronian method
for making an oration, the best-developed and most self-conscious pedagogical model of thinking. The new *artes* also continue to shape the way the
boys read, "observ[ing] the examples of the hardest points in Grammar, of
the arguments in Logike, of the tropes and figures in Rhetorike, referring
every example to his proper rule, as before" (233). Any text they take up
will now appear to them as a made thing of many parts, assembled in
persuasive structures:

> he must observe in authors all the use of the Artes, as not only the words
> and phrases, not only the examples of the arguments; but also the axiome,
> wherein every argument is disposed; the syllogisme, whereby it is concluded;
> the method of the whole treatise, and the passages, whereby the parts are
> joyned together. (233)

The basic procedures of analysis and classification—breaking things down
and identifying their kinds within the threefold framework of grammar, logic, and rhetoric—have been combined and elaborated, even as
Kempe pays increasing attention to the large-scale schemes that reveal the
"method" of the text as a whole.

Such attention to logical and rhetorical constructedness brings reading
and writing ever closer together: what students are taught to see in a text
is the way it was assembled, from parts that they can reuse.[15] Exercises in
composition now demand that they specify "all the arte" of a model—parse

14. Ramus sought to sharpen a blurred boundary between the two by assigning *inventio*
and *dispositio* to logic, *eloquentia* and *pronuntiatio* to rhetoric; rhetoric was thereby effectively
limited to the schemes and tropes. See Howell, *Logic and Rhetoric in England, 1500–1700*, esp.
146–72.

15. A point made by Terence Cave in *The Cornucopian Text*: "In imitation . . . the activities
of reading and writing become virtually identified. A text is read in view of its transcription as

it, construe it, and type its rhetorical and logical structures—then assay a new topic while following the original "phrase for phrase, trope for trope, figure for figure, argument for argument, and so of the rest" (234). The latitude for variety steadily increases, permitting students to omit and add material and alter "the method, forme of syllogismes, axiomes, arguments, figures, tropes, phrases and words" (236). Mere repetition, so tenacious at earlier stages, is no longer an adequate move in the game. The variations may be more or less formulaic, but the boys must at the very least quarry their commonplace books. Finally the ladder is kicked away altogether: "let him assay otherwhiles, without an example of imitation, what he can do alone by his owne skill alreadie gotten by the precepts and the two former sorts of practise" (237). The scholar is still guided by the artificial precepts that he has so thoroughly studied, but there is no longer any Ciceronian model waiting on the other side. Kempe and Erasmus are closest at this final stage, and the schoolboy's words are closest to being action in the world—at least, rhetorical action.

———

Such is the career of Kempe's schoolboys, roughly from the ages of five to sixteen. There is much more to say about the texture of daily life in the school, its mechanisms of discipline, the boys' own social arrangements. Some of that will be salient in later chapters. For the moment I am concerned specifically with what the boys did to texts to prove their understanding, the routines of *repetition, catechism, analysis, classification, epitome, drill, translation, disputation,* and *composition.* In pointing out these operations— the operations I will shortly treat as the elements of a poetics—I have also tried to anticipate some ambiguities in their definition. One source of such ambiguity is the stubborn undertow of mere repetition. The accounts Kempe gives of what his boys do may strike us as ambitious, like his permutational drills or his imitations of Cicero, but on the basis of his descriptions it is difficult to rule out completing the exercise simply by echoing the teacher or by reproducing the oration's text word for word. Such tacit substitution of repetition for more complex operations is a perdurable feature of schooling, and it leaves its traces in *The Education of Children in Learning.* It may afford the teacher flexibility to adjust the difficulty of the exercise to the ability of the student; more often, it simply redefines learning itself as a transparent and tractable exchange. No knowledge is easier

———

part of another text; conversely, the writer as imitator concedes that he cannot entirely escape the constraints of what he has read" (35).

to prove. The forces that reduce learning to repetition on the scale of the exercise are kin to those that define education itself as a project of reproduction, making each student from the same mold.

The other ambiguity I want to emphasize—like the first, a functional ambiguity—is generated by the curious relation between imitation and precept.[16] *Imitatio* is the name for what the schoolboy does when he writes after an ancient text, and as I suggested above it invokes the undeliberate, habitual learning of the young child, the almost bodily having-into that Aristotle describes. Its poetic forms attract such metaphors as digestion or the bees making honey in the fastness of their hive. As a matter of its schoolroom practice, however, and particularly as Kempe defines it, *imitatio* is a method: a step-wise, rule-based project in which every stage ought to be present to the mind of the imitator, and demonstrable to his teacher.[17] Rules—at least as the humanist *artes* typically conceive them—are themselves texts, and following them is a conscious and deliberate business, a kind of reading-into-action. The distinction undergirds two very different ideas of what learning is like. Having drawn that distinction, however, it sometimes seems that classroom practice is devised principally to blur its boundaries. Is the Ciceronian text a whole to pattern yourself after? Or is it an example of principles you can in turn apply elsewhere? One way of understanding school *imitatio*—and it is a way particularly well suited to Kempe's curriculum—is as a method developed to regulate and even displace the instinct that it nonetheless claims as its mainspring.

What is learning, then? Is it the forming of habits by imitation? Is it learning the rules, and applying them; having your head full of their texts and reading them out into action? The schoolroom has no answers for these big questions, or at least, it never asks them. Instead it has its particular, practical routines. Learning is breaking something into its parts, or reducing it to its sententious essence. Or learning is just saying it back again. What I want to suggest is that the ambiguities both in the large definition of the project and the demands of its particular exercises are ways of *not seeing* what the whole enterprise can in practice come down to. (This argument ought to recall one made by Anthony Grafton and Lisa Jardine, when they claim that the techniques of humanist reading obscure

16. I borrow the phrase "functional ambiguity" from Annabel Patterson, who uses it, in *Censorship and Interpretation*, to describe strategies of evading censorship; I adapt it here to refer to a way of obscuring or not recognizing a practice that is at odds with the terms in which it is characteristically defended.

17. Thomas Greene discusses the tension between these ideas of imitation in *The Light in Troy*, 54–55.

the more challenging content of ancient texts—about which more below.)
The poets I will consider in subsequent chapters are preoccupied by the
misrecognitions entailed in received procedures of understanding. They
attend to the costs of reading as you have been taught to read, and to what
you will not recognize if you play it by the book. But it is worth observing—
for the moment, without either sympathy or censure—that almost any
school exercise could be interpreted as an instrument of not-knowing as
surely as it is an instrument of proof. To specify the kind of response a
student can give to a question or a text, to define a scene of instruction in
order to provoke a particular representation of understanding, is to decline
to recognize a whole range of other criteria, responses, symptoms, even
persons. Without such constraints, our classrooms would be chaos. We
properly spend considerable effort training students not to give the wrong
kind of answer, and by our specificity—by the care with which we structure
the scene of instruction and test what happens there—we exclude much of
the idiosyncrasy, bathos, and extravagance of their responses. And indeed:
who would want to know what our students *really* think?

A Poetics of Pedagogy

What licenses my reading humanist pedagogy as a poetics, admittedly a
peculiar way to study the enterprise, is first of all the purposes of the chapters
following: I want to judge its influence on works of literature, and I take
that influence to be not least a matter of the representational conventions
it offers to (or presses on) the poet-as-teacher. But equally important is
the idea that scenes of instruction are built to produce representations,
signs of having learned, of understanding, that allow us to move on to
the next exercise, or to the next year, or to confer degrees. This poetics
will be grounded in the categories of exercise I have derived from Kempe,
but I will draw now from a wider variety of sixteenth- and sometimes
seventeenth-century sources: the manuals of schoolmasters and of theorists
like Erasmus, but also school statutes, textbooks, commonplace books,
and references to school in other kinds of writing. What follows will be
more about school than about literature, but the question of time—of
narrative—will be more and more insistent, foreshadowing what I take
to be romance's most important reproach to the training of its schooled
audience.

It should be said, however, that the exercises I will discuss should not
be thought of solely within a framework of representation. The schoolboy,
after all, lives *inside* them, and the adult hardly escapes when he graduates.

Pedagogical routines establish deeply embedded habits of reading and understanding. The framework of habitus—what Pierre Bourdieu calls "the system of structured, structuring dispositions . . . which is constituted in practice"—is more directly answerable to such claims.[18] The techniques of instruction I will go on to describe are inseparable from postures and rhythms of the body, and from the larger, collective rhythms of the institutions where they are housed. If exercises have, as a rule, articulable rules, nonetheless the great majority of what a schoolboy does between dawn recitations and evening prayers is learned differently—more, one might say, by imitation. The mostly unarticulated habits of deference, civility, competition, even cleanliness that are manifested in ordinary behavior are arguably the most important and deepest-laid lessons. They are dispositions, or attitudes (of body and mind), that both reflect and propagate the institution that houses them. They are what prepare him to take his place in a society whose hierarchy is imitated in the classroom's local forms of order.[19]

Still, it will not serve my purposes to dissolve learning altogether into habitus, for as I have already suggested there are moments in the school day—structured by particular exercises—that all participants will point to in order to say, this boy understands, and this boy does not. It is to account for these, and for their reach into the rest of life, that I will elaborate a framework of representation. The best way to think about the relation between these two approaches, representation and habitus, is to recognize

18. Bourdieu, *The Logic of Practice*, 52. His book attempts to supplant structuralist social analysis, and more generally the project of trying to understand social or psychological patterns by making models of them: "this hermeneutic philosophy . . . leads one to conceive action as something to be deciphered, when it leads one to say, for example, that a gesture or ritual act *expresses* something, rather than saying, quite simply, that it is 'sensible' (*sensé*) or, as in English, that it 'makes' sense" (36–37). He prefers a concept of practice that, he acknowledges, is "not easy to speak of . . . other than negatively" (80), but that is characterized by an acknowledgment of life in time, and a refusal to abstract rules for following from rules immanent in activity. This idea of practice is indebted to Wittgenstein's "form of life." I want not to reject the model-making of the structuralists—nor mimesis as a project of understanding more generally—from the vantage of habitus, but to think of the two as competing frameworks of interpretation that will be invoked at different times, for different motives, and with varying degrees of self-consciousness.

19. Although I have not introduced it explicitly here, in formulating this account of school exercises I have had in mind Wittgenstein's conception of a language game; my intermittent use of the word "game" is best glossed by his *Philosophical Investigations*. An exercise, like a language game, is often a kind of tendentious model of mental activity—but of course, where Wittgenstein's games are heuristic, exercises are instituted in practice and can constitute the self-understanding of the student. See e.g., §2 and §53–56.

that they come from distinct analytic vantage points, good for different problems at different times. (They are themselves not altogether unlike the paradigms of rule following and imitation.) Some of that doubleness of perspective is captured in "exercise" itself. "Exercise" is a word for structured preparation, a model of a desired, real-life capacity. But it also means to *do* something. The same is true for the word "practice," upon which Bourdieu depends so heavily: there is both practicing the violin, and practicing the law. So too with the Latin *exercitatio*, which is central to the ancient pedagogical vocabulary. Because I am moving toward an account of literary texts, I will favor the language of representation—perhaps I will be trapped in it the way my subjects are. The claims of habitus, however, will not fall away. They will return with particular authority near the end, in the guise of ordinariness.

There is something else at stake in the difference between these two perspectives. Let us say that habitus is an attempt to capture a form of life from the inside, or at least to avoid imputing to those who live it a systematic account of its governing principles. There is unavoidably a hint of projected innocence here. The participants do not know what they are doing, at least not the way that the detached observer can know; they do not need to know that way, because their knowing consists in the activity. Representation, by contrast, avowedly considers its objects *ab extra*, making pictures, models, systems in order to understand them. Even if you study yourself in these terms, you are trying to step back, out of your own shoes: the activity and the act of understanding it are alienated from each other. This alienation is a necessary condition of representation—which is nothing more or less than saying there is a sign and a signified, and that they are different orders of experience. One might think of the first condition (knowledge as practice) as capturing the experience of the tractable schoolboy, for whom the school routine is natural, a matter of habits. No question of the representativeness of his activities arises, because there is no active sense of an outside. At the other end of a spectrum we might imagine a mature, perhaps disillusioned adult, who stands outside—and more importantly, after—his schooling and regards it as a system of rules; he asks, what are these rules for, whom do they serve, what do they stand for?

School itself is constructed as a representation. It gives to the young an account of what the world is going to be like. There are people for whom that account serves all their lives: its forms are the natural forms of understanding, the way to think, the way to read. They will never think of it as a representation, because they will never ask, and will never feel the need to ask, what is behind it. There are others who, for whatever reason, come to think of its picture of the world as a false one, and from this alienated retrospect ask of every task they undertook, *what did it mean? Whom was it for?* And then, there is the gray territory in-between, occupied by those who can articulate, endorse, or dispute what their education has given them, who have enough detachment for critique, but whose thinking and writing remain—on terms chosen or unchosen—structured by its forms. This middle ground is the awkward terrain of the rest of the book. If what comes next is a poetics, it is at the same time a set of habits, whose authority cannot be altogether a matter of choice for the men who learned by them to read and write.

$$a \rightarrow a$$

We are obliged to start again with routines of *repetition*: exercises where the student is asked to give back what he has been given. Such repetition is arguably the essence of education, and arguably its opposite. Either way it has a uniquely powerful status as a trope of learning, what learning comes down to, or back to. (Though perhaps one should say it is an antitrope, the resistance to figuration.) Kempe's petty school instruction begins with routines in which students repeat letters and syllables that the master has said aloud. The same fundamental operation persists, working on more or less complicated matter, up and down the curriculum. Students memorize the rules in Lily word by word from the beginning of grammar school, and are often called upon to recite them, apropos of particular features of a text or for their own sake. The timetable at Eton in 1530 reserves the hour after noon on Friday for "renderyng of ruls lernyd the hole weke," even as late as the sixth form, when the rules would include principles of logic and rhetoric as well as grammar.[20] *Sententiae* are also common matter for memorization, and students memorized by heart longer passages from their lectures and from texts they were reading—the boys at Winchester were responsible for twelve lines of Ovid every week, which seems to be

---

20. Leach, *Educational Charters and Documents 598 to 1909*, 451. Also from Eton, T. W. Baldwin cites a description of the daily routine: "In every of the said Forms the Rules shall be said in the Morning, and by and by more Rules given unto them." He quotes from Mulcaster's *Positions* to reinforce the point: "'The morening houres will best serve for the memorie & conceiving: the after noone for repetitions, & stuffe for memorie to worke on.' So the morning hours were to be used for getting, the afternoon for repeating and setting, this being the usual sixteenth-century routine" (*Small Latine*, 1:149).

on the low end.[21] They would "prove" their knowledge, in the idiom of the statutes, by reciting to the master or usher.

There are some important variations on these simple games: whether the students repeat immediately or from memory, what cues for repetition the master gives (the text itself, a command like "give the sentence," or, as in catechism, below, a scripted question). But the rudiments are the same. This is not imitation, if imitation implies (1) a difference and (2) that sense of habituation, approximation, bodily having-into, slower time. Nor is it rule-following, for there is no requirement that the student produce the precept governing the routine. Repetition is somehow below both of them. To each of the kinds of exercise I describe here I will want to put the questions, what picture of knowledge does it have to offer? What picture of learning, and of the student's mind? The answers in this case—as I have already suggested—are plain ones. Knowledge is a string of text; learning it is hearing or reading it; knowing it is repeating it; the mind is the place those words are stored, as a vessel holds liquid or a tablet receives words. One could say that repetition is a *sign* of understanding, but that would be according the practice a kind of epistemological curiosity with which it does not necessarily keep company. Better to say: repetition *is* understanding, one thing we can mean or demand when we ask, do you understand? Have you learned?

Nothing would dismay the humanist reformers more than this *reductio*. Erasmus's much-used manual for letter writing, *De Conscribendis Epistulis*, asks, "what is the point of repeating parrot-fashion [*psitaci more*] words that are not understood?"[22] A century later Brinsley insists, as part of a growing chorus of his contemporaries, "*Legere & non intelligere negligere est*": to read without understanding is neglect.[23] Such complaints are a *topos* of the

---

21. T. W. Baldwin, *Small Latine*, 2:419. And from the statutes of the Bangor School, closely based on those at Bury St. Edmunds: "The said Scholars shall daily use to commit to their memory and care without the book by the Schoolmaster's or Usher's appointment all petty sentences within their ordinary lectures which the Schoolmaster or Husher may require and hear without the Book at the time appointed for the rendering of their said ordinary Lectures." Students also "shall learn perfectly by heart the articles of the Christian faith, The Lords prayer, the ten commandants [*sic*] . . . and the Schoolmaster with the Husher shall every Saturday in the afternoon make proof and instruct their Scholars for their perfectness therein" (*Small Latine*, 1:307, 309). David Riggs discusses these practices with an emphasis on how "drawn-out, compulsory routines of transcription and regurgitation dissolved the antithesis between physical and mental labour" (*The World of Christopher Marlowe*, 37–38).

22. Erasmus, *Works*, 25:194. The curriculum at Bury St. Edmunds seems to echo Erasmus: "Those who are being instructed in the first elements of grammar are not to utter words at random and without understanding like parrots" (T. W. Baldwin, *Small Latine*, 1:301).

23. Brinsley, *Ludus*, G1v.

literature, and I have already suggested in the preface that their increasing frequency and the specificity of the reformers' remedies—the efforts to find pedagogical techniques that guarantee *real* understanding—are a historical phenomenon, a late sixteenth-century second wave of humanist reform. In one way or another all the exercises I describe below are part of that phenomenon, efforts to address that anxiety. But repetition is tenacious, insidious, and in many cases perfectly useful. It is easiest of the kinds of learning to recognize; in its simple rigor it is always ready as a mode of proof and a mode of discipline. It subtends the idea of education as a project of mere reproduction: raising boys to be the same as their teachers, their fathers, and one another; to hold and to voice the same beliefs.[24]

The trouble between such an idea of learning and romance fiction is easy to anticipate. Unalloyed repetition is the enemy of narrative, narrative that can tell time only by producing difference: where the same thing happens again and again, there is no story. Mere repetition is likewise the enemy of figuration. If to know *is* to repeat, then, what can *The Faerie Queene* be but a long, corrosive forgetfulness?

$$"q \rightarrow a"$$

The game of *catechism* is very close to mere repetition: it is based on a memorized script, which provides particular questions as cues for particular answers. The northern Reformation's zeal to promulgate points of doctrine to the ordinary worshipper accounted for its rapid spread. Its historians, however, argue for origins in medieval grammar teaching, and in the latter half of the sixteenth century religious catechisms were well installed in school.[25] There is an engraved image of a schoolroom—featuring

---

24. On the question of "education as reproduction," Margaret Ferguson takes a useful survey of the work of such theorists as Pierre Bourdieu, Jean-Claude Passeron, and Louis Althusser, as well as some dissenters, in "Teaching and/as Reproduction." This strain of educational thinking is grounded in Marxist theory, and the idea that education functions chiefly to reproduce existing class structures. See also Halpern, *The Poetics of Primitive Accumulation*, esp. chapters 1 and 2, where he discusses the relationship between ideological reproduction and stylistic reproduction.

25. Ian Green describes how the interrogatory catechism becomes the standard English form over the course of the sixteenth century in *The Christian's ABC*, 62; on Donatus's *Ars Grammatica* and other roots of the form, including Luther's catechism and humanist dialogue, see 16–18. On catechism in the Reformation generally see Strauss, *Luther's House of Learning*, 153–73. On the role of religious catechism in schools see Watson, *The English Grammar Schools to 1660*, 69–85, which includes a digest of school statutes prescribing the practice, usually for Saturdays. See also Charlton, *Education in Renaissance England*, 98.

a boy, his head cocked deferentially, declaiming to the bearded master—on the frontispiece of Alexander Nowell's *Catechism*, which was decreed the national standard in 1571. The participants inside are identified as Master and Scholar:

MAISTER: Tell me my childe of what religion thou art.
SCHOLER: Of the same religion, whiche Christ our Saviour taught, whereof I am
    called, and doe trust, that in deede I am a Christian.
MA: What is Christian religion?
SCH: Christian religion is the true worshipping of God, and keeping of his
    commaundementes.[26]

Like all of the catechisms published for use in and out of school in the period, Nowell's follows this script form. The master's questions are memorized cues to particular memorized responses. The answers—to the chagrin of reformers—were often ponderous and intricate.[27] The exercise is more ritual, liturgical, antiphonal than the simplest forms of repetition ($a \rightarrow a$), but whether the matter is doctrine or grammar everything hangs on getting the words just right.

What kind of knowledge is this? The scholar's answers are repeated verbatim: one could again invoke many of the familiar metaphors of pedagogical reproduction to account for them, tablets and vessels and so on. The fact that they are cued by the master's questions, however, makes a difference, for it ties them to a particular two-part performance. You know the catechism in the saying of it; you prove your command—your knowledge of doctrine, and perhaps even your faith—by a specific performance. The lesson is identical with its test.[28] That identity has obvious practical advantages for the master: like the simplest repetition games, it provides a clear answer to that question, *how do I know you understand?* All the scholar has to do is hold up his part; his answers can be checked against the script. But for just this reason it is also a kind of knowing that seems particularly beholden to the circumstances of instruction—one that is rigidly shaped

26. Nowell, *A Catechisme, or Institution of Christian Religion*, A2v.
27. See I. Green, *ABC*, 246. Brinsley's pedagogy of "short questions" (*Ludus*, G3r) is an address to this tendency.
28. See Strauss, *Luther's House*: "From the very outset it [catechism] prepared the learner for the examination that tested its results at the end of the learning process" (173). This identity of lesson and test is a particularly clear instance of the general problem of a lesson that is difficult to extract from the scene of instruction, and that, if cleaved to, may compel the student to impose the shape of that original classroom scene on the world beyond.

by the configuration of the classroom where it is learned. Dissatisfaction with the inflexibility of the form is increasingly evident among reformers in the late sixteenth and early seventeenth centuries, and there are various attempts to loosen it from rote recitation.[29] But as always, the reformers' zeal is best evidence of the tenacity of the practices they deplore.

Boys did sometimes catechize one another in schools, at least in grammar: it was possible, that is, for the scholar to play the master's part.[30] Still it remained the master's part, whoever played it, as Nowell's script would remind any reader. That stubborn difference between roles raises another peculiarity of knowing for two voices: which of them is yours? Can they both be owned? If only the answerer's, then to whom—when you are out there in the world—does the questioner's belong? Is the questioning voice to be understood as something like the prompting of circumstance, which the believer rejoins with professions of faith? Or does it remain the voice of a particular, honored authority, now implanted within you but no less alien? (Sidney has a canny phrase for this problem, the "inward father."[31]) These are questions again about how a particular kind of knowing, a schoolroom game of question and answer, allows us to know the world precisely by giving the world that schoolroom's shape. It is a problem Lyly and Sidney confront when they use the script of catechism to represent the business of inner deliberation.

a . . . c . . . e→g

Grammar *drills* are another kind of understanding again. ("Drill" in this sense is a nineteenth-century coinage, gathering for my purposes a category of exercise the schoolmasters did not clearly distinguish.) They are the

29. In *The Christian's ABC* Green observes that there is "no shortage of evidence for the importance attached to constant repetition and simple memorization" (236), but that "By the turn of the sixteenth century and increasingly from the mid-seventeenth century...we find distinctions being drawn between, on the one hand, the mechanical parroting of words and, on the other, a real understanding of their meaning and commitment to their implementation" (232). Catechism became over time a more sophisticated practice as the interpolation of longer texts, use of both reading and hearing, and other devices came to modify the basic structure of question and answer: "By the late sixteenth or early seventeenth centuries, 'catechizing' was not a single operation but a whole range of overlapping and interlocking activities" (5).

30. See the Harrow statutes of 1580: "The Schoolmaster shall every day, for the space of an hour, hear either the third, fourth or fifth forms amongst themselves propound questions and answers one to another of cases, declinings, comparison of nouns, conjugations, tenses and modes of verbs" (Watson, *Grammar Schools*, 93–94).

31. Sidney, *The Countess of Pembroke's Arcadia (The Old Arcadia)*, 292.

routines of declining and conjugating that were a staple of the schoolboy's work. We have seen Kempe's students ring changes on *pater bonus diligit filium probum*. At Rivington, "the Usher shall daily exercise [the students] with diversity of words in every comparison, declension, gender, tense, and conjugation"; at Bury St. Edmunds, students quiz each other "two and two . . . in the searching out the declinations of nouns with their due articles and Genders in the seeking and finding out of the conjugations with their preterits and supines."[32] Lily's *Grammar* makes ambitious suggestions about how these questions should be posed: "every waye forewarde, backwarde, by cases, by persones, that neyther case of noune, ne persone of verbe can be required, that he can not without stoppe or study telle."[33] Such rigor is systematic and permutational: like a musician practicing a difficult figure, first straight, then backward, then upside down, then transposed by thirds, by fourths, and so on. These exercises make for a kind of systematic mimesis of chance, forcing the student to adapt to new conditions, to keep making new forms. They are also displacements of chance, a way of domesticating it.

That power to imitate chance is important to all exercises, and it will be useful to keep such ambitions in mind, for of course nothing is more ambitious that way than romance. Their ingenuity—"forewarde, backwarde, by cases, by persones"—reflects a determination to outwit mere repetition. Drill would seem to be the purest case of rule-following in the Tudor schoolroom: the rules of grammar not merely as matter for memory, but as ways of making and acting. There is a parallel strain of skepticism, however, about precepts in the pedagogical literature, strongest in the earliest decades when Erasmus was most influential, but persistent into the next century. The founder of St. Paul's school, John Colet, concludes his *Aeditio* of 1509 by insisting that students "busily learn and read good Latin authors of chosen poets and orators, and note wisely how they wrote and spake, and study alway to follow them, desiring none other rules but their examples."[34] Erasmus promises that "aided by . . . rules you will notice much for

---

32. M. Kay, *The History of Rivington and Blackrod Grammar School*, 184–85; T. W. Baldwin, *Small Latine*, 1:308.

33. Lily, *Grammar*, A3r. See also Brinsley's *Ludus Literarius*: "aske the same questions backe againe, the last first. . . . Then aske the questions as it were backward thus" (H4v); "make them as perfect in their Genders forwards and backwards" (I1v).

34. He continues: "For in the beginning men spake not Latin because such rules were made, but contrariwise because men spake such Latin upon that followed the rules were made. That is to say, Latin speech was before the rules, not the rules before the Latin speech. Wherefore, well-beloved masters and teachers of grammar, after the parts of speech sufficiently known in your schools, read and expound plainly unto your scholars good authors, and show to them

yourself" but cautions not to "follow . . . slavishly." Even Ascham, always keen after a good precept, wants "a volume of examples, a page of rules."[35]

The reformers' main anxiety about rules is that they will be nothing more than matter for memorization, as of course they often were, and that if they are applied—whatever, exactly, that might mean—they will prove too rigid for the play of circumstance to which the orator must always hold himself accountable. The language of imitation serves as a way of easing these worries, even in cases where the activity of *imitatio* is most highly methodized. This recourse to instinct reflects how underdeveloped most humanist reflection on rule-following tends to be (a matter that will become particularly important in chapter 3).[36] One might discriminate among the kind of understanding that is proved by saying the rule, the kind of understanding proved by acting in accord with it, and (best of all) the kind of understanding proved by doing both. But the difference between the first two—saying the rule and following it—is surprisingly elusive, as though rule-following were understood merely as a kind of saying-into-action. Recent scholarship has emphasized that the modes of reading taught in the humanist classroom were pointedly directed toward praxis.[37] The corollary is that action was often understood on the model of speech, acting out as reading out, the recitation of a maxim in the language of the deed. On this straitened account of action Sidney in particular will brood.

art→a / r / t

The next three kinds of exercises—the next three ways of proving understanding—are aspects of that larger routine of "unfolding" a text that Kempe describes: presenting a lecture, declaring its "argument and scope," construing and parsing the grammar, observing rhetorical ornament and logical structure. The canonical account of this procedure is from Erasmus's *De Ratione Studii*, where his example is a comedy by Terence. Before beginning

---

every word, and in every sentence what they shall note and observe, warning them busily to follow and to do like both in writing and in speaking, and be to them your own self also speaking with them the pure Latin very present, and leave the rules" (quoted in Hunter, *John Lyly*, 19–20).

35. Erasmus, *Works*, 24:670; Ascham, *Letters of Roger Ascham*, 270–711.

36. Judith Anderson's *Words that Matter* explores how the systematic grammar (especially syntax), and emphasis on the mind generally, in scholastic thought gives way to a concern with referentiality, the matter of words, among the humanists (esp. 7–42).

37. See esp. Grafton and Jardine, "'Studied for Action': How Gabriel Harvey Read His Livy." This idea will return in chapters 2 and 3.

to work on the language, he advises, inform your students about the life and characteristic style of the author, the laws of the genre, and explain "as clearly and concisely as possible the gist of the plot [*summam explicet argumenti*]."[38] The teacher should go on to point out unusual features of rhetoric and instances of imitation, before turning to philosophy in order to "bring out the moral implication of the poets' stories" and identify "patterns [*exempla*]" of conduct.[39] Whenever the school statutes and timetables refer to an author, it is a good bet that something like this routine was used to bring his language before the boys: Terence, Cicero, Virgil, Ovid, all entered the classroom by these stairs.

John Brinsley takes the time to explain each step. He uses the term *analysis* for the first half of a process he calls "*Analysis* and *Genesis*; that is . . . resolving and unmaking the Latine of the Author, and then making it againe just after the same manner, as it was unmade." Taken all together this operation is very close to what Ascham calls "double translation," but for the moment I want only to borrow his phrase "resolving and unmaking." "Unmaking" is the word Kempe uses for breaking down a word into syllables, in preparation for learning to write.[40] The "unmaking" of analysis can refer more broadly to reducing anything to its fundamental parts, particularly where the process is guided by the assumption that those parts were the units of its original making (or "genesis"). This is another powerful idea of what it is to understand something: bringing a complex structure to the point where there is nothing complex left, only simples, its building blocks. The humanist passion for grammatical and rhetorical disassembly has led critics like Mary Thomas Crane to conclude that schoolboys were "taught to view texts as containers of fragments that could be possessed by memorization and transcription in a notebook."[41] Success at this delimited

38. Erasmus, *Works*, 24:683. The *Collected Works'* translation of *argumentum* as "plot" risks anachronism, but gives some indication of how narrative might be assimilated to the nontime of argument.

39. Ibid., 24:682–83. Erasmus's instructions are worth comparing with the revealingly partial version given by Cardinal Wolsey in his 1529 statutes for the Ipswich Grammar School, which was reprinted in some editions of John Colet's *Grammar*. See also Mack, *Elizabethan Rhetoric*, 15–16.

40. Brinsley, *Ludus*, O4v; Kempe, *Education*, in *Four Tudor Books*, ed. Pepper, 223. The terms "analysis" and "genesis" suggest Ramist influence. See also Coote, *English Scholemaster*, C3r.

41. Crane, *Framing Authority*, 86. Anthony Grafton and Lisa Jardine's *From Humanism to the Humanities* is the most influential site for this argument; see for example their account of the pedagogy of Guarino Guarini in fifteenth-century Ferrara as "an overwhelming preoccupation with a profusion of tiny details. . . . When we try to imagine what it felt like to be trained in rhetoric by Guarino we are faced with this mass of disparate information hung on a frame of one or two key texts" (20). See also Kintgen, *Reading in Tudor England*, 43. Richard Halpern argues

game is a matter of showing you can cut out the right bits. Kempe—who repeatedly expresses his interest in mastering larger structures of argument too—would be dismayed at her conclusion, but Crane is right to diagnose a characteristic devolution of the humanist program, as well a prominent direction in its theory. Just as mere repetition can count as learning, so can mere analysis, a practice that will inevitably obscure wholes by a multiplication of bright parts.[42]

$$a\,/\,r\,/\,t \;\longrightarrow\; \text{A B C} \ldots \text{Q R S T U} \ldots$$

The idea that I can understand something simply by breaking it apart is stubbornly autonomous: that brute conviction underlies, for example, the dichotomizing of the Ramist program (as we will see in chapter 5). It is parodied at moments in Spenserian allegory. In schoolroom routines of "unfolding," however, analysis is usually linked to *classification*: I know X because I recognize it not only as a distinct part of the text, but as an instance of Y. Such recognitions are necessary for parsing, when students (as at Rivington) "give a reason why every word is put in such gender, number, person, case, tense, and conjugation."[43] Those "reasons" are precepts of grammar, and the words are sorted out among them—the precepts function as categories. The typing of rhetorical phenomena, identifying the schemes and tropes, is a similar business. The more highly developed schemes of classification are those associated with schoolroom practices of note taking and the commonplace book. Students often identified features of texts, particular tropes and schemes, by a system of marginal notations. They also kept separate commonplace books—sometimes only one, sometimes two or even three—for the storage and ready retrieval of fragments of their

---

that humanist pedagogy "decomposed" texts "into harmless, inert atoms" (*Poetics*, 47). Peter Mack offers a qualification: "Thus although the general tendency of the commonplace method is to fragment a text into short reusable segments, it can also encourage readers to explore connections and contrasts of ideas within a text, to discover preoccupations and connections beyond the level of linear plot"; "In their commentaries schoolmasters gave considerable emphasis to the structure and narrative order of set texts" (*Elizabethan Rhetoric*, 44, 47).

42. Roger Ascham testifies both to humanist discomfort with this tendency and to its prevalence in a letter to the Strasbourg schoolmaster Johann Sturm, in which he discusses his ambition to write a book of examples as complement to *The Schoolmaster*: "I want something else [than books of rules], I require more. We need an artisan and an architect who knows how by an artful method to bring the parts together, to polish the rough spots, and to build up the entire structure" (*Letters*, 270).

43. Kay, *The History of Rivington and Blackrod Grammar School*, 185.

reading.[44] The matter they transcribed there could include *sententiae*, brief anecdotes, or exempla; choice rhetorical ornaments might be stored in another notebook, or interspersed. The schemes of classification varied, with the most typical being likely topics for debate, such as "courage" or "justice," arranged alphabetically.[45]

It is a confusing aspect of the theory of these books—not uncomplained-about by contemporaries—that both the categories and the matter that filled them could be called "commonplaces," or *topoi*, or *loci*.[46] A place, that is, could be put inside another place. What this ambiguity demonstrates is the extent to which any piece of text might itself be treated as a paradigm waiting for instances. "Fortitude" is a category; but so, once it has been transcribed under "Fortitude" in your commonplace book, is the maxim, "As Iron doth bruse all other mettalles: so fortitude doth overcome all kinde of daungers."[47] By virtue of having been picked out and recorded, those particular words can themselves now be recognized as a general case within which some aspect of our experience might fit—a place where that experience can be put.

Understanding, then, is a matter of making connections, subsuming instances under headings, putting things in the right place. You prove you know by the proper ordering of a commonplace book and the true classifying of a given case. Taken together the commonplaces make "a mode of apprehending the world," as Ann Moss puts it, a grid for experience with a place for every new thing: Erasmus can promise that if you "first provide yourself with a full list of subjects," you will be ready for anything.[48]

44. See Mack, *Elizabethan Rhetoric*, 44, for a concise account.

45. On schemes of classification in commonplace books see Moss, *Printed Commonplace-Books and the Structuring of Renaissance Thought*, esp. 192–95.

46. As Richard Sherry testifies: "the varietie of authors hath made the handlynge of them [commonplaces] sumwhat darke, because among them selves they can not wel agre, neyther of the names, neyther of the number, neyther of the order" (*A Treatise of Schemes and Tropes*, F4v). See also T. W. Baldwin, *Small Latine*, 1:126–27. Sister Joan Marie Lechner distinguishes between the 'analytic' and the 'subject' topic in *Renaissance Concepts of the Commonplaces*: "[The 'analytic' topic is] usually thought of as a concept which could be used in asking oneself questions about a subject and which would generate ideas concerning the subject: for example, such 'places' as definition, division, etymology and relation, when applied to a particular subject, would 'spin out' the full meaning of that subject. The 'subject' topic or heading, on the other hand, represented a heading more usable for organizing material gathered in a commonplace book, where one 'located' an argument named according to the subject matter of its contents, such as virtue, physics, peace, or ethics" (229–30).

47. Meres, *Palladis Tamia*, M2v.

48. Moss continues: "The commonplace-book is revealed as a mode of apprehending the world, and a mode which is beginning to stabilize into a mental set. The commonplace-headings themselves may be varied and they may be increased in number and range, but

That grid is also a powerful de facto model of the mind, a subdivided space within which useful knowledge can be stored by its kinds, a less vividly imagined but perhaps more deeply founded version of the memory palace.[49] This space is the most important contribution rhetorical pedagogy makes to the set of ways that the period pictures what thinking is like and where it happens. There will be more to say about its dimensions shortly; here what is most salient is that the attendant idea of memory is fundamentally synchronic. By organizing matter according to topic in space, the commonplaces displace not only other, chronologically based orders but also the sedimented and time-bound nature of untrained memory. The first page and the last page of a diary, or of the old *Arcadia*, plot points on an arc of time. What is to be found on the first and last pages of a commonplace book is a relatively arbitrary function of its indexing procedure. Like repetition and analysis, the classification of commonplaces takes the time out of the matter to which it is applied.

One more operation native to the routine of unfolding: *epitome*, deriving from a text a shorter formulation that captures that text's meaning or essence. Ascham uses the word to mean "cutting away words and sentences" in making summaries, a practice he scorns as "a way of study belonging

---

the universe to which they refer is assumed to constitute an array of morally interrelated concepts, susceptible to an arrangement which supplies a rhetoric of argumentation geared to put the case for and against any proposition or course of action, to persuade and dissuade, to praise and blame" (*Printed Commonplace-Books*, 123). Erasmus's words are from *De Copia*, in *Works*, 24:635. He elaborates a few pages later: "So prepare for yourself a sufficient number of headings, and arrange them as you please, subdivide them into the appropriate sections, and under each section add your commonplaces and maxims; and then whatever you come across in any author, particularly if it is rather striking, you will be able to note down immediately in the proper place, be it an anecdote or a fable or an illustrative example or a strange incident or a maxim or a witty remark or a remark notable for some other quality or a proverb or a metaphor or a simile." His own example is "the heading 'Changeableness' or 'Irresolution'" (*Works*, 24:638, 642). Roger Ascham asserts that "books of commonplaces be very necessary to induce a man into an orderly general knowledge, how to refer orderly all that he readeth *ad certa rerum capita* and not wander in study" (*Schoolmaster*, 107). One hears in "wander" an echo of his complaint against romance, to which the *capita rerum* are an antidote.

49. See Strauss, *Luther's House of Learning*: "This kind of reductionism, which pictured the mind as an efficient engine with discrete parts and a tidy division of mechanical operations, made matters considerably easer for pedagogues" (83). Jessica Wolfe discusses the analogy of mind and method to mechanism in her *Humanism, Machinery, and Renaissance Literature*, 26, 135ff. The analogy is not much found in the pedagogical literature itself.

rather to matter than to words, to memory than to utterance."[50] He is not the only schoolmaster to be skeptical of such exercises, but the deeper idea behind them—that understanding is an effect of condensation—is commonplace and powerful. It is a small step from excerpting *sententiae* from a text to taking them, by synecdoche, for its meaning. Brinsley calls such maxims the "summe" (as Erasmus calls them the *summa*), and such a sense of their importance would come naturally to students trained in the early forms on Aesop, where a sententious moral typically provides both narrative closure and an account of what the tale meant.[51] Likewise for students expected to elaborate arguments from the seed of a maxim. Once again there is a simple intuition at the root of these practices: to understand a big thing, a thing too big to think about all at once, take a small but representative piece of it, or make a small model of the whole; either way, something small enough to grasp, as though in the palm of your hand.[52] The resulting epitome, typically in the form of *sententia*, can be stored among the commonplaces. It is fit for memorizing. And again, when it derived from a text that is narrative in character, it takes the time out.

So, another three ideas of knowing: taking a text apart, classifying its pieces, making it small enough to hold all at once. They are interwoven in the practice of unfolding a text in the classroom. But their separability is important: each, in its own circumstances, generates a different answer to that question, *do you understand?*

$$a \rightarrow \alpha \ (\rightarrow a)$$

We come now to *translation*, a practice at the heart of the humanist classroom, and yet an abiding matter of uneasiness there. The late sixteenth century was a great age of translating in the larger culture: all kinds of books were being Englished at London's busy presses, from Elyot's Plutarch to courtesy books to the Italian tales against whose "subtle, cunning, new, and

---

50. Ascham, *Schoolmaster*, 109, 106. Howell, *Logic and Rhetoric*, quotes a testy Richard Montague on the subject: "The Abridgements that have beene made long since, and of late, are held to be one of the chiefe plagues of Learning, and learned men. It maketh men idle, and yet opiniative, and well conceited of themselves. He that can carry an Epitome in his pocket... imagineth mightily, that he knoweth much, and yet indeed is but a *ignaro*" (201). Mordechai Feingold discusses Ascham's epitomes in relation to Ramism in "English Ramism: A Reinterpretation," 160–64.

51. "Also cause them to make you a report of what the summe of the Epistle is... as was said of the Fables" (Brinsley, *Ludus*, Y4v).

52. On fables, as well as on *sententiae*, handbooks, and hands, see chapter 3.

diverse shifts" Roger Ascham railed.[53] The rhetoric of their prefaces almost universally advertises the profit and instruction got by the new ease of access. R. F. Jones surveys the propagandizing of this industry and concludes that the "process of education was thought to consist largely in putting into the vernacular any book whatsoever."[54] He touches on a deep idea, that translation may be *in itself* both a kind of teaching and a kind of learning. A kind of teaching, in that the translator accommodates something difficult and foreign to the powers of the reader, making it familiar, carrying it across a boundary from otherness to self. A kind of learning, because the *activity* of translating, on the student's part, might itself count as understanding. Translation is an obvious engine against the risks of mere repetition, proving that grasp of the matter is independent of a particular order of words. A student who carries the same *sententia*—here *sententia* in its most general sense of "meaning"—from Latin to Greek to Hebrew and round to Latin again, as Ascham dreamed that students would, must have a strong and flexible comprehension of the argument as well as the languages. To understand something, this game suggests, *is to know it in more than one way;* as Erasmus says, "to pour the same subject-matter from one form of poetic container into another."[55]

Translation of various kinds was ubiquitous in the Elizabethan classroom. There was the routine of construing, providing word-by-word equivalents as a first stage of reckoning with a new text (English in the earliest forms; later, Latin synonyms and paraphrase). "[F]or all your constructions in grammar schools be nothing else but translations," observes Ascham.[56]

53. Ascham, *Schoolmaster*, 69.

54. Jones, *The Triumph of the English Language*, 40.

55. Erasmus, *Works*, 24:303. While anxiety about the divorce of *res* and *verba* is regularly expressed by humanist educators—most famously in Ascham's plea that "Ye know not what hurt ye do to learning that care not for words but for matter" (*Schoolmaster*, 115)—separating the two for the purposes of variation and copia is a notion that underwrites a wide range of school exercises. See also Vives: "Then let them change the words and keep the same idea" (*Vives: On Education*, 110). On problems of *res* and *verba* generally, see Terence Cave's reading of Erasmus in *The Cornucopian Text*, where he meditates on the precariousness of the project of distinguishing them: "*Res* and *verba* slide together to become 'word-things'; the notion of a single domain (language) having a double aspect replaces that of two distinct domains, language and thought" (21).

56. Ascham, *Schoolmaster*, 83. John Stockwood's *The Treatise of the Figures* (first printed 1609) gives a picture of what schoolroom construction was like: "*Figura* a figure *est* is *forma* a kind *dicendi* of speaking, *novata* made new *aliqua arte* with some art" (A4r). Lawrence D. Green notes that Stockwood was headmaster of the Tunbridge Grammar School in the 1580s, and that his textbook "is clearly the work of a teacher who has had hard experience in the classroom" ("*Grammatica Movet*: Renaissance Grammar Books and *Elocutio*," 111). See also Brinsley's examples of parsing in *Ludus*, O3r.

Exercises in more elaborate paraphrase and in "metaphrasis," turning passages from prose to verse and vice versa, were also widely used.[57] Such regimens are continuous with an Erasmian program of copious variation, recasting a single sentence 146 ways, and ultimately with the more sophisticated imitations I will treat under "composition" below.[58] Still, there was a strong suspicion of translation per se: Brinsley observes that "translations were generally in disgrace in Schooles."[59] Particularly for the stricter Ciceronians, translating could only carry students away from the best Latin into inferior style or, worse yet, out of Latin altogether into the vernacular. Such traffic might contaminate Cicero's idiom with the depredations of English word order; it was certainly of limited usefulness in teaching students to write and speak a new tongue to be forever returning to the old.

Roger Ascham is most closely identified with the humanists' characteristic solution: so-called double translation, which he describes with great care in the *Schoolmaster*.[60] This exercise begins with the usual routine of unfolding a Latin text, the master construing and parsing; "by and by" the scholar imitates him "that it may appear that the child doubteth in nothing that his master taught him before." Then master and scholar separate:

> the child must take a paper book and, sitting in some place where no man shall prompt him, by himself, let him translate into English his former lesson. Then, showing it to his master, let the master take from him his Latin book,

57. Erasmus in *De Copia*: "It will be of enormous value to take apart the fabric of poetry and reweave it in prose, and vice versa, to bind the freer language of prose under the rules of metre" (*Works*, 24:303). On versifying see Brinsley, *Ludus*, Bb3vff., and Riggs, *Christopher Marlowe*, 51–53.

58. We can see the overlap of the agendas of translation, permutational variation, and copia in exercises prescribed in Erasmus's *De Ratione Studii*, for example: "Sometimes they should express, again and again, the same proposition in different words and style. Sometimes they should vary the expression of the same proposition in Greek and Latin, in verse and prose. Sometimes they should express the same proposition in five or six kinds of metre.... Sometimes they should recast the same proposition in as many forms and figures as possible" (*Works*, 24:679).

59. Brinsley, *A Consolation for Our Grammar Schooles*, F3r. He elaborates on the same page: "First, that our usuall translations did direct the young Scholars uncertainly, and sometimes amisse, being oft rather to expresse the sense, then the words in anie right order of Grammar; and that the learners must go by memorie, and as it were by rote, more then by anie certaintie of Rule, unlesse they were of better judgement."

60. On the history of the practice see W. E. Miller, "Double Translation in English Humanist Education." Miller points out that there were earlier accounts of double translation in Vives, and that the practice can be traced to Cicero; he also cites a description of a very similar routine in the Rivington statutes of 1566 (169).

and, pausing an hour at the least, then let the child translate his own English into Latin again in another paper book.[61]

Variations on this sequence might include having the master make the English translation first, as Kempe does; in any case at the end of the exercise the master will be able to point to the Ciceronian original "wherewith he shall conferre... and correct" the translation.[62] As with Kempe, Ascham is vague on exactly what constitutes the final form of the exercise, "the like shape of eloquence."[63] Is it an idiomatic variation? A copy? Again, this seems to be a functional ambiguity. But Brinsley's account of *Analysis* and *Genesis*—"resolving and unmaking the Latine of the Author, and then making it againe just after the same manner"—is more specific. He wants to see "the very same latine of their Authors," coming back to the same words. The process is like retracing the steps of a journey, "for there is the same waie from Cambridge to London, which was from London to Cambridge."[64] Brinsley manages to combine the journey of translation with the safety of repetition. In canceling the difference between the exercise and the original by conferring and correcting, the scholar is returned to where he started: he is like a prodigal son, who has ventured out into the vernacular but is now come home safe to a London, or an ancient Rome, that has been waiting, unchanged and immemorial, for his return.

This tendency of double translation to resolve to repetition is yet another instance of an exercise that cancels time, not in this case by reducing a narrative text to an anarrative form, but by returning the student at the end of the process to the very text with which he began. Any time taken or lapsed could only be legible in a difference between the beginning and the end, and that difference is effaced by correction. There is, all the same, a stubborn middle to these exercises: an "hour at the least" between the first translation and the second for Ascham, and for Kempe, "three or foure houres."[65] The question of what this meantime is for—for remembering? for forgetting?—will recur as part of a general problem of the difference between teaching time and learning time.

61. Ascham, *Schoolmaster*, 14–15.
62. Kempe, *Education*, in *Four Tudor Books of Education*, ed. Pepper, 230.
63. Ascham, *The Schoolmaster*, 87.   64. Brinsley, *Ludus*, P1r, O4v–P1r.
65. Kempe, *Education*, in *Four Tudor Books of Education*, ed. Pepper, 227.

The summit of these schoolroom exercises and the synthesis of the boys' training in grammar, logic, and rhetoric was *composition*: of themes, letters, sometimes verse, and ultimately orations. The oration in particular is closest to the action in the real world that supposedly waited outside, the persuasive authority of counselor or governor held up to the schoolboy as the reward for his diligence. Such forms are also closest to literary imitation: in the latest stages of his curriculum at Plymouth, Kempe goes so far as to propose that "imitation may bee exercised in verse likewise. . . . As we see Virgil to have imitated Homer in method."[66] This kind of composition offers the most resistance to pedagogical reductions. It is harder to fit the student oration to the simplest metaphors of mind—to read back from the finished product to anything like a slate, or a vessel of wine. The idiom of literary imitation, outside school, defers to this difficulty. Poesis is usually described not as method, but by metaphor, digestion or honey making or other concessions to the inner alchemy by which reading becomes writing. The belly and the hive are secret spaces, and if they have a method, we cannot see it at work.

But again it is characteristic of the humanist program to render visible what is hidden by such metaphors. That is what it means to make such a complex process as composition teachable. The five-stage Ciceronian program, which Kempe adapts for his upper degrees, is the answer, with its steps of *inventio*, or finding arguments; *dispositio*, ordering them; *eloquentia*, ornamenting them with the schemes and tropes; *memoria*, committing everything to memory; and *pronunciatio*, the graces of performance.[67] The process draws on all of the exercises that lead up to it, offering the student a procedure by which the memory-structure of the commonplaces may be put to work in argument. Of the five stages, *inventio* is generally considered the most important—so says Cicero—and it provides the larger culture with the most elaborated and specific pedagogical model of what it is like to understand, or just to think about any question at all. (The other stages seem to have much less of a hold on the poetic imagination; they are in any event much less directly associated with poetry as an art of inventiveness.) For these reasons, and because it is so often used to figure thinking in fiction, I will take *inventio* here as a synecdoche for the problem of method in composition generally.

66. Ibid., 236.

67. The earliest Latin treatment of the five stages is the *Ad C. Herennium Libri Quattuor De Arte Rhetorica*, usually known as the *Ad Herennium* and attributed in the Renaissance to Cicero; other sources included Cicero's *De Inventione, De Oratore*, and *De Partitione Oratoria*, and Quintilian's *Institutio Oratoria*. See Howell, *Logic and Rhetoric*, 66–68.

The verb *invenire* means "to find," and this first step is the gathering of matter for making arguments. It begins with a question: in school, typically a set subject for a theme, something like "Ulysses should urge the Trojans to give back Helen rather than endure the war." The writers of the logic and rhetoric handbooks treat what happens next as a physical event in a mental space. "[Y]ee must drawe the wordes of your question through the places," says Ralph Lever, and Abraham Fraunce advises, "If we shall for exercise sake use to draw any one word through these generall places of invention, it will breede a great plentie and varietie of new argumentes."[68] The "places" to which both men refer are the commonplaces, here understood as a set of relational categories, or ways other matter might bear on the question at hand. (John Brinsley's simplified list in *Ludus Literarius* is pitched to the schoolroom: "Causes, Effects, Subjects, Adjuncts, Disagreeable things, Comparisons, Notations, Distributions, Definitions, Testimonies."[69]) The words of the question—words like "Helen" and "war"—are one by one drawn through those places as through a succession of rooms, where association, like a magnetism between proximate objects, finds out related arguments. Drawing "war" through the *topos* "cause," for example, might yield the argument, "As the wings of birds being clipt, in time do grow out againe: so warlike forces doe continually gather head, except thou often curbe them and keepe them under."[70]

Not only does this method offer a way to start to think about the question, but the darkness of the other mind, the student's mind, is lit up for the master (and for the student) to see. The process evidently relies on that mind being exceptionally well stocked with commonplaces. How did it work in practice? Aphthonius's widely used *Progymnasmata* contains exercises in such intermediate genres as fable and *chreia* (or anecdote-making), and Lorich's schoolroom edition models for students the process of drawing sample questions through the places *a causa*, *a contrario*, and so on.[71]

68. Lever, *The Arte of Reason, Rightly Termed, Witcraft*, P1v; Fraunce, *The Lawiers Logike*, 81v. See also T. W. Baldwin, *Small Latine*, 2:5, and for a useful general survey Langer, "Invention," in *The Cambridge History of Literary Criticism: Volume 3, The Renaissance*, ed. Norton, 136–44.

69. Aristotle's predicaments were popular for this purpose, as was the set recommended by Aphthonius's *Progymnasmata*; see Moss, *Printed Commonplace-Books*, 192–95.

70. Meres, *Palladis Tamia. Wits Treasury*, Gg3v. Cicero defines an argument simply as a "plausible device to obtain belief [*probabile inventum ad faciendam fidem*]" (*Cicero*, ed. Loeb, 4:315). See also Lanham, *A Handlist of Rhetorical Terms*, 170.

71. See for example an exercise in *chreia* that starts from Genesis 50:1, Joseph weeping at the death of his father Jacob; drawing this verse through the place *a contrario* yields a meditation on false tears (Aphthonius, *Aphthonii Sophistae Progymnasmata*, D7v–D8r). See also Riggs, *Christopher Marlowe*, 52–54.

Brinsley advises that scholars closely follow these given examples to start: "These very Theames may be written on, first for incouragement; after, others of like matter to be imitated, according to the same places." His faith in the sufficiency of students' commonplace books for more adventurous composition is limited, and he advises that they rely on a wide range of printed compilations for the "choysest sayings."[72] Many of the books he recommends—like Wrednot's *Palladis Palatium Wisedoms Pallace* (1604)— are organized by topics like "Quietnesse" or "Resurrection." This means that students might simply draw the words of the question through the alphabetical index of such a book; it seems likely they often did, the more so as these collections proliferated.

The question is often asked about invention, and about the five-stage method generally: is it a way of considering an open question, or a technique for marshalling and organizing evidence to support a position determined in advance? One can find arguments for both, in the period and the present day.[73] The tendency of the second to disguise itself as the first is a particularly interesting problem, and one to which we will find Sidney attentive when he stages his forest disputations. We might also pose a parallel question: is *inventio* an artificial method, one thing the mind can do, or does it capture the nature of thinking itself? Here too there is some division. For many educators, invention's relation to thinking more generally is not of particular interest; it is a discipline, in every sense, and if students are doing it then at least their minds are not wandering. But others sound more like Joseph Hall, whose devotional handbook *The Art of Divine Meditation* (1609) Brinsley praises for its account of *inventio*: "I had rather to require only a deep and firme *Consideration* of the thing propounded . . . through all, or the principall of those places which natural reason doth afford us: wherein, let no man pleade ignorance, or feare difficulty: we are all thus farre borne Logicians."[74] That is to say that *inventio* is a true representation

---

72. Brinsley, *Ludus*, Aa4v, Bb2v. Charles Hoole, writing well into the seventeenth century, seems even more uneasy about the students' ability to gather sufficient matter, and advises that they pool together what they invent (*A New Discovery of the Old Art of Teaching Schoole*, N3r). See Clark, *John Milton at St. Paul's School*, 218–19.

73. See Ullrich Langer, "Invention," in *The Cambridge History of Literary Criticism*, 136–37; Howell, *Logic and Rhetoric*, 68.

74. Hall, *The Art of Divine Meditation*, D5r–D6v. Hall's "*Consideration*" is a word particularly suited to *inventio*-as-thinking, assembling the constellation of related ideas. Hall believes in method, but does not fetishize it: "For as the minde, if it go loose and without rule, roves to no purpose; so if it bee too much fettered, with the gines [engines] of strict regularity moveth nothing at all" (D6r). See also Sidney's friend Abraham Fraunce in his *Lawiers Logike*: "I say, that mans soule hath in it a naturall power and abilitie, whereby it is apt to conceive any thing,

of the operation of the mind, a practice that can be refined by attention and study, but which admits of no alternative save "rov[ing] to no purpose."[75] What school has to teach, then, is what thinking really looks like, how it really works. If, as a poet, I mean to write a scene of deliberation, surely this is how I should conceive it.

Classroom composition remains more complicated than this sketch of invention can compass. It entails any number of other de facto measures of understanding (I understand X because I can make something useful out of it; I understand Y because I can persuade you that it is true; I understand Z—by way of Erasmus's *copia*—because I can dilate it, amplify it, constitute or reconstitute persuasive speech from an atom of argument; and so on). I have suggested that this very complexity—the practical difficulty of judging an oration, as opposed to a grammar exercise—motivates the explicitness of the method of *inventio* and its successor stages. Let us in any event say that as a young, well-educated man in Elizabethan England, you think this way, or think you think this way; when you look inside your own mind, you see what you were taught to see; when you make a mistake, you rebuke yourself for a lapse from this method. What would be the consequences? One, much commented on, is that you will tend to approach any problem as a debate on which you must take a side. This is a cliché of the rhetorical mind-set generally.[76] Another is that you will assume that matters are to be decided or contests won by appeal to a store of shared, often ancient wisdom. Finally, and most important to my argument, *there will be something fundamentally atemporal, anarrative, even ahistorical about the arguments you make.* Even when you draw the words of the question through the place *a causa* you are seeking after commonplaces rather than a narrative, and seeking in a space of memory that is not stratified or sedimented with time, but laid out in a topical field. The mind so represented it a timeless place.[77]

---

if it bee directed, turned, applied, and bent thereunto. . . . But to him onely, as Tully sayth, will these generall predicamentes or Categories of argumentes become profitable indeede, which hath beene a travailed and a well experienced man in matters of importance" (81v). As Ann Moss remarks, this idea of methodical invention as the nature of thinking is characteristic of Agricola and Ramus: "Commonplaces are not only 'sedes argumentorum,' but 'sedes naturae.' The headings in the student's commonplace-book are a key to chapters in the book of nature itself" (*Printed Commonplace-Books*, 121).

75. Hall, *Art*, D6r.

76. On such mind-sets see Richard Lanham's introduction to *The Motives of Eloquence*, 1–35.

77. Timothy Hampton describes a version of this problem in his book on the rhetoric of exemplarity, *Writing from History*: he argues that "humanism is marked by an essential paradox" (16), on the one hand acutely sensitive to historical distance, on the other committed to a model of exemplary instruction that ignores that distance. Examples will be the subject of chapter 4;

a *vs.* b

The last routine in this taxonomy, the game that looks most like a traditional game, is *disputation*, where understanding equals winning—the schoolboy equivalent of trial by combat. Contests of one kind or another were a regular feature of school life from the earliest forms, and Erasmus praises the salutary effects of "mutual rivalry," or *aemulatio*.[78] The first exercises in this vein are often close to catechism: Edmund Coote's *English School-Maister* (1596) provides a script for a debate about spelling, and in a marginal note advises, "When your Scholers first learne this Chapter, let one read the questions, and another the answer. When your Scholers oppose one the other, let the answerer answer without booke."[79] Brinsley likewise suggests that students rehearse from memory the "disputations of grammar" from Stockwood's *Quaestiones* (1592).[80] As students progress, disputations become formal, competitive occasions, where success and failure dictate classroom standing, and even the order of seating.[81] These formal debates demand that scholars draw on the same technical powers of invention to fashion their arguments. For their pains, other prizes might be available too: at Sandwich the statutes provide for a once-yearly public "disputacions, upon questions provided by the Master," with the winner to receive a silver pen worth 2s. 6d.[82]

If understanding here looks like winning, there were also subtler ways in which this game might get inside the student's head. Like catechism, it presents thinking as an affair for two voices, and the literary representation of decision-making as an inner debate *in utramque partem* is a familiar

---

here I am trying to understand how pedagogical practices contributed to this emptying of time from texts in the classroom.

78. Erasmus, *De Ratione Studii*, in *Works*, 24:682; see also *De Pueris*: "The motives of victory and competition are deeply embedded in our children, and the fear of disgrace and desire for praise are also deeply rooted, especially in children who have outstanding intellectual abilities and energetic personalities. The teacher should exploit these motives to advance their education.... In short, by alternating praise and blame, the instructor will awaken in his pupils a useful spirit of rivalry, to use Hesiod's expression" (*Works*, 26:340). Also *De Copia*, in *Works*, 24:303.

79. Coote, *The English Schoole-Maister*, E4v.

80. Brinsley, *Ludus*, Dd1v.

81. For a general discussion of English disputations see Watson, *English Grammar Schools*, 91–97. Sanction could be found in ancient sources, including Quintilian: "Having distributed the boys in classes, they made the order of speaking depend on ability, so that the place in which each of them declaimed was a consequence of the progress which they thought he had made. Judgements were made public" (*The Orator's Education*, 1:93).

82. Quoted in T. W. Baldwin, *Small Latine*, 2:378.

convention long before the Renaissance. The prominence of printed dialogues in the curriculum—Cicero's, Erasmus's, and a host of others written
specifically for the classroom—is another tributary of this practice.[83] In the
works I will consider here, the ruminative exchanges one finds in Erasmus's
Colloquia, which tend to feature an authoritative speaker and a neophyte,
are less common than a more competitive, forensic back-and-forth. For
the solitary thinker faced with a moral dilemma, as, for example, Lyly's
Euphues, making up his mind means importing the old classroom inter-
locutor and staging a debate. The habit is one more sign of the hero's
beholdenness to the particular space of his training, that resonant wooden
box that gets reconstructed in the strangest places.

From this taxonomy of exercises—repetition, catechism, drill, analysis, epitome, translation, composition, disputation—one might derive a set of even
more fundamental figures of understanding: *repetition*, for one (again not
properly a figure at all: it is the absence of trope, of turn), and then a set of
tropical or schematic defenses against it, *reversal* (or other formal, positional
variations), *translation*, *contraction*, *dilation*. Each is something fundamental
one might do with knowledge—knowledge however understood—to prove
a grasp of it. Having those tropes in mind will be useful when we get to the
romances, which experiment with them on the levels both of rhetoric and
of narrative. But by moving to such a schematic extreme, notwithstanding
my efforts to ground these concepts in daily exercises, a vast territory of
school life has already been excluded, including a wide variety of practices
that might bear on this question of what counts as having learned something. Take, for example, the classroom performance of drama. Putting
on plays was fairly common in the period, and Spenser's teacher, Richard
Mulcaster, was particularly known for the holiday and court productions
at Merchant Taylors'. Fluency of physical movement and dramatic affect
would have signaled to the audience something about which students got
it and which didn't, and some of the same criteria must have been applied
on an even more regular basis in the evaluation of *pronuntiatio*, the actual
declaiming of orations. A couple of steps deeper into the everyday brings
us to manners, a theme in many of the statutes.[84] There is also the matter of

83. On dialogues in English schoolrooms see T. W. Baldwin, *Small Latine*, 1:724–26. See
also Wilson, *Incomplete Fictions*.

84. At Westminster in 1560, for example, one of the prefects "carefully inspects each boy's
hands and face, to see if they have come with unwashed hands to school. . . . This order [*ordo*]
shall be kept every day" (Leach, *Charters*, 507–9). Early humanists, it should be said, had some

punishment. Even the most day-to-day routines, attendance, moving in an orderly way through the classroom, the school's habitus, are kinds of understanding.[85] (Certainly it is said of the student who keeps transgressing them, deliberately or accidentally, that he just doesn't understand—what to do, or that this is for his own good.) All of this is to say that my taxonomy is a long way from being an ethnography of the Elizabethan classroom.

Nor does it exhaust, or come close to exhausting, the frameworks within which the problem of learning presented itself to the Elizabethans. There were rival discourses in natural philosophy, theology (especially the question of conversion), medicine, and even magic for questions of what knowing is and how to recognize it when it happens. The vocabularies of rhetoric and pedagogy were by no means sealed off from these other frameworks by the classroom walls, and some of them will necessarily make appearances in the pages to follow.

But the reductiveness and relative independence of my scheme is still very much the point. For these reductions—like language games in their schematic simplicity—were enforced in practice. All sorts of disciplines and social spaces may aspire to give accounts of the self, from natural philosophy to common law.[86] Some have the worldly authority to impose them, and school is one of those. The interest of some scholars in establishing overarching historical paradigms of subjectivity—especially under the influence of Michel Foucault—can have the effect of distracting us from how the variety of local conceptions interact from case to case, even moment to moment.[87] Capturing that flux of admittedly partial, de facto selves, selves

---

work to do to elevate reading to the importance of manners, as Sir Thomas Elyot complains in his free translation of Plutarch: "Finally is it not a great foly and madnes that where we do accustome our chyldren to take meate with the ryght hande, and if they do put forthe the left hand, anone we correct them: and for to make them to here good and commodious lernynges, we make no provision nor be circumspecte therin?" (Elyot, *Education*, in *Four Tudor Books*, ed. Pepper, 17).

85. Bourdieu and Passeron's *Reproduction in Education, Society, and Culture* considers how much of school life is organized by instilling manners, routines, and other subcurricular school practices.

86. Elizabeth Fowler writes that "'Character' is the literary representation of person, and we should understand it as comparable to the representations of person in other spheres of cultural practice" (*Literary Character*, 28). I have not adopted her larger analytic framework here—an account of person modeled on genre theory—but I do want to think about school as one of those spheres, within which many different ideas of self are current.

87. Katherine Maus's *Inwardness and Theater in the English Renaissance* is a useful portal into questions of Renaissance subject formation, a debate I will not engage directly. I am interested in the variety of ad hoc subjectivities erected in particular scenes of instruction. Maus observes that "'Subjectivity' is often treated casually as a unified or coherent concept when, in fact, it is

as they are defined by particular social and especially pedagogical transactions, is what I hope to be able to do—it is, I believe, happening all the time in the fictions I will be most concerned with. We are always treating people *as if*, shifting the terms on which we acknowledge them, taking account of them in different lights according as they impress, seduce, frighten, hurt, or love us. We set terms for our interactions that admit, exclude, and sometimes durably shape aspects of our interlocutors. The scene of instruction has its own particular terms and urgencies for these dynamics. To be asked merely to repeat the master's words is different from being asked to imitate Cicero, or to dispute with a classmate; if, after having been licensed to declaim at the head of the class, you are constrained to a regime of catechism, you will feel it as a failure to acknowledge your powers, even an assault upon them. Teachers have the power to open and close parts of their students by how they teach—at least at the scene of instruction, and that is an important scene, and one that ramifies.

Telling Learning

I have managed to elaborate this taxonomy without commenting on the diagrams that divide it, an unsystematic mix of mock-algebra and pictograms that I have used to stand for the fundamental kinds of exercise. I intend them as an ad hoc heuristic, a way of capturing the elementary character of the ideas of understanding I take to underwrite the day-to-day practices of the schoolroom. Their reductions are at least analogies to the reductions inherent in the practices themselves. They also share a quality that I claim for most of those practices, in that, by their nature as diagrams, they *take the time out*, representing a time-bound routine or set of routines as an all-at-once picture. For, one way or another, these exercises are almost all pitched against time: repetition conforms the end to the beginning, as does most double translation; epitome, analysis, and classification are all time-independent ways of grasping a text; composition and debate rely for their matter on the synchronic inner landscape of the commonplaces. My diagrams are not themselves humanist artifacts (though there will be something to say about humanist diagram in chapter 5), but as a group they figure an important tendency in the practices they stand for.

------

a loose and varied collection of assumptions, intuitions, and practices that do not all logically entail one another and need not appear together at the same cultural moment" (29). I want (a) to describe a set of those assumptions connected to the classroom, and (b) to talk about what happens when these parts are taken for the whole.

The idea of understanding as an abstraction from time is ancient and durable, written deeply enough into thinking in the West that it can be hard to recognize. It is intuitive: if we are in the middle of events, experiencing them as they sweep past or involve us, surely we cannot understand them. We must step outside, or stand above, or slow down, and develop some account—some representation—upon which we can reflect at our leisure. It must moreover be a representation that we could potentially carry away and apply to similar events at a different time and in a different place. To have that representation is to understand, in a way that subtends most of the other nonce-accounts of understanding I have offered. That representation might take the form of a law, a rule, a moral (in the sense of maxim), or a diagram, but in any case it lifts us gratefully out of both the time of events and the time of narrative. Following Jerome Bruner, we might call this kind of understanding *paradigmatic understanding*, which satisfies us by providing some kind of detemporalized paradigm—again, be it rule, moral, exemplar, picture—to which we can contract and compare the flux of experience. Such understanding "is based upon categorization or conceptualization," writes Bruner, "and the operations by which categories are established, instantiated, idealized, and related one to the other to form a system."[88] In one way or another most of the routines described above produce or traffic in such paradigms.

Because the agenda of this book is to think about how the lessons that the schoolroom teaches find their way into fiction, the most important questions in the chapters to follow will turn on the relation between the varieties of paradigmatic understanding that school cultivates and something we might call (again following Bruner) *narrative understanding*—a mode steeped in time and circumstance, and particularly native to romance.[89] The schoolroom's own distinctive relation to questions of time and story is important to framing this contrast, for what I am ultimately describing is a kind of competition between them over how to *tell learning*. This contest is not only a matter of how narrative fictions are treated when they are brought into the curriculum—we have seen the ways in which Virgil, for

88. Bruner, "Narrative and Paradigmatic Modes of Thought," 98. A parallel line of argument in a more explicitly literary-critical context is made by Karlheinz Stierle in his influential essay, "Story as Exemplum—Exemplum as Story: On the Pragmatics and Poetics of Narrative Texts." He distinguishes between "systematic texts" like maxims and proverbs, and narrative texts.

89. Bruner argues that narrative understanding "deals in human or human-like intention and action and the vicissitudes and consequences that mark their course. It is essentially temporal rather than [like paradigmatic understanding] timeless" ("Narrative and Paradigmatic," 98–99).

example, can be resolved into a collection of commonplaces. It is equally a question of how a classroom reckons time; whether what goes on there is thought of in narrative terms, as a story or set of stories; whether the curriculum itself might be thought of as a kind of story, and how, as a plan for the development of a young man, it might compare to other modes of telling growing up, such as, say, romance.

Central to this project is a distinction between two kinds of time, *teaching time* and *learning time*. The first is the time of instruction; the second is the time within which that instruction becomes useful, meaningful, understood. It will be immediately obvious how much more tractable the first is than the second. Teaching time is best exemplified by lecturing: putting a given matter into an order of words and speaking them out. Lectures may be reliably set to clock time, which governed—usually by way of the local church bell—the ordinary hours of the Tudor classroom, according to schedules that were widely shared among schools.[90] But lectures are also normally paced with at least some attention to the students' powers of receiving them, and it is a reformers' *topos* that teaching should not go too fast for learning. This is where the gamelike structure of exercises comes in, as a way of synchronizing teaching and learning. Exercises allow for proofs of understanding within a manageable compass; they are games you can play to their finish within an hour, a day, a year, and within a long room filled with eighty boys. What gets taught, and what counts as knowing it, will be profoundly shaped by the local conditions of this demand for proof. Schools are not a place for slow time; they are impatient to know what (or better, whether) their students know.

One could think of all of this apparatus, the whole structure of school, as a defense against an alternative conception or recognition of learning time, which treats it as something much less definite, much more contingent: the kind of learning that must wait for its proof, wait until that moment when it can be somehow unfolded in action, or for that belated, years-later epiphany, *ah, now I understand!* "Time will tell," we say, or *veritas filia temporis*. Such patience over an indefinite *meantime* allows lesson and proof to be profoundly disjunct, and the idea of proof itself becomes more dilated and obscure, perhaps closer to the romance ambition of Spenser's Redcrosse—"his hart did earne / To prove his puissance" (*FQ* 1.1.3)—than to the "probation days" at the Merchant Taylors' school.[91] (*Probare* means

---

90. See, for example, the various timetables in the statutes collected by Leach in *Educational Charters*, esp. for Eton in 1530 (451) and Westminster in 1560 (507–17).

91. Probation days were an annual feature of the school year at Merchant Taylors' from its founding, including Mulcaster's tenure there; see Draper, *Four Centuries of Merchant Taylors'*

"to try" or "prove"). This kind of learning time is open to hazard and fortune, even defined by it. The schoolroom is built to shut it out.

This is not to say that the long Tudor school day admits no time but teaching time. Every schoolmaster recognizes that the boys cannot be exercised all day, that there must be intervals of play. Brinsley considers daily breaks useful because "honest recreations" improve the boys' concentration at their proper tasks; they "gaine so much time every day, as is lost in those intermissions."[92] Such breaks are worthless or "lost" in themselves, but they are a necessary condition for the success of the lessons they interrupt, a kind of pastime or meantime. Learning as play is also an important humanist idea: Ascham is one of many who recommend folding *ludus* and *labor* together.[93] But the most revealing alliance of teaching time and meantime is one we have already glimpsed, those three or four hours Kempe allows to lapse between the two phases of double translation. What are those three or four hours *for*? For remembering in, perhaps, to test the memory across a blank interval. (The students were surely occupied with other tasks, but were not being taught the matter on which they would shortly be tested.) But is that time not equally for forgetting—that is, isn't it the point of this scheduled meantime that one *might* forget? How can it be justified except as a window of necessary risk, of chance? Such indeterminate middles acknowledge the vagaries of learning time within a regimen that otherwise tends to insist on its synchronization with teaching. They pay tacit tribute to the relation between proof and time itself, setting boundaries to that time but not attempting to define what will happen in it. There is an analogy to the plot of the prodigal son, where the teaching resides in the frame, but the

---

School, 1561–1961, 248. The exercises administered on these days were eventually collected and published under the title *The schools-probation: or, Rules and orders for certain set-exercises to bee performed by the scholars on probation-daies* (1661).

92. Brinsley, *Ludus*, Qq2r.

93. Roger Ascham may disparage the "pastime and pleasure" of reading "certain books of chivalry" (romance is for him paradigmatic of lost time), but he elaborates a classical and Erasmian theme in arguing that learning itself can be a kind of play (*Schoolmaster*, 68; see also Quintilian, *Orator's Education*, 1:75, and in his *De Pueris* Erasmus writes, "If a gentle method of instruction is used, the process of education will resemble play more than work [*ludus videatur, non labor*]," *Works*, 26:324). Submerging the ends of exercise in the structure of game—substituting extrinsic purposes for intrinsic pleasures—allows him to blur the boundaries between the two. He recounts how Socrates spent his last days in the practice of metaphrasis, turning "prose into verse" as his "exercise and pastime . . . when he was in prison" (*Schoolmaster*, 98). Other writers, like Mulcaster in his *Positions*, praise the lessons to be had from a variety of physical exercises, from archery (one of Ascham's favorites) to vigorous laughter.

meaning of that teaching *might* be thought to depend, however obscurely, on the hazards of the middle.

Richard Mulcaster allows himself to ponder this problem in earnest. His treatment of time is one aspect of a general concern for the responsiveness of teaching to "circumstance." He insists, as many others do, that the readiness of students for school not be determined by mere calendar years: "ripenes in children, is not tyed to one time."[94] But he also allows himself to meditate on time in more fundamental ways. "Time of it selfe," he declares, "is the noblest circumstance wherwith we have to deale," the most important and demanding contingency—a challenge he conceives on the model of the orator's responsibility, a moral and political responsibility, to his occasion. The proper instruction at the proper moment "profiteth the *common weale* by perfiting all"; time demands the educator's respect as "the *prerogative* to thought: the *mother* to truth: the *tuchestone* to ripenesse: the *enemy* to errour: mans only stay, and helpe to advice."[95] Time is the medium of thinking; truth unfolds there and error is confuted. Again and again he insists that it is in time alone that we can know what we have learned, and *that* we have learned: "the time to prove well learned [is] long," and "proofe travell in time will perfourme."[96] At least at these moments Mulcaster entertains a different idea of proof than that of the set exercises given on probation day at his own school. He is Spenser's teacher, after all.

But one searches in vain for another Elizabethan educator who does more than recycle the *topoi* of pedagogical timeliness, and even Mulcaster's *Positions*—which he thought of as only a prologue to a full account of grammar teaching—never gets around to showing in any detail how this expansive sense of learning time might be written into the curriculum. The general claim I made in anatomizing the classroom's exercises stands: that they are constructed to impose atemporal conceptions on time-bound materials. If this is true, then, what does that mean for conceptions of *narrative*, for time as it is figured in the telling of a story? Granted, school characteristically rewrites stories in nonnarrative forms. But perhaps these exercises themselves, as events in time, have their own, so far unrecognized narratives—with their beginnings and endings, and the contingent middle before the scholar's answer? And what about the arc of the curriculum, from first beginnings in petty school to the heights of the sixth form? Are stories embedded in the structure of school?

---

94. Mulcaster, *Positions*, 31.
95. Ibid., 257.

96. Ibid., 144, 39.

I think not. I want to adopt a more demanding definition of narrative than the mere tripartite structure of beginning, middle, end—one better suited, in particular, to describing romance. Following Aristotle, let us say that narrative is a structured mimesis of life in time. (So far, of course, the same could be said of school.) Narrative is structured in the sense that it is the imitation of an action that is complete in itself, or at least carries expectations about closure and origin—the sense of an ending, as Frank Kermode would say, and the sense of a beginning, even if neither is realized.[97] But I want particularly to emphasize what Aristotle identifies as the change of fortune within those bounds, change that can take the form of a complex plot of *peripeteia* (a reversal of conditions) or *anagnoresis* (a reversal of knowledge, or recognition).[98] Romance multiplies reversals under the sign of error. Such transformations, and the sense of contingency they produce, are essential to narrative's mimesis of time, to the experience of fictional time. It is the feeling of doubt, expectancy, not-knowing, and other states of suspension—states that nonnarrative discourse is mostly concerned to exclude—that endows narrative with its capacity to express duration, and makes it host to the kind of long time, learning time, within which something we do not yet understand will prove out.

Such a definition might permit these school games to be seen as minimal narrative structures, framing as they do the indeterminacy of the student's performance. But even if we allow this, still they exert a palpable antinarrative pressure by telescoping the long time of learning to the short term of teaching. What about the bigger picture, the curriculum as narrative, the pattern of the grammar school student's progress through the forms? There is, to be sure, a necessary order to his career, a beginning and an ending and eight or so years in between. But what happens to the student over that time is typically imagined by educators in one of two ways. First, as the careful safeguarding of an original innocence, by protecting the student from bad influences and exposing him to good. This optimism is characteristic of Erasmus in most of his moods, and identified with humanism more generally, especially at its Italian origins. Second, and conversely, the project may be viewed as the constant correction of a childish nature congenitally disposed to stray, the formation of habits of rectitude by steady discipline. This is an older, one might say Augustinian strain, but both are legible, in different proportions, in most educators.[99] Neither story—if we can call

---

97. Aristotle, *Poetics*, 1450b20ff; Kermode, *The Sense of an Ending*.
98. Aristotle, *Poetics*, 1452a20ff.
99. Gerald Strauss traces these two lines to Quintilian's optimism on the one hand, and Augustine's "extreme pessimism" on the other, while acknowledging that other readings of

them that, and I would suggest we should not—gives scope for reversal, for a kind of recognition that is specifically the transformation and overturning of a previous understanding. Neither one is a plot that makes the necessary space for error.[100] They are rather cycles of repetition that add up, year to year, to a set of good habits and capacities.

The point then of this meditation on classroom time is to describe how deeply what critics have identified as the antinarrative bias of humanism is inscribed in the order of school itself, in the way school taught students to understand the texts they read, even narrative texts, and in the implicit account the curriculum gave of what growing up was like.[101] There were, to be sure, differently shaped narratives of growing up available. Some of the allegorizations of the *Aeneid*, like Landino's, took Virgil to describe the hero's maturing into his responsibilities as a founder of nations, and then there were stories like *Daphnis and Chloe*, the Greek romances.[102] But from our modern vantage, in the long wake of the bildungsroman, it is important to recognize that for the sixteenth century, education—learning, over time, to be an adult—simply was not the sort of thing you typically told a story about, and even less was it conceived of as by its nature narrative. For Fielding's Tom Jones, growing up (to the extent that he does) cannot happen except by means of a narrative structure, with its reversals and recognitions; that is the natural shape of learning. His maturity is not a matter of rejecting experience but of being shaped by it. That was not at all obviously so for Pyrocles or Redcrosse Knight or even for Hamlet. The 1580s and 90s are an essential moment in the history of the bildungsroman, but a moment when its possibility is only struggling to be born, and mostly, tendentiously, failing.

Behind such failures, and we will see many of them, is the conflict between those two kinds of understanding: paradigmatic understanding, particularly as it is rooted in the forms taught in school, and narrative understanding. Paradigmatic understanding abstracts its object from time; it is the text as already read, understood according to its topoi, its laws. It is

---

Augustine were available (*Luther's House*, 51). The more pessimistic side of Erasmus is on display in his *Institutio Principis Christiani*, about which more in chapter 3.

100. Ascham is interested in error as an element of learning, though only as an opportunity for correction: "For I know by good experience that a child shall take more profit of two faults gently warned of than of four things rightly hit" (*Schoolmaster*, 15).

101. Kinney discusses this antinarrative bias in the course of constructing an alternative in *Humanist Poetics*, 3–38. See also Helgerson, *Elizabethan Prodigals*, 1–19. C. S. Lewis argues that "the great literature of the fifteen-eighties and nineties was something which humanism . . . would have prevented if it could" (*English Literature in the Sixteenth Century*, 19).

102. On allegorizations of the *Aeneid* see D. C. Allen, *Mysteriously Meant*, 142–54.

powerful, useful, and deserves sympathetic recognition: we certainly could not ever live without it. But under the particular circumstances I am studying here, generic and historical, it becomes identified with an institution and a program of reading that writers have reason to resist. Narrative understanding refuses both paradigmatic abstractions and their institutional origins in favor of a kind of explanation that insists on time and circumstance. The difference between them is the difference between answering a question by stating a maxim and by telling a story. The insistent demand of works like *Arcadia* and *The Faerie Queene* for narrative understanding can be read in their sheer resistance to criticism, how, as critics reading one another's work, we can always go back to the narrative to point out some nuance of plot that casts doubt on our general claims. They are built specifically for this: they solicit and flatter trained reading, while at the same time satirizing it both within their stories and in their rhetoric and structure. On some deep level—perhaps it should be said, paradigmatically, for such is the fate of criticism—they are artifacts and prisoners of an unresolved opposition between story and school.

A Culture of Teaching

It remains to ask—why *this* generation of writers? Poets had been going to school for centuries. Why should these three men, students in the grammar schools of the 1560s and 70s, have been so haunted by the scene of their own instruction? One answer is that some version of this study might indeed be written about any age, and perhaps about any genre, too. Lyly, Sidney, Spenser, and their romances make up just one episode in that eternal struggle between art and education.[103] But there are reasons why it is a pivotal episode. The first of them, as I have already suggested, has to do with the new centrality of secular poetry to the curriculum. A poet coming of age in those first generations of institutionalized English humanism would have had to decide, willy-nilly, whether he wanted to be read as he had been trained to read. But there were also broader, political reasons why these young men might have looked at school differently than their predecessors had; why they might be more inclined to be suspicious of its role in a new social order, an order that was to balk, in different ways at different times, the ambitions of each of them. G. K. Hunter tells such a story about the youthful disillusion of John Lyly. As the grandson of the William Lily who wrote the nation's grammar book, John had more reasons

---

103. The last phrase is T. S. Eliot's, from his essay "Blake," in *The Sacred Wood*, 154.

than most to credit the dream that good Latinity was the road to political advancement. He came of age, however, at an awkward moment. "[T]he myth of state-service as the natural end of a training in the humanities" had become "so well established that the up-and-coming literati cannot escape from it," writes Hunter, even as the government was growing "sure enough of itself to dispense with their sometimes embarrassing services."[104] There were hardly places enough in the Tudor bureaucracy for all the new men trained up this way.[105] The young Lyly struggled to find his.

Variations on this story can be told of Philip Sidney, whose gifts of wit and learning were often more of an impediment to his advancement than a help, and of Edmund Spenser, who went from Merchant Taylors' to Cambridge to provincial Ireland, never lastingly to return.[106] Richard Helgerson's account of the proliferation of romances of the prodigal son—books by young men trying to call attention to their gifts by ingeniously squandering them—testifies to an anxiety that the ordinary paths to advancement were blocked. (Writers like Gascoigne, Greene, and Lodge fit Helgerson's pattern too, along with Lyly and Sidney.) The frustration of these generations must have been compounded by an awareness that the schools that had betrayed them were more than ever an instrument of the government they hoped to serve. Elizabeth's reign had seen an explosion in foundations, with 130 new grammar schools (for a total of about 360) and over £250,000 contributed to school endowments by 1603. These schools enrolled more and more sons of the better gentry and aristocracy, as part of a concerted strategy to get promising young men off horseback and onto benches.[107] As Helgerson puts it, "In no other period of English history has pedagogy been so directly the concern of government."[108] Not only did Elizabeth prescribe a grammar and a catechism, but also the Privy Council kept close watch on the substance of the curriculum. In 1582, for example, it troubled itself to issue an edict against the reading of Ovid's *Ars Amatoria*

104. Hunter, *John Lyly*, 15.

105. Still valuable on the predicament of the educated gentry is Stone, *The Crisis of the Aristocracy*, esp. 183–232. See also his article "The Educational Revolution in England, 1560–1640," esp. 70–71. David Riggs treats the question in his biography of Christopher Marlowe, 61–62.

106. There is a useful summary of the debate about Spenser's advancement in Ireland in Richard Rambuss, "Spenser's Life and Career," in *The Cambridge Companion to Spenser*, ed. Hadfield, 30–31.

107. Alexander, *Growth of English Education*, 185. On the Tudor project of bringing the aristocrats into schools, see Stone, *Crisis*, 303–31; on that transition over a larger historical scale see Orme, *From Childhood to Chivalry*, esp. 217ff.

108. Helgerson, *Elizabethan Prodigals*, 29.

and *Tristia*, recommending Christopher Ocland's somewhat less humid *Anglorum Praelia* instead.[109]

Recent literary and historical scholarship has emphasized the ways in which humanist pedagogy—its practice, on the day-to-day level of exercises—was adapted to this consolidation of autocratic power. Even in those classrooms from which Ovid was exiled, the curriculum still prescribed texts of great moral and political complexity, Virgil and Cicero prominent among them. But Cicero's republicanism or the anti-imperial pathos of Dido were easy to evade, so the argument goes, under the intensely philological regime by which they were read. Among all the grammatical, logical, and rhetorical timber the plots of the old *silvae* are hard to see. As Anthony Grafton and Lisa Jardine put it, such study

> stamped the more prominent members of the new elite with an indelible cultural seal of superiority, it equipped lesser members with fluency and the learned habit of attention to textual detail and it offered everyone a model of true culture as something given, absolute, to be mastered, not questioned—and thus fostered in all its initiates a properly docile attitude towards authority.[110]

However they may have celebrated the public eloquence of the Roman forum, the schools were better set up to produce good bureaucrats, and in England they were producing more of them than the market could bear. The long shadows of Foucault and Fritz Caspari fall across such explanations.[111] I am persuaded by Rebecca Bushnell's caveat that "pedagogical

109. "in all the grammer and free schooles within their severall Dyoces the said bookes *de Anglorum proeliis* and peaceable governement of her Majestie maye be, in place of some of the heathen poetes nowe read among them, as *Ovide de arte amandi, de tristibus*, or suche lyke, may be receyved and publickly read and taught by schoolemasters unto their schollers in some one of their formes in the schooles fitte for that matter" (edict of the Privy Council, April 21, 1582; quoted in T. W. Baldwin, *Small Latine*, 1:112).

110. Grafton and Jardine, *From Humanism to the Humanities*, xiv.

111. Foucault's interest, especially in the middle of his career, in "disciplinary technologies" has particularly shaped the way literary scholars have interpreted humanism, and inspired the increasing scrutiny of particular classroom practices. See, for example, Halpern's *The Poetics of Primitive Accumulation* and Stewart's *Close Readers: Humanism and Sodomy*. Caspari's *Humanism and the Social Order in England* argues for the fundamental conservatism of humanism as a movement: "During the sixteenth century, English humanists evolved a social doctrine with which they tried to defend and improve the existing order of society. They used their knowledge of Plato and Aristotle, of Cicero and Quintilian, to justify the aristocratic structure of English society, the hierarchy of 'order and degree' in the state" (2). Rebecca Bushnell reviews this skeptical line in the introduction to *A Culture of Teaching*, "Humanism Reconsidered," 10–22.

texts oscillated between play and work, freedom and control, submission and mastery," and that for the schoolmasters this was a "*functional* ambivalence," expressing an unpredictable mix of impulses to individuation and conformity.[112] But what follows will show a bias toward the skeptical side of this debate, because I take it that it was in this direction that the former schoolboys I will study tend to err.

The challenge is to capture that double sense of debt and resentment that these poets, whose greatness depended so deeply on their education, felt toward their teachers and their teachers' legacy. On one side of a spectrum is the freedom of being at home in your own training: its rules seem natural, it fits the life you lead, and its prescribed ends align with your desires. On the other, the freedom of critique, of finding a vantage outside that training from which it is legible as a representation, and from which you can ask disinterestedly, representation *of what*? Once again, the middle is the territory of this book, where you feel somehow misled or betrayed, miseducated, and struggle for terms to think and write about that predicament that are not its own terms.

There is at least one more historical reason why that struggle might have been so acute for the generation of Sidney and Spenser. My own development of Bushnell's phrase "a culture of teaching" is intended to register the deep and distinctive sense in which humanism conceives of all knowledge pedagogically. This is starkly visible, for example, in the routines of catechism, where instruction and test are identical—to know the catechism, to know your faith, is to be able to recite your part in the script, to do exactly the thing you do in school. The same problem is writ large in Paul Oskar Kristeller's widely accepted claim that humanism is not so much a philosophy as an educational reform movement, a pedagogy, a method.[113] The imperatives of teaching exercise enormous authority over the shape of knowledge generally.

Something of what is at stake in saying that humanist knowledge is pedagogical knowledge may emerge from a modern parallel. Twenty-first-century science records and conveys knowledge in a variety of forms, from learned articles to searchable databases. A relatively small portion of its materials—considered just in terms of what gets printed and circulated—is

112. Bushnell, *Culture of Teaching*, 19.

113. "Renaissance humanism was not as such a philosophical tendency or system, but rather a cultural and educational program which emphasized and developed an important but limited area of studies" (Kristeller, *Renaissance Thought*, 10). On the reception of this claim see Nauert, "Renaissance Humanism: An Emergent Consensus and Its Critics."

prepared specifically in order to provide instruction, as opposed to information. It is a familiar lament among curricular reformers today that much science teaching is merely the delivery of facts, often in a form and sequence ill-adapted to the needs of students. Humanist scholars made similar complaints about the pedagogy of scholasticism. By contrast, they celebrated their own success in putting materials in the best order, making them swift and easy of apprehension. (The limit of that project may be the Ramist diagrams of the curricular *artes*, where the arts' native structure and the order of their proper instruction are indistinguishable. More on this in chapter 5.) This convergence of knowing and teaching is part of what Victoria Kahn refers to as the humanist "resistance to theory"—the preference for practical reason over speculative systems, where practice increasingly, as she describes, took the form of pedagogical method. (She too finds the culmination of the humanist culture of teaching in the thinking of Ramus, where "pedagogy . . . is not simply the means of instruction: it is the subject matter as well."[114])

Or another, still blunter way of putting it: for this generation, books were teachers, and to read was to be taught. With cheaper books and ever higher rates of literacy, a wide range of other readerly motives was sinking hardier roots into the culture, but—as the endless pedagogical rhetoric in the prefaces to the most pleasurable and trivial volumes testified—all acts of reading were still under the shadow of school and church. In a way quite foreign to us, any scene of reading was a scene of instruction.

This is to say that when a poet circa 1580 set about to write a poem to fashion a gentleman in true and noble discipline, his culture had an elaborate script for him, ideas about teaching and learning that were written more deeply into his training and intellectual culture than it is easy for us moderns to imagine. This script marked him; it also dictated the way his readers would understand what they read. The first of the poets in this study to wrestle with that challenge will be John Lyly. Since the argument that has gotten us this far is a complicated one, it will be worth briefly summarizing its premises one more time before turning to him:

1   At the heart of education is an epistemological problem, the teacher's question, *how do I know you understand?*

114. Kahn, "Humanism and the Resistance to Theory," 159. Ramus is simultaneously the "death of humanism" for Kahn, insofar as rhetoric is so profoundly subordinated to logic in his thought. See also her *Rhetoric, Prudence, and Skepticism,* esp. 135.

2 Pedagogical practices are constructed to answer that question by providing specific representations of what knowledge is and what it looks like to know it.

3 Such routines—the exercises that school students in the practices of trained reading—also make larger representations of knowledge, knowing, learning, and thinking, representations that define but also carry beyond the scene of instruction.

4 Such exercises, and the reading practices they cultivate, also represent the student as learner, and in so doing offer what amount to ad hoc theories of the self, which will shape the master's teaching and the student's self-understanding; these likewise define and also carry beyond the scene of instruction.

5 It is a common tendency of these exercises to render narrative or historical texts in anarrative forms: they share an idea of understanding as taking the time out.

6 They likewise offer an account of education itself as an a- or antinarrative process.

7 Romance, as the quintessentially narrative mode, offers itself as a way of thinking outside or against this kind of training: a way of testing given understandings and exploring alternatives by reinvesting them in time.

In his *De Ratione Studii*, Erasmus writes to an audience of teachers that the best way to know a subject is to teach it: "For there is no better means of grasping what you understand and what you do not. Sometimes new ideas occur to one in preparing a lesson [*commentanti disserentique*], and everything is more firmly fixed in the mind when teaching."[115] Any teacher can recall moments when an idea seemed to achieve a new depth, clarity, or connectedness under the pressure of explaining it; and conversely, moments when a student's question, or just the unexpected faltering of one's own confident stream of talk, exposed lapses of memory or reasoning. So much still seems natural to us today. But the idea that teaching is the *best* way of knowing—there is something about this that is both the glory and the curse of humanism. By teaching, and teaching well, I may just assure myself that you know what I want you to know; even that we know the same thing. I consolidate my confidence in a set of ideas about what knowledge is. But is it also only by teaching—teaching you? declaiming in the classroom of my own mind?—that I can ever be sure that I know myself?

115. Erasmus, *Works*, 24:672.

CHAPTER TWO

Experience

The subject of this chapter is experience, experience as the opposite of school; what school is intended to prepare for, or perhaps to prevent. The occasion is a dispute between John Lyly and the dead schoolmaster Roger Ascham over whether it is possible, or wise, to learn from experience. The fictional terrain is the tangled streets of Naples and an England seen through foreign eyes. Yet the story begins, as it will end, in a hermit's cell.

That cell should seem like a straitening frame, if experience is to be associated with romance's grand canvas of wanderings and shipwrecks. But if one searches the works of Lyly's heirs for a figure of experience—a figure who bandies the word or even bears the allegorical name—it is the hermit who keeps turning up, in Barnaby Rich or Robert Parry or Emanuel Forde or Robert Greene.[1] Greene's two-part romance, *Greenes Never Too Late; or, a Powder of Experience* (1590), offers a particularly sage and serious specimen: "his haires were as white as the threds of silke in *Arabia*" and "many yeeres had made furrows in his face, where experience sate and seemed to tell forth

---

1. See for example Parry's *Moderatus* (where the hero "descryed a good olde man, sitting in a seate digged out of the hard Rocke, his hoarie haires [being messengers of the winter of his age] seemed to cover a treasurie of experience" [N1r]); Rich's *Don Simonides* (the hero again: "for that I see, you carie the Hayres of Experience, and your yeares, betoken staiednesse, and my selfe have neede of counsell, I beseeche you recount me the cause of your abode here, the Discourse of your trouble, and the intent of your solitarynesse" [C2v]); or Forde's *Parismus* (where it is a woman, and a somewhat better listener, who encounters the hermit: "The old man hearing her speeches, made this answere: Faire Ladie, my homely Cell is not woorthie to receive your person, but such as it is, you shall be hartily welcome thereto: for I desire to live no longer, then to extend my small assistance to such as are in distresse, but especially to such harmelesse creatures as your selfe: therefore pleaseth you with kindnesse to accept what succour my abilitie will afford, or what counsel my experience may give you" [I2r]).

oracles"; he is "the perfit Idea of a mortified man."[2] The tale begins when a traveling palmer happens upon this forbidding figure and is treated to a lesson that is mortifying indeed. The hermit strikes a series of edifying poses with familiar props of skull, hour glass, and Bible, and follows each with a sententious speech that plays variations on the theme of memento mori: "When then I see that earth to earth must passe, / I sigh, and say, all flesh is like to grasse."[3] The speeches are in verse, and the palmer explains that while the sentiments are the hermit's, the words are his own, a translation from the "rough hie Dutch" made in order better to remember the old man's wisdom.[4] The palmer has learned his lesson by translating it.

This recollected scene of instruction is part of a complicated frame narrative surrounding what is otherwise a mostly conventional prodigal tale. The palmer is a guest at the house of the narrator, and it is there that he unfolds first his encounter with the hermit, then the story of Francesco, a likely young man who gets himself into trouble in the mock-London of "Troynovaunt." Francesco's story occupies most of the work. He is a country schoolmaster who marries the virtuous Isabel, and seems to be embarked on a career of blessedly plotless virtue before he makes his trip to the big city. There, under the influence of the courtesan Infida, he falls so low as to become a playwright before his wife finally wins him back to country life. The prodigal cycle is completed by his rustic reformation.

At the far side of this tale, there is another scene of instruction. Now it is the narrator whose learning is at stake: he is anxious that he will not remember, or perhaps does not yet grasp, the moral of the story, and he asks the palmer to leave "certaine testimonies on these walles, whereon whensoever I looke, I shall remember Francescos follies and thy foresight."[5] This request plays to a humanist commonplace, painting and carving sententious wisdom on the scholar's walls, but the palmer's variation on the practice is unusually severe. He draws his own blood to make the ink, and what he goes on to write recalls the mortifying lessons of the hermit, a zodiac of twelve brief poems (accompanied in the text by twelve woodcuts) that trace the cycle from Aries to Pisces, from youthful ignorance through the winter of age to a kind of spring in the acceptance of death. The lesson is gratefully received: "The palmer had no sooner finished his circle, but the Host over read his conceipt, and wondering at the excellencie of his wit, from his experience began to suck much wisedome."[6]

2. R. Greene, *Greenes Never Too Late*, C2v.   4. Ibid., C2v.
3. Ibid., C3r.   5. Ibid., K4r.
6. Ibid., L2v. The "Host" is the narrator, who has spoken in the first person throughout the narrative, but who is now, at this moment of lesson-making, translated to the third: perhaps

Like all prodigal tales, Francesco's sums to a circle, beginning and ending in the security of his wife's virtue. The contingency of its meantime—its "paths of error"—is wound tight on the zodiacal wheel of the palmer's conceit.[7] This is what the *lesson* of experience looks like, as distinct from the *narrative* of experience: circular, not veering or extravagant; a lyric or an emblem, not a romance. The narrator is now free to fashion himself as a bee sucking wisdom from a flower, a favorite humanist pedagogical trope.[8] The schoolroom paradigms for this operation are translation and epitome, rewriting and compressing. Such transformations are what it is to understand narrative, to understand experience: a generic modulation out of romance into (in this case) lyric condensation.[9] The lesson is both the end and the antidote to the story, and the book as a whole is a kind of tutorial in good reading.[10]

This hermit presents in little a problem that beset humanist educators as a matter both of theory and practice. That problem is what to do with experience: how to regulate an essential but unruly category in their own discourse, and what to do about traditions of education, new and old, that emphasized getting boys out of the classroom and into the world. On the one hand, most humanists prized the term. It was a way of talking about their distance from the vain abstractions of the scholastic philosophy, and among the ancients they admired it was a concept of considerable

the chain of instruction, hermit to palmer to narrator, is now extended to the "I" of the reader.

7. Ibid., K4r.

8. On the apian metaphor for imitation, see Crane, *Framing Authority*, 57, 59, and Pigman, "Versions of Imitation in the Renaissance," 4–7.

9. This is something of what Greene means by his title, "a powder of experience," where a powder is a kind of medicinal preparation, decocted from the messier stuff of Francesco's misadventures. *Experimentum* could be used in the period to refer to "a recipe or formula of some sort used to bring about a non-natural change in the course of natural events" (Schmitt, "Experience and Experiment: A Comparison of Zabarella's View with Galileo's in *De Motu*," 87). Here I am using "genre"—as I mostly do, when talking about romance—in something like Rosalie Colie's sense of a set toward experience, a repertory of "'frames' or 'fixes' on the world" (*Resources of Kind*, 8). Some critics, more or less closely following Northrup Frye, would describe the difference as between a category into which whole works are placed (genre) and the participation of a given text in a recognizable kind of literature without that kind necessarily defining the whole (mode). So Alastair Fowler: "The terms for kinds [or genres], perhaps in keeping with their obvious external embodiment, can always be put in noun form ('epigram'; 'epic'), whereas modal terms tend to be adjectival" (*Kinds of Literature*, 106). My approach to romance is more modal.

10. It should be said, the hermit is no simple humanist exemplar; if he personifies experience, it is as a monitory emblem, hardly the hero or the public man often held up before students. Greene's romance may conform itself to humanist ideas of instruction in many ways, but the knowledge it produces at its end is a stark *contemptus mundi*.

prestige. On the other hand, experience was often invoked as the opposite of school, associated with debauchery and travel to the Catholic south. This problem gets particularly tricky in the vicinity of romance, and for Roger Ascham, author of *The Schoolmaster* (1570), the two become so closely tangled that he is prepared to reject experience altogether. "[E]xperience," he writes, "is the common schoolhouse of fools and ill men." He deplores its inefficiencies and its risks, its liberation of desires and its hostility to good precepts. "Learning teacheth more in one year than experience in twenty, and learning teacheth safely, when experience maketh more miserable than wise."[11]

Greene's hermit offers an answer that stops short of repudiation: he rescues experience by translation into allegory. Under his tutelage romance is made straight again, and we are reassured that its extravagances ultimately yield only his unenviably timeless and deathward wisdom. But one hears a very different answer to Ascham in the first of Lyly's prose romances, *Euphues: The Anatomy of Wit* (1580). Ascham is on Lyly's mind from the title page—he borrows his hero's name from Ascham's account of the qualities of a good student—and halfway though the book, he takes on *The Schoolmaster* directly: "It is commonly said, yet I do think it a common lie, that experience is the mistress of fools; for in my opinion they be most fools that want it."[12]

So just what is at stake in Lyly's attempt to rescue experience from the schoolmasters, and to claim it for fiction? What he sets out to defend can be glimpsed as a kind of shadowy ideal: the power of experience to teach Euphues what he needs to know to live a good life; the power of romance narrative to tell that experience as it accumulates or develops over time. For Greene's hermit the fruit of experience is the rejection of experience, and of narrative itself. Euphues promises to be something more like the hero of a bildungsroman. Such a story of his education in the world would justify romance by showing how its accidents can amount to fashioning, or at least contribute to wisdom; it would give us romance as a mode of empirical knowledge, the accumulating foundation of a potentially virtuous life. Lyly's work fulfills the critical side of this grand promise, offering a shrewd satire of its hero's humanist training. But over the long arc of the *Anatomy*

11. Ascham, *Schoolmaster*, 51, 50.

12. "[E]uphues . . . Is he that is apt by goodness of wit and appliable by readiness of will to learning" (Ascham, *Schoolmaster*, 27–28); Lyly, *Euphues: The Anatomy of Wit; Euphues & His England*, 111. *Euphues* is the first of the seven qualities Ascham seeks in the good student, a list he adapts from Plato's *Republic*. Subsequent citations to the *Euphues* romances are given by page number in parentheses in the text.

and its sequel, *Euphues and His England,* that larger dream of an education by experience is unrealized—specifically and even tragically unrealized. Lyly identifies an area of potential in his chosen genre, and fails, tendentiously, to fulfill it. The story of this failure will give first shape to an opposition that will haunt this whole book, between the habits of mind I am identifying with school and the less formulated, quasi-empirical ambition to learn by being in the world. The dream he will test is the dream that narrative could capture that latter potential, and resist appropriation by the kind of trained reading that the palmer, tutored by his hermit, demonstrates at the end of Greene's tale.

Having set such a course for the chapter, it will already be obvious that the word "experience" is being pulled in many directions. Before embarking for Naples with young Euphues, it will be useful to provide a preliminary anatomy of experience itself.

The Senses of Experience

If we find in England no explicit scholarly quarrel about "experience" of the kind that *romanzo* engendered in Italy, still the word's usage gives evidence of a contest across the culture over its proper definition and its contribution to knowledge. That contest bears on a number of volatile areas of intellectual life, from the stirrings of an experimental science to the debates that shaped Protestant theology.[13] It will flatter the schoolmasterly side of this project to consider that range in terms of the word's grammar. Not its literal grammar, exactly; rather, the properties of voice, tense, and person that together define the axes of meaning on which particular uses may be plotted. "Experience" as the sixteenth century had it could be active or passive, present or past, first or third person.[14]

13. I will not treat Reformation senses of "experience" in any detail here, but see, for example, Barbara Lewalski's account of Protestant meditation in *Protestant Poetics*: "Essentially, the Protestant concern in both categories of meditation, occasional and deliberate (as in the sermon) is to trace the interrelation between the biblical text and the Christian's own experience. . . . The Christian's experience is to comment upon the biblical text, and the text upon his experience" (154–55). From the beginning it is an important category for Luther: "Not scripture alone . . . but experience also. . . . I have the matter itself and experience together with Scripture. . . . Experience alone makes a theologian," he says in his *Table Talk* (quoted in Gerrish, *Continuing the Reformation*, 186).

14. This way of thinking about the concept owes a debt to Raymond Williams's distinction between experience present and experience past in his *Keywords*, 126–29. The most detailed recent exploration of the word's history and philosophical permutations is Martin Jay's *Songs of Experience*; in some ways I am trying to carry his story, which begins with Montaigne, back a

To begin with voice, then, and a point of actual grammar: the Latin *experior* is a deponent verb, member of a class of verbs that has active meanings and passive forms. This fact makes a little allegory of the word's poise between active and passive senses. *Passive experience* will be most familiar to a twenty-first-century speaker: experience as an encounter with the world beyond the self, the unconditioned or unmediated. "Fortune" is one name for how that world impresses itself on us; "chance," "accident," "error," and "wonder" are others. An important idiomatic strain, as common then as now, roots this kind of experience in the senses: "see by experience," "feel by experience," "know by experience."[15] In these ordinary phrases it is almost as though experience were a faculty of sensory reception.

Such unconstructed openness—to characterize it at its limit—can be pleasurable; it can also be associated with suffering. "We know by experience itself that it is a marvelous pain to find out but a short way by long wandering," writes Ascham, borrowing again from Erasmus, whose *Institutio Principis Christiani* (*Education of a Christian Prince*) proclaims, "The ancients said that it is a wretched sort of wisdom which is acquired by experience [*experientia*], because each person reaches it through his own misfortune."[16] Erasmus has in mind such writers as Hesiod, Aeschylus, and Plato. This line in the classics harmonizes with the widely diffused Christian sense of *contemptus mundi*, which turns the believer away from a world of helpless suffering toward an afterlife of bliss. Together these broad cultural currents give us experience—and being in the world generally—as pain, unwanted and unchosen, definitively passive. Pain taxes the hope that we can communicate what we feel with others, and hence contributes to the sense that experience is ultimately private—that it cannot be told or shared, but only had.

Less familiar to modern-day speakers is *active experience*, the word's mostly obsolete senses of trying, probing, or proving. These meanings have since passed to "experiment," a transition that happened gradually over the seventeenth century as the vocabulary of the new science developed and took hold. At the end of the sixteenth century, "experience" and "experiment" were in free variation, and to experience something could mean to put it to the test.[17] Education writing shows evidence of efforts to

---

few decades to describe how the word is wrestled over in the particular pedagogical context of English humanism.

15. For example, "see by experience" finds its way into in the fictions of George Pettie (*A Petite Pallace*, C5r), Robert Greene (*Morando*, F1v), and Henry Roberts (*Honours Conquest*, B2r).

16. Ascham, *Schoolmaster*, 50; Erasmus, *Works*, 28:218. For Erasmus's Greek sources see *Works*, 27:512 n.47.

17. So Thomas Elyot in his *Castel of Helthe*: "In extreme necessitie it were better experience some remedy, than to do nothynge" (quoted in *OED*, "experience" I.1.a). In a study of the

point the word toward this more active sense, and thereby perhaps separate it from the kind of learning-by-experience that puts the young mind at the world's mercy. Sir Thomas Elyot concludes his treatment of schooling in *The Boke Named the Governour* with an allegory of prudence that exemplifies this tendency.[18] His stepwise method—worked out, remarkably enough, in the language of dance—is intended to explain how we may make a regulated progress from invention to action, and he calls the final stage "experience . . . to whom is committed the actuall execution." He goes on: "For without her, Election is frustrate, and all invention of man is but a fantasie. And therefore who advisedly beholdeth the astate of mannes life, shall well perceive that all that ever was spoken or writen, was to be by experience executed."[19] He wants to identify experience with action: to experience something is not to suffer it, but to *do* it.

As I have described them so far, these varieties of experience, active and passive, are both in the present tense: the moment in which the self may be asserted in action, or overcome by suffering or pleasure. Experience past—experience mediated or constituted by memory, habit, or even writing—broaches subtler questions of how we are made up by and in the world. Probably the single most influential account for the Renaissance of the relation between the tenses of experience comes from Aristotle's *Posterior Analytics*: "So from perception there comes memory, as we call it, and from memory (when it occurs often in connection with the same thing), experience; for memories that are many in number form a single experience. And from experience . . . there comes a principle of skill and

relation between "experience" and "experiment" in the works of Zabarella and Galileo, Charles Schmitt observes that "it must still be emphasized that in the sixteenth century there was yet an unresolved ambiguity between *experientia* and *experimentum*, as used in the philosophical and scientific literature" ("Experience and Experiment," 90). In his *New Atlantis* even Francis Bacon refers to the investigatory activities of Salomon's House as both experiments—"we have three that take care . . . to direct new experiments, of a higher light, more penetrating into nature than the former"—and experiences: "we have consultations, which of the inventions and experiences which we have discovered shall be published" (*Works*, 3:165).

18. The allegory is too complex and suggestive to do justice here: having begun with an account of how social order is predicated upon the strict observation of degree, Elyot works out his theory of prudence—which amounts to a theory of how deliberation and action fit together—on the model of the dialectical relation of masculine and feminine qualities in dance. Of the successive stages of deliberation that are mapped onto the motions of dance, the last is experience itself. One might expect the term therefore to be a register of what is bodily about Elyot's chosen metaphor, the kind of learning that happens by the habituation of physical motion. But Elyot seems to intend the student to be an observer rather than a participant, third person rather than first person, watching rather than embodying, and "experience" turns out to mean something quite different.

19. Elyot, *A Critical Edition of Sir Thomas Elyot's the Boke Named the Governour*, 102.

of understanding."[20] Aristotle begins in the present with the senses, but treats experience proper as a matter of memory, and more specifically a sediment of coordinated memories that together make a skill or *techne*. The self made by experience is the self qua craftsman, the practitioner of an *ars*. Such an account of self-fashioning is not narrative, but a gradual refinement of repetition into expertise, for the purposes of which identity is coextensive with a particular learned skill. Like the curriculum, it allows us to conceive of growing up without telling a story.

Such an account has the merit of transforming the hectic manifold of sense experience into the stability of a skill that is also a social role, just as mastery of the *artes* of grammar, logic, and rhetoric might be expected to do for the schoolboy. Such mastery effects a transition from passivity to activity, and in so doing it tells you who you are. Some humanist theorists project the same dynamic into the history of knowledge, as Juan Luis Vives does in his *De Tradendis Instituendis*:

> In the beginning first one, then another experience [*experientia*], through wonder at its novelty, was noted down for use in life; from a number of separate experiments [*experimentis*] the mind gathered a universal law, which after it was further supported and confirmed by many experiments, was considered certain, and established. Then it was handed down to posterity.[21]

The history of the *artes* is founded on a moment when experience—understood as something like the shock of the new—is, by a process of "separate experiments," reduced to universal law. The resulting relation between experience and law is not an ongoing dialectic; it is not reenacted by each generation. Rather, it is a historical event that happens once and for all:

---

20. Aristotle, *Works*, 100a3–9.

21. Vives, *On Education*, 20. For another, more widely circulated version of the same idea see the introduction to the ubiquitous *Distycha Catonis*, here in an English translation of 1560: "Long life maist thou have and many thinges maist thou by experience and practise learne, yet peradventure in readynge some fruitfull woorke thou shalte perceyve more witte and judgement, then ever coulde by experience be attained unto, or by anye manne hereafter invented forasmuch as graces and giftes are nothyng so plenteous as thei were in the beginnyng of the worlde when god did make manifeste his wonderfull power and myghte in the wittes of the Heathen, for the better instruccion and confirmacion of the faithe of the christians to come" (C2v–C3r). William Baldwin's *A Treatise of Morall Philosophie* (1547) states in its preface that "Necessitie as I judge (& that not without cause) was the first fynder out of morall Philosophye, & Experience, which is a good teacher, was first master thereof, & taught such as gave diligence to marke & consider thi[n]ges, to teache and instruct other therin" (A4r). That instruction presumably takes the ultimate form of the maxims that fill Baldwin's book. On the origin of the arts in experience generally see Manley, *Convention*, 21, 32–33.

before the foundation of the *artes* we were obliged to learn by experience, but now we learn by precept. Such experience past is truly past, and though Vives acknowledges our first wonder at its novelty, it is ever after quarantined by history.

Vives can stand for a general tendency to invoke the authority of experience to support a regime of precept, likewise to substitute for the immediacy and passivity of sense experience the practical mastery of the arts. (In neither case does the idea of *experience as narrative* ever arise: again, as in the schoolroom, mastering an art is not a story.) Still another humanist version of experience past moves us to a consideration of the third grammatical axis, that of person. Sense experience is first-person by definition, as is the kind of learning by experience that Aristotle describes; precept, which may be taught, moves us into the third. No one claims that precept *is* experience: the two are always conceptually distinct. But such claims *are* made for history. Here again Sir Thomas Elyot is an astute commentator: he allows both "experience whiche is in our propre persones" and also experience that is "actes committed or done by other men, wherof profite or damage succedynge, we may (in knowynge or beholdinge it) be therby instructed to apprehende the thing, which to the publike weale, or to our owen persones, may be commodious."[22] Vives makes the same distinction: "Experience is either personal knowledge gained by our own action, or the knowledge acquired by what we have seen, read, heard of, in others."[23] Humanism is a culture of the book, and both of these thinkers look to recruit the power of experience—even the prestige of the word—to the mediations of reading. Experience can be got, that is, in the safety of the schoolroom or the study, from the exempla (or even the stories) of history: *his* experience (or *hers*) can be *mine*. Not just knowledge, or learning, but experience itself.[24]

So we find experience as doing and as suffering; as the immediacy of the present moment or as the lessons drawn from a succession of such moments; as what cannot be had except by being there, and as something that can be and may best be drawn from books. Then as now, this perplexing word, in the sum of these meanings, is a formidable philosophical provocation. Take an everyday phrase like "see by experience," adduced above as evidence of the grounding of experience in the senses. Might it not just

22. Elyot, *Governour*, 250, 246.   23. Vives, *On Education*, 228.

24. Arthur Ferguson observes: "the humanists seem to have entertained a more than ordinarily high regard for the power of historical study artificially to extend the experience of the individual and to serve as an inexhaustible mine of example upon which the more practical teachings of moral philosophy might be firmly founded" (*The Articulate Citizen and the English Renaissance*, 193).

as well mean that seeing is always conditioned by past experience, by what has already happened to you, what you have already read? That it is not in the eye but in the mind? (Might not "see by experience" even describe the impossibility of seeing anything new?) We are almost compelled to consider the play between memory and the senses. Other languages may divide such meanings among different words (as German does between *Erfahrung* and *Erlebnis*); English concentrates them in one, and has for hundreds of years.[25] Taken together they imply a profoundly dialectical conception of how we come to know. And yet—in practice, particular sixteenth-century usages are partial and polemical, or at least vulnerable to polemical construction. Experience is either passive or active, present or past, first person or third. The word is a controversy unto itself. Ascham and Lyly will each take sides in this tug-of-war in the pages to come, and it is to this contest that young Euphues proves to be a martyr.

One other way of describing this controversy: it might be said to be a dispute over the *authority* of *experience*. These two words sit uneasily together, as Chaucer's Wife of Bath reminds us ("Experience, though noon auctoritee").[26] At one limit they are perfect opposites: experience is always calling authority into question, dissolving or simply obviating its claims by a super- or prevenient immediacy. This antiauthoritarian experience is present, passive, and first person. At the opposite limit, however, experience is an attribute or even a badge of authority. Ascham tells a maddening little story in illustration of the latter case. Sir Roger Cholmley, onetime chief justice of the King's bench, sits in judgment over some reckless lads brought before him for "certain misorders" at the Inns of Court. Knowing him to have been a "good fellow in his youth," they plead for leniency: "wise men before us have proved all fashions, and yet those have done full well."

25. There is an influential tradition of debate in German philosophy over the problem that gets translated into English as "experience": from Wilhelm Dilthy onward it has turned on the relation between *Erlebnis* (roughly, something lived inwardly and intensely) and *Erfahrung* (external events and the wisdom, practical knowledge or rules derived from them). We can recognize elements of the grammar of "experience" in each. The terms are polemically defined and redefined on their way from Dilthy to Walter Benjamin, their senses sometimes transferred or even reversed. Martin Jay's *Cultural Semantics* concisely traces a tradition of debate about these terms from Dilthy's distinction between "the discrete stimuli of mere sensation" and "the internal integration of sensations into a meaningful whole available to hermeneutic interpretation" (48) to Benjamin's attempt to subsume both under *Erfahrung* and thereby "find for knowledge the sphere of total neutrality in regard to the concepts of both subject and object" (50). The story is told at greater length in his *Songs of Experience*, chapters 6 and 8.

26. Chaucer, *The Riverside Chaucer*, 105. Of course, the Wife is only searching for alternative grounds for her own authority, and is not above invoking a textual tradition when it suits her purposes.

Cholmley concedes that "in youth I was as you are now," but explains that of his boon companions from those days, "not one of them came to a good end. And therefore follow not my example in youth, but follow my counsel in age, if ever ye think to come to this place."[27] The story resembles Vives's account of the origins of the arts: there is a phase of experience (Cholmley's "example in youth") and its translation into law ("my counsel in age"), after which wisdom may ever after be transmitted by precept. The young men are barred experience of their own in favor of the lessons of the aged. Cholmley himself becomes a figure of experience in the manner of the hermit, hardier and more public-minded, but equally forbidding.

The question for the most ambitious romancers—for Lyly, and later for Sidney and Spenser—is whether there is any space between these two accounts, between experience as the corrosive opposite of authority and as the badge of authority. It is the question of whether we can ground knowledge in ongoing experience: can what we gather ad hoc from the unstructured world amount to learning? There is a kind of answer-in-waiting in the idea of scientific method, a procedure of experiment under which we know the world by gathering observations and testing assumptions.[28] Another answer—readier to hand in 1578—might come by way of romance narrative. To tell a *story* of learning by experience is at least potentially to mediate, in time, between the surprises of the next moment and the wisdom that remains afterward. Lyly's question is therefore about narrative, and also, necessarily, about the formation of literary character in narrative, and about how characters learn.

The Schoolmaster and the Anatomy of Wit

To Euphues, then, by way of the dispute that may well have given him birth. Here is what Ascham's *Schoolmaster* has to say about experience, that schoolhouse of fools and ill men:

> Learning teacheth more in one year than experience in twenty, and learning teacheth safely, when experience maketh more miserable than wise. He

27. Ascham, *Schoolmaster*, 51.

28. So Bacon, who moves through Ascham's anxieties on his way to an account of experiment in the *Novum Organum*: "Experience is blind and silly, so that while men roam and wander along without any definitive course, merely taking counsel of such things as happen to come before them, they range widely, yet move little forward . . . the right order of experience is to kindle a light, then with that light to show the way, beginning with experience ordered and arranged, not irregular and erratic, and from that deriving axioms, and from the axioms thus established deriving again new experiments" (*Novum Organum*, ed. Urlach and Gibson, 78–79).

hazardeth sore that waxeth wise by experience. An unhappy master he is that is made cunning by many shipwrecks; a miserable merchant, that is neither rich nor wise but after some bankrupts. It is a costly wisdom that is bought by experience. We know by experience itself that it is a marvelous pain to find out but a short way by long wandering.[29]

These sentences are the climax of three pages or so of diatribe, and part of their surprise, as I have already suggested, is that *experientia* elsewhere is made so congenial to the practical orientation of humanism—often by main strength, as the likes of Erasmus, Elyot, and Vives redirect or wrest the word toward action.[30] Experience is associated with the *uses* of the past, as Elyot explains in his *Governour*: "The knowlege of this Experience is called Example, and is expressed by Historie, whiche of Tulli is called the life of memorie."[31] In its present senses it keeps company with words like *casus*, *kairos*, and prudence, words that describe the orator's alertness to the particulars of his circumstance.[32] Humanist experience is paradigmatically active; its past is written history, its present that of deliberate action. It stands easily for the commitment to political efficacy and usefulness, a kind of pivot between the languages of history and rhetoric.[33]

Why then would Ascham sacrifice this hard-won territory? The answer is that he wants, first of all, to use the word against a particular, practical target: the growing custom of sending young men to the Continent to finish their educations, what would later come to be called the Grand Tour. (He likely also has in mind the older regimes of household training for aristocrats that still competed with the schools for the minds of well-born young men, or

29. Ascham, *Schoolmaster*, 50.

30. Surprising, but not without parallel. In *De Pueris Instituendis*, Ascham's immediate source, Erasmus writes, "You might also ponder the fact that philosophy can teach more within the compass of a single year than the most diverse range of experience stretched over a period of thirty years. Moreover, the guidance of philosophy is safe, whereas the path of experience leads more often to disaster than to wisdom" (*Works*, 26:311). See also Francis Clement, *The Petie Schole* (1587), in *Four Tudor Books*, ed. Pepper: "Thou therfore that now neglecteth to be learned of me, shalt then be taught by experience (a lure in deede, but a severe Schoolmistresse)" (85–86); and the 1602 translation of Pierre de la Primaudaye's *The French Academie*: "That prudence, which is gotten onely by use, and by a man's own experience, it is too long, dangerous and difficult, because it is not able to make us wise but after our own perill" (165; quoted in Manley, *Convention*, 111).

31. Elyot, *Governour*, 246.

32. See Manley, *Convention*, esp. 112–26, and Kahn, *Rhetoric, Prudence, and Skepticism in the Renaissance*, 23ff. on prudence and rhetorical praxis.

33. As Arthur Ferguson writes in *The Articulate Citizen and the English Renaissance*, "it is important to notice that the essential link between humanistic learning and practical citizenship lay in the emphasis he [Elyot] and his fellow humanists placed on experience" (192).

even something like Prince Hal's "haunting all companies," the scion's license to linger in taverns.[34]) In each case the claim of experience to teach threatens the authority of the schoolmaster as gatekeeper, whose school was only precariously established in the 1560s as a pathway to power in Tudor society. The color Ascham gives to this bad experience is the color of literary romance. Such venturing, he insists, is full of risk, misery, and misspent time; the young traveler makes a bad bargain, one that can only lead to shipwreck, wandering, and, in a perfect phrase, "marvelous pain." These romance motifs are crossed with the language of Ovidian metamorphosis, a vivid fantasy of what will happen to the English traveler in the "Circe's court" of Catholic Italy: "he shall sometimes fall either into the hands of some cruel Cyclops or into the lap of some wanton and dallying Dame Callypso, and so suffer the danger of many a deadly den.... Some Circe shall make him, of a plain Englishman, a right Italian."[35]

As this polemic continues, romance becomes not merely the instrument of Ascham's critique but increasingly its object. He turns his scorn first upon "bawdy books ... translated out of the Italian tongue," but takes in the Arthurian matter of Malory as well, and a preemptive defense of Homer's *Odyssey* raises suspicions of its kinship, too.[36] Such filiations were discussed explicitly in Italian quarrels over the *romanzo*, but rarely among Englishmen: Ascham is a precocious genre theorist in spite of himself.[37] He evidently believes that these books court the Ovidian transformations

34. On the old, aristocratic training see Orme, *From Childhood to Chivalry*, esp. chapters 1 and 2; also J. H. Hexter's account of how the education of aristocrats changed over the sixteenth century (and the widespread belief that it had *not* changed) in "The Education of the Aristocracy in the Renaissance," 45–56. I return to this subject in chapter 6.

35. Ascham, *Schoolmaster*, 63, 62.

36. Ascham assures us: "And yet is not Ulysses commended so much nor so oft in Homer because he was *polytropos*, that is, skillful in many men's manners and fashions, as because he was *polymetis*, that is, wise in all purposes and ware in all places; which wisdom and wariness will not serve neither a traveler except Pallas be always at his elbow" (*Schoolmaster*, 62).

37. There is no direct evidence that Ascham read in the voluminous debate on the *romanzo* emerging in Italy. But he claimed he had read at least some books by Giovanni Pigna—his work on Horace and his *Sophoclean Questions*—and Pigna's *I Romanzi* (1554) made a central contribution to the controversy (*Letters*, 279–80). Ascham's biographer Lawrence V. Ryan notes that he seems to have read the prose romance *The Four Sons of Aymon* as a child (*Roger Ascham*, 13). His anxious gathering of texts is as good a definition as any for the senses of romance I intend in this study; my working definition tends toward the loose rather than the strict construction, with an emphasis on the multiple plot and wandering error, though occasionally as above I will touch base with debates about the term *romanzo* in the period. For the most modal of accounts, see Parker, *Inescapable Romance*; Barbara Fuchs surveys the problems of definition—which, it might be said, are partly constitutive of romance, and from which strict construction might be said to flee—in her *Romance*, 3–9. I take Wittgenstein's notion of family resemblance to be a good way of thinking about how such diverse texts as the *Odyssey* and the

that he first associates with travel, turning the young man into an "Inglese Italianato": "ten *Morte Darthurs* do not the tenth part so much harm as one of these books made in Italy and translated in England. They open, not fond and common ways to vice, but such subtle, cunning, new, and diverse shifts . . . to teach old bawds new school points, as the simple head of an Englishman is not able to invent."[38] Here we catch the note of what must be Ascham's deepest anxiety. These books are teachers too, bringing the Catholic sophistications of scholastic philosophy ("school points") to the arts of seduction; they are not merely distractions from good precepts, but rivals. For Ascham, the school of experience is the school of romance, an evilly compounded enemy of the schoolmaster.[39]

Antipathy to experience is written into Ascham's very style. He is one of the English masters of the Ciceronian period, and *The Schoolmaster* is full of textbook elaborations and subordinations variously drawn out. But look again at the long passage quoted above, "Learning teacheth more in one year." There he is curt and sententious; his maxims, one after another, exemplify a kind of teaching antithetical to the career of accident they deplore, a terse and provident wisdom, like coins hoarded to rebuke a spendthrift young man. The next chapter will puzzle at much greater length over what happens to such maxims when they actually find their way into fiction. Here we can glimpse how they might constitute a kind of didactic countergenre, one that might immunize the student against romance.

It is against Ascham's contempt for experience that Lyly the romancer makes a stand: it is a common lie, that experience is the mistress of fools. Critics tend to agree that this accusation is a reply to the old schoolmaster, eleven years dead in 1578.[40] That Lyly is a categorical enemy of Ascham's

---

Italian novella might be pulled together under such a rubric: see A. Fowler, *Kinds of Literature*, 40–44.

38. Ascham, *Schoolmaster*, 68. Within a page of declaring that "Learning teacheth more in one year than experience in twenty" Ascham concedes something like the opposite: "Thus experience of all fashions in youth, being in proof always dangerous, in issue seldom lucky, is a way, indeed, to overmuch knowledge" (51).

39. Martin Jay notes: "Insofar as 'to try' (*experiri*) contains the same root as *periculum*, or 'danger,' there is also a covert association between experience and peril, which suggests that it comes from having survived risks and learned something from the encounter (*ex* meaning a coming forth from)" (*Songs of Experience*, 10).

40. Lyly's editors suggest that "Lyly's first paragraph seems meant, in fact, as an answer to the long passage in Ascham in which he makes this quotation" (*Euphues*, 111). See also Maslen, *Elizabethan Fictions*, 214–15. Arthur Kinney, in *Humanist Poetics*, is more inclined to see the two works as ideologically compatible, both engaged in a "tough reexamination of humanism" (176).

larger project is much less obvious. Indeed, there are many ways in which *The Anatomy of Wit* seems almost fawningly loyal to Ascham's script. Lyly's brilliant young hero, his *homo rhetoricus*, leaves the university at Athens (read: Oxford) for Naples, and overgoes the Englishman Italianated in making himself a man of all nations: "What countryman am I not? If I be in Crete I can lie, if in Greece I can shift, if in Italy I can court it" (13). The amorous freedoms he permits himself there likewise have an Ovidian complexion: "Love knoweth no laws. Did not Jupiter transform himself into the shape of Amphitryon to embrace Alcmene; into the form of a swan to enjoy Leda; into a bull to beguile Io; into a shower of gold to win Danae?" (78–79). The story of his giddy career and inevitable comeuppance seems tailored to flatter Ascham's polemic rather than to overturn it. After all, Lyly was the grandson of William Lily, who gave his name to the ubiquitous grammar. There was ink in his veins.

Nonetheless—I want to take up Lyly's defense of experience as if it were a manifesto, a statement of his determination to explore the power of romance narrative to call received modes of teaching and learning into question. It will turn out to be somewhat perverse to construct a reading of *The Anatomy* along these lines, but revealing all the same. A turn to its sequel, *Euphues and His England*, will eventually make clear how a deeper ambition to rethink the terms of his didactic project underwrites both romances, however balked that ambition turns out to be.

Euphues: The Anatomy of Wit is now a book mostly studied for its style, the addiction to isocolon and natural similes that came to be known as "euphuism." There will be occasion to touch on these matters here, but it is with the structure of the narrative—a founding instance of Helgerson's prodigal plot—that I will be mostly concerned.[41] We already know a great deal about its structure from the title page: "wherein are contained the delights that Wit followeth in his youth by the pleasantness of love, and the

41. Helgerson's is still the most useful book on the fictions of this period. His central argument is that the plot of the prodigal son, with its stages of virtuous upbringing, license, and repentance, serves Elizabethan writers as a way of containing their own conflicted purposes: "If both civic humanism and courtly romance were to figure in a single life or a single literary work, they could not often do so as parts of a coterminous union, but rather in some dialectic of opposites, in a structure like that of the prodigal son story, with its pattern of admonition, rebellion, and guilt" (*Elizabethan Prodigals*, 41). The book ingeniously and convincingly suggests that this model could be applied to a career too, as I discuss in chapter 1.

happiness he reapeth in age, by the perfectness of wisdom" (1). This is to be a classic, three-phase prodigal tale. A quick skim through the book's pages, however, reveals something peculiar about its proportions. The phase of repentance, when Euphues is back at his desk in Athens, occupies, by way of his writings there, fully half of the book's length. This means that in considering how Lyly represents experience—and what kind of storytelling might make good his claim that we can learn from it—there are two distinct places to look, the prodigal middle and this protracted, epistolary aftermath.

First to the middle, the romance proper, where another layer of detail can be added to the long title's forecast. Euphues arrives in Naples and promptly encounters an old man named Eubulus, a kind of urban hermit, if there can be such a thing, who is full of counsel for the gifted but reckless young man. Euphues spurns this advice, naturally, and his next encounter is with a more immediately congenial spirit, the young Philautus. The two form a fast friendship, in both senses of "fast," and soon they are inseparable. Inseparable enough that Philautus persuades him to come along on visits to woo his beloved Lucilla, with the predictable result that Euphues is soon acting in his own interest and Lucilla is smitten with the witty newcomer. This liaison presently comes to light and the friends fall out, only to find that Lucilla has gone on to batten her affections on the ignoble Curio. There is a bitter exchange of letters between the spurned rivals, then a chastened reconciliation, and finally Euphues returns repentant to the university to take up divine studies.

It would be possible to add more detail still to such a summary: but actually, not very much. One of most striking aspects of the *Anatomy* is how streamlined its events are. A comparison with the technique of one of its most influential predecessors, George Gascoigne's *The Adventures of Master F. J.*, makes Lyly's narrative minimalism patent. F. J. is also a story preoccupied with courtship; here is a typical bit of business in which F. J. discovers that his rapier is missing (it has been playfully stolen by Lady Frances, pander in the book's love triangle):

> Eche one parted from other, to prepare themselves, and now began the sporte, for when *F. J.* was booted, his horses sadled, and he ready to ryde, he gan mysse his Rapier, wherat al astonied he began to blame his man, but blame whom he would, found it could not be. At last the Ladies going towardes horsebacke called for him in the base Court, and demaunded if he were readie: to whom *F. J.* aunswered. Madames I am more than readie, and yet not so ready as I would be, and immediatly taking him selfe in trip

[catching his own mistake], he thought best to utter no more of his conceipt, but in hast more than good speede mounted his horse, and comming toward the dames presented him self, turning, bounding, and taking up his courser to the uttermost of his power in bravery.[42]

Gascoigne manages this little episode expertly: the quotidian sequences of booting and saddling, the misplaced blaming of the servant, and F. J.'s half-recovered slip all linger out the discovery. His fear of shame is expressed alike in his words, his thoughts, and his curveting braggadocio; everything is slowed down with a helping of ordinary detail. Lady Frances and Gascoigne conspire together to make the reader wait. Compare this mix of realism and artful delay with a typical piece of narrative in the *Anatomy*:

> But Lucilla, who now began to fry in the flames of love, all the company being departed to their lodgings, entered into these terms and contrarieties. (39)

Or:

> But it happened immediately Ferardo to return home. Who hearing this strange event was not a little amazed; and was now more ready to exhort Lucilla from the love of Curio, than before to the liking of Philautus. Therefore in all haste, with watery eyes and a woeful heart, began on this manner to reason with his daughter. (86)

This is about as much space as the *Anatomy* ever gives to reporting event: characters enter and leave rooms (here, "immediately"), or go from house to house, but it is rarely more than a line or two before they start talking to one another or to themselves. Fictional space serves Lyly only to coordinate dialogue, and the book moves with conspicuous, schematic haste through its love plot.[43]

---

42. Gascoigne, *A Hundreth Sundrie Flowres*, 172. On some relations between *F. J.* and *Anatomy* as novellas, see Mentz, "Escaping Italy: From Novella to Romance in Gascoigne and Lyly." Mentz argues that there is a turn to romance in *England*, sacrificing the Italianate novella's experiments in favor of "a form that is simple, coherent, structured, and transparent—i.e., premodern" (170). I have preferred a more expansive definition of romance, allowing for its own experiments.

43. Richard McCabe comments on what he calls the "meagre" narrative: "the work is not a novel but an anatomy, or analysis, of a problem central to humanist thought: the relationship between eloquence and truth" ("Wit, Eloquence, and Wisdom in *Euphues: The Anatomy of Wit*," 299).

How then does the *Anatomy* ever fill the sixty-six pages between Euphues's arrival in Naples and his return to Athens? The answer is *talk*, and in particular, argument and inward deliberation. Take for example the first encounter between Euphues and Philautus: there is no description of this young gentleman, only the narrator's announcement that Euphues is determined "to enter into such an inviolable league of friendship with him as neither time by piecemeal should impair, neither fancy utterly dissolve, nor any suspicion infringe." From there we plunge immediately into the commonplace book of Euphues's reasons. "'I have read,' saith he, 'and well I believe it, that a friend is in prosperity a pleasure, a solace in adversity, in grief a comfort, in joy a merry companion, at all times an other I'" (28). Drawing mostly from Cicero's *De Amicitia*, he deploys a phalanx of immemorial *sententiae* in defense of a friendship that "time by piecemeal" cannot impair, *sententiae* that effectively take the place of telling how their friendship happens.[44] This suddenness is characteristic of Lyly as a narrator, but here it is also a clear object of his satire, an ill-starred substitution of Athenian book-learning for what Euphues himself calls the "trial [that] maketh trust" (29).

The forming and breaking of such bonds is the stuff of the rest of the plot. Euphues's affair with Lucilla proceeds along the same lines, with the same speed: he suffers a "sudden change," she a "sudden sorrow" (39), and they soon separate to vent long monologues weighing the propriety of this new affection. A cento of paragraph heads captures the shape of Euphues's deliberations: "What is he, Euphues . . . but will rather punish thy lewdness than pity thy heaviness?"; "O ye gods, have ye ordained for every malady a medicine . . . leaving only love remediless?"; "But O impiety!"; "Aye but, Euphues"; "Shall I not hazard my life to obtain my love?"; "Tush, the case is light where reason taketh place"; and at last, inevitably, "Well, well" (43–48).[45] Ranks of commonplaces fill in the rest. The timeless character of these *topoi* is underscored by Lyly's dependence on natural similes: "hath she not heard . . . that the greatest mushroom groweth in one night; that the fire quickly burneth the flax?" (45). Even as they figure the unseemly haste of Euphues's affections, these comparisons lift us out of narrative contingency into the absolutes of natural law. It is not the last time we will see Lyly ridiculing in his hero an attribute endemic to his own style.

44. Compare this catalogue with the gathering of wisdom on friendship that Erasmus offers in *De Ratione Studii*, which inoculates the student against the notorious homoeroticism of Virgil's second eclogue (*Works*, 24:683–87).

45. I have followed Croll's edition for pagination and spelling, as elsewhere, but have adverted to the 1578 printing for paragraphing.

There is some sense in which the Neapolitan Euphues has never left Athens: these debates and monologues are nothing if not school exercises, more turbulent and self-contradictory than the typical five-part oration, but full of forensic ingenuity. The majority of *disputationes* are implanted into the mind of a single character, and decision-making comes to look very much like two gifted schoolboys in combat. Such two-part inventions are the book's real model for thinking, and dazzling fence takes the place of narrative: most pages of *The Anatomy of Wit* occupy the non-time of argument, a version of the non-time of school. If Euphues's performances do have a distinctive temporality, it is the prematurity and effervescence of wit itself. Wit, too, is a kind of enemy of narrative; its time is now, and it is both reckless of the future and indifferent to the past. As experience it is pure present tense; it is not learned over time, but a gift of nature from the beginning. The net effect is to make the *Anatomy* the most untimely of romances.[46]

So if we are to find evidence of an education by experience—evidence of the difference experience makes—we will evidently have to look elsewhere than the prodigal middle of the *Anatomy*. For notwithstanding its moment of protest, the story of Euphues in Naples manages to flatter Ascham's critique in *The Schoolmaster*, plunging its hero into the perils of the Englishman Italianated without ever actually indulging in what it describes, the pointless narrative wandering, the waste of time. It is a particularly neat trick, and if Lyly looks less adroit than Gascoigne as a storyteller, we do well to consider that his aim may have been to undo the story in telling it. The only question left is: can we find some account of the good of experience in the phase of Euphues's repentance, the remainder of the book? Does Lyly have a way of showing in his hero's penitence the *particular difference* experience makes; how Euphues's wisdom is tempered by his trials? Does the quality of his virtue show anything of the passage by which he has attained

46. Ascham prefers "hard wits"—"hard to receive but sure to keep," their knowledge like engraving in "wood and stone...aptest for portraiture"—to giddy, improvising quick wits (*Schoolmaster* 24–25); Lyly draws from Plutarch in leveling the same censure: "he that taketh upon him to speak without premeditation knoweth neither how to begin nor where to end, but falling into a vein of babbling uttereth those things which with modesty he should have concealed, and forgetteth those things that before he had conceived. An oration either penned, either premeditated, keepeth itself within the bounds of decorum" (124–25). This preference for the written over the extemporaneous is an important strain in humanist thought: see for example Cave, *The Cornucopian Text*, 125–56, and Crane, *Framing Authority*, 13–38. Of course, rhetoric smiles on good improvisers as well; see Quintilian, *Orator's Education*, 10.7.1–29.

it? Or does experience merely burn away the passions to leave wisdom unchanged amid the ashes? There is plenty of space for posing these questions: Euphues repents on page seventy-five, with more than a hundred pages left to go.

The beginning of this long ending is signaled by Euphues's proclamation of repentance. He is friendless and unbeloved as he leaves Naples, and he turns back to his studies in what could be described as a kind of moral panic:

> I will to Athens there to toss my books, no more in Naples to live with fair looks.... Philosophy, Physic, Divinity shall be my study.... The Axioms of Aristotle, the Maxims of Justinian, the Aphorisms of Galen have suddenly made such a breach into my mind that I seem only to desire them, which did only erst detest them. (85)

Euphues repairs to the same device Ascham wields to fend off romance: the pithy wisdom of the axiom, maxim, or aphorism. Perhaps this is the same kind of generic modulation that ends Greene's *Never Too Late*, learning from the story by reformulating it in sententious lessons; though that said, these maxims do not seem to crystallize what has happened to Euphues, just to provide a formal alternative. At any rate they suggest at least a minimum lesson of experience: do not trust it; perhaps even, do not learn from it; stick to your maxims instead. More tendentious and large-scale modulations of genre are to come. Euphues begins in his scholarly fastness to write letters: to Philautus and to several other friends, moralizing epistles that imitate classical sources from Ovid's *Remedia Amoris* to Plutarch's *De Exilio*. There is also a report of a dialogue with an atheist, and a tract on education adapted from Plutarch called "Euphues and His Ephebus." G. K. Hunter observes that Euphues "vanishes from sight in a cloud of Biblical references" when he argues with Atheos, and something similar could be said about the other imitations, too.[47] The hero has become an author, an author of texts his best-trained readers could have been expected to recognize from their school days. Meanwhile the more-or-less unobtrusive narrator who has carried the story since its beginnings in Naples—what story there has been to carry—fades away, and the remaining pages are a succession of documents from Euphues's own pen.

There are precedents for books ending this way, with letters. Manuals of letter writing often finished with an anthology of examples, and perhaps

---

47. Hunter, *John Lyly*, 62

Lyly's romance invites us to consider assimilating it to that most practical of didactic kinds.[48] There is also Antonio de Guevara's exceptionally popular life of the emperor and Stoic philosopher Marcus Aurelius, which was printed many times in England, first as *The Golden Boke of Marcus Aurelius* and later as *The Diall of Princes*, and which ends with a selection of the emperor's letters.[49] Lyly clearly read Guevara—both writers close their books with a letter to a woman named Livia—but there are telling differences between them. In Guevara's book, the letters are dated throughout the emperor's life, and are to be read as supplements to an already completed story. Euphues's life actually *becomes his letters*: the narrative stops, the letters and tracts begin, and we can know him from that point forward only through what he writes.

And what he writes are essentially school exercises: imitations of the classical texts over which precocious boys were bent at their desks all across England. I have been pressing the question of how we might know that Euphues has learned something from experience; to test the promise, made at the beginning of "Euphues and His Ephebus," that experience is something other than the schoolhouse of fools and ill men. I have been looking for a specifically literary, and specifically narrative, mode of representing such learning, an alternative to the systems of representation encountered in the classroom. What the *Anatomy of Wit* offers instead is a perfect return to those schoolroom instruments.[50] Far from offering a new kind of knowing proper to its romance experiment, the book finally congratulates its audience by according us the vantage of the schoolmaster, and we can sit in judgment, if we choose, on the grace and decorum of Euphues's *imitatio*.

48. See, for example, Fulwood's *The Enimie of Idlenesse Teaching the Maner and Stile How to Endite, Compose and Write All Sorts of Epistles and Letters* (1568).

49. The first was translated by John Bourchier (the second Baron Berners), and printed in 1535; the second by Sir Thomas North, printed in 1557. Judith Rice Henderson's "Euphues and His Erasmus" summarizes the long debate over Guevara's relation to the *Anatomy* (136). The fact that both books end with letters to Livia is among the strongest pieces of evidence for influence. On Guevara's style as an influence on Lyly's, and their common sources in Medieval Latin, see Croll, "The Sources of the Euphuistic Rhetoric," in *Style, Rhetoric, and Rhythm*, 278–79.

50. Henderson makes a similar suggestion: "Lyly's model was the humanist school curriculum, especially the composition exercises described by Desiderius Erasmus in *De Ratione Studii, De Duplici Copia Verborum ac Rerum*, and *Opus de Conscribendis Epistolis*" ("Euphues and His Erasmus," 138); "The appended letters and treatises in *The Anatomy of Wyt* are the *raison d'etre* of the narrative" (145). Henderson sees Lyly as finally, however, more sympathetic to Euphues's training, and his own: "In *The Anatomy of Wyt* Lyly tests the value of humanistic education and even satirizes the misuse of humanist rhetoric, as recent criticism of his prose fiction has recognized. He does not, however, reject humanist precepts as some have claimed.... The treatises and letters appended to the narrative show Euphues gradually achieving the wisdom offered by humanist education" (159).

That Euphues himself takes on the tone of a schoolmaster, hectoring Philautus for his sins, only increases the pleasure to be had in judging him. Lyly seems to default entirely and ingeniously on the promise to defend experience. The *Anatomy* is a book for Roger Ascham after all.[51]

It is primarily in looking at the sequel, *Euphues and His England*, that it will be possible to think again about the success of this strategy: on its own terms, it appears formidably achieved. But I have already tried to point to ways in which the sins of Euphues—especially his untimely recklessness— might be identified with features of the book's style more generally. At the beginning of "Euphues and His Ephebus," right after Euphues has made his defense of experience, there is another hint that his reformation may make a problematic example. He states his intention to "set down a young man so absolute as that nothing may be added to his further perfection" (112), and defends the story of his own lapses: "To the intent, therefore, that all young gentlemen might shun my former looseness, I have set it down; and that all might follow my future life" (113). He assumes authorship of the foregoing third-person narrative, a surprising revision, but it is the final locution—"follow my future life"—that is most peculiar. Euphues is proposing himself as an exemplar, but the example is not yet. We think of following *past* examples, a notion central to the humanist account of the value of history. Recall Elyot's claim that "The knowlege of this Experience is called Example, and is expressed by Historie"; he describes a process by which past experience becomes a useful model. Following a *future* life is a neat trick. Perhaps we are meant to keep just a step behind Euphues as he shows the way; he seems confident that somehow that future is already determined in its virtue, as good as lived. But what this promise really achieves is a perfect and perfectly self-conscious abrogation of the authority of experience, past or even present, by translating the concept into nonsense.

Euphues in England

The Euphues of the *Anatomy* is not a particularly well-developed character, certainly by the standards of the modern novel or the soon-to-be-born Shakespearian stage. It is one of Lyly's deep jokes that his hero is

---

51. Although this proclamation risks understating some of the comedy even of the tracts and letters themselves, which Theodore Steinberg describes well in "The Anatomy of *Euphues*": "*Euphues*," he writes, "is essentially a comic work: it is an 'anti-courtesy book,' a parody on the usual works in the genre and a guide which should not be followed" (38).

transformed from a reckless, sententious schoolboy to a sober, sententious schoolmaster at a stroke: there is no in-between, it takes no time, and to follow his life-to-come is to be pointed into a blank futurity. As it turns out, however, that future has a more specific narrative content than the closure of the first prodigal plot could predict. In 1580 Lyly published a sequel, *Euphues and His England*, in which his hero and Philautus journey from Athens to the country of their readership, reentering the story he seemed to have escaped in his retreat to the library. In doing so he raises again the question of what difference experience makes, now in the form, what difference does the *Anatomy* make to *England*? By virtue of what continuities is this the same Euphues; is he wiser, or more foolish, or changed at all for having gone once through the prodigal cycle? Has he learned anything? Lyly's sequel allows us to ask how the straitened, partial models of self associated with particular pedagogical strategies might unfold in a more ambitious narrative context. The extent of Lyly's engagement with this problem, as a matter of literary technique, emerges already in the ligature between the two books, the "Epistle Dedicatory" that Lyly wrote to the Earl of Oxford. He is concerned there with whether his new Euphues will be recognizable at all.

This anxiety about recognition begins in an anxiety about timing. Prefaces to sequels are always hybrids of beginning and middle, and it is common, especially in the period, for them to celebrate the speed or lament the delay of their arrival in the reading public's hands. Lyly imagines himself as the mother of two untimely children: "Of the first I was delivered before my friends thought me conceived; of the second I went a whole year big, yet when everyone thought me ready to lie down I did then quicken" (193). The peculiar sexual politics of this conceit aside, he is evidently defensive about how long it took him to produce *England* (which a brief postscript to *Anatomy* had promised—Euphues's epistolary disappearing act notwithstanding—"within one summer" [183]). The first book, he tells us, was "hatched in the hard winter with the halcyon, the other not daring to bud till the cold were past like the mulberry" (195); still more uncomfortably, "My first burden coming before his time must needs be a blind whelp; the second brought forth after his time must needs be a monster" (193). The untimeliness of his books is monstrous and perverting. They are too early or too late; they fail to make a claim to the useful present, and they are disconnected from one another, belated or premature but never meeting in the middle.

We are already back in the sheer unease with time that is such a defining feature of the *Anatomy*. Lyly reaches (as he often does) for the analogy of painting to explain his predicament, expressing anxiety about the fidelity of his portrait. Will Euphues *look* like Euphues?

> Wherein I am not unlike unto the unskilful painter who, having drawn the twins of Hippocrates (who were as like as one pease is to another), and being told of his friends that they were no more like than Saturn and Apollo, he had no other shift to manifest what his work was than over their heads to write, "The Twins of Hippocrates." (194)

"So may it be that had I not named Euphues," he goes on, "few would have thought it had been Euphues" (194). This is a maker's complaint against himself, fearful that he wants the skill to render the resemblance. But already he has transposed the problem to his advantage, taking the literary challenge of continuing Euphues's story and comparing it to portraying identical twins in the simultaneity of a single pictorial plane. Painting allows Lyly to *deny* that the problem of the two Euphueses is a problem of time and narrative. It becomes instead something closer to mere repetition, the same thing twice, making Euphues (2) look like Euphues (1).

Lyly's alertness to this reduction becomes patent by the sheer weirdness of another excursus into visual imagery, when he conjures a pair of paintings to describe how he solved his problem: "So that at last I was content to set another face to Euphues; but yet just behind the other, like the image of Janus, not running together, like the Hopplitides of Parrhasius, lest they should seem so unlike brothers that they might be both thought bastards" (192). The Hopplitides are athletes, and the paintings are described in Pliny's *Naturalis Historia*: "a runner in the race in full armour who actually seems to sweat with his efforts, and . . . a runner in full armour taking off his arms, so lifelike that he can be perceived to be panting for breath."[52] It would seem that there could be no more straightforward representation of our life in time than these two images: they are patently a sequence, the same runner during and after his exertions. They make, that is, a minimal narrative; and one could also say, a minimum representation of experience, in which the hard breathing of the second picture is explained by the running in the first. There is no real question of their proper order. Lyly's perversity is to treat this difference—so obviously a difference of *time*—as though it were something like the problematic difference of kinship, as though these were two *different* soldiers who might be proper brothers, or might both be bastards. He reimagines them sharing a pictorial plane such

---

52. Pliny, *Natural History*, 35.36.71.

that we can test their resemblance in seeing them side by side. He has taken the time out. And then he goes on to tell us that this double portrait is the wrong way to conceive of the project after all, too open to charges of infidelity, poetic and paternal. Better to think of it as that Janus face, with Euphues (2) set "just behind the other," Euphues (1). This image has the advantage of being temporal: Janus looks both forward to the future and back into the past. But again there seems to be no proper link between them, no continuity in their opposite-facing; if indeed they *are* facing in opposite directions, for that "behind" may just as easily suggest the relation of face and mask.

The puzzle, in reading Lyly, is just how far to press these conceits. It can be hard to tell when they are keys to his design, and when they are under-determined, almost accidental side effects of his compulsive copia. Perhaps his revision of Pliny's Hopplitides is rooted in a mistaken memory. Still it seems safe to say that in the aggregate these prefatory musings point to a radical concern about narrative continuity, a concern that expresses itself first in the groping after a mode—painting—in which the problem might be imagined as not arising at all. But it cannot be avoided, for Lyly must get on with the telling of Euphues's story. Like the project of education, this telling presents problems of sameness and difference, the continuity of character over time—the transformation of experience present to the experience past not of written history, but of self. We have seen how the representational strategies of the classroom can cancel narrative, and that is how Lyly uses them in the *Anatomy*. *England* will not let him escape from his story so easily.

———————

Euphues and His England is unabashed about its return to romance, begin-ning as it does with a sea voyage. Lyly's twist is that the voyage is not from the moral capital to the periphery, but the reverse: the Athens-cum-Oxford that served as the *Anatomy*'s center of gravitas is displaced by England, the nation of the book's readership. This reversal of romance trajectory antici-pates how complicated the book's treatment of genre will become. Like the *Anatomy* (and *Never Too Late*), *Euphues and His England* will undergo generic modulations that demand consideration as a kind of lesson-making, a translation of its narrative into more properly didactic terms. Unlike those works, it never leaves that main narrative altogether behind. The book tests the capacity of a romance plot—defined by Italian theorists in terms of its tolerance for multiplicity and variety—to contain and reconcile a variety of matter, to weave *dulce* and *utile* more closely than the alternating phases of the prodigal plot can do. This promise of synthetic power is something like the promise of "experience" itself to gather the range of its own possible senses, making a reconciliation of past and present, active and passive, first and third person. This synthesis is another idea of learning, a possible self-fashioning dialectic with the world. It is also another challenge—after the *Anatomy*'s ingenious capitulation—to the humanist intuition that the lesson has to be *different in kind* from the experience that occasions it.

England's durable main narrative, though richer in event, busier, and far less predictable in outcome, is again simple in outline. When Euphues and Philautus arrive in England—after a voyage on which Euphues beguiles the time with more prodigal tales while a seasick Philautus curls up on the deck—they encounter a former courtier named Fidus. Fidus is suspicious of the newcomers, like any good Englishman, but once they have won his confidence he tells them the story of his courtship of Iffida, her noble continence and tragic end, and the resolution that turned him to his present occupation as a beekeeper. Enlightened by this most un-Neapolitan narrative, the travelers journey on to the court and fall in there with a quintet of younger men and women, who welcome them into their virtuous circle. In what follows there are two threads: the relations that develop among Euphues, Philautus, and the young members of the English court, and the course of the friendship between the two men. That friendship is already altered from the days of the *Anatomy*. Philautus has become a deferential sidekick to the newborn moralist, evidently cowed, if not altogether convinced, by the authority of the epistles directed at him from Euphues's study. Once an "other I" (20), he is now a restless pupil.

There are signs that Euphues is intent on keeping his quasi-anthropological encounter with England on a strictly textual basis. He takes as his guidebook Caesar's *Bella Gallica*, a comically out-of-date "humanist Baedeker" (as Richard Helgerson puts it), and he recommends treating the new country as the kind of bookish garden one finds everywhere in education writing: "When we come into London we shall walk in the garden of the world, where among many flowers we shall see some weeds, sweet roses and sharp nettles.... I had rather thou shouldest walk among the beds of wholesome pot-herbs than the knots of pleasant flowers" (287).[53] This is travel as reading, picking out useful rhetorical *flores* from the world's garden while leaving untouched what is useless or corrupt.[54] If romance

---

53. Helgerson, *Elizabethan Prodigals*, 76.
54. On the network of tropes that connect reading, teaching, and gardening, see Bushnell, *Culture of Teaching*, 73–143.

is wantonly syncretic, it can be countered by the diligent and discriminating anthologist, who transplants its finest blossoms into the taxonomical seedbeds of his commonplace book. Perhaps, for all this traveling, we need not yet leave the classroom defined by the end of the *Anatomy*.

When they arrive at the court, however, Euphues and Philautus find themselves in a moral landscape for which neither schoolmasterly injunctions nor the slights of Naples have quite prepared them. The company they join consists of three women and two men: the somewhat older Flavia, who presides, and a courtier named Martius, matched to her in age; the Lady Camilla and her consort Surius, to whom, it will turn out, she has pledged her heart; and Mistress Frances, who is conspicuously unattached. Together they present the travelers with a new combination of sociability, feminine appeal, and virtuous conduct that has its ultimate source in the civilized games of Castiglione's *Book of the Courtier*.[55] Theirs is a civilized space sheltered by the virtuous island, not the margin of some romance landscape to which Euphues's voyaging might be expected to take him (romance landscapes being, after all, mostly margin).

One can think of this court as a potential reconciliation of the binary, learning and love, conventionally estranged by the prodigal plot. The great achievement of *Euphues and His England*—so different from the *Anatomy*'s perverse ingenuities of structure—is the unexpected delicacy and even compassion with which Lyly renders Euphues's transformation within this new space. There was no question of character change in the *Anatomy*, and we have seen how *England*'s dedicatory epistle descends into absurd ekphrastic convolutions trying to think about the second Euphues's relation to the first. Now, however, he and Philautus find themselves frequenting the court "almost every day for the space of one month," and Euphues takes "such delight that he accounted all the praises he heard of it before . . . to be partial in not giving so much as it deserved" (290). He is becoming *over time*—albeit a swift month—something of a courtier himself. His conversations with Philautus are changed, almost giddy: "In sooth, my good friend, if I should tarry a year in England, I could not abide an hour in my chamber. For I know not how it cometh to pass that in earth I think no other Paradise, such variety of delights to allure a courtly eye" (299). It is a moment of possibility in many registers. Euphues opens himself to his own past—to his experience, to the *Anatomy* itself—in confessing the folly

---

55. For an account of Castiglione's games in the sense intended here, and the resilience of the society they define, see T. M. Greene, "*Il Cortegiano* and the Choice of a Game," in *The Vulnerable Text*, 46–60.

both of his love for Lucilla and of his misogynistic letters to Philautus. Even as he tells Philautus "thou shalt not shrive me like a ghostly father" (299–300), his spontaneous confession restores a lost reciprocity to their intercourse. And above all, he seems to have changed his mind about love: "An heretic I was by mine invective against women, and no less than an hypocrite for dissembling with thee; for now, Philautus, I am of that mind that women——" (300).

The dashes are Lyly's: he has taken his reader to the very threshold of a new book. At this threshold, the defenses against narrative are on the point of being brought down. Euphues is poised to recant, and in so doing to acknowledge his own history; Philautus, for his part, is chafing with resentment at the moral bit he has worn since his friend, not so long ago a traitor to the idea of friendship, became his tutor. It is difficult to overstate how different this moment is from anything in *The Anatomy of Wit*. The plot of that first book was perfunctory, generically prescripted, almost parodically inevitable. Here a complex history pours into a decisive moment, and everything is balanced on two dashes.

What happens next, if our sympathies have not been altogether dulled by the relentlessness of the rhetoric, is terribly sad. Philautus takes up the hint of hypocrisy with a vengeance, and accuses Euphues of being in love. Upright Euphues is shocked—for this, he is not quite ready—and he summons his injured dignity to issue a consummately euphuistic response: "experience teacheth me that straight trees have crooked roots" (311), he tells Philautus, impugning his friend's own motives, and folding that fragile word "experience" back into the aphoristic texture of the prose. (Euphues is no arborist: experience doesn't teach him this, the maxim does.) By the time he reaches the end of a withering rebuke he has returned to his old modes of self-discipline. "I will absent myself, hire another lodging in London, and for a time give myself to my book" (315). Euphues returns, that is, to his chamber, just as he did in his moral panic after Lucilla's betrayal in the *Anatomy*. There is the sense of something stillborn, and the fragile generic compound of the Castiglionian English court is fragmented. Euphues becomes again the figure of a textual, sententious, cloistered humanism, for whom the only secure idea of virtue is the life of a scholar. Philautus meanwhile is precipitated into a hectic and futile renaissance of romance: he pursues Camilla by all the old tricks, secreting messages in pomegranates and consulting a magician about a charm to win her love. The old prodigal binary is emphatically reinstituted as a breach between the two friends.

But if Euphues and Philautus have reverted to old patterns, the book has not, quite. Lyly's portrayal of their gradual reconciliation has some of the same melancholy tact as the telling of Euphues's first thaw. Spurned by Camilla, Philautus hurls himself at his friend's feet again; forgiveness comes by stages of maddening and poignant indecision. The first petition (in an obsequiously euphuistic style) leaves Euphues "as one in a quandary" (365); he reads the second over and over, "being in a mammering what to answer. At last he determined once again to lie aloof" (369). It all takes time; the quandaries and the mammering are a kind of nondeliberative suspension—not one side or the other of an argument, but a poise between them—alien to the plotting of the *Anatomy*. In this new narrative resourcefulness *England* has become capable of telling change in Euphues, or at least tantalizing us, and him, with the possibility: the book has escaped the classroom idioms of exercise and disputation. Still the artifact of his own good training, however, he seems unable to take advantage.[56]

The forking of Euphues's and Philautus's paths—back to the scripted roles, respectively, of precisian and libertine—is enacted on a larger, generic scale in the book's final episodes. Things come to a head at a dinner party. The guests are a slightly awkward seven: Flavia and Martius, Camilla and Surius, Frances, Philautus, and Euphues. Philautus still pines for the unattainable Camilla, Frances is unattached, but Euphues remains somehow the odd man out, and when they proclaim an after-supper game to beguile the occasion he is made the judge. These courteous games are the sort of learned, witty, aristocratic sport that makes up the tissue of class solidarity in Castiglione. As Surius puts it, "there can be nothing either more agreeable to my humour or these gentlewomen's desires than to use some discourse as well to renew old traditions . . . as to increase friendship, which hath been by the means of certain odd persons defaced" (385). Their form is courtly disputation, and the subject of course is love. Competition is sublimated on such occasions, and the principles of dialectic are not the court of highest

56. For a counterargument, see Stephanson, "John Lyly's Prose Fiction: Irony, Humor and Anti-Humanism." Like most critics, Stephanson takes Lyly to be satirizing Euphues's humanism, but he credits the two parts as together unfolding a proper defense of experience: "It is the wisdom of common sense, experience, and much learning through suffering that comes to occupy the vital didactic strain of Lyly's prose fiction" (16). Richard McCabe, in a reading of *Wit*, agrees: he sees a "pattern of education underlying the story, the movement, prompted by 'experience,' from willful 'wit' to deliberate 'wisdom'" ("Wit, Eloquence, and Wisdom," 300).

appeal: the point is instead the tacit accommodations that can be achieved by airing difficult matters in highly conventional, stylized terms. The failure of formal argument to resolve practical questions is a bitter joke in the *Anatomy*. Here, it is a benign and strategic compact.

If Euphues's appointment as judge suggests that he is not quite of this playful company, still the deference with which he is treated is mixed with affection. He is a welcome guest; we might be forgiven as readers for forgetting the young, beautiful, dangerously witty rake who arrived in Naples, but he is little more than a year removed from the height of his reckless appeal, and still might command a place at love's table. In England, however, he mistakes the occasion. As each of the participants speaks— on one side or the other of such problems as where love comes from, lover or beloved, and "whether in love be more required, secrecy or constancy" (400)—Euphues confutes them in turn, and finally, courteously, judges the whole proceedings: "I thus begin to conclude against you all; not as one singular in his own conceit, but to be tried by your gentle constructions" (405). Camilla wonders (as Philautus has before her) if there is not some hypocrisy in his dismissal of love: "One may easily perceive that you have been of late in the painter's shop, by the colours that stick in your coat" (407). But the game is effectively over; once again, Euphues has succeeded in imposing the criteria of his learned training on a scene that is ill-suited to such rigors. As judge, he positions himself somewhere between the severe schoolmaster and the contentious schoolboy, debating each point; Castiglione's comity is overwritten with the competitive ranking of the classroom, where upright Euphues once again takes the first bench.[57]

He also confirms himself as an outsider, and shortly after this dinner he is somewhat mysteriously called back to Greece on business. The new psychological subtlety of *England* allows us to wonder if he is not making a graceful excuse, sheltering his tender dignity from such insinuations as Camilla's. Returned to Athens, he consolidates his remove by taking up his pen again. "Euphues' Glass for Europe" is a paean to Elizabeth, adapted from William Harrison's *Description of England*: we are back in the

---

57. See Helgerson: "Euphues is forced to change his ideas more than any other Eubulean sage ever was. He does not, however, change enough. He remains an alien figure in England. He is respected; his company is sought; his advice respected; but he is, nevertheless, an outsider" (*Elizabethan Prodigals*, 76). Catherine Bates, by contrast, takes Euphues to be a full participant in this courtly ideal: "For Euphues the discursive practices of courtship—including 'discourses of love'—are a civilizing phenomenon because they alone can restrain concupiscent desires, conversation acting as a surrogate for sexual passion. Philautus, for his part, argues for 'bourgeois' love-making that is to be legitimized by marriage" ("A Large Occasion of Discourse," 485).

interpolated, nonnarrative genres with which *Anatomy* ended (though no longer, it should be said, in the territory of the classical curriculum). Meanwhile, as letters between them inform us, life goes on for Philautus. With his schoolmasterly friend gone, it is not long before the sensible redirection of his passions from Camilla to Frances fits him into the waiting scheme of multiple marriages. Euphues needs only to be cleared out of the way, it seems, for the book to lapse into comedy.

Comedy might be said to be one of *England*'s endings. Can it answer the question about the representation of learning by experience? Philautus does seem to have wised up; after so many pages of agon with Euphues, he side-steps into what promises to be a good enough marriage. But comedy in general has a sharp epistemological horizon. It is about getting married, not being married, and whatever happens afterward is none of its business. It has its own defenses against experience, the sort of ongoing, dialectical experience promised by romance, and against narrative too. Ferardo's infidelity in *Never Too Late* makes for a satisfying prodigal story, but what we hope for in marriage—at least, generically speaking—is for there to be no more plot at all. (Another way of saying this: there may be a kind of experience proper to marriage, but it is first person and incommunicable.) Lyly makes these limits clear: "What Philautus doth they can imagine that are newly married," he says, delicately averting his eyes; indeed it "may be that Philautus would not have his life known which he leadeth in marriage" (462). Perhaps Philautus has learned something, but the genre of his new knowledge constrains us from ever knowing if it is useful or not. His is hardly the proper fate for a good humanist.

———

What then of Euphues? He greets Philautus's news with an epistle of marriage advice in close imitation of Plutarch. This is Lyly's last joke at his hero's expense: of what could Euphues have less experience than of marriage? He speaks from purely bookish, schoolmasterly authority, interspersing the *Conjugalia Praecepta* with gems from Erasmus's *Adagia* and other worthy sources, as Athens taught him to do. These aphorisms are his final safety. And yet—the narrative opens up one more time for him, on the book's penultimate page:

> This letter dispatched, Euphues gave himself to solitariness, determined to sojourn in some uncouth place until time might turn white salt into fine sugar; for surely he was both tormented in body and grieved in mind. And so I leave him, neither in Athens nor elsewhere that I know. But this order he

left with his friends, that if any news came or letters that they should direct
them to the Mount of Silixsedra. (462)

Silexsedra can be translated "seat of flint": Euphues has left his library for
the severest wilderness, becoming, finally, a hermit. We are back to where
we started, with humanist fiction's archetype of experience. It may be with
some surprise that the reader realizes this transformation has taken all of
two months, from the beginning of the sea voyage on December 1, 1579, to
the final letter dated February 1. Euphues remains nothing if not untimely;
it is as though he has aged to senescence in that span, and he commits
himself to the gradual time of turning white salt to sugar. Perhaps we see
in this slow alchemy the new color of his hair.

One more time: "It is commonly said, yet I do think it a common lie,
that experience is the mistress of fools; for in my opinion they be most fools
that want it." But has Euphues learned anything from all this experience?
Is this retreat the final image of his wisdom, a kind of achievement? One
can imagine Lyly turning his hero into a character like Greene's sententious
hermit, or even smug Roger Cholmley, purveying precepts to the young at
the base of the mountain where their own prodigal errancies carry them.
But this is not what happens. He is instead as silent in his way as Philautus
in his nuptial bower:

> two friends parted, the one living in the delights of his new wife, the other
> in contemplation of his old griefs. What Philautus doth they can imagine
> that are newly married; how Euphues liveth they may guess that are cru-
> elly martyred. I commit them both to stand upon their own bargains. . . . I,
> gentlewomen, am indifferent, for it may be that Philautus would not have
> his life known which he leadeth in marriage, nor Euphues his love descried
> which he beginneth in solitariness; lest either the one being too kind might
> be thought to dote, or the other too constant might be judged to be mad. But
> were the truth known I am sure, gentlewomen, it would be a hard question
> among ladies whether Philautus were a better wooer or a husband, whether
> Euphues were a better lover or a scholar. (462)

I have described the parting of the two friends as a generic division: first
along something like the old prodigal lines, libertine and scholar; now,
more fundamentally, into comedy and a kind of tragedy, the tragedy of
self-exile. There is the tantalizing hint of a new love nourished in solitariness, a hook perhaps to hang another sequel on. But the ground note is
his suffering. Euphues's knowledge, whatever else it is, is tragic knowledge,

belated and incommunicable, no good to him or anyone else. He has been "cruelly martyred," Lyly tells us, and we might ask, to what? To the unbending rectitude of his self-reformation? Martyred, even, to *The Schoolmaster*? Thomas Peacham, in his handbook *The Garden of Eloquence*, identifies martyrdom as a rhetorical trope: "*Martyria* in Latine *Testatio*, is a forme of speech by which the Orator or Speaker confirmeth some thing by his owne experience."[58] Perhaps Euphues is a martyr to the very idea that experience could prove anything. Perhaps he has suffered for a word that cannot know itself.

It is Roger Ascham's move to identify experience with romance, where romance's always irregular boundaries can compass the likes of Painter, Malory, and the *Odyssey*. He constructs a partial, polemical view of "experience" in the process: one that acknowledges its rivalry with school in terms that make school's superiority and greater safety clear. I have tried to unfold a deeper analogy between the two over the course of this chapter, one that turns on their common syncretism. When Italian apologists define romance, much is made of this native variety, the capacity to contain a multiplicity of incident; that appetite for variety includes the assimilation of other genres into itself, pastoral or lyric or comedy or tragedy.[59] Romance has distinctive markers of its own, shipwreck or foreign marvels, but it is partly held together across its many differences by this tolerance for internal difference. Such capaciousness is part of what Lyly's books exploit in their own variety, even when the materials they admit seem antithetical to that very tolerance. "Experience" as a category is likewise divided by the grammatical oppositions I have described, present and past, active and passive, first and third person. The neighborliness of these senses holds out the possibility that they will be thought dialectically rather than as polemical opposites. What I have called learning by experience is one version of such a dialectic, in which the passive encounter with the world constitutes over time an active, competent self. It seems like a simple thing, learning by trial and error, not once and for all but ongoingly; the syncretic aspect of romance suits telling it better than any other kind of writing could. Such a story would be one in which the middle makes a difference to the end. It is the sort of story that puts a person together. But Lyly cannot tell it; it is the story he most of all cannot tell.

---

58. Peacham, *Garden*, 85.

59. See Weinberg, *History of Italian Literary Criticism*, where variety and the multiple plot are central to Weinberg's account of the debate over Ariosto and Tasso (see esp. chapters 19 and 20). The preface to Sir John Harington's translation of *Orlando Furioso* defends the multiplicity of "tales that many thinke unartificially brought in" (12).

CHAPTER THREE

Maxim

It is never very hard to find Philip Sidney in his own works: a telltale pun points to the frustrated lover Astrophil in his sonnet sequence, *Astrophil and Stella*, and again to the melancholy Philisides in both versions of *Arcadia*. The part of the disappointed young man seems to have suited him. All the same, it may be that the first role he wrote for himself was that of a school-master, in the little pastoral drama called *The Lady of May*. *The Lady* was mounted for the Queen's visit to the Wanstead estate of Sidney's uncle, the Earl of Leicester, in the spring of 1578 or 1579. In design it is very much like the sort of play or pageant schoolboys might stage for royal visits: an elab-orate disputation between the shepherd Espilus and the foster (or forester) Therion over the right to marry the May Lady, with the queen as audience and ultimate judge.[1] The rivals take up a classic debate *topos*: "Espilus is the richer, but Therion the livelier," as the Lady says; the shepherd offers prosperity and predictability, while the foster, swashbuckling thief of veni-son from the nearby forests, "doth me many pleasures" and yet "grows to such rages, that sometimes he strikes me, sometimes he rails at me."[2] Much criticism of the play has focused on this pair, and especially on the possi-bility that Therion stands for the gifted but impetuous Sidney himself, in a plea for favor and indulgence.[3] Neither candidate, however, has all that

1. For a survey of school theater see Cartwright, *Theatre and Humanism*, esp. 13–16. Sidney's headmaster at the Shrewsbury School was Thomas Ashton, who had been a fellow of St. Johns, Cambridge, and brought that college's dramatic tradition to his school in 1561. See Oldham, *A History of Shrewsbury School, 1552–1952*, 5–6.

2. Sidney, *Miscellaneous Prose*, 25.

3. Stephen Orgel, "Sidney's Experiment in Pastoral," first proposed that Sidney represented himself in the foster as a bid for favor, and that he would have been dismayed when Elizabeth (as

many lines to speak; by far the greatest share goes to the schoolmaster, Rombus.

What a schoolmaster might be doing in this rustic idyll is not immediately obvious, but the question doesn't trouble Rombus, who asserts himself with a learned filibuster:

> I am, *Potentissima Domina*, a schoolmaster; that is to say, a pedagogue; one not a little versed in the disciplinating of the juvental fry, wherein (to my laud I say it) I use such geometrical proportion, as neither wanteth mansuetude nor correction, for so it is described: *Parcere subjectis et debellare superbos*. Yet hath not the pulchritude of my virtues protected me from the contaminating hands of these plebeians; for coming, *solummodo*, to have parted their sanguinolent fray, they yielded me no more reverence than if I had been some *Pecorius Asinus*: I, even I, that am, who I am. *Dixi. Verbum sapiento satum est.*[4]

This buffoon is a stock figure out of school satire, and his Latin is embarrassingly mangled; Sidney, the favorite son of the Shrewsbury School and Christ Church, Oxford, must have enjoyed sending up his own exquisite rhetorical training. For all Rombus's ridiculousness, however, he proves surprisingly tenacious. Dismissed for his presumption, he nonetheless hangs around, coaches the participants, and finally makes his bid to decide the matter, almost displacing the authority of the queen herself. In one of the two surviving texts of the play he returns even after this heresy, offering a hasty, fawning epilogue and an agate necklace to Elizabeth. Rombus is enough of a would-be stage manager, even would-be author, that critics have speculated Sidney might have taken the role himself.[5] That speculation—and more importantly, the parodic ambitions that prompt it—point to a constitutive fact of Sidney's career: that in taking up his pen he was not only committing himself to "teach and delight," as his *Defence of Poetry* promises,

---

manuscripts record) chose the shepherd. Louis Montrose largely concurs with Orgel's reading, identifying the two as "the pliable placeman and the impetuous free spirit" ("Celebration and Insinuation: Sir Philip Sidney and the Motives of Elizabethan Courtship," 15).

4. Sidney, *Miscellaneous Prose*, 23.

5. On the relation between the printed text of 1598 and the Helmingham manuscript, see *Miscellaneous Prose*, 17–20, and Kimbrough and Murphy, "The Helmingham Hall Manuscript," esp. 106–7. S. K. Heninger writes that, "Within the world of the play, it is he [Rombus] who accepts the poet's responsibility for the performance and keeps things moving" (*The Poet as Maker*, 400). Alan Hager goes so far as to speculate that Sidney took the role of the schoolmaster in the actual performance ("Rhomboid Logic: Anti-Idealism and a Cure for Recusancy in Sidney's *Lady of May*," 488).

but that his own idea of literary instruction was fatally tangled with the work of the schoolmaster.[6]

There are no schoolmasters in the *dramatis personae* of the old *Arcadia*, but the problem of Sidney's identification with the role is diffused through the work at every level, from the brilliant surface of its rhetoric down to its deep structure. Rombus's self-undermining brand of schoolmasterly authority is everywhere. I want to follow his tracks, and outline the book's larger struggle with its own didacticism, by attending to a particular trope he favors: the preeminent feature of *Arcadia*'s style, the *sententia*, or moral maxim. *Sententia* is the self-important figure that crowns Rombus's first speech, "I, even I, that am, who I am. *Dixi. Verbum sapiento satum est.*"[7] The English half of this assertion is a brazen tautology, parodying the proud autonomy that marks the ethical posture of Stoicism. "I, even I" looks built to stand perfectly and necessarily on its own. On inspection, however, it does seem to lean a little on the adjacent Latin *sententia*, "a word to the wise man is enough." The relation between them is metonymic; however garrulous this schoolmaster, he stakes his identity on the claim that the man is the motto and the motto is the man. I am I am my word. It is a lesson in ethics, particularly Stoic ethics, upon which *Arcadia* will brood in a thousand ways.[8]

Ascham and Lyly both show how this figure may serve as a kind of compressed countergenre to romance: it has a pith and universality that are perfectly antagonistic to narrative discovery. It is a possible opposite or antidote to experience, and if there is an essence to humanist pedagogy, *sententia* is it. This chapter will be an occasion to consider what happens when school *sententiae* become, perversely enough, the very texture of a romance, the signal feature of its dialect. C. S. Lewis wrote fifty years ago that "maxims of law, government, morals, or psychology . . . are scattered on nearly every page" of *Arcadia*, and his "nearly" represents something of an undercount.[9] They are everywhere, and they are a key both to Sidney's bearing toward the culture of teaching in which he was raised, and to the antididactic project of this first draft of his pastoral romance.

6. Sidney, *Miscellaneous Prose*, 80.

7. Ibid., 23. Rombus's bad Latin and bad memory are particularly striking here; he treats *satis* as though it were a declinable adjective, and the present participle *sapiens* as though it called for second rather than third declension endings. The *sententia* is a school tag, found—in the form *dictum sapienti sat est*—in Plautus, *Persa* IV.vii.19 and Terence, *Phormio* III.iii.8, among other places.

8. On the association between *sententia* and Stoic ethics as a matter of style, see Croll, "'Attic Prose' in the Seventeenth Century," in *Style, Rhetoric, and Rhythm*, 87.

9. Lewis, *English Literature*, 335.

A Notable Figure

One could begin almost anywhere in *Arcadia*, from Euarchus's juridical decrees down to the demotic proverbs of Dametas. But it may be useful first to offer a definition, a guide for spotting this particular rhetorical specimen among all the other trees in Sidney's *sylva*. Erasmus—always the first authority in these matters—treats *sententia* as a subclass of the hundreds of sayings gathered in his *Adagia*, the influential compilation he published in ever-expanding editions between 1500 and 1536. An adage, he explains, is "a saying in popular use, remarkable for some shrewd and novel turn"; a *sententia* is an adage that bears particularly on "instruction in living."[10] The rhetorician Henry Peacham offers a more detailed definition in his *Garden of Eloquence* (1593):

> Gnome, otherwise called *Sententia*, is a saying pertaining to the maners and common practises of men, which declareth by an apt brevitie, what in this our life ought to be done, or left undone. First it is to be observed, that everie sentence is not a figure, but that only which is notable, worthie of memorie, and approved by the judgement and consent of all men, which being such a one, maketh by the excellency thereof the Oration not onely beautifull and comely, but also grave, puissant, and full of majestie.[11]

There are four features of this description worth picking out. (1) *Sententia* has moral force; it not only pertains to our manners and practices, but it also declares—with an "apt brevitie"—what we should and should not do. Peacham allows that "everie sentence is not a figure," and that one can make moral claims without figuration: "sentence" in this case would mean something like the bare idea, without its clothing of words.[12] But (2) as a figure it is "notable," or "remarkable [*scita*]," as Erasmus puts it. It stands out from its context and sticks in the memory, as a function not only of its brevity but of a grave and forceful style. *Sententiae* are also (3) elegant, "beautifull and comely," often structured by schemes like isocolon or antithesis. (But "not onely" elegant, says Peacham: *sententia* should not be mistaken for mere ornament). Finally (4) *sententia* has an authority that arises from the judgment and consent of all men, expressed as power and "majestie." There is a tense politics-in-little in the way Peacham voices this

---

10. Erasmus, *Works*, 31:4. See also Aristotle's *Rhetoric*, 1412b20–33.
11. Peacham, *Garden of Eloquence*, 189.
12. Terence Cave is mostly concerned with this sense of the word in *The Cornucopian Text*, 28.

last claim, a grounding of majesty in consent (or perhaps in what Erasmus calls "popular use [*celebre dictum*]") that touches nearly the civil order of Arcadia.[13]

The importance in the classroom of *sententia*'s moral dimension cannot be overstated. In his dialogue on the reform of Greek pronunciation, Erasmus has one of the interlocutors, a lion, summarize an ideal grammar-school program. His friend Bear suspects an omission: "No ethics?" he asks. "Ethics will be taught by means of aphorisms [*aphorismis*]," replies Lion, "especially aphorisms that refer to the Christian religion and to one's duties towards society."[14] We have seen how in the English grammar schools' culture of the commonplace book *sententiae* were matter for memorization, kernels of themes, morals of stories. They were the most prestigious of the many figures boys were taught to handle, arguably both cornerstone and capstone of the curriculum, the first lesson and the last harvest of reading.

In fiction the situation of *sententia* is much less integral or easy to specify. Peacham's claim for the universality of the trope is an ancient commonplace: Aristotle says its use "amounts to a general declaration of moral principles," and Quintilian speaks of its "universal voice [*sententia universalis est vox*]."[15] This autonomy—this claim to being everywhere and always true—is the source of strange effects when it is introduced into narrative. Even when a maxim is spoken in a particular situation, by a particular character, it bids to stand outside or above the flux of fictional motives and events. Its truth value does not depend on who speaks it or why; by its nature it makes claims beyond its local situation.[16] This detachment

---

13. Blair Worden discusses the centrality of precept to Sidney's political interests in *The Sound of Virtue*, 3–22, and he detects an impatience with "the Polonius-figures who had trained him for unremitting public commitment" (6).

14. Erasmus, *Works*, 26:387. Of Reformed schools on the Continent, Gerald Strauss writes, "For the great majority of schoolboys these sayings contained the sum of the education they received" (*Luther's House*, 190).

15. Aristotle, *Collected Works*, 1395b10; Quintilian, *The Orator's Education*, 1.9.3. See also for example the English Schoolmaster Nicholas Udall, who calls *sententiae* a "universall sorte of wrytynges" in his preface to Erasmus's *Apophthegmes*, **6v.

16. In his account of the eighteenth-century French novel, Geoffrey Bennington identifies problems that I take to be equally characteristic of Elizabethan fiction, if differently inflected: "It is clear, for example, that a series of narrative and descriptive sentences could make up a novel in the absence of any sentitious proposition, whereas a series of sentitious propositions could in no sense be described as a novel. The first formal approach to sentitiousness suggests that if maxims, aphorisms and other sentitious forms can indeed be found in abundance in novel texts, then they are no more than a non-essential adjunct to the 'essence' of the novel. . . . [But if] a certain type of analysis of the novel tends to relegate sentitiousness to the status of a non-essential adjunct, then sentitiousness seems to take its revenge by insisting on its own universal validity, compared with which it is the narrative-descriptive complex that becomes

contributes to its preeminent suitability for excerption, and its value as a gem in a commonplace book. It is the quality Rombus appeals to with his "I, even I," claiming to rise above the distasteful social tangle in which he finds himself. It locates *sententia* peculiarly between the utterance of a character and, we might almost say, of the reader himself, or of the reader's culture.

———————

These problematical sentences are what the princes Pyrocles and Musidorus have most in their mouths when they enter the fiction, set down by Sidney at the border between school and romance narrative. They have spent eleven years at study in Thessaly, given "wholly over to those knowledges which might in the course of their life be ministers to well doing."[17] Having finally been summoned back to the court of Pyrocles' father, King Euarchus of Macedon, they take advantage of a happy shipwreck to make their dilatory progress over land, defending ladies and succoring the oppressed as they go. Now they are come to Arcadia, latest stop on a kind of Grand Tour that takes in the "strength and riches" of each country, "the nature of the people, and . . . the manner of their laws" (12).[18] Musidorus, slightly the

———————

the 'rest'" (*Sententiousness and the Novel*, 5). He owes a debt in this analysis to Derridian ideas of supplementarity.

17. Sidney, *The Countess of Pembroke's Arcadia: The Old Arcadia*, ed. Duncan-Jones, 10. Subsequent citations are given in parentheses in the text. It is worth pointing out that while Sidney's description borrows from the language of schooling, his princes do not go to school— they are brought up in the household of Euarchus's dowager sister. The absence not only of schoolmasterly but of masculine authority generally is conspicuous. I can only speculate that while Sidney is concerned throughout to parody conventional aspects of the princes' education, when he actually describes it he indulges himself in an idyll opposite to school, the two princes bringing up each other with a mutuality like what I will shortly describe with the Pygmalion simile. Contrast Philisides' account of his upbringing in the fourth eclogues (290–91), which sounds a good deal more like Sidney's own.

18. Sidney echoes a much-echoed line from the beginning of The Odyssey, "Many cities of men he saw and learned their minds" (*Odyssey*, 4, in Fagles's translation). This line is a humanist commonplace, usually mediated through its quotation in Horace's *Ars Poetica*, "qui mores hominum multorum vidit et urbes" (*Satires, Epistles, Ars Poetica*, l.142). To follow its circulation under these dual auspices is to tell a story in little of humanist anxiety about travel and romance. Roger Ascham repaired to it frequently as secretary to Sir Richard Morrison, the English ambassador to the court of Emperor Charles V: "When my lord sees me greatly delighted by the second line of Homer's second work," he writes to his friend and teacher John Cheke, "he readily promises that I am to go . . . to Italy" (*Letters*, 137; see also 127, 132, 145). Erasmus adapts the line in his *Institutio* even as he insists, "do not imagine that, with Ulysses, you must travel across all lands and seas" (*Works*, 27:277). In his *On the Education of Princes* the Strasbourg schoolmaster Johann Sturm gives the line over to Horace altogether, writing that "Ulysses in place of histories, which in his time did not exist, learned about the flaws of many

elder, praises his cousin Pyrocles' studious travel habits: how he has been "wont, in all the places you came, to give yourself vehemently to knowledge of those things that might better your mind; to seek the familiarity of excellent men in learning and soldiery; and lastly, to put all these things in practice both by continual wise proceeding and worthy enterprises, as occasions fell for them" (12–13).

Contra Ascham, book learning and Grand Tour seem to fit naturally together here; the hastily sketched romance trajectory (filled in later in the book) makes both a stage for the exercise of the princes' well-cultivated virtues and a garden of new knowledge to be harvested by careful comparison of one state with another. Musidorus's praise for his cousin sounds a good deal like the advice that Sidney—who spent three years on the Continent after leaving Oxford—gave in a letter to his younger brother when Robert's turn came to travel abroad. "[F]urnish yourself with the knowledge of such things as may be serviceable to your country, and fit for your calling . . . which certainly stands in . . . the right informing your mind with those things that are most notable in the places which you come unto."[19] It is no coincidence that looking for things most "notable" in the "places" you visit borrows from the language of the commonplace book. Worldly Elizabethans were urged to keep such books for travel as well as reading, books where (as Sidney puts it in another letter to Robert) a man might transcribe information and "lay it up in the right place of his storehouse."[20] This travel-as-reading—recall Euphues and Philautus picking wholesome *flores* from the "garden of the world" when they first come to London—overlays the rhetorical *topoi* onto the geographic and political topography of new lands. The double sense of "places" in mental and physical space captures a hope that the world might be known by bringing the two into alignment.

This is the sort of travel that even Ascham might approve of: the categories of the commonplace book are always interposed between the young man and experience. It does not take long, however, for this ideal to come under pressure. Notwithstanding his former good habits, Pyrocles has stalled in Arcadia, unexpectedly addicted to a particular, melancholy grove.

---

peoples' customs. For he saw the customs of many men's cities according to Horace" (*Johann Sturm on Education*, 180–81).

19. Sidney, *Sir Philip Sidney*, ed. Duncan-Jones, 284–85. This letter was reproduced, alongside a letter of advice for travelers from Robert Devereux, the Earl of Essex, in a volume titled *Profitable instructions describing what speciall observations are to be taken by travellers in all nations, states and countries* (1633).

20. Ibid., 292.

Musidorus expresses his concern at this "slacking of the main career you had so notably begun and almost performed" (12). When good counsel has no effect, he tries a school trick, baiting his friend into an ad hoc disputation on another old theme, *otium* vs. *negotium*, and accusing him of lapsing into an unbecoming solitariness. "A mind well trained and long exercised in virtue," he admonishes, "does not easily change any course it once undertakes ... for being witness to itself of his own inward good, it finds nothing without it of so high a price for which it should be altered" (12). What Musidorus values in his cousin is a self-consistency established by training and exercise, and maintained by a kind of inward witnessing, the self regarding the self in order to assure its own unity. This precarious autonomy (precarious not least because of the doubleness already implicit in its self-regard) sounds the Stoic note so common in ethical reasoning throughout *Arcadia*.

Pyrocles, meanwhile, listens none too attentively to this lesson, giving himself over instead to reverie in praise of the place where he lingers. As he dilates its virtues, we listen in on Musidorus's thoughts:

> [Musidorus] framed in his mind a reply ... in the praise of honourable action (in showing that such kind of contemplation is but a glorious title to idleness; that in action a man did not only better himself but benefit others; that the gods would not have delivered a soul into the body which hath arms and legs (only instruments of doing) but that it were intended the mind should employ them; and that the mind should best know his own good or evil by practice; which knowledge was the only way to increase the one and correct the other; besides many other better arguments which the plentifulness of the matter yielded to the sharpness of his wit). (15)

What the reader is allowed to overhear is the process of *inventio*: Musidorus is arguing by the book, gathering matter from the commonplaces of his memory, whence he retrieves, of course, *sententiae*. But even as he stocks his quiver, he realizes that Pyrocles' thoughts are "rather stirred than digested," and he adapts his tactics accordingly, substituting a mild *concessio* for the fusillade he had planned: "Your words are such, dear cousin, so sweetly and strongly handled in the praise of solitariness, as they would make me likewise yield myself up unto it" (15). It is altogether a formidable rhetorical performance for Musidorus, full of controlled power and delicate adjustment. He continues in a gentle, unsententious vein until, in passing, he utters the fateful word "lovers"—whereupon Pyrocles can at last no longer conceal the true source of his torment. The younger prince breaks down and confesses that he has fallen in love with the princess Philoclea, and that he plans to disguise himself as an Amazon in order to woo her away from the paranoid pastoral court of Arcadia's Duke Basilius.

This is a most unwelcome revelation for Musidorus, and everything changes at once, in his speech and in the plot of *Arcadia* itself. Pyrocles' impending transformation is an ethical emergency. Love by its nature makes a breach in the autonomy that he has just been celebrating—it "utterly subverts the course of nature in making reason give place to sense, and man to woman" (18)—and Pyrocles overgoes the usual dangers (or perhaps literalizes them) by proposing to become a woman. Now Musidorus's response is densely sententious: "For to say I cannot is childish, and I will not womanish"; "your behaviour can never come kindly from you but as the mind is proportioned unto it"; "there is no man suddenly either excellently good or extremely evil, but grows either as he holds himself up in virtue or lets himself slide to viciousness" (18); and so on, more than ten of these maxims in the space of a modern page and a half. The scene hammers home that idea of *sententia*-as-antidote already encountered in Lyly and Ascham. It is the trope of ethical constancy and autonomy, of the self that finds "nothing without it of so high a price for which it should be altered" (12). The sickness it is meant to cure is metamorphosis, what Ascham would regard as a Circean transformation.

This opposition will structure the rest of the chapter: *sententia* and metamorphosis, a figure for constancy and a twist of plot. *Sententia* will continue to associate itself with Stoicism, as the rhetorical form of an ethical attitude, an attitude whose gospel of autonomy and *apatheia* was widely received in Renaissance humanism (and not least in classroom instruction).[21] But

---

21. Gordon Braden's *Renaissance Tragedy and the Senecan Tradition* gives a wonderful account of Stoicism as a philosophy of the will: "Throughout Stoicism the operative values are, time and again, power and control: we restrict our desires less because they are bad in themselves than in order to create a zone in which we know no contradiction" (20). He relates this authority to the motives of empire, and Seneca's *imperare sibi maximum imperius est* (21), but also notes that an ethic of *apatheia* can be adapted to the needs of the oppressed citizen. On the reception of Stoic thought in England—via Seneca, but also Marcus Aurelius and Epictetos—and on its braiding with Christian *contemptus mundi*, see p. 70. See also William Bouwsma's "The Two Faces of Humanism," an account of the relation between Stoicism and Augustinianism that is not overly concerned to disguise its sympathy with Augustine, and Jill Kraye, "Moral Philosophy," in *The Cambridge History of Renaissance Philosophy*, ed. Schmitt, 360–74. Sidney's friend Fulke Greville read *Arcadia* as a book for Stoics: "I know his purpose was to limn out such exact pictures of every posture in the mind that any man, being forced in the strains of this life to pass through any straits or latitudes of good or ill fortune, might (as in a glass) see how to set a good countenance upon all the discountenances of adversity, and a stay upon the exorbitant smilings of chance" (*Prose Works*, 11).

even as Musidorus dips into his store of Stoic wisdom, it is worth observing something peculiar about how he presents the maxims he gathers, something that almost undermines the project from the start. He does not give Pyrocles a single, ringing formula to identify with, a single *verbum sapienti*, as the opposition with metamorphic copia might suggest. Instead he delivers himself of a torrent. We might well ask: what is Pyrocles supposed to do with all this wisdom? For his predicament is something like our own, we readers who are doused with maxims on every page of *Arcadia*. To understand better what Sidney is up to in posing this problem—a problem of sheer sententious plenitude—we will have to look beyond the rhetoricians' accounts of the trope to consider how it was used, especially to teach.

Maxim and Metamorphosis

John Brinsley offers a script for the classroom handling of *sententiae* in his *Ludus Literarius*:

Q: What is that, that will overcome all things?
A: Love.
Then bid him give the sentence.
A: *Amor vincit omnia.*
Or thus: Is there any thing that can overcome all things?
A: Yes; Love.
Or thus more particularly, to put delight and understanding into them;
Q: What is that which will overcome learning, & make it our owne?
A: Love of learning, or loving our bookes.
Q: Give me a sentence to prove it.
A: *Amor vincit omnia, &c.*[22]

This excerpt, at which I glanced in chapter 1, is characteristic of Brinsley's method of "short questions," by which the scholar may "understand and remember any morall matter." He is intent on breaking down the catechetical routines students produce by rote, replacing them with an interrogation "forwards and backwards" in the manner of drill.[23] The first two questions already supply most of the words of the answer, though the second version is nominally more open than the first; the third applies the sentence to its immediate context. Together they might be said to go at least some way to unfolding its possible meanings. But there is something circular about the

22. Brinsley, *Ludus*, T4r.   23. Ibid., L14r, I1v.

procedure: *amor vincit omnia* is both the source of the student's knowledge and its proof. Does the *sententia* need explaining, or is it itself an explanation? Which would count as understanding it? This little dilemma points to two major strains in Renaissance thinking about what the trope is good for. Sidney will play them off against each other.

Erasmus can give us an account of the first, and indeed he likely stood for it in the minds of most sixteenth-century educators. His *Adagia*—the collection of sayings he built up over more than thirty-five years—reflects a profound respect for the density of these figures. He regards the best of them as a kind of radically compacted knowledge, a lapidary summary of ancient wisdom polished by generations of popular use. They have an almost magical, hieroglyphic intensity of significance.[24] His repeated descriptions of them as gems or seeds—metaphorical commonplaces inherited from the classical rhetorical tradition—figure this fascination with their concise complexity. They are so perfect as to be almost singular; in their concision and untranslatability, they are a border category between *res* and *verba*, with something of the unmistakable, indivisible fact of a simple physical thing about them.[25]

What do you do with such a thing? The *Adagia* acts out its answer: most of the sayings are followed by prose descriptions of their origins, history, meaning, and likely use, often running to several pages. In their meandering style and range of association some of these accounts are sophisticated enough to be regarded by critics as precursors to the essays of Montaigne or Bacon.[26] What you do with a maxim, then, is think about it, write about it,

24. Erasmus invokes Aristotle's authority: "They [adages] were preserved, he thinks, partly because of their brevity and conciseness, partly owing to their good humour and gaiety; and for that reason are to be looked into, not in sluggish or careless fashion, but closely and deeply.... Plutarch too in the essay which he called 'On How to Study Poetry' thinks the adages of the Ancients very similar to the rites of religion, in which things which are most important and even divine are often expressed in ceremonies of a trivial and seemingly almost ridiculous nature" (*Works*, 31:14). Thomas Greene describes Erasmus's "fascination with the hard, secret, precious, time-resistant capsule of signification," to which he attributes "something theurgic, mysteriously and uncannily powerful," in his essay on the adage "Festina lente" in *The Vulnerable Text*, 4.

25. Bacon later gives a defense of aphorisms not for their plenitude but for their fragmentary character: "Aphorisms, representing a knowledge broken, do invite men to inquire farther; whereas Methods [the 'Magistral' style of the rounded period], carrying the shew of a total, do secure men, as if they were at furthest" (*Works*, 3:405). See Altman, *Tudor Play of Mind*, 43. In both cases *sententiae* are a provocation to more thinking and writing.

26. Rosalie Colie, pointing to the use of sententiousness in Montaigne, locates one origin of the genre of the essay in the Erasmian sense of *multo in parvo*: "The essay is, really, in part a fulfillment of the implications of adage-making; by working from adages into new context, it developed into a form of its own" (*The Resources of Kind*, 36).

and ultimately write with it. It will afford no obvious path to understanding, let alone to action, but read rightly will provoke patient deliberation,
fulfilling its potential when it is richly reintegrated into the world of its
reader. In a collection called the *Apophthegmata*—this one devoted specifically to maxims of moral force—Erasmus emphasizes the potentially dark,
gnomic quality that occasions such interpretive labor. (Recall that *gnome* is
Peacham's Greek name for the trope.) The schoolmaster Nicholas Udall's
1542 translation explains that *sententiae* "rather by a colour signifie then
[than] plainly expresse a sence"; they work on the reader more obliquely,
and by their own agency: "as thei . . . dooe lightly synke and settle in the
mynde, so dooe thei contein more good knowelage and learnyng in the
deepe botome or secrete privetee, then thei shewe at the first view."[27] Here
too there is a sense that interpreting a *sententia* can take time: the process
by which it imparts its wisdom is as opaque as the saying itself, for it must
settle into the bottom of the mind before it will disclose the bottom of its
own wisdom. Whether the model is the *Adagia*'s patient commentary or a
seed growing in the dark space behind the eyes, the very unobviousness
of the trope—its almost successful resistance to the understanding—is what
makes it useful.

In both the *Adagia* and the *Apophthegmata* this interpretive or unfolding
time is figured on the page: the sayings are separated by commentary, sometimes pages of it. That space stands for contemplative time. Schoolroom
themes that begin from maxims provide the student a similar opportunity
to dilate one of these pregnant phrases, to bring its compacted wisdom into
a larger (if not usually a narrative) order. Such models favor the idea that
sententiae are to be taken one by one: a word to the wise man is enough.
In plenty of contemporary printed collections, however—beginning with
the *Sententiae Pueriles*, a basic text in so many schools—one finds ranks of
sayings one after another, often organized by topic and presented without
leisure for comment. In form they follow the school commonplace book,
which did not often pause for annotation. Perhaps their relentless advice
has a counterpart in the hectoring barrage Musidorus directs at his meta-
morphosing friend.

What is the good of *these* maxims—the same words, but in such a different context, so hard and fast upon one another? In the *Apophthegmata*—its
own essayistic bent notwithstanding—Erasmus entertains a very different
way of thinking about how *sententiae* might work. Shortly before his meditation on the color of the trope he makes an analogy to wrestling. Wrestlers,

27. Erasmus, *Apothegmes*, **6v.

he points out, must have "at all tymes certain suer poinctes and wayes bothe to catche holde, and also to wend out of holde"; in the same way,

> thei that travaill in the busie occupacions of peace and of warre must of congruence have in a readynesse suer rewles [*certas rationes*], by whiche thei maye bee putte in remembreaunce what is in that presente case nedefull or expediente to bee dooen, and what not.[28]

Here is no talk of a maxim settling or sinking in; instead, *sententiae* are sure rules, and they may be applied like wrestling holds. This characterization of the trope as a *rule* is another topos of the tradition. That is what Puttenham calls them—"such rules or sentences"—and he translates the Greek *gnome* as "the Directour."[29] In Erasmus's example these rules are so ready-to-hand that they may be applied in the heat of combat. Such readiness entails its own idea of understanding, as though the maxims were grasped not in the mediating mind but in the very organ of action, the hand.[30] There is no interpretation; they could not be more obvious.

Yet another of Erasmus's tracts, the *Institutio Principis Christiani*, sheds some light on the relation between these two accounts, the *sententia* as an object for interpretation and as a sure rule. He wrote the *Institutio*, which was printed in 1516, for the guardians of the young Prince Charles, son of the Emperor Maximilian. It is a book in its way much closer to a particular scene of instruction than either the *Apopthegmata* or the *Adagia*. It is also more directly exposed to the political sensitivities of the schoolmaster's mission, bringing up children who will eventually have their say in the fate of nations.[31] Both pressures are legible in the style: the prose is densely sententious, again a bit like listening to the outraged Musidorus; almost

28. Ibid., *6r.

29. Puttenham, *The Arte of English Poesie*, 235–36.

30. The idea of the hand as an organ of understanding—one that can somehow elide doubt and deliberation to put what it grasps into immediate practice—recurs in the commonplace literature. Printed commonplace books were often issued in portable quarto or octavo formats; Thomas Palfreyman, who expanded William Baldwin's *Treatice of Moral Philosophy*, is among the writers who emphasize their portability, how easily they fit in the hand; he speaks of "finding in his hand a booke" (A3r), of how it should be "easy in the hand to be caried" (A4r) and how the reader "shoulde take any suche woorke in hand" (A4v), even how too bulky a book would be "more unhandsome of thexact [the exact] reader to be caried" (A4r). Richard Taverner worries about the hand taking the place of the mind in his preface to the *Catonis Disticha* (1553): "I perceyved, that of the most part it is rather borne in the handes, then imprynted and fixed in the memorie" (A2r); "beare it hence forth, not onely in hande, but also in mynde" (A2v).

31. Bushnell discusses this problem in her chapter on George Buchanan's job as school-master to the future James I, in *A Culture of Teaching*, 44–72.

every sentence is a maxim. There is no talk of interpretation or unfolding. Maxims should be inscribed above the prince's crib and on the rim of his drinking cup; "it is not enough just to hand out the sort of maxims which warn him [the prince] off evil things and summon him to the good. No, they must be fixed in his mind, pressed in, and rammed home [*infigenda sunt, infulcienda sunt, inculcanda sunt*]."[32] *Sententia* is an inherently conservative figure, and this is by far the most conservative account of pedagogy to be found in the Erasmian corpus. That conservatism is a direct response to the stakes, for all of Europe, of Charles' rule. Erasmus fears tyranny above all, the arbitrariness of the tyrant's will; his answer is sure rules. From the *Apophthegmata* again: "for a manne born to bee a prince and a governour, it is necessarie that a readie and shorte waye to learne vertue bee quickely dispeched, and not at leasure disputed & reasoned in woordes."[33] It is as though Erasmus imagines maxims here—under the pressure of politics— as an alternative to disputing or reasoning, even an alternative to words themselves. They are not gnomic but *obvious*. All you need to do is follow them, and for "follow," read "obey."

The *Institutio* offers a model of the circumstances under which interpretive leisure—a gift not least simply of time—is sacrificed, and the bottomless *gnome* becomes a rule to be followed. Such straitening is more generally symptomatic of a wide range of anxieties: not only the politics of faction and nation but the precarious polis of the schoolroom, and even Musidorus's fear for the sex of his intimate. Such doubts press *sententiae* from koans for meditation toward rules, from obliquity toward obviousness, and at the same time cause them to multiply anxiously. This effect—the devolution of the *sententia* to rule under pressure—might be formulated as an axiom, if not a maxim.

---

32. "Then at those points where he feels the boy is inclined to go wrong let him [the tutor] especially fortify the young mind with healthy precepts and relevant principles and try to guide its nature, while still responsive, in a different direction.... But it is not enough just to hand out the sort of maxims which warn him off evil things and summon him to the good. No, they must be fixed in his mind, pressed in, and rammed home. And they must be kept fresh in the memory in all sorts of ways: sometimes in a moral maxim, sometimes in a parable, sometimes by an analogy, sometimes by a live example, an epigram, or a proverb; they must be carved on rings, painted in pictures, inscribed on prizes, and presented in any other way that a child of his age enjoys, so that they are always before his mind even when he is doing something else" (*Works*, 27:210).

33. Erasmus, *Apothegmes*, *5v.

So Musidorus's maxims are something like orders shouted in a burning building. Pyrocles is not supposed to comment on them, or make them, to borrow a phrase from the *Defence*, the "ground-plot of a profitable invention."[34] They are for following, meant to be obvious, scripts for immediate action. Under their barrage Pyrocles becomes a schoolboy again, who "no more attentively marked his friend's discourse than the child that hath leave to play marks the last part of his lesson" (19). Already we can tell what space of play has been sacrificed here to the rescue of a Stoic self. But the very schoolmasterliness of the rebuke also raises questions about how well such rules sort with the Stoicism they seem intended to shore up, insofar as Stoicism is an ethics of independence. Not only are there too many of them, but what are we to make of the fact that they seem so strenuously imposed from outside—aren't they Musidorus's rules, not Pyrocles'? Erasmus may have deployed *sententiae* against tyranny, but Milton (in his "On Education," as many years later) would call them "tyrannous," instilling the "barren hearts" of their followers "with a conscientious slavery."[35] Peacham's definition points to just this tension between the "majesty" of the trope and the "consent of all men" that underwrites it. The problem is writ large in *Arcadia*'s well-documented concerns with Protestant resistance theory, the grounds on which a monarch's authority rests and on which it may be overturned.[36] It is writ small in the debate between this ad hoc schoolmaster and his pupil. Are these rules that Pyrocles can give to himself? Or is this kind of moral instruction merely a form of conscientious slavery? (Is Stoicism itself finally, as T. S. Eliot has it, "a philosophy suited to slaves"?[37])

Or yet another way of putting the question: what agency do *sententiae* allow their speakers? For the debate turns out not really to be about *action*, notwithstanding its beginning in Musidorus's critique of solitude and *otium*. As it proceeds, his harangue is more and more an exhortation not to act but to *remember*. One of the maxims Musidorus invokes—"the gods would not have delivered a soul into the body which hath arms and legs (only instruments of doing) but that it were intended the mind should employ them" (15)—has already been identified as central to their upbringing in Thessaly, where, "taking very timely into their minds that the divine part

34. Sidney, *Miscellaneous Prose*, 103.   35. Milton, *Complete Prose*, 2:375–76.

36. On Sidney's interest in Protestant resistance theory—not least through his would-be mentor Hubert Languet, likely author of *Vindiciae, Contra Tyrannos*—see Worden, *The Sound of Virtue*, 51–57, 281–94. See also McCoy, *Rebellion in Arcadia*, 11–28.

37. Eliot, "Shakespeare and the Stoicism of Seneca," in *Selected Essays*, 112.

of man was not enclosed in this body for nothing, [they] gave themselves wholly over to those knowledges which might in the course of their life be ministers to well doing" (10). Pyrocles is in fact being asked to *remember* something he has already learned. Musidorus explains that this recollection is all that is really necessary for a moral recovery: "Therefore, to trouble you no longer with my tedious but loving words, if either you remember what you are, what you have been, or what you must be . . . I doubt not I shall quickly have occasion rather to praise you for having conquered . . . than to give you any further counsel how to do it" (19).

We are deeper still into the book's *reductio* of Stoic ethics. Virtue is the autonomy that comes from being like yourself. To fall from virtue is to forget yourself; to recover is to remember, even re-member, restoring those "arms and legs (only instruments of doing)" (15) to the proper governance of a unified wit and will. There is a hint here of Plato's account of learning as recollection in the *Meno*, where, with some prompting from Socrates, a slave boy derives for himself the principles of geometry. But in the *Meno* the content of that recollection is demonstrable, a set of axioms drawn in the dirt. The closer Musidorus gets to the heart of his advice, the less he says he has to say; he wants "to trouble you no more with my tedious but loving words" (19).

So just what is Pyrocles supposed to remember, again? Musidorus's advice—"remember what you are, what you have been, or what you must be" (19)—sounds not unlike a question posed by Thomas Palfreyman to his readers a few years before, in 1571: "Shoulde not the remembraunce of our selves, what wee are, & what wee have, bee in us continually quick and lively?"[38] Palfreyman asks in his capacity as the editor of the much-printed *Treatice of Moral Philosophy*; what he has to offer there are maxims, his contribution to the growing ranks of printed commonplace books on London booksellers' shelves. He evidently takes its contents to fulfill his imperative to self-recollection. *Remembering yourself is remembering your maxims.* Their peculiar status as universal wisdom, equally the property of everyone, allows them to stand in for a personal virtue, and even when I urge them on you I am giving you something already properly your own. They make a kind of solution to the content problem of the Stoic's circular self-assertions, just as Rombus's empty "I, even I" leans on his maxim *verbum sapiento satum est*. The most famous scene of sententious instruction in

---

38. W. Baldwin, *A Treatice of Moral Philosophy* (1571), A5v. First published in 1547, the *Treatice* went through several editions; Palfreyman not only added a preface but also augmented the text.

Renaissance literature is a parody of exactly this problem. *Hamlet*'s Polonius plies his son Laertes with maxims on the eve of the young man's departure for France: "give thy thoughts no tongue, / Nor any unproportioned thought his act"; "neither a borrower nor a lender be"; and so on. He crowns his advice with the injunction, "This above all, to thine own self be true."[39] What is that self, what account of it do we have, if not the catalogue of common virtues he has just recited?

The point of following out this *reductio* is not only to show the flimsiness of Musidorus's resources against love. It is to show how Sidney bears down on the schoolmasterly practice of instruction by moral maxim. (Recall again how this regime makes Pyrocles the child who fails to mark "the last part of his lesson" [19].[40]) The Erasmian essay has no room to unfold here. Nor do we quite know what to do with a rule, supposing *that* is what these maxims are. As at the end of Lyly's *Anatomy*, we are constrained by the epistemology of the schoolroom—we can know learning only by the classroom's codes—and remembering a maxim is the sole measure of learning, even of virtue. This constraint has its comedy, and its charm, for Musidorus is about to undergo a transformation of his own, one that will propel him ostensibly far beyond his schoolboy priggishness.[41] But *Arcadia* itself will never outgrow its own compulsive sententiousness.

———

There is of course another side to *Arcadia*, an alternative to this straitening rhetoric, in the energy of its disguises, its playful experiments with sexual identity, and the dazzling ingenuity of its plot. One gathering term for these impulses might be romance. Another is metamorphosis, of which there is

39. Shakespeare, *Hamlet*, 1.3.55–81.

40. "Pyrocles' mind was all this while so fixed upon another devotion that he no more attentively marked his friend's discourse than the child that hath leave to play marks the last part of his lesson, or the diligent pilot in a dangerous tempest doth attend to the unskillful words of the passenger" (19). There is a deft and easy-to-miss witticism in the way these analogies line up: the child is the pilot, and the schoolmaster the unskillful passenger. Like so much of Sidney's dazzling rhetoric, it seems like a clever trick played under the teacher's nose.

41. He never altogether escapes, however. At the moment of his most dramatic self-assertion, when he elopes with Pamela, Musidorus and his beloved are ambushed (even as Musidorus seems poised to take advantage of her trusting slumber) by a group of rebels who have been hiding out in the forest after their failed coup. Musidorus holds them off, but one slips behind him to put a knife to Pamela's throat, whereupon the prince casts away his sword like a "poor scholar . . . at the child-feared presence of a cruel schoolmaster" (267). That the schoolmaster emerges at this moment of crisis for Musidorus—the double failure of erotic self-control, and of military prudence—suggests how much he is always behind the scenes.

a good deal in the book, not only all the fantastical dressing up but scraps of Ovid too, mostly introduced to make fun of characters who do not know how to change. The sententious Musidorus is rendered speechless by Pyrocles' transformation, "even as Apollo is painted when he saw Daphne suddenly turned to a laurel" (16); later Duke Basilius is rebuked by Pyrocles and left standing speechless "as the old governess of Danae is painted, when she suddenly saw the golden shower" (100).[42] Metamorphosis here is an instrument of satire, deployed against the same kind of moral stasis that gets figured as the stubbornness of *sententia*.

But that opposition—*sententia* and metamorphosis—does not get us altogether outside the schoolroom, both because Ovid is something of an insider there, and because the structure of the opposition savors somewhat of the lamp. Principally on the strength of his mock-didactic *Ars Amatoria*, Ovid was known as the *praeceptor amoris*, or as Stephen Gosson has it, "the amorous schoolmaster."[43] His peculiar pedagogical authority carries over to the *Fasti* and the *Metamorphoses*, which were read as historical and mythological compendia as well as for what the Spanish humanist Juan Luis Vives conceded was the "wonderful ease [*mirae facilitatis*]" of their style.[44] Vives—who served briefly as tutor to Mary Tudor—is nonetheless alarmed by Ovid's place in the canon:

> Plato casteth out of the commonwealth of wise men which he made, Homer
> and Hesiod the poets, and yet have they none ill thing in comparison unto
> Ovid's books of Love, which we read and carry them in our hands, and learn
> them by heart, yea, and some schoolmasters teach them to their scholars,
> and some make expositions and expound the vices.[45]

Ovid is not only a seducer; he actually traffics in bad precepts. (The reformed Euphues praises the English for a love "not tied to art but reason, not to the precepts of Ovid but to the persuasions of honesty."[46]) And to top it off, he was taken to be a bad student himself, as Vives again testifies: there are some poets who "rejoice to get bound up in their work; there

42. For a discussion of Sidney's acquaintance with the painting, of which several versions existed throughout Europe, see Duncan-Jones, "Sidney and Titian."

43. Gosson, *The Schoole of Abuse*, 29.   44. Vives, *On Education*, 159.

45. Vives, *Vives and the Renascence Education of Women*, 61.

46. Lyly, *Euphues*, 374. See also Robert Greene in his *Vision*: "And cause he [Ovid] would the Poet seeme, / That best of Venus laws could deeme, / Strange precepts he did impart, / And writ three bokes of loves art" (*Life and Complete Works*, 12:199–200).

are others who look remiss and as if they were doing something else, and who, loose and free, do not wish to exert themselves; such were Ovid and Lucilius as Horace bears witness."[47] If he is an insider, he is a dangerous and unpredictable one.

And there is another reason for the special antagonism of educators, one more specifically connected to the *Metamorphoses*. Leonard Barkan writes of the poem that "the principal change is sexuality.... Myths of magical change, again and again, will be stories celebrating the unfamiliar forms of the sexual impulse, with all their terror and allure."[48] He goes on to note that the stories are often allegorized as *rites de passage* from child-hood to adulthood, where sexual awareness or awakening (or a frozen denial of the impetus to change) are at stake. Alarmed by such transforma-tions, Vives fears that Ovid's obscene verses might "infect whatever they touched," and asks, "Is it then wrong to exclude those verses from Ovid, which would make a young man worse than he is?"[49] His myths propose an alternative account of how we may cross the boundary between innocence and experience, and they do so by appeal to a kind of knowledge that is un- or half-chosen, category-defying, sensuous rather than rational: "they only know it which inwardly feel it" (11), as the narrator says of Pyrocles' love. In the terms of the last chapter, metamorphosis is paradigmatic of the knowledge got by experience—first person, present tense, sometimes active and sometimes passive. It is very close to the kind of knowledge we now call carnal.

At moments Sidney seems simply to give himself over to this opposi-tion as it would have been constructed for him by his training—a training to which rhetorical habits of binary opposition were so fundamental.[50]

47. Vives, *On Education*, 75. The opening of Ben Jonson's *Poetaster*, where the student Ovid lays aside his law books for poetry, is in the same tradition (1.1.1–18). For more on Ovid in the schoolroom see Riggs, *The World of Christopher Marlowe*, 97–107.

48. Barkan, *The Gods Made Flesh*, 13. He later observes that "There is what we might call a grand homology between the materials of romance and those of Ovidian mythology" (173).

49. Vives, *On Education*, 128. Ascham links Ovid, as we have seen, with the dangers of sur-render to experience, and Elyot advises replacing him with Horace: "in the saide two bokes [*Fasti* and *Metamorphoses*], a longe tyme shulde be spente and almost lost: which mought be better employed on such authors, that do minister both eloquence, civile policie, and exhortation to vertue. Wherfore in his place let us bring in Horace in whom is contayned moche varietie of lernynge and quickenesse of sentence" (*Governour*, 46).

50. It is worth noting, however, that Shrewsbury was unusual among grammar schools for not having Ovid in the curriculum; see T. W. Baldwin, *Small Latine*, 1:390. Perhaps this omission only enhanced Sidney's sense of the complexity of Ovid's position, whenever he first became aware of it.

Metamorphosis is what Pyrocles proposes to undergo, from man to woman and from Macedonian to Amazon; he eventually confesses as much to Philoclea when he goes to her bed ("Behold here before your eyes Pyrocles, prince of Macedon, whom you only have brought to this fall of fortune and unused [i.e., unaccustomed] metamorphosis" [105]). Such change is what his cousin Musidorus most fears about love, the power to "transform the very essence of the lover into the thing loved" (18).[51] Like love, metamorphosis is self-loss, the end of autonomy. As such it is the perfect opposite of the centered self of Stoicism.[52]

But Sidney's most sustained, direct use of Ovid in *Arcadia* betrays a deeper restlessness, an ambition not just to take the side of Ovid against the schoolmasters—and it is by no means clear, as the plot unfolds, that Ovid's side is the right one, in any simple way—but to reconfigure the terms of the opposition. This revisionary impulse works itself out in two allusions to the Pygmalion story, the first of which comes at the very end of the princes' inaugural debate. There is no winner there, at least as a matter of forensics: the back-and-forth accelerates from set speeches into stichomythia before it finally reaches a breaking point, and Pyrocles faints. (Not for the last time is an argument in *Arcadia* solved by a swoon.) When Pyrocles revives, Musidorus repents of his hard reasoning and rededicates himself to his cousin's cause, going so far as to help him into his Amazonian disguise. And something new happens. "For my part, I promise you," says the elder prince, "if I were not fully resolved never to submit my heart to these fancies, I were like enough while I dressed you to become a young Pygmalion" (25). The other allusions, to Daphne and Danae, emphasize the asymmetry of metamorphosis. Someone is changed, someone remains the same, and someone is condemned merely to watch. With Pygmalion, however, there is a hint of another possibility, for the transformation—even if Musidorus seems to be good-humoredly fending it off—is mutual.

Sidney continues to explore this Ovidian story at another pivotal moment of recognition and reconciliation, the bedside conversation when

51. He prefers a Platonic account, by which "the love of heaven makes one heavenly, the love of virtue, virtuous," but this account is difficult to separate from something more Ovidian: "this effeminate love of a woman doth so womanize a man that, if you yield to it, it will not only make you a famous Amazon, but a launder, a distaff spinner" (18). In the new *Arcadia*'s revision he puts metamorphosis at the front of his concerns when he first sees his cousin the Amazon: "What was the causer of this metamorphosis?" (*New Arcadia*, 132).

52. I borrow this phrase from Thomas M. Greene's treatment of Ben Jonson's Stoicism, "Ben Jonson and the Centered Self," in *The Vulnerable Text*, 194–217.

Pyrocles, having won Philoclea's confused heart by his Amazon disguise, discloses his metamorphosis. With this revelation another change begins:

> The joy which wrought into Pygmalion's mind while he found his beloved image wax little and little both softer and warmer in his folded arms, till at length it accomplished his gladness with a perfect woman's shape, still beautified with the former perfections, was even such as, by each degree of Cleophila's words, stealingly entered into Philoclea's soul, till her pleasure was fully made up with the manifesting of his being, which was such as in hope did overcome hope. (106)

At first the joy described seems to be Pyrocles'; it is natural enough to assume that he is the male figure in the simile. But with the gradualness of melting wax—most Ovidian of figures—it becomes clear that Philoclea is the sculptor, imaginatively refashioning the Amazon in the image of a young prince while she listens to his story. As the terms of the allusion resolve, the gracefully managed confusion metamorphoses each lover into the other, and the effect is a mutuality in which each is both sculptor and quickening statue. Three hundred years later W. B. Yeats would ask of Leda's ravishment by Jove, "Did she put on his knowledge with his power," reminding us that one of the asymmetries that define Ovid's metamorphoses is that of knowledge.[53] Metamorphosis is a fundamentally hierarchical business, even when it inverts hierarchies, and in this it is like teaching. Sidney suspends this contest by giving each role—rapist and victim, sculptor and statue, perhaps even master and student—equally to each of his friends and lovers, letting them inform one another.

Arcadia performs at this moment a metamorphosis of metamorphosis. If we turn back to the princes' debate, and to the scene of dressing Pyrocles, this revisionary Pygmalion looks like a radical solution to their forensic dilemma. Not only does it evade the dyad of sententiousness and metamorphosis, but it rewrites Ovid as the sponsor of a third way, a mutual fashioning, and in so doing escapes the learned habits of antithesis and *disputatio* that underwrite the rhetorical order of the book. C. S. Lewis writes that Sidney yearns not for "a reverie but a structure," a remark quoted with approval by Nancy Lindheim when she describes how he carries antithesis to a fineness of discrimination that ultimately expresses the "harmonious,

53. Yeats, *Poems*, 215.

synthetic nature of his vision of the ideal."[54] Here, however, the ideal *does* seem like a reverie, fleeting, fragile, surrendered to rather than achieved. It recalls the "sweet emulation" (9) of the princes' growing up together in Thessaly, imitating only each other. The sterile circle of Stoicism is enlarged by the admission of one loved companion, and for a moment that is enough.

Three Fates of Sententiousness

A line of thinking would seem to be completed with this image of Pygmalion and his statue. The empty rigorism of sententiousness and the inconstancy of metamorphosis are overcome by an idyll of unhierarchical making, first in homoerotic and then in (perhaps correctively) heterosexual terms. But these momentary, imagistic stays are frail against the forces of plot set in motion by the princes' arrival, and, before that, by the abdication at the root of the book's turbulent politics. Moreover, the work's addiction to the trope, the constant recurrence of sententious formulae, continues unabated. As readers we have been equipped with a critical framework for thinking about sententiousness, but the most important consequences of talking—and thinking—that way are yet to be played out. Ultimately I want to follow those consequences down into the deep structure of the work, and outward into its reception. But first it will be worth watching what happens to *sententia* within the plot, three fates of moral rhetoric in *Arcadia*. The first two are in the mouths of very different characters, Philoclea and Euarchus; the third reconnects the trope to what I have identified as its opposite term, metamorphosis.

––––––

Philoclea first, who is conspicuously uneducated. Her sister Pamela is bookish and principled, foreshadowing the upright orator who becomes such a central figure in the revised *Arcadia*, but she herself is a creature of prelapsarian innocence "whose eyes and senses had received nothing but according as the natural course of each thing required, whose tender youth had obediently lived under her parents' behests without the framing (out of her own will) the forechoosing of anything" (95). If the princes are always already

54. Lindheim, *The Structures of Sidney's Arcadia*, 38, 41. The *Defence* provides examples of this habit of mind: how poetry is the ideal synthesis of the powers of history and philosophy; how English is "fit for both sorts" of prosody, ancient quantities, and modern "number (with some regard of the accent)" (*Miscellaneous Prose*, 120, 119). Synthesis is for Sidney the highest modality of praise.

products of a learned culture, then Philoclea is an experiment in starting from the beginning, and as such she is crucial to the book's questions about learning. (Indeed, she might be said to be the only character who learns anything.) Her fall from innocence naturally begins with the stirrings of bewildered love for Pyrocles, whom she still takes to be an Amazon. Sidney writes a remarkable scene in which the weeping princess revisits a grove where, a few short days before, she had inked a hymn to chastity on "a fair white marble stone" (96). There she finds that the text of her lyric "was already foreworn and in many places blotted" (97), her immemorial vow effaced by the ordinary insults of the weather. It is the first sign of a fall into what Sidney figures as the specifically textual pathos of humanism: Philoclea is looking at an old text to try to recover an old self, and finds too much time in the way.

The famous tangle of love, misrecognition, and gleefully intricate plotting that fills the second and third books ultimately brings Pyrocles to her bedchamber, the scene over which Pygmalion and his answering statue preside. They lie together that night, making honorable promises of marriage, but before they wake the next morning Basilius's man Dametas discovers them in bed. He steals Pyrocles' sword, and bars the doors while he goes to summon the duke; Philoclea's secret lapse is now on the verge of being made public. Pyrocles, first to wake, sizes up the situation and determines—by a peculiarly Stoic logic—that he must kill himself to save her reputation, choosing a loose window bar as his instrument: "O bar... since thou couldst not help me make a perfecter escape, yet serve my turn, I pray thee, that I may escape from myself" (253). This self-escaping is an interesting business. On the one hand, it is a kind of perfection of Stoic self-control, and the ultimate sacrifice for his beloved Philoclea. On the other, it could be read as a panicked reaction to his exposure as a failed master of his own appetites. Suicide offers itself as the ultimate act of self-annealing in the face of his own heteronomy; escaping oneself becomes a perverse version of remembering oneself.[55] But he botches the job, and the effort wakes his astonished beloved. When she rouses him from his not-so-serious swoon an exchange of speeches on the *topos* of suicide ensues.

It is a wonderful debate, even better than the princes', impressively handled on both sides. To the extent that Sidney was still writing for an imaginary audience of his old schoolmasters, they could not have but been pleased. There is a bias to the contest, however, tipped in part by an important shift in Philoclea's rhetoric. Searching for grounds to convince

55. On the Stoic affinity for suicide, see Braden, *Renaissance Tragedy*, 24–25.

her beloved, she comes up with a few *sententiae* of her own: "truly, my Pyrocles, I have heard my father and other wise men say that the killing oneself is but a false colour of true courage, proceeding rather of fear of a further evil, either of torment or shame" (255). Never mind that her father hardly exemplifies the true color of courage: this tentative maxim gets at something in Pyrocles' motives, and she pursues the tactic:

> Whatsoever (would they say) comes out of despair cannot bear the title of valour, which should be lifted up to such a height that, holding all things under itself, it should be able to maintain his greatness even in the midst of miseries. Lastly, they would say God had appointed us captains of these our bodily forts, which without treason to that majesty were never to be delivered over till they were redemanded. (255)

These are fine examples of a form the reader has by now become well used to. What is different about them—strikingly different, once you see it, and unexampled among the countless other instances in the book—is that Philoclea provides an attribution. She is alone among *Arcadia*'s speakers in citing her sources, and also alone in her pragmatic commitment to the minimum condition of earthly love, that both lovers be alive.

One might conclude that this scrupulousness is a mark of her tentative progress toward the full rhetorical authority of the princes. The good student learns to kick away the props and treat such wisdom as his own: it becomes him, and he becomes it. But this incomplete appropriation is also a muted challenge to the way *sententia* is used everywhere else in the book. If the princes go happily along with the idea that *"Know thyself* descended from the skies," as Erasmus puts it, Philoclea remembers where she heard the words first.[56] Such attribution, which qualifies the sense both of the universality of the *sententiae* and their identification with their speaker, at least holds open the possibility of thinking *about* them, as opposed to thinking only *by means* of them. It is a fragile moment, in its way like the brief idyll of the Pygmalion image. It does not ultimately make much of a difference: Pyrocles is "not so much persuaded as delighted by her well conceived and sweetly pronounced speeches" (259), and he is deterred from taking his own life only when Philoclea wraps herself around his legs to stop him. But Sidney's concertedness in raising these questions—thrice repeating an

---

56. "They were so deeply respected in old time, that they seemed to have fallen from heaven rather than to have come from men. 'And *Know thyself* descended from the sky' says Juvenal" (Erasmus, *Works*, 31:13). Note that Erasmus coyly offers an attribution.

attribution used nowhere else in his sententious book—is unmistakable. In the words of a young woman innocent of schooling, he gives us a glimpse of how this trope might be otherwise.[57]

Philoclea suggests how sententiousness might be tempered by being reintroduced into narrative, reattached to the contingencies of character, time, and circumstance. Euarchus is a complementary study in the consequences for narrative of perfecting sententious detachment. As his name suggests, he is the good king of Macedon and father of Pyrocles, kept offstage throughout the first four books in his role as the original destination of the princes' journey—a kind of mark that their growing up aims at. By the end of the fourth book they have gone far astray indeed. Pyrocles is captured in Philoclea's bedroom, and Musidorus has been waylaid while trying to escape with Pamela, eventually passing into the custody of the duke's deputy Philanax. Basilius's apparent death on the morning of Pyrocles' capture precipitates the whole plot into the complex trial that occupies the last phase of the book. The princes stand accused both of adultery—which is a capital crime under the strict laws of Arcadia—and of conspiracy to murder. Into this mess, the narrative at its maximum of complexity and misrecognition, Euarchus is introduced in the midst of a progress that brings him to Arcadia at the crucial moment. Petitioned by Philanax, he consents to sit in judgment at the trial.

The narrator's admiration for Euarchus is unqualified, and the terms of his praise perfect the language of Stoic self-similarity that has half-comforted and half-rebuked the princes all along:

> the reward of virtue [is] in itself; on which his inward love was so fixed
> that it never was dissolved into other desires, but keeping his thoughts true
> to themselves, was neither beguiled with the painted gloss of pleasure nor

57. In the following chapter we will see another, more oblique instance of the woman idealized precisely for her lack of education in Spenser's portrayal of Britomart in Book III of *The Faerie Queene*. The original *Arcadia* is dedicated to Sidney's sister Mary, and sometimes the narrator addresses an audience of women; Sidney calls his book an "idle work." On the rich question of a female audience, see Lucas, *Writing for Women: The Example of Woman as Reader in Elizabethan Romance*, esp. 118–34. The book was read by educated men, however, as though it were written for them: Fulke Greville, in his *Dedication*, says that "his end . . . was not vanishing pleasure alone, but moral Images, and examples" (*Prose Works*, 134); Gabriel Harvey, in *Pierce's Supererogation*, exhorts readers to take up the book, saying, "He that will loove, let him learne to loove of him that will teach him to Live, and furnish him with many pithy and effectuall instructions" (G. Smith, ed., *Elizabethan Critical Essays*, 2:263).

dazzled with the false light of ambition. This made the line of his actions
straight and always like itself, no worldly thing being able to shake the
constancy of it. (309)

Euarchus's autonomy and self-consistency are apparently irreproachable.
It should be no surprise, then, that his legal reasoning makes for the most
densely sententious language in the book: "since between prince and subject there is as necessary a relation as between father and son, and as there
is no man a father but to his child, so is not a prince a prince but to his
own subjects," he opines; "they that will receive the benefit of a custom
must not be the first to break it, for then they can not complain if they
be not helped by that which they themselves hurt"; "For no proportion it
were of justice that a man might make himself no prince when he would
do evil, and might anew create himself a prince when he would not suffer
evil." He has been called upon to "pronounce . . . sentence" (349), and he
aligns the rhetoric of his wisdom with the rigors of Arcadian law. John
Hoskins—who made a rhetoric handbook, *Directions for Speech and Style*,
from Arcadian examples thirteen years after Sidney's death—observes that
"*sententia* is better for the bench than the bar," better for judgment than for
pleading.[58] If this is so, in Euarchus, empowered to decide the fate of all
the main characters, Sidney realizes in full the legislative potential that has
only been latent in the trope up to now.

His judgment is famously severe: Pamela is unpunished, but Philoclea is
condemned to the convent, and the princes to death. The duchess Gynecia
will be buried alive with her husband. Nor does he delay, "not needing to
take leisure for that whereof a long practice had bred a well grounded habit
in him" (349). This is not the speculative dilation of Erasmus's *Adagia*,
but—finally—the rigorism of rule-following. It takes no time, and promises
a swift, determinate execution. Euarchus renders his sentence in ignorance
of the princes' identities, for they reveal nothing of their birth, and he
has not seen them in ten years. But when their lineage is discovered his
judgment is unaffected. He is the very monarch Erasmus has in mind in his
sententious *Institutio*: "The good, wise, and upright prince is simply a sort
of embodiment of the law," a man who can "disregard emotional reactions
and use only reason and judgment. . . . the prince should be removed as far
as possible from the low concerns and sordid emotions of the common
people."[59]

58. Hoskins, *Directions for Speech and Style*, 40.
59. Erasmus, *Works*, 27:264, 221.

As many critics have pointed out, and as most readers will feel, this judgment is calculated to create the maximum dissonance between the sympathies cultivated over the hectic course of the narrative, and the unbending ethics embodied by those maxims that have all along been like troublesome stones in its rushing stream. The revelation of what a judgment truly like itself is truly like is a shock, and may make us long for the comically impotent sententiousness of Musidorus's screeds: the sentence of the bar, not the bench. But *Arcadia* knows no proper grounds for questioning Euarchus's authority. Sidney's interest in resistance theory might have provided him with justifications for unseating the tyrant or the wastrel, but Euarchus is neither of these. His speech is by its very sententious nature "approved by the judgement and consent of all men," to invoke Peacham's words again.[60] He has not violated his trust by reckless appetites or religious deviance. Quite the contrary: he is a harrowingly strict interpreter of the laws of the country. The story brings us to an appreciation of the limits of the law, perhaps the limits of *any* universal law, absent clemency or equity. If we have been able to laugh at the abuse of *sententia*, by the end of the trial we cannot wish for its true use.

———

Philoclea and Euarchus, then, both carry this trope to a different dead end. The third fate of sententiousness brings it back into contact with its original opposite, metamorphosis. Again, the contest between the two can be seen to animate the whole book, with its disguises and unmaskings, escapades and punishments. It is one way of describing a large competition between stasis and change, order and energy, autonomy and desire. But for all the vigor of this competition, it is the ultimate fate of sententiousness—not in the mouth of a particular character, but as it is diffused through the rhetoric of the whole—to become more difficult to separate out from the turbulence it aspires to govern. This problem has already begun to assert itself in that first debate, and it becomes particularly clear in the trial of the final book. At that trial, which is intended to clamp down on the princes' ever more ingenious shifts, there is one more costume change, when the two take on the roles of the royal Palladius and Timopyrus (identities they long ago prepared for such exigencies). When they appear before Euarchus the narrator surrenders himself to the glamour of their new selves, lovingly itemizing the detail of their princely garments. Pyrocles wears "a long coat of white velvet reaching to the small of his leg, with great buttons of

60. Peacham, *Garden*, 189.

diamonds all along upon it" and a diadem "closed up at each end with the richest pearl were to be seen in the world"; Musidorus wears Tyrian purple and is crowned by a "Persian tiara all set down with rows of so rich rubies as they were enough to speak for him" (326). The trial begins with a fashion show.

There is something unmistakably comic about all this dressing up, and about the reaction of the narrator, whose hard judgments are swept away on the hem of that long white velvet coat. In his distraction he dwells particularly upon jewels. Indeed, the same might be said of *Arcadia* as a whole, and not just here; the book features these ornaments again and again at pivotal moments. They are invariably associated with personal emblems, like Pyrocles' figure of the dove and eagle (24) or Pamela's "perfect white lamb tied at a stake" (34). They are also produced as tokens or proofs of identity, used by both Pyrocles and Musidorus to vouch for their noble origins. One might even say that they function something like *sententiae*, insofar as they are instruments for stabilizing identity, physical equivalents of characters' mottos. And if one were to say as much, it would only be following an analogy—jewel to *sententia*—that we have already seen to be rife in the rhetorical literature. Quintilian and Erasmus both refer to maxims as gems; Peacham observes that "excellent sentences ought to be esteemed as precious pearles and costly jewels in princely vestures."[61] Musidorus's rubies play on this association explicitly: they are "enough to speak for him" (326). Both princes arrive in the courtroom bedizened with articulate ornaments.

A deep plot coordinates this fine-spun web of association. If there is something diverse and scattering bright about this particular spectacle, it is not the first time we have been so dazzled; we are back to the problem of the proliferation of *sententiae*, the splendid excess that seems to come at such cost to the figure's Stoic ambitions. In his *Defence of Poetry* Sidney mocks the keepers of "Nizolian paper-books" who "cast sugar and spice upon every dish that is served to the table—like those Indians, not content to wear earrings at the fit and natural place of the ears, but they will thrust jewels through their nose and lips, because they will be sure to be fine."[62] Hoskins's *Directions for Speech and Style* makes the same complaint: "It is very true that a sentence is a pearl in a discourse; but is it a good discourse that is all pearl? It is like an eye in the body; but is it not monstrous to be all eyes?"[63] These remarks are typical of rhetoricians' cautions about the

---

61. Ibid., 191.

62. Sidney, *Miscellaneous Prose*, 117.

63. Hoskins, *Directions*, 39.

overuse of the trope.[64] They also share a peculiarly metamorphic vision of the consequences, whether it is transformation into an Indian (implicit in Sidney's simile), or to an Argus-eyed monster out of Ovid's story of Io. Hoskins's grotesque image of the body all eyes is borrowed from Quintilian: "Personally, I think these highlights are in a sense the eyes of eloquence [*oculos eloquentiae*]. But I do not want there to be eyes all over the body, lest the other organs lose their function."[65]

What happens in this scene is only what is in danger of happening everywhere in *Arcadia*: its moral rhetoric, which Peacham advises be "verie sparingly sprinkled in the Orations of the most eloquent Orators," has become a habit of overdress, or even grotesquerie.[66] This *contaminatio* of the trope of constancy by the myth of change, or vice versa, might be taken as another instance of that turn of mind that Nancy Lindheim describes as Sidney's "temperamental need for synthesis," the tendency of his dichotomies to strain toward a "harmonious, synthetic . . . vision of the ideal."[67] This synthesis is characteristic of his praise, as with the elegantly counterbalanced virtues of the princes and princesses. But in this case, the collapse, or proliferation, of *sententiae* into rhetorical decadence is another instance of his satire.

Fore-Conceit and Afterlife

Sidney's anatomy of the abuses of *sententia* is concerted and thorough; the elegance of its instances (and Sidney does write a beautiful maxim) is systematically undercut by the uses to which they are put. It remains to consider how these concerns penetrate to the level of the work's structure—how *Arcadia* conceives and critiques the *shapes of understanding* that underwrite its idiom—and finally, what it all might mean for the reader. That project can begin with an account of the shape of the book. It is a critical commonplace that the old *Arcadia* falls into two parts, though there is some disagreement about how to make the division. Richard Helgerson, for example, regards its five books together as a kind of trap for the reader, baited by the princes' charm in the first three, and sprung by the narrator's sharp judgment at the beginning of the fourth. We are seduced and then rebuked *seriatim*. Anne Astell emphasizes the transition from the *telling* of the main story to the

---

64. See also Peacham's "caution": "Now in a sentence heede must be taken . . . that they be not too oft used" (*Garden*, 191).

65. Quintilian, *The Orator's Education*, 8.5.34.

66. Peacham, *Garden*, 191.　　　　67. Lindheim, *Structures*, 6, 41.

retelling of the trial, when all of the preceding events are redescribed to suit the interests of prosecution and defense. The reader's judgment is exercised in comparing them.[68] I want to move the pivot slightly earlier in the third book, to the double moment of the princes' seductions. Up to that point *Arcadia* is all fabulation, a giddily intricate narrative increasingly driven by the inventiveness of the princes' own plotting. In the third book, each prince reaches the point of his desire, Pyrocles in Philoclea's bedchamber and Musidorus with his near-kiss, or near-rape, or whatever it is, of Pamela in the forest. From this moment of satisfaction or near-satisfaction, the storytelling begins all over again, now in the mode of justification, ratio-nalization, and finally legal argument. A diagram of that chiasmus would look like this:

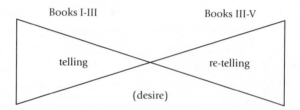

The book has the shape of a bow tie, or an hourglass on its side. At its crux is desire.

The old *Arcadia* cannot be fully described by any one such model; there is also, for example, something like a five-act dramatic structure behind its five books, and the advisedly plural title of Nancy Lindheim's study of the revision—*The Structures of Sidney's Arcadia*—describes the original too.[69] The shape I have diagrammed, however, has a particularly interesting relation

68. It is with the fourth book that Helgerson takes *Arcadia*'s "trap" to snap shut on the reader. Three books of more-or-less sympathetic representation of the princes' adventures give way to a pitiless anatomy of their crimes: "the narrator manipulates his readers into sharing the guilt and the awareness of guilt that characterizes Pyrocles, Musidorus, and Sidney himself" (Helgerson, *Elizabethan Prodigals*, 136). Ann Astell focuses on the trial as a recapitulation of the main action in an effort to describe the *Arcadia*'s "didacticism." She argues that what is at stake for readers is not just an interpretation of the book, but self-knowledge, because we will already have formed judgments parallel to those rendered in the trial. Full of mistakes, lies, and other goads, the testimony probes our interests in the narrative: "As the reader goes through the process of reconstruction and invention, he suddenly confronts his own blind-ness. . . . The reader feels how gullible he has been" ("Sidney's Didactic Method," 45). Alan Hager describes this as a fundamental procedure in Sidney's works, which he calls "retroactive reading": "Once we realize we have, in a sense, been seduced by a mask, our medical cure has taken, and we must go back and reinterpret and reevaluate the experience" (*Dazzling Images*, 130).

69. On the five-act structure generally see Hunter, *John Lyly*, 55.

to Sidney's ideas about reading, ideas in which *sententiae* are implicated. He describes how to read an epic poem in a famous passage from his *Defence of Poetry*:

> for any understanding knoweth the skill of each artificer standeth in that *idea* or fore-conceit of the work, and not in the work itself. And that the poet hath that *idea* is manifest, by delivering them [heroes such as Orlando, Cyrus, and Aeneas] forth in such excellency as he had imagined them. Which delivering forth . . . so substantially it worketh, not only to make a Cyrus, which had been but a particular excellency as nature might have done, but to bestow a Cyrus upon the world to make many Cyruses, if they will learn aright why and how that maker made him.[70]

The fore-conceit is a kind of essence of the text, conceived in the poet's mind before composition: an abstract compound of its meaning, its worth, its purpose, and its design. This idea—idea in a Platonic sense—is embodied in the actual text, in the sequence of its words and the person of the hero. The written work delivers the idea to the reader, who can in turn make many Cyruses if he will learn "why and how that maker made him." The original conception of the author, that is, is essential to the reception of the work.

Sidney often talks about meaning as though it were something inside the text, a kernel in an ornamental shell.[71] His account of the fore-conceit makes it possible to follow the career of that kernel. It begins as the pregnant idea in the poet's mind, which is given body by his composition, incarnate in an order of words. The reader, in turn, extracts that idea from the text in the process of reading. Next—as Sidney puts it later in the *Defence*—the reader makes the narration "an imaginative ground-plot of a profitable invention."[72] That is, he makes himself a Cyrus, realizing the heroic

---

70. Sidney, *Miscellaneous Prose*, 79.

71. "[T]hough the inside and strength were philosophy, the skin, as it were, and beauty depended most on poetry"; "Plato and Boethius . . . made mistress Philosophy very often borrow the masking raiment of Poesy" (*Miscellaneous Prose*, 75, 93).

72. Sidney, *Miscellaneous Prose*, 103. George Chapman, a careful student of the *Defence*, provides a gloss on this use of "ground-plot" in the Sidneian introduction to his translation of the *Odyssey*: "yet is the Structure so elaborate and pompous that the poore plaine Groundworke (considered together) may seeme the naturally rich wombe to it and produce it needfully" (2:5). Forrest G. Robinson discusses fore-conceit and ground-plot in his study *The Shape of Things Known*, where he argues that they have a fundamentally visual character: "The poem is merely a verbal medium through which the poet's mental pictures are made delightfully accessible to the eyes of his audience. An adept reader will invert the creative procedure" (123).

fore-conceit in his own action. By this exemplary action he may in turn
make many Cyruses like him, if those men have the wit to recognize the
how and why to derive once again, that is, the fore-conceit. This trajectory compasses the extended career of what we have seen other humanist
thinkers describe as reading for action. The pattern of reducing a text to its
essence—so often a maxim—then reexpanding it by translation or imitation
is familiar enough from the classroom; here that latter phase of dilation
takes the form of action in the world. If we think about this kind of reading
as an activity unfolding in time, we come up with a familiar shape:

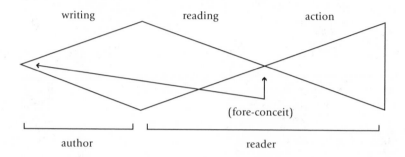

The shape of reading here (the hourglass of the rightmost two-thirds of the
diagram describes the reader's experience) is homologous with the diagram
of *Arcadia*'s plot. No coincidence: Sidney constructs the old *Arcadia* as a
process of reduction and dilation (analysis and genesis, Brinsley would
say) that maps what would be a deeply familiar readerly habit. Anyone
trained as he had been at Shrewsbury could recognize in the total order
of the fiction a picture of his own procedure, almost as though the book
had been read for him in advance. If this is so, *then the fore-conceit*, the crux
or turning point between its phases of reading and action, its essence and
meaning, *is desire* itself—or as Pyrocles puts it in that first debate, "enjoying."

At least one textual clue could be adduced to support what might be
thought of as a large-scale, structural joke about the particular profit of reading this "idle work" (as Sidney described it to his sister [3]), and about the
shapes of understanding that would be brought to it. In the first eclogues,
the bitter old man Dicus unveils before the gathered company of shepherds
a revisionary emblem of Cupid, depicted as a figure with a laurel crown in

---

That inversion, represented in my diagram, is the translation of the author's fore-conceit into
action.

one hand and a purse of money in the other, "painted all ragged and torn, so that his skin was bare in most places, where a man might perceive all his body full of eyes, his head horned with the horns of a bull, with long ears accordingly, his face old and wrinkled, and his feet cloven." The assembled company laugh, but the narrator allows that the emblem might well be the fruit of "a better judgment, which saw the bottom of things" (57). Cupid, as it turns out, is indeed the bottom of things in *Arcadia*: desire is what all the princes' machinations come down to. This figure of Argus returns once more in the poem, just at that narrative crux when Pyrocles finds himself in bed with Philoclea, "beginning now to envy Argus's thousand eyes, and Briareus's hundred hands" (211). The filament between the two scenes is stretched thin, but we can look to John Hoskins, whose *Directions for Speech and Style* has so many Arcadian examples, for someone who seems to have thought along the same line: "It is very true that a sentence is a pearl in a discourse; but is it a good discourse that is all pearl? It is like an eye in the body; but is it not monstrous to be all eyes? . . . And if a sentence were as like to be an hand in the text as it is commonly noted with a hand in the margent, yet I should rather like the text that had no more hands than Hercules than that which had as many as Briareus."[73] Hoskins reminds us of the rhetorical discourse within which Argus was a persistent figure for sententious excess. That watchful beast squats at the desiring center of *Arcadia* as though to suggest the problem of sententiousness is there too, or there especially.

————

The texture of the old *Arcadia* mocks the ethical ambitions of *sententia* by a proliferation that flies in the face of the rhetoricians' caution about overuse; Euarchus's sententious verdict explores the contrary risk of singular rigorism. The parody of reading enacted in the book's hourglass structure addresses itself to the deep habits (or models) of mind by which the whole enterprise sustained itself. Why should a book have a motto; why should it come down to a single idea, a single maxim or (as Ramus would put it) "dialectical ratiocination"?[74] Why should understanding be a making-

73. Hoskins, *Directions*, 39. Marking *sententiae* in the margin with a pointing finger or sometimes with what we now call quotation marks in the margin was a familiar convention. Hoskins's juxtaposition of Briareus and Argus is most unlikely to be a borrowing from Sidney, since he worked with the published new *Arcadia*, from which this scene in the old was excised. The pairing may have been conventional: see e.g., Shakespeare's *Troilus and Cressida*, 1.2.27–28.

74. Walter Ong shows how Ramus's analytic method can strip Cicero's *Pro Milo* down to the singular "dialectical ratiocination" at its heart: "It is permissible to kill a criminal."

small, a taking-the-time-out; as opposed, say, to an experience of reading? The implication of Sidney's parody is that any such act of reduction-as-understanding will necessarily misrepresent his narrative. Desire may be the engine of *Arcadia*, but surely it is not all that is to be learned there. His satire is directed at the most fundamental aspects of the antinarrative impulse in humanist pedagogy, and he makes his fiction a mirror in which his well-trained readers can see an image of their own costly efficiencies. To profit by *Arcadia* one cannot simply carry away the kernel of wisdom at its heart. What we should do with it instead is less obvious; it is not clear that Sidney himself could have said.[75] But at the very least, we cannot extricate ourselves from the narrative.

Certainly Sidney did not; he was three books into a revision of the old *Arcadia* when he died. (That revision, which transforms his orientation toward the project of teaching, will be the subject of chapter 5.) An incomplete, "new" *Arcadia* was published in 1590, and then in 1593 came an edition that provided some awkward closure to the story by tacking on the remainder of the original text. But this is not how *Arcadia* was first read. The first Arcadian sentences to find their way into print appeared two years before, in Abraham Fraunce's 1588 *Arcadian Rhetorike*. Fraunce sets Sidney alongside the likes of Homer, Virgil, and Tasso as an exemplar of the various tropes and schemes, and though he is interested in all sorts of rhetorical effects, a handful of the excerpts he includes qualify as *sententiae*. From that point forward Sidney's maxims became a staple of the industry of the printed commonplace book: they are to be found in Francis Meres's *Palladis Tamia: Wits Treasury* (1598), Nicholas Ling's *Politeuphuia, Wits Commonwealth* (1612), and in hosts of other compilations that followed. No Englishman of his era had anything like this success making himself portable and quotable; his wisdom became the most valuable coin in this particular economy of learning. It was a kind of literary triumph, whose causes were many, and certainly included his genuine gifts as an aphorist.

But to be taken up this way in the commonplace books, if my argument is right, is also a kind of failure. For Sidney wrote a fiction designed—in its plot, its structure, and its style—to satirize the kind of trained reading

---

"We might say today that this is the 'meaning' of the oration *For Milo*, for everything beyond such summary statement, according to Ramus, is ornament" (*Ramus, Method, and the Decay of Dialogue*, 191). On Sidney's Ramism see chapter 6.

75. He did not, in any event, in his *Defence of Poetry*, which can be read as an antitext to the *Arcadia*, a guide to the strategies of reading that the fiction will flout. See for example Hager, *Dazzling Images*, 115–29, for an account of the *Defence* as a praise of folly.

that pursued above all the gems most prized by the commonplace books' makers. Among his tactics is persistently to recall his readers to the schoolroom origins of that training, to suggest the way instruction in and by that figure makes his readers students again, and to ask them to think twice about what they learned and how they learned it. Sidney himself, of course, had thrived in that schoolroom, by all accounts. His biographer Thomas Moffet relates how "the master commanded his delight and joy" at Shrewsbury, and how at Christ Church "He was never seen going to church, to the exercise ground, or to the public assembly hall (where he frequently employed himself), except as distinguished among the company of all the learned men."[76] In the years after his death it was only more common for promising young aristocrats to be brought up in school. But when he came to write the first *Arcadia*, he must have felt betrayed by all that learning.[77] In many ways the old *Arcadia* remains a book to impress Sidney's teachers, had they condescended to admire a fiction in the vernacular, and to forgive its dalliance with romance. As a sustained, elegant, and acrobatic exhibition of the fruits of a training in high rhetoric it is exceeded in the history of English letters only by its revision. But it wants no part of the schoolmaster's profession.

76. Moffett, *Nobilis; or, a View of the Life and Death of a Sidney*, 73, 78.

77. Katherine Duncan-Jones's biography *Sir Philip Sidney, Courtier Poet*, tells the classic story of Sidney's disappointments at court. Alan Stewart's *Philip Sidney: A Double Life* pays particular attention to Sidney's reputation abroad and his success as a diplomat, balancing but not canceling the familiar account of his domestic frustrations.

CHAPTER FOUR

Example

The last two chapters map limits of the Elizabethan pedagogical imagination. On the one hand, instruction by moral maxim, installing in the student's memory a set of *sententiae* that can be read out into good conduct. (Action, if you like, as reading aloud.) On the other hand, the idea of an education by experience, a growing-up-in-the-world that has no use for school—tantalizing as a prospect, more palpable, especially for the likes of Roger Ascham, as a threat. Romance narrative affords a literary space for testing these limits against each other. Its generic habit of subjecting settled ideas to the disruptions of error and marvel makes it something like a mimesis of empiricism, full of the "proving" and "testing" that are already native to the chivalric vocabulary. Among the things Lyly and Sidney test are the techniques of reading brought to their books by their educated peers.

To define the test this way is to see it mainly as a rivalry between poets and schoolmasters, a rivalry that is the principal concern of this book. That said, a version of the same contest is also played out within the humanist schoolroom. To regard the schoolroom as simply "instilling . . . barren hearts with a conscientious slavery," as Milton puts it, slights the variety of instruction in the best classrooms, classrooms like Richard Mulcaster's at Merchant Taylors'.[1] Humanism as a reform movement widely proclaimed its interest in preparing students for the challenges of experience, even for providing some version of experience on the premises (albeit in the form of historical writing). If the schoolmasters were unwilling simply to commit the young to the hazards of the world, neither, of course, are we. They

---

1. Milton, "Of Education," in *Prose Works*, 2:376. In this particular context Milton is talking about training in law.

were looking for ways to make school a useful preparation for a specific set of practical challenges. And if the definition of those challenges, even of "action" itself, carried ideological freight with which Lyly and Sidney took issue, nonetheless the dilemma of perilous experience and empty sentence was the schoolmasters' dilemma, too.

There was a characteristically humanist answer to that dilemma: example. This workaday piece of pedagogical furniture—a compromise between experience and maxim—was treated with exceptional reverence by education writers. We might provisionally think about it as a piece of experience, a sample cut from the world's cloth in such a way that it somehow bears a lesson. An example has a boundedness that raw experience lacks, and a point, and it excludes or at least circumscribes whatever might be harmful in the context from which it is drawn. In all these ways it is a middle category between the pedagogical limits this study has so far surveyed. We have seen that each limit had its critics: men suspicious of the vain proliferation of *sententiae* on the one hand, of experience and its correlates (the Grand Tour; the old, aristocratic education) on the other. But example, the middle ground, knew no reproach. Admiration runs high among the rhetoricians: "No kinde of argument in all the Oratorie craft, doth better perswade and more universally satisfie than example," writes Puttenham.[2] It runs higher still among schoolmasters like Ascham, who was prepared to bet almost everything on the middle way: "I demand a volume of examples, a page of rules," he wrote to his friend Johannes Sturm, the Strasbourg schoolmaster.[3] Ascham never drafted that volume, a successor to his *Schoolmaster*, but his ambition can stand for the romance of his class with its projected contents.

Of the three poets who are my own examples here, none was as profoundly and variously interested in teaching and learning as Edmund Spenser, none as skeptical of how his audience was trained to read (and not only in school). Example—or as Spenser spells it, "ensample"—is a peculiarly intense focus for that skepticism.[4] One could very roughly map the major terms of the last two chapters (experience and maxim) onto the

2. Puttenham, *Arte*, 39.

3. "I want something else [than books of rules], I require more. We need an artisan and an architect who knows how by an artful method to bring the parts together, to polish the rough spots, and to build up the entire structure.... And I will not be content with one or two examples, but I am looking for many of them, varied in kind.... I allow my *Schoolmaster* to be sparing in laying down rules, provided that he shows himself liberal and generous ... with offering examples" (Ascham, *Letters*, 270–71).

4. By way of the Old French *essample*, "ensample" may be traced back to the Latin root, *exemplum*; the OED proclaims that, along with "sample," "example" and "ensample" are "ultimately

cardinal opposition in Spenser's polymodal poem between romance narrative and personification allegory. His six-and-some books are a kind of perpetual contest between the two, unfolding, reforming, and corroding one another, the allegory tending toward an abstract, axiomatic order, the erring course of the narrative toward unstructured experience.[5] Example—example as a piece of experience—is a fragile middle category, and it tends to come into play when the relation between those larger forces is most troubled. The poem's self-scrutiny is at its most intense when it shows examples being made.

We know far more about Spenser's teacher, Richard Mulcaster, than about any of Sidney's teachers, or Lyly's. Mulcaster is in many ways the most interesting of the schoolmasters who left a record of his method, as he did in two treatises from the early 1580s (*Positions Concerning the Training Up of Children*, 1581, and *The First Part of the Elementarie*, 1582). There are reasons to think that Spenser owed him a substantial intellectual debt.[6] Nonetheless, this chapter will not be about that relationship. Spenser had left school far behind by the time he finished the first installment of his romance, in Ireland, three hundred miles and twenty-one years from the precincts of Merchant Taylors'. The knights of his fiction set out from the court of the Faerie Queene, not from the university at Athens or home schooling in Thessaly. This chapter must instead consider the stubborn authority of humanist habits of mind and ideas of teaching long after school; the function of the schoolroom here, and from here on out, will be more heuristic. Spenser does sometimes compose scenes of instruction that look like how a young gentleman in his own England might have been taught. But generally speaking his pedagogical inquiries are translated more completely than Lyly's or Sidney's into the language of romance. The tests he posed

---

the same word." "Sample" in its modern sense can serve to remind the reader of *exemplum*'s derivation from the verb *eximere*, to take out or excerpt.

5. See Teskey, *Allegory and Violence*, esp. 23. In *The Choice of Achilles* Susanne Wofford conceives this opposition in terms of figure and action in epic more generally: her reading of *The Faerie Queene* "consistently opposes the apocalyptic and hierarchical structure of allegorical imagery with an anti-apocalyptic, metonymical narrative" (228–29). Both critics have had a substantial influence on my argument in this chapter and elsewhere.

6. I have discussed the sophistication of Mulcaster's attitude toward time in teaching in chapter 1. He is also the most flexible-minded of the schoolmasters in thinking about the competing claims of authority and experience; his confidence in the latter makes a strong contrast with Ascham. For example: "It is not enough to rule the world, to alleadge authorities, but to raunge authorities, which be not above the world, by the rule of the world, is the wisemans line" (*Positions*, 22). See also DeMolen, *Richard Mulcaster and Educational Reform in the Renaissance*, and by the same author, "Richard Mulcaster and the Profession of Teaching in the Sixteenth Century," where he calls Mulcaster "an ebullient and choleric reformer" (129).

for his Elizabethan readers would not always have recalled them to their classroom days; still, they bring that classroom's legacy under the closest scrutiny.

What Can Redcrosse Read?

As with experience and *sententia* in previous chapters, one objective here will be to construct a wide-ranging account of how school-trained readers thought both about and with example. But the project of assessing what that cherished piece of didactic technology means to *The Faerie Queene* confronts a distinctive obstacle, the presumption that the allegorical agents that populate it cannot learn, or even cannot change. They are fixed ideas; what happens in the poem is a matter of their interaction, or perhaps their unfolding, but not their transformation. So far I have focused on scenes of instruction that operate simultaneously inside and outside the text, in representations of learning among characters and designs on the reader. Can we expect a representation of the "inside" in the landscape of person-ification allegory? Susanne Wofford offers a strong and valuable caution: "characters do not know they are in an allegory, and cannot and do not 'read' the signs of their world as figurative pointers to another arena of understanding. . . . The 'heroic ignorance' of the characters is absolute."[7]

I will return to Wofford's claim repeatedly, sometimes to reinforce it, sometimes to point out how hard—how significantly hard—it is to swallow. There is a useful, preliminary test case in Book I's conveniently named Ig-naro. He is the porter who greets Arthur, most unhelpfully, when the Prince enters Orgoglio's dungeon: old and blind, with his head on backward, "His name *Ignaro* did his nature read aright" (1.8.31). He makes for an especially pure instance of what Angus Fletcher calls the "daemonism" of the alle-gorical agent, the tyranny, almost like demonic possession, of a single idea over his aspect and actions.[8] His ignorant name and his ignorant nature are one and the same. Arthur's belated and half-comic recognition of this limit reminds us that there are different orders of character in the poem:

---

7. Wofford, *The Choice of Achilles*, 220. See also her chapter on *FQ* I–III in *The Cambridge Companion to Spenser*, esp. 116-19. Isabel MacCaffrey offers a slightly softer version of this claim: "The fact that a character's experience occurs in a particular setting and a particular pattern that is allusive *need not* (and ordinarily *does* not) signify its dramatic 'meaning' in the character's consciousness" (*Spenser's Allegory*, 101–2). For a counterargument, see Quilligan, *Milton's Spenser*, 51–52.

8. Fletcher, *Allegory*, 25–69. On Arthur "reading" Ignaro see Miller, *The Poem's Two Bodies*, 84.

the prince's mounting frustration is checked when, after several fruitless requests for directions, "He ghest his nature by his countenance" (34). This guess would seem to be a very modest sort of allegorical reading of one character by another, *contra* Wofford. But Ignaro himself, without doubt, is incapable of such self-transcendence or self-knowledge. His name reads his nature, and we read his name; he means without intending. He cannot change without becoming unintelligible. (What would we make of a knowledgeable Ignaro? The whole allegorical edifice would come tumbling down.)

If Ignaro is paradigmatic of character in *The Faerie Queene*, then whatever is didactic about this poem must be played out in another register. And indeed, he has a clear value for the reader, as a definition of what ignorance is—even a kind of icon for thinking with, a means of holding and moving the concept "ignorance" within the mind. This last view entails an idea of allegory as a mimesis of thinking, an approach to the poem that has been important to many of its critics: "a model of the mind's life in the world," as Isabel MacCaffrey puts it.[9] The characters are concepts, and the poem thinks by combining and recombining them in the logic, or the stream of consciousness, of its narrative. The poem advertises this idea of itself with particular clarity in such moments as the progression of the seven deadly sins, the centerpiece of the House of Pride (1.4.16–36). The sins each have Ignaro's emblematic fixity, and successive stanzas place them in a significant order, so that Idleness leads to Gluttony leads to Lechery and on to other, grosser villainies. Their arrangement in fictional space is meaningful, too: the first six draw the cart in teams of two, and its axle makes the distinction between the forward or active vices (Gluttony, Lechery, Wrath) and the froward or passive (Idleness, Avarice, Envy). Allegory serves as a method of analysis, and narrative is its handmaiden, obediently moving from case to case without troubling the exposition with any reversals. The mind of the poem is free to think its thoughts in the most schematic, universal terms.

Such a concept of allegory has affinities with the models of mind available in the ordinary pedagogy of the classroom.[10] It depends on such operations as analysis and epitome; like the synchronic inscape of the commonplaces, it establishes relations of place at the expense of relations of time. If we accept this account of allegory as adequate to the poem, then it is

9. MacCaffrey, *Spenser's Allegory*, 6. Gordon Teskey calls it "a heuristic instrument for exciting the mind to activity" (*Allegory and Violence*, 99).

10. Allegory is rarely a presence in the classroom, probably because it would have seemed medieval to humanist temperaments. Sir Thomas Elyot's allegory of dancing, discussed in chapter 2, is a notable exception.

apparent how beside the point it is to ask what Ignaro knows or doesn't know, let alone whether or what he might learn. His mode is being, or perhaps meaning, but certainly not knowing. He doesn't need to know himself any more than a thought or an idea needs to know itself. (The *reductio* of a thought knowing itself, particularly if it must know itself by another thought, quickly becomes absurd.) *The Faerie Queene* thinks *with* these characters, or agents, or emblems, and it proposes that very thinking to its readers, as though we could adopt it as our own cognitive dialect. We can not only think the same thing as the poem, but think it the same way. If this is the poem's grand project, then we can simply stop worrying about what the characters learn or do not learn, and concentrate, as the "Letter to Raleigh" would have us do, on the thoughts it makes us think—one way to let it fashion us.[11]

But *The Faerie Queene* is also a story, a romance. Over the three books of 1590 the analytic self-confidence of such set pieces as the procession of sins is shaken again and again. The poem is more profoundly dedicated than any work considered here, perhaps than any work of literature, period, to exploring the tensions between paradigmatic and narrative modes of understanding. Moreover—and the more central a character is, the more telling this concern—the narrative is attended by the stubborn expectation that it will represent something we might as well call *Bildung*. Redcrosse is a "clownishe younge man" who will eventually slay a dragon.[12] To do that, he has to change; to grow up and grow wise, not just to unfold; and the story has to make that happen. I mean *Bildung* in no stronger, and no weaker, sense than this.

So let us for a moment make the opposite assumption, that Spenser's characters can in fact learn. This book has been preoccupied with how learning can be made visible: what might it look like in the fictional environment of *The Faerie Queene*? One answer—and the terms will hardly be surprising at this point in the study—is paradigmatic, a change to the appearance or the characteristic actions of the agent-as-emblem. So Ignaro's head

---

11. Angus Fletcher's study of poetic thinking, *Colors of the Mind*, describes such accounts of mind as a "simplistic but complicated allegorical structure . . . becoming the preferred image of the mind's complete workings" (50), a tendency he takes novels to resist. He observes: "Thinking the poem implies such things as taking the poem as an occasion for thought; thinking through the poem; being aware of one's thoughts as one reads the poem; looking for some logic in the poem; allowing a poem to trigger certain lines of thought; looking in the poem for what Coleridge called its 'implicit metaphysic'" (111–12). Spenser's poem proposes all these possibilities, but over and against the narrower authority of the allegory itself as that preferred image.

12. So Spenser calls him in the "Letter to Raleigh," in *The Faerie Queene*, ed. Hamilton, 719.

might be turned right way round again; he might remember the key that Arthur needs; he might even be rechristened *Sapiento,* to account for his new nature. He could be seen under the aspect of a new paradigm. The problem here is that such changes amount to a new character, while what we think of as learning—certainly, as *Bildung*—requires a continuity of self, the persistence of some things while others change. (This is Lyly's problem, how to knit his two Euphueses together.) Another possibility, still under the auspices of paradigmatic understanding, is the gradual resolution of the emblem out of more mixed and ambivalent narrative materials. So Redcrosse or Guyon might be seen gradually to take on more and more of the qualities of their virtues as the story proceeds, until at the end they are constituted as adequate allegorical representations: Redcrosse can finally stand for Holiness, Guyon for Temperance. The sign of having learned is the consolidation of the emblem. This is a relatively common view of the matter in the criticism, one that might be said to synchronize the character's learning with the reader's, the one becoming and the other deriving a satisfying final image from the end of the story.[13]

The alternative is learning as narrative, learning that cannot be separated from the story in which it is told, that *is* that story, for the character who lives it—who is portrayed by its means and medium—and for the reader. I have mostly approached that idea by the *via negativa,* glimpsing it, for example, in the reversing mirror of Euphues's tragic rigorism. *The Faerie Queene,* with its plot of error, makes it possible to be more specific about the antagonisms between narrative understanding and conventions of formal instruction. So much of what happens in school, and what happens in so many everyday instances of teaching, is underwritten by that fundamental idea of learning as repetition. So much comes down to being able to say it back, do it again: *do you understand? Say it back to me.* In the landscape of Spenserian romance, where error is the norm, the opposite is the case: repetition is precisely the sign of the failure to learn. It is to their continual cost that characters pursue their daemonic compulsions, in spite of changing circumstances; time and again, they take their armor off, or fall asleep at unpropitious moments, or kindle in irascibility, and suffer for it. Success—scarce as it is in the poem—would seem to depend on a flexible adaptation to events as they happen. Such adaptability is what it would mean to be, in Arthur's words, "ware

13. See, for example, Donald Cheney's account in *Spenser's Image of Nature*: characters in *The Faerie Queene* "may appear to be embodiments of the virtues in their dealings with others—showing the operation of Holiness or Justice on those who supplicate or challenge them—and at the same time they are human figures struggling to realize their own identities in terms of these virtues" (6).

of like agein" (1.8.44), wary not least of the seductions of likeness itself. Learning is figured in variety, and change, and it is not so much a discreet, preparatory phase as it is an ongoing bearing toward the world.

These are two now-familiar models. Does Redcrosse learn anything, according to either of them? Does either entail reading the allegory from the inside? I will put these questions to two episodes, first the end of Book I—a natural place to look for signs of learning—and then the House of Pride. In the latter, the matter of example will begin to move to the foreground.

The story of Redcrosse's decline is just that, a story. There is the overconfidence of the defeat of Errour, the all-too-human loss of faith in Una, the defensive pride that makes him so vulnerable to Duessa's seductions and to everything that ensues. These events follow one another in a chain of causation, bringing him, over time, to his nearly fatal encounter with Despaire. Still he goes on to defeat the dragon, a victory that argues some kind of change in his character, the kind of change that we are tempted to call learning. (Certainly many of the poem's critics call it that.[14]) Moreover, before he goes to fight the dragon, he undergoes the disciplinary rigors of the poem's most concerted didactic edifice, the "schoolhouse" (1.10.18) of the House of Holiness. Some instruction must be going on.

The structure of that schoolhouse has been much discussed, in its three stages: a severe purgation with Fidelia and Speranza, the more benign tuition of Charissa and the Seven Beadsmen, and finally the vision of the New Jerusalem vouchsafed him by the hermit Contemplation. A variety of different kinds of teaching is implicated in this sequence, but I want to concentrate on a pattern of pedagogical closure that has been pointed out by Darryl Gless. Gless observes that despite the apparently progressive structure of the house, Redcrosse's tuition is repeatedly described as though it were already complete. Fidelia, for example, "unto him disclosed every whitt," and she is able "with her wordes to kill, / And rayse againe to life the hart, that she did thrill" (1.10.19). This power brings the reborn knight "To such perfection of all hevenly grace" (21) that he is overcome again by suicidal despair. Later he is whipped and scourged by Penaunce until "no one corrupted jott" (26) remains; again it sounds as though his reform is fully accomplished. Then the seven beadsmen instruct him in charity until

---

14. For a recent example of this reflex, see Hester Lees-Jeffries, "From the Fountain to the Well: Redcrosse Learns to Read."

"so perfect he became, / That from the first unto the last degree, / His mortall life he learned had to frame / In holy righteousnesse, without rebuke or blame" (45). Gless accounts for this proliferation of finalities as a rebuke to the idea that works might make a difference to the status of our souls.[15] Salvation, too, is not a story, in the sense that its end is not caused by the worldly events of the meantime spent on earth.[16]

Something similar happens in the dragon fight. It is a pitched battle of three days, the first two of which end the same way, with the knight overwhelmed by a blast from the "infernall fournace" (1.11.44) of the dragon's fiery breath. The first time, Redcrosse stumbles backward, seared by his own armor, into the *well of life* (29), the waters of which have the power to restore the dead and "guilt of sinfull crimes cleane wash away" (30). He arises the next morning as a new man, with emphasis on the "new": "So new this new-borne knight to battell new did rise" (34). On that second day, it is a "trickling streame of Balme" that receives his fall, a stream that issues from the base of the Tree of Life (for the battle is fought on the ancient site of Eden) and that can "reare againe / The sencelesse corse appointed for the grave" (48). Reborn from this second death, Redcrosse is finally fit to dispatch the dragon, which he does without particular difficulty on the third day. Scholars have associated the first of these revivifying waters with baptism, the second with communion; certainly they are sacramental.[17] What I want to emphasize is that preparing this knight for his final victory, both in his instruction at the House of Holiness and in the fight itself, is a matter of killing and reviving him, again and again. He is subsumed into a transfiguring, ritual pattern, a sacramental structure, and *this* is how the poem imagines the change that enables his victory. What is sacrificed is any

15. Gless, *Interpretation and Theology*, 154–63. "Nothing prevents readers of Catholic or unselfconscious Pelagian leanings from reading merit into the knight's actions in I.x, or readers of humanistic biases from remaining puzzled by the canto's apparent contradictions," he writes. "If the House of Holiness is viewed as a metaphoric representation of Protestant doctrines of holiness, however, *The Faerie Queene* I.x will be found to embody the overall implication that works in this world are important, admirable, eagerly to be pursued, and yet contribute nothing to justification" (150).

16. On the Protestant reformation of genre, including romance, and the problem of narrative see J. King, *Spenser's Poetry and the Reformation Tradition*, esp. 200–202.

17. King offers a sterner, Protestant account of Redcrosse's career as the recognition of his own election: "The overall movement of Redcrosse's experience traces the trajectory of Protestant spiritual life from the initial conviction of sin to confidence that one is the chosen recipient of divine grace" (*Spenser's Poetry*, 60).

idea of education, indeed any idea of a subject of education. The newborn knight succeeds because he is new. Change is not learning, but rebirth.[18]

I have held tight through this account to the expectation of a narrative of education, as though Redcrosse's assumption into the rituals of Holiness could only be a default, like Euphues's retreat into the schoolroom at the end of the Anatomy. The poem is brought to the expedient of changing modes in order to represent the knight's prophesied success. His fall may be a story, but his redemption is willfully stripped of narrative syntax. (His redemption has no middle, just a succession of beginnings and a sudden end.) But there is something perverse about reading this as a failure of the poem. Isn't the very point of the Book of Holiness to strip Redcrosse of self-hood in order to perfect his superlunary virtue? Perhaps the narrative language of romance is suited only for describing the dismantling sadness of experience. If so, then what actually happens to the knight gives an account of learning—of knowing—to which experience not only makes no difference, but to which experience is anathema. You have learned when you have been purged of its corruptions, when you have become an exemplar. (Perhaps this is a version of Wofford's "heroic ignorance.") The repetition of Redcrosse's ritual rebirths—how he is new each time—is a way of insisting that his story (if not *the* story) has been broken. The paradigm of Holiness is instituted in its place.

If you stop reading for the night at the end of the battle with the dragon, you will likely go to sleep thinking that a career of fruitless error has been resolved into ritual knowledge—that what you have witnessed is the purging of experience and the consolidation of an exemplar, and that the proper question now is not what Redcrosse knows, but what he is, or better, what he stands for. So much for *Bildung*. But if that is the poem's orthodox doctrine, or at least the first book's, reading a little further inevitably raises some trouble, with Redcrosse's disquietingly selective narration of his own adventures (if experience does not matter, why rewrite it?), the return of Archimago, and the open-endedness of the very end. There are episodes along the way, too, that offer proleptic cautions about what it would mean to abstract the knight from his story. Most important among them is the

---

18. Michael McKeon's *Origins of the English Novel* describes such a pattern as characteristic of romance in its difference from the novel: "romance character development tends to proceed by discontinuous leaps between states of being—by 'rebirths'—and to be signified by the successive divulgence or alteration of name" (39).

House of Pride, the home of those deadly sins, where Spenser meditates at least as intensely on instruction as he does in Charissa's schoolhouse. It is there that example first appears as a serious instrument for thinking about learning. The episode begins with the declaration, "For unto knight there is no greater shame / Then lightnesse and inconstancie in love, / That doth this *Redcrosse* knights ensample plainly prove" (1.4.1); it ends when Redcrosse's dwarf "ma[kes] ensample" (1.5.52) of the house's victims; and, in a kind of coda, the next canto starts off with the simile of a sailor whose ship has narrowly avoided a "hidden rocke," and who looks back "halfe amazed . . . Having escapt so sad ensamples in his sight" (1.6.1). These "ensamples" are a kind of frame for everything that happens in between.

Framing will be much to the point in what follows. If an example is a piece of the world, then it must have a boundary that marks its difference; it must be possible to tell it apart from miscellaneous experience, to say where it begins and ends, as a preliminary to saying what it means. That said, surveying the hundred or so stanzas between those signposts does not make it immediately obvious what the example is. First, there is simply a great deal of material to be found there: the story of Redcrosse's seduction by the chivalric ethos of Lucifera's house, and his combat with the knight Sans Joy; also the allegorical pageantry that seems to define the life of the place. Is *all* of this the example? Can a narrative be an example? There is the complex, emblematic tableau of the sins, too. Are they examples? Can an allegory be an example? We might think of these questions as turning on the preposition in the phrase *example of*, and they are compounded, in this case, by questions entailed by the preposition in the phrase *example for*. At the beginning of the episode, it looks like Redcrosse himself is the intended audience for what will follow: "Young knight, what ever that dost armes professe, / And through long labours huntest after fame, / Beware of fraud, beware of ficklenesse" (1.4.1). By the end of the same stanza, however, this expectation is less secure: "That doth this *Redcrosse* knights ensample plainly prove" (1). It could be that the possessive "knights" tells us this example is his to interpret. It is more idiomatic, however, then and now, to read it as saying that he himself *is* the example. We are back to the question of what Redcrosse can read—especially, whether he can read himself.

The final stanzas of the episode—the far side of the frame—show one way that an answer can be made to all these questions. Redcrosse has won his victory over Sans Joy, and his wounds are soothed with flattering balms of wine and oil. Una's dwarf, meanwhile, goes snooping around the foundations of the place, and there he finds a dungeon stocked with the victims of Pride. The next six stanzas present the fruits of *inventio* on the topic, a catalogue of the overweening from the Bible (Antiochus, Nimrod, Ninus) and Rome (Tarquin, Caesar, Pompey), to proud women (Semiramis, Sthenoboea, Cleopatra), and finally nameless routs of overspending courtiers. When the catalogue is finished the dungeon becomes a scene of instruction for the knight: "Whose case whenas the carefull Dwarfe had tould, / And made ensample of their mournfull sight / Unto his maister, he no lenger would / There dwell in perill of like painefull plight" (1.5.52). As when Arthur makes his sermon after Duessa's capture, there is a good deal of didactic technology in play here, a "case" which is "told," then an example "made . . . of their mournfull sight." Does Redcrosse actually see the translated spectacle for himself? That doesn't seem like quite the right question: the lesson is of the sort that most estranges us from the poem's capacities for realism, from our sense that it portrays persons in places. There is little liveliness in Nimrod or Tarquin here. Nevertheless—or therefore?—its warning is clear, and Redcrosse leaves posthaste. (It may not even occur to the reader that Pride's victims go unrescued; that is a question that will not be so easily escaped in Book II.)

If this dungeon tableau counts as an example, then example is difficult to distinguish from emblem. There is no particular sense that the victims of Pride are cut from the cloth of experience. But Redcrosse's sojourn is not quite over yet. The young knight flees under cover of darkness by way of a "privy Posterne" (1.5.52), scrambling along a "fowle way" that is "like a great Lay-stall," littered with a "Donghill of dead carcases" that have come "to shamefull end" (53). The scenery is surprisingly scatological, his exit alimentary: it is as though Redcrosse were being shat out of the shameful end of the House of Pride.[19] This indigestion goes directly to the question of what the knight has learned, for digestion is the favorite humanist trope for assimilating new knowledge. Here, that trope is willfully inverted. Not only does Redcrosse not digest what has been shown to him in this space, but the promise of his understanding is turned inside out, and he is discharged from his own experience as matter that is inassimilable, untransformable, and above all, oblivious. The scene is a perfect opposite, a perfect travesty of learning.

Perhaps *this* is the example, then; and perhaps this is how example gets made. If Redcrosse's "ensample" was supposed to "plainly prove" that "there is no greater shame / Then lightnesse and inconstancie in love"

---

19. As Mark Rose observes: "the knight sneaks away through what is in effect the fundament of the House of Pride" (*Spenser's Art*, 73).

(1.4.1), certainly that shame, or shaming, has been realized. Which is not to say that the knight is represented as experiencing shame. Indeed, the peculiar possibility that this scene raises, and on which I want to continue to dwell, is that making an example—making an example *of* someone—comes and even must come specifically at the example's expense. The example's instructive potential is directed outward, toward some audience, but it is unintelligible from the inside. There would therefore have to be something almost deliberately mocking about hanging a sign at the end of the episode— the alexandrine identifying "that sad house of *Pryde*" (1.5.53)—that characters cannot read. Recall that the episode begins as though it were addressing the young knight himself. It ends by satirically, humiliatingly expelling him, while denying (or sparing) him any sense of his own humiliation.

Such a sampling of Redcrosse's career—in the House of Holiness, in the dragon fight, in the House of Pride—shows how many kinds of reading *The Faerie Queene* solicits, playing them off against one another, flattering and then unsettling the expectations that we bring to the work. We get caught up in the story, and find ourselves confuted by a sacramental allegory; we square up our emblem of Holiness, then find that the story has swallowed him again. Examples get made at the seams of this project, and their doubleness promises to bridge the differences. But Spenser has concerns about examples, too. They raise for him the question, who gets to read them? How are they made? And out of what, out of whom? The expulsion of Redcrosse from the House of Pride may not be so different from the heroic ignorance of the perfected hero in the last canto. That uncomfortable equation recalls us to Wofford's claim that characters "cannot and do not 'read' the signs of their world," a claim it seems both to confirm and to color more darkly. I want to register that confirmation, while still holding open the possibility of exceptions—or at least acknowledging again how strong the temptation is to make a reader of Redcrosse, and how indispensable that temptation is to the poem's design. And at the same time I want to venture a step further along the path Wofford marks, by way of suggesting that *The Faerie Queene* may unsettle us with the possibility, not only that characters cannot read the allegory, but that *we must read it at their expense*: not only do they never know what we know, but they suffer for our enlightenment. That is what it is to make an example of someone.

The Boundaries of Example

Book I puts a few questions about examples into play: how they are framed; whom they are for; what they are made of. These questions become central to the education Guyon receives in Book II. It will sharpen our sense of Spenser's motives for scrutinizing the figure, however, if we first look more closely at what the schoolmasters made of it. Example was humanism's longed-for bridge from precept to praxis. John Colet, founder of St. Paul's School, saw in it an antidote to the aridity of rote rules in language teaching: "if any man will know, and by that knowledge attain to understand Latin books . . . let him above all busily learn and read good Latin authors of chosen poets and orators . . . desiring none other rules but their examples."[20] Examples might replace rules altogether, so long as they are cut from the true cloth of the classics. Roger Ascham, meditating his book of examples, waves the same banner forty years later: "surely one example is more valuable, both to good and ill, than twenty precepts written in books."[21] Sometimes educators speak as though the importance of example were such that the principal work of the schoolmaster might simply be the gathering of fit specimens. "The master, like a diligent bee, must fly round through all the garden plots of knowledge," writes Juan Luis Vives, "and, particularly for his pupils' sake, gather and collect examples which he has observed."[22] The example—properly chosen? properly excerpted? properly shaped?—can do the rest by itself.

So what is the source of this high regard; what exactly would these men have understood by an example? For it is the peculiar sanctity of example that I want to explain, and that troubles Spenser most. Two main accounts come down to the sixteenth century from antiquity, one from Plato, one from Aristotle. In keeping with his doctrine of the forms, Plato's principal legacy is example as *paradigma*, a model or standard. Present-day theorists often speak of this sort of example as *vertical*, an instance that embodies and points to an ideal.[23] Aristotle's concept is more rhetorically oriented. He treats example as a mode of proof, or more properly, of evidence. It functions by providing the instance or instances from which a general principle may be inferred: "When we base the proof of a proposition

20. Colet, *Aeditio*, quoted in Hunter, *John Lyly*, 19–20.
21. Ascham, *Schoolmaster*, 55.
22. Vives, *On Education*, 179. In *De Copia* Erasmus likewise emphasizes the teacher's responsibility to gather appropriate matter (*Works*, 24:635).
23. The distinction between vertical and horizontal example is summarized by Alexander Gelley in his introduction to his collection *Unruly Examples*: "Whereas the Platonic model displays a vertical directionality, from a primary exemplar down to multiple instantiations, for Aristotle example involves something like a lateral movement" (1). See also John D. Lyons, "Circe's Drink and Sorbonnic Wine: Montaigne's Paradox of Experience," 88–89 in the same volume.

on a number of similar cases, this is induction in dialectic, example in rhetoric."[24] The Roman rhetoricians take up this line, a kind of *horizontal* example: Cicero declares that it "involves a certain principle of similarity running through diverse material"; Quintilian agrees.[25]

These two kinds—vertical and horizontal—correspond roughly to two basic accounts of what example is used for. Horizontal example persuades: it makes cases in politics or law by providing parallel instances that confirm a proposition. (It may also be understood to instruct, if the student's task is to derive the rule from the instance or instances.) Vertical example is more characteristically pedagogical, offered up as a model for imitation, an exemplar. The exemplar does not so much prove a case as it embodies qualities after which we can pattern ourselves; it solicits imitation. On the side of persuasion, we have already heard Puttenham declare that no "argument . . . doth better perswade and more universally satisfie then example." He uses "argument" in something like Cicero's sense of a "plausible device [*inventum*] to obtain belief," which is to say, anything—example or maxim or perhaps even scheme or trope—that may be invented (in the technical sense) to argue with.[26] An example is one of the things you can put in a commonplace book, and by virtue of having been put there in one category or another it is already an example *of* something. (Under the heading "courage," it is an example of courage, and so on.) It is set to work by likening "one case to another," as Puttenham says, fitting it either to another case under discussion or to a proposition.[27] It has the power to convince because it is more obvious in its meaning than the doubtful case it serves. The most effective examples will therefore be the most familiar, the subjects of the greatest cultural consensus; they will function best as evidence if they are self-evident.

Where can you find such examples: concise, forceful, above all obvious in their meaning? The favorite humanist answer is history. The best examples, says Puttenham, are "the lively image of our deare forefathers"; they allow us to "draw the judgements precedent and authorized by antiquitie as veritable . . . into similitude or dissimilitude with our present actions and affaires."[28] Sir Thomas Elyot takes them to be nothing less than the useful form of the past: "The knowlege of this Experience is called Example, and is expressed by Historie, whiche of Tulli is called the life of memorie."[29]

24. Aristotle, *Rhetoric*, 1356b14.
25. Cicero, *De Inventione*, 1.30.49; Quintilian, *Orator's Education*, 5:11.
26. Cicero, *De Partitione Oratoria*, 2:5.   28. Ibid., 39, 245.
27. Puttenham, *Arte*, 245.   29. Elyot, *Governour*, 246.

History *is* example—that is, example is the form by which we can know about times before our own. Enthusiasm for the "liveliness" of such examples—lively images, the life of memory, and so on—has a twofold importance. First is the vitality attributed to the trope, as a way of accounting both for its power to move us and also for its meaning. (An example is not just an inert piece of experience; it has a point, almost an intention.) Second is the conviction that examples can capture *real* life, what *really* happened.[30] Their persuasive force may be traced to their historical origins and authority. That appeal to historicity arouses a companion anxiety about fictional examples, a worry Peacham articulates in his *Garden of Eloquence*: "Fained examples and Apologies, ought to be used verie seldom," he writes, and "regard ought to be had, that they be not alledged in the forme and countenance of true histories, whereby the truth is violated, and the simple and silly hearer seduced."[31] Example is the real thing. Tampering with it is accordingly discouraged.

The paradigm of humanist example, then—at least the forensic, horizontal kind—is a little self-evident story from history. Puttenham again: "as if one should say thus, Alexander the great in his expedition to Asia did thus, so did Hanniball comming into Spaine, so did Caesar in Egypt, therfore all great Captains and Generals ought to doe it."[32] Alexander, Hannibal, Caesar are the life of memory: lively, again, because they are taken from life; also because their conquests are stories, because they move, and can tell us something about a world in motion around us. For just this reason, however, humanist examples always contain within themselves a miniature version of this study's animating conflict between paradigmatic and narrative understandings. Karlheinz Stierle is among the present-day theorists who make such a diagnosis, treating the example as a "minimal narrative unit" that is ideally compound with precept but never perfectly subject to its control.[33] Timothy Hampton associates humanist pedagogy in particular

30. See also Peacham, who combines both aspects: "they [examples] present to the view and contemplation of our minde, the true and lively Image of time past, for by them it is that we know and see what was done long before our birth" (*Garden*, 187).

31. Ibid., 189.   32. Puttenham, *Arte*, 245.

33. "The exemplum as a minimal narrative unit relates to the minimal systematic unit of the moral-philosophical precept in such a way that they virtually form a compound"; on premodern history generally, he observes, "Whenever history takes on a concrete form, it does so in a manner related to its subsumption under categories of the moral system" (Stierle, "Story as Exemplum—Exemplum as Story," 400). See also Nichols: "Reducing narrative mode almost to a zero state, or attempting to do so, the example offers itself as a temporally neutral or else proleptic descriptor of human behavior"; that is, it aspires to the atemporal universality that

with the ambition to reduce example to the minimum of a bare name.[34] Puttenham's "Alexander... did thus, and so did Hanniball" works in that direction; that tendency is even more patent in Spenser's *inventio* of Pride's victims. There is a pressure, in humanist examples, out of story; out of time, into universals; toward name but also toward maxim. It is even possible for Erasmus, at one moment in *De Copia*, to classify maxim itself as an example.[35]

All this suggests how precariously close to paradox this bridging figure comes. That is part of its pedagogical power, but also its vulnerability: horizontal example traffics in history for its force, and yet it tends to reduce history to a ringing name, a name we already know. As Montaigne says—Montaigne who is the most clear-sighted, if gimlet-eyed, Renaissance theorist of these questions—"example is lame."[36] It cannot quite stand on its own. Its prized obviousness is always vulnerable to misconstruction, and the more it is focused toward its moral, the more stripped of story, the less it is distinctively an example—the less *lively* it is. Brinsley among the educators registers this problem with particular directness. He insists on communicating what he repeatedly calls the "force of the examples," even their "life," identifying something that is meant to be both essential and obvious yet must still be pointed out, as it were separately. (In cases where a particular grammatical point is at issue, he suggests that "the words wherein the force of the examples doth lie, [be] printed in differing letters."[37]) Here is the example, he says, that piece of the real thing. And *here* is its force, its life.

───────────

The need for persuasive example to be both lively and obvious—and above all, to be self-sufficient—generates this tension between the stability of its meaning and its authenticity as an excerpt, a piece of experience. A similar

chapter 3 associated with maxim ("Example vs. *Historia*: Montaigne, Eriugena, and Dante," in *Unruly Examples*, ed. Gelley, 54).

34. Hampton, *Writing from History*: "On the one hand, the humanist veneration of antiquity sanctions a model of reading in which the reader actualizes tradition by opening the exemplar up, by calling to mind the great deeds as they are stored in the name, by replaying the entire narrative of the heroic life. On the other hand, at the same time, the moralism of humanist pedagogy favors a gesture of closure that fixes the name's ideological significance" (27).

35. Erasmus's most expansive list of examples in *De Copia* includes "stories, fables, proverbs, opinions, parallels or comparisons, similitudes, analogies" (*Works*, 24:607).

36. "[T]out exemple cloche" (*The Complete Essays of Montaigne*, 819).

37. Brinsley, *Ludus*, M1v; see also M3r, R4r, X3r.

problem arises when the example is considered as an object of imitation. Writing about education is full of historical figures and even fictional heroes who are forwarded as models for the student: *be like this*. Identifying such models for imitation was part of how students were taught to read, and framing them was part of teaching. Erasmus, in his *Institutio*, offers a limit case, proposing an ideal for the young prince's contemplation: "Then let him [the master] paint as it were a picture. . . . Let the teacher therefore depict a sort of celestial creature, more like a divinity than a mortal: complete with every single virtue."[38] The *Institutio* is laden with precept, as we have seen in chapter 3, but here the point is to construct a model—to paint a picture—that will be a comprehensive object of imitation, including every virtue, leaving out no grace or strength that the prince should cultivate. Such examples, or exemplars, are preeminently vertical, in the sense that the student's likeness to the exemplar corresponds to the exemplar's likeness to the virtue itself, in a kind of Platonic hierarchy. Sidney draws up a conventional list of the candidates for such a model in his *Defence*—Cyrus, Alexander, Aeneas—and praises their ability to propagate themselves by inciting readers to imitation: "so far substantially it worketh, not only to make a Cyrus, which had been but a particular excellency as nature might have done, but to bestow a Cyrus upon the world to make many Cyruses."[39]

In the fashioning of these vertical exemplars, however, there is once again inevitably a swerve away from the idea of example as a piece of the real thing, whether or not it is acknowledged. As Timothy Hampton writes, "[e]very moment in the life of the exemplar . . . becomes a kind of synecdoche of the 'complete life,'" which is another way of saying that exemplarity tends to disintegrate the narrative of its subjects' lives to produce a series of emblematic actions, or even poses.[40] This kind of exemplarity tends to attract the language of visual description—"the true and lively Image of time past," says Peacham—and hence to remove itself still further from our life in time.[41] As the example is purified—by stringent excerption,

38. Erasmus, *Works*, 27:223.

39. Sidney, *Miscellaneous Prose*, 79. Sidney's "it" is the fore-conceit (discussed in chapter 3), which might be identified here with the "force" of the example.

40. Hampton, *Writing from History*, 24. In addition to Hampton, Stierle, and Gelley, cited above, the debate on what Hampton calls the "crisis of exemplarity" has been carried forward in a special issue of the *Journal of the History of Ideas* (vol. 59, no. 4, 1998). See esp. Francois Cornilliat, "Exemplarities: A Response to Timothy Hampton and Karlheinz Stierle," and Michel Jeanneret, "The Vagaries of Exemplarity," which is particularly good on Erasmus's interest in the polysemy of examples and on the historicity of examples generally.

41. Peacham, *Garden*, 187.

by rewriting, by transposition toward painting—it becomes more and more like fiction, or a certain kind of fiction. As Erasmus writes:

> poetry also offers passages which no one would deny are fictional, but since it is generally accepted that they were invented precisely for the purpose of functioning as examples, and what is more were invented by great writers, they have all the weight of examples; I mean things like the goddess Envy, Rumor, Discord.[42]

By the end of this description what Erasmus has arrived at is personification allegory. He has gotten there by degrees, but the kind of reading involved has changed qualitatively: for allegory is a mode better suited for analysis than for imitation; our response to the likes of Envy, Rumor, and Discord is properly more detached, neither viscerally imitative nor viscerally aversive. Certainly what liveliness these emblems have no longer comes from their being simply cut from real life.

To this imitation of exemplars—*be like this*—must be added one more variety of pedagogical example. The injunction most distinctive to humanist teaching is *write like this*. Schoolboys were encouraged to master the style of classical authors, in particular Cicero's, and in many classrooms to assimilate a much broader range of voices. That project demanded an encounter with extended passages of those authors' works: not just *sententiae*, or the teacher's epitomes, but the contiguous pages of text necessary to the recognition of a style.[43] This is a different kind of example again, and it tacks back against the drift toward allegory. Since the great project of humanism, after teaching (and perhaps the dream of counsel), was textual editing, there was an ethic of accuracy pervading the enterprise. If students are to be given something to imitate, it should be as close to its original, historical form as possible, Colet's "good Latin authors" in the best possible texts. The schoolmaster was free, that is, to cut and to frame, but less free to rewrite. An impressive instance of this scruple is to be found in Erasmus's *De Ratione Studii*, where he provides elaborate, prophylactic instructions for reading the homoerotic elements of Virgil's second eclogue—rather than simply censoring bits of it, or skipping it altogether.[44]

---

42. Erasmus, *De Copia*, in *Works*, 24:614.

43. Hence not only Ascham's book of examples, but the extended passages of Terence or Horace to be found in *The Schoolmaster* itself; Kempe likewise introduces extended passages of Cicero into his manual (see chapter 1).

44. *Works*, 24:683–87.

Such compunctions about textual accuracy contribute further to that peculiarly strong sense of the example's sanctity. Example is not only forceful, not only lively, but it has a kind of integrity in relation to its source. That account persists even when the example is pressed furthest toward allegory, and away from excerption, so long as it is still understood *as* an example. (And this is equally true of negative examples.) The text of the example itself may still be understood according to the usual routines of humanist reading, parsing and epitome and so on. But it is a piece of the original, and the concept of example, not least on this account, retains a principled association with the word-for-word of the past. Reverence for the figure—as humanism's signal, practical difference from scholastic teaching—is central to the propaganda for the new pedagogy. It is this learned habit of deference to its boundaries that will most arouse Spenser's suspicions in Book II.

Making Examples

"[W]e have not the wit to pick out and put to use what happens before our eyes, and to judge it keenly enough to make it an example," complains Montaigne.[45] Making examples—picking them out and hewing them from their surround so we or others can learn from them—is the preoccupation of Book II. For this reason, among others, it is a book about boundaries and limits, and so of course it begins with the hero Guyon's dangerously inchoate and unbounded encounter with a dying woman, an encounter that first delineates what will be the ethical challenge of his education over the rest of the book.

When the knight discovers Amavia in a forest clearing, she makes a "Pitifull spectacle" (2.1.40), her husband Mortdant dead at her side, her own knife in her breast, and their infant child playfully bloodying his hands at the wound. Guyon's immediate reaction is a kind of mirror of her suffering: "His hart gan wexe as starke, as marble stone, / And his fresh blood did frieze with fearefull cold, / That all his sences seemd berefte attone" (42). This is only the first time that Guyon, faced with a spectacle of pain, is paralyzed with—well, with what? Perhaps he suffers the existential assault of a circumstance he cannot redeem, as a knight errant whose role it is to save the damsel. "[H]elp never comes too late" (44), he assures her two stanzas later, and he is patently wrong. Or perhaps there is a sudden contagion of affect, a moment of sympathy across the protective boundaries

45. Montaigne, *Essays*, 828.

of the allegory, across the characters' different meanings: an outbreak of compassion, which comes near to annihilating the knight.

Such compassion is a peculiar vulnerability of the Spenserian character. Human solidarity has everything to do with the ability to convince ourselves that we feel the same things. We regard a spectacle of suffering together, and are touched with the same pity; we argue with one another, and share feelings of strained love and anger. At least we like to think so. Within a strict system of personification allegory, however—a system invoked, if never fully realized, by Spenser's poem—that sense of feeling-with is a threat to identity. If Anger storms into a room, followed somewhat later by scuffling Regret, we have a little allegory of the costs of losing your temper. But Anger cannot feel regret, nor can Regret feel anger, without the risk that the system of argument they inhabit together will lapse into incoherence. There is a structural prohibition against such commonalities. It is not strictly enforced, for Spenser's poem does not altogether play by its own rules, but the undersong of loneliness derives not least from the burden of these laws.

Let us say then that Guyon is paralyzed by compassion, by the existential threat of Amavia's claims on his emotions. He recovers himself by action: he snatches the knife from the wound and stops the bleeding, ministering to Amavia until she begins to breathe again. The rescue is a virtuous deed. As the passage proceeds, however, an emerging pattern of imagery discovers how transgressive it is—transgressive in the etymological sense of a crossing of boundaries or borders. The narrator calls the scene a "sad pourtraict / Of death and dolour" (2.1.39), a "Pitifull spectacle" (40); Guyon describes it as an "ymage . . . Of ruefull pitty, and impatient smart" (44). This language is formal, compositional, kin to the emblem books. The pictorial boundaries that these words erect are reinforced (as Susanne Wofford has shown) by hints that the structure of the scene borrows something from drama—from spectacle, "Tragedie" (2.2.1), and pageant (Amavia imagines her death as staged for an audience of gods who "take delight / To see sad pageaunts of mens miseries" [2.1.36]).[46] The boundary resembles the one between players and audience as well as between image and looker. The effect of this juxtaposition of emblem and stage is to *frame* the prospect doubly, setting it off from the rest of the poem's action even more emphatically than Spenser's usual allegorical tableau-making would do. When he first sees

---

46. Wofford, *The Choice of Achilles*, 247. I have discussed this scene with reference to the idea of theater in *The Faerie Queene* more generally in "Spenser and the Troubled Theaters," 181–90.

Amavia, Guyon stands on one side of a strongly marked threshold, whether
the threshold is the edge of a stage or of a picture. Standing there, he is
a reader, or an audience member. When he crosses that line, he becomes
something else.

The theatrical analogy suggests one problem with Guyon's strongly
taken action. If he is the audience, then his intervention is like leaping on
stage in the middle of the play, as though to save Desdemona or remind
Albany to look after Cordelia. But it is also possible to imagine that so long
as he stands on the safer or cooler side of that line his position is that of
a student, and in that case the frame marks off something he is supposed
to study. Altering its contents will spoil the lesson just as surely as wresting
away Othello's pillow will spoil the play. To learn from such an image, such
a spectacle—such an example?—it is necessary to recognize that it belongs
to a different order of experience, or even that it is outside experience, and
to stand back.

Guyon does not recognize these signals at first; he just hurls himself
forward, as chivalric script and "inward paine" (2.1.42) dictate. But Amavia
dies despite his efforts, and he is plunged back into a debilitating grief,
wreathing his head in his arms to block out "so heavie sight" (56). This
time he rescues himself by a contrary strategy: "Then turning to his Palmer
said, Old syre / Behold the ymage of mortalitie" (57). He retrenches, that
is, behind the dotted lines that the narrator has drawn around the scene,
and in so doing identifies another way of overcoming the double threat of
impotence and compassion presented by Amavia's violent despair. There
is both framing and pointing in that exhortation, "Behold the ymage": it
is a teaching gesture. By these means he makes of this scene a didactic
occasion, one that can now be ground through the mill of the stanza to
yield a sententious motto: "The strong through pleasure soonest falles, the
weake through smart" (57). Amavia has become a lesson. She has been cut
out of the world of experience, with its ambiguous and continual moral
claims, and repositioned in an ad hoc schoolroom that Guyon has built
hastily in the little clearing. It is this act of instruction—a kind of example-
making—that allows the knight to move on.

Spenser is working out some ideas about the formal structure of the scene of
instruction here, ideas bound up, as we will shortly see, with the book's cardinal virtue of temperance. He is also thinking about the psychology of such
scenes, and from that vantage it is worth registering the unexpectedness of
Guyon's teacherly pose. For most of the book, the knight is obviously

the student, and the figure to whom he directs his lesson, the Palmer, is his black-robed tutor. The relationship between the two will turn out to be marked throughout by such subtle jostling for authority. The Palmer has always particularly puzzled critics, not least because he is a presumptively Catholic pilgrim in a presumptively Protestant poem. It helps to recognize the pedagogue in him, with his robes and a staff that he carries to "*point* his way" (2.1.34; italics mine). Among his roles is that of the gray and sober tutor who is a *topos* of the education literature from Plutarch to Mulcaster, a figure—not quite a schoolmaster himself, but endowed with a school-masterly authority—who not only takes charge of the young aristocrat in his chamber, but also accompanies him through the world. He is plentiful in the literature of the late century: we will see him again, for example, on the battlefields of Arcadia, where he is still advising his grown-up ward Amphialus.[47]

But this pilgrim-tutor, compounded of his social roles, is also often taken to be a figure of Reason, the sort of practical reason that makes the calculations of temperance. If he is Reason, too—if he is both a companion and a faculty of mind—then he is both outside and inside the hero. This doubleness, a symptom of the poem's endless, productive indecision between psychomachia and social mimesis, is particularly useful for its thinking about the dynamics of instruction. It allows Spenser to consider how our teachers are always both outside and inside us. The problem is like that of the catechism as I described it in chapter 1: can the student appropriate, own, or author the catechist's words, or do they remain forever another man's question ringing in his head, a question he must nonetheless answer in word or in deed? Does learning a lesson consist in preserving that alien voice within himself in its strangeness, or in eventually assimilating it, absorbing it, or even, in the language of imitation, digesting it? (The same problem haunts *sententia* in *Arcadia*.) For such questions psychoanalysis has the language of introjection and the formation of the superego. *The Faerie Queene* is in its way a still more flexible instrument, for it never lets us rest

47. For this tradition see Plutarch (*Education*, trans. Elyot, in *Four Tudor Books*, ed. Pepper, 12–17), Elyot (*Governour*, 33), Mulcaster (*Positions*, 246). Amphialus is still ruled by his "old governor" in the new Arcadia (*New Arcadia*, 495). Nohrnberg recognizes the teacher in him: "the Palmer's powers derive from his wisdom, the kind of developed foresight and expertise that a pupil finds in a preceptor or mentor" (*The Analogy of The Faerie Queene*, 290). Paul Cefalu gives an account of the Palmer as a kind of mis-educator (as well as a survey of accounts of his identification with reason and prudence) in *Moral Identity in Early Modern English Literature*, 56–64. Anne Prescott discusses an illuminating parallel (to Redcrosse as well as Guyon and the Palmer) in "Spenser's Chivalric Restoration: From Bateman's Travayled Pylgrime to the Redcrosse Knight."

easy knowing whether a given encounter is with a real person or an aspect of ourselves that we misrecognize as a real person. (And when, in what we call real life, can we ever be sure about that?[48]) The plot of Book II is set up to experiment with this puzzle in the register of instruction, separating and recombining the two characters, knight and palmer, with an almost clinical curiosity.

So when Guyon turns to the Palmer to say, "Old syre / Behold the ymage of mortalitie" (2.1.57), it is a complicated moment. Perhaps he is speaking Reasonably. Proper detachment is the good of having the Palmer by his side, and keeping that company is the sign of his rationality, a sign that teaches us as readers to interpret what he says as good counsel. But there may be just a hint of condescension in "Old syre," a provocation to another kind of psychological reading. Pretending to teach your teacher is a way of proving that you understand, but it is hardly the most evolved; it cannot but be touched with resentment, even sycophancy. Spenser hints at a kind of adolescent rivalry in Guyon, one that continues in the ensuing debate about whether or not Amavia should be given her burial rites. The question of who speaks which lines here is difficult to sort out, as editors attest—difficult in a way that at first flatters the assumption that there is a kind of conceptual unison developing between them.[49] But the sides of an argument do emerge, with some work, and the result seems more than a little gratuitous. Amavia should be given proper burial because she acted in anguish, says the Palmer; but no! says Guyon, she should be buried because we are not fit to judge. This is the narcissism of minor differences. Guyon tests his independence, but not so far as to disagree, or disappoint.

———————

All of this—the careful boundaries of the lesson, the boundary testing of teacher and student—is a way of containing the debilitating horror of Amavia's death. The lesson-making allows Guyon to leave the scene and continue the quest set for him back in Cleopolis by the Palmer. The episodes that follow have the character of intermediate exercises in this new discipline of boundary-making. There is the house of Medina, a schematic

———

48. Wofford again is the critic who pursues this question most directly: "To learn to read Spenser's poem is to learn that everything—a person in the story, a place, a house, a tree or a giant—can represent an aspect of the hero's own psyche" (*The Cambridge Companion to Spenser*, 116). I have tried to develop the ethical and psychological issues at stake in cases where there is a strategic confusion between these two possibilities, social mimesis and psychomachia; that confusion is itself mimetic of our daily difficulty telling the difference.

49. See Hamilton's notes in his edition of *The Faerie Queene*, 169.

representation of temperance as an ethical mean, where Guyon intervenes between two contrary knights "and rare ensample made" (2.2.25) of his own good conduct. Then there is the brief, turbulent operetta played out among Pyrocles, Furor, and Occasion, which ends with Guyon smiling at the defeated fiery knight and preaching, "henceforth by this daies ensample trow, / That hasty wroth, and heedlesse hazardry / Doe breede repentaunce late, and lasting infamy" (2.5.13). Guyon's lines echo Arthur's outside Orgoglio's castle, the "daies ensample" that will inscribe "this lesson deare" (1.8.44). He is studying to make—or just to recognize?—examples. He is also learning temperance, and Lauren Silberman's account of the workings of that virtue in Book II suggests how the two lessons may conspire with each other. She is interested in the calculating aspect of temperance, its detached specification of the mean between extremes. "The use of Temperance as a design for ethical living," she writes, "becomes a series of exegetical defenses against experience."[50] She emphasizes how mechanical (and in that respect un-Aristotelian) temperance in Book II typically is, and how its version of reason enforces, or licenses, distance from the immediate claims of an ethical situation. In this detachment, temperance is like allegory. One must stand back to calculate, just as, with allegory, one stands back to read.

Or to teach, or to learn. Every scene of domination or subordination, seduction or abstinence, mercy or punishment, is also a scene of instruction in this book, and in every scene the degree of proper detachment is at stake. Example is Spenser's subtlest instrument for investigating this problem, and it comes most to the fore when Guyon and the Palmer are separated—the test of whether Guyon as a character has incorporated, or could incorporate, the meaning of his guide. Two episodes unfold before they are reunited, the first of them taking place on the lovely island in the midst of the Idle Lake. Here the island's giddy *spiritus loci*, Phaedria, advertises its virtues to Cymochles before Guyon arrives:

> It was a chosen plott of fertile land,
> Emongst wide waves sett, like a litle nest,
> As if it had by Natures cunning hand,
> Bene choycely picked out from all the rest,
> And laid forth for ensample of the best:
> No dainty flowre or herbe, that growes on grownd,

---

50. Silberman, *"The Faerie Queene, Book II and the Limitations of Temperance,"* 9. See also Gohlke's "Embattled Allegory: Book II of *The Faerie Queene.*"

No arborett with painted blossomes drest,
And smelling sweete, but there it might be fownd
To bud out faire, and throwe her sweete smels al arownd. (2.6.12)

The island is a gilded vitrine, but the account of example is subtly tendentious. These flowers are choicely picked out, and grow on a chosen plot; they
are the fruit of labors perhaps more like the schoolmaster's than like the
gardener's, blooms culled rather than cultivated. The rhetoric sounds a lot
like the fulsome prefaces of the period's printed *florilegia*, which promised
the choicest bits of the best authors, a "garden of wysdome conteynynge
pleasaunte floures, that is to saye, propre and quicke sayinges of pri[n]ces,
p[h]ilosophers and other sortes of men," as Richard Taverner puts it; flowers "truely collected and diligently gathered together" to make a "very
necessarie and profitable" anthology, in the words of John Northbrooke.[51]
Phaedria is something of a saleswoman, and one can almost imagine her
hawking such a book among the stalls at St. Paul's.

And that's not all: not only is the perilous work of choosing already
done, and done by nature's own hand, but two stanzas later it appears
that these "ensamples of the best" have actually chosen themselves. "Behold, O man, that toilesome paines doest take / The flowrs, the fields,
and all that pleasaunt growes, / How they them selves doe thine ensample
make" (2.6.15). These lines are themselves flowers from Scripture, adapting Christ's Sermon on the Mount, and the ideal they express is what we
might call a *natural* example: the example that needs no special trimming
or shaping, but that grows in the wild for us to recognize and be instructed
by.[52] It points itself out, points to itself. The particular merit of such a natural example is that it allows us to forget that example might be, or must be, a
made thing. It is choice—choice in the sense of select, ideal, perfect—without
having to have had a chooser, let alone a maker.

When Guyon arrives on the island he proves impervious to Phaedria's
seduction and her "ensample of the best." Why? Perhaps because they
come with such clearly inscribed boundaries about them—because Guyon's
instruction in example is a kind of progressively acquired immunity, a way
of recognizing the parts of the poem that he should not touch. What could

51. Taverner, *The Garden of Wysdome Conteynynge Pleasaunte Floures*, A1r; Northbrooke,
Spiritus Est Vicarius Christi in Terra. The Poore Mans Garden, A1r.

52. This idiom, "natural example," is occasional in the period; one can find a specimen of
its ideological work in Sir Thomas Smith's *De Republica Anglorum* (1583), when he describes
the ancient patriarchs as "the first and natural example of an absolute and perfect king" (C4r).

be easier to resist than the items in this display case? His detachment is becoming almost natural.

Guyon faces one more test alone before he is reunited with the Palmer: the temptations of wealth and power in the Cave of Mammon. The knight does have company, however, if not guidance, for he is led through the cave's three chambers by the solicitous money god himself. Once again the scene has its pedagogical dimension. Mammon is not a teacher so much as a father (or father-in-law), calling the young knight "Sonne" (2.7.18) and ultimately offering him his daughter's hand in marriage. The byplay between them—Mammon's cajoling, Guyon's rectitude—might just glance at another *topos* of education writing, the interfering attentions of parents. Spenser's teacher Mulcaster complained how "parentes and freindes, wilbe medlers somtime, to further their young impes," and he had a long tradition of irritated educators behind him.[53] Here father Mammon tries to sidetrack Guyon by interrupting his discipline with all manner of worldly goods and favors.[54] Guyon's resistance takes the form of a blank and unin-clining wonder (of a kind that there will be occasion to think about again, with Britomart). No schoolmaster needs to intervene now. And indeed, here as on Phaedria's island, Guyon exhibits considerably less evidence of temptation than he does in any other part of the poem. The quality of the temptation is one difference, for Guyon turns out to be far more vul-nerable to the appeals of suffering women than to the promise of riches. But Spenser is also continuing to think about the dynamics of teacher and student: it appears to be easier for the knight to indulge his temptations to desire and violence alike when his teacher is near to check him. Alone, he is much more abstemious, more conservative, more timid.

---

53. Mulcaster, *Positions*, 29. He puts this renunciation in a nationalist key later in the book: "But though everie parent be thus affected toward his owne child, as nature leades him to wish his owne best, yet for all that everie parent must beare in memorie that he is more bound to his country, then to his child, as his child must renounce him in countermatch with his countrie" (141–42). It should be said that there is another strain in education writing that emphasizes how teachers should be like fathers in their authority; see for example Vives in *De Tradendis*, "He [the master] will be of a fatherly disposition towards his pupils, so they may be to him in the place of sons" (*Education*, 56). And while the Palmer has no daughter for Guyon to marry, he does once call his charge "sonne" (2.5.24).

54. Mammon's ambitions for the young man are interesting. Notwithstanding his own appearance as an "uncivill wight" (2.7.3), he seems to have civilizing designs: "Sonne . . . leave the rudenesse of that antique age . . . Thou that doest live in later times, must wage / Thy workes for wealth, and life for gold engage" (18). Money is the means by which both human society and one of its scions can grow up, and also the sign of that maturity.

Which might be a way of saying that he has, after all, learned something. The shape of the lesson is clearest when he enters the third of Mammon's chambers, the Garden of Proserpine. The garden is a kind of photographic negative of Eden, decked in poisonous, black foliage and stocked with the usual roster of sinners, one of whom is thrashing energetically in the dark river. Ever-curious Guyon climbs up on the bank to get a look. What he sees is a man half-submerged, groping after fruits that recoil from his grasp, stooping to drink from waters that recede before he can taste. "The knight him seeing labour so in vaine, / Askt who he was, and what he ment thereby" (2.7.59). The answer, of course, is that this is Tantalus, who begs his questioner for food or drink—begs him, once again, to cross the distance between them, the frame of that riverbank, to minister to his conspicuous needs. That boundary could be just as permeable as the open space between any two bodies. But Guyon knows better now:

> Nay, nay, thou greedy *Tantalus* (quoth he)
> Abide the fortune of thy present fate,
> And unto all that live in high degree,
> Ensample be of mind more temperate,
> To teach them how to use their present state.
> Then gan the cursed wretch alowd to cry,
> Accusing highest *Jove* and gods ingrate,
> And eke blaspheming heaven bitterly,
> As authour of unjustice, there to let him dye. (2.7.60)

Guyon has already asked "who he was, and what he *ment* thereby" (59; italics mine); he begins the encounter as a reader, inquiring after meaning.[55] He seems to recognize that he is moving through an allegory, if not perhaps to recognize his implication in it, or to read it with much comprehensiveness or skill. And having so constituted the encounter, he neither freezes in horror behind the boundary of the riverbank, nor lunges across it. The "ensample" of Tantalus would seem already to be an emblem, already an allegory, the opposite of Amavia's sympathetic claims—safely incommensurate and altogether beyond care. Or *almost*. For Guyon's act of motto-making, "Ensample be of mind more temperate," is also an exhortation to reform. Here is the moral distinctiveness of example, its tenaciously equivocal,

---

55. Compare a comic version of the same question, posed by an uneasy Archimago when, disguised as Redcrosse, he takes up with Una: "all the way they spent / Discoursing of her dreadful late distresse, / In which he askt her, what the Lyon ment" (1.3.32).

middle position, partaking both of experience and precept. Tantalus might yet change; this example is unstable enough, poised between two worlds, that Guyon might yet allow—might yet hope?—that they could share the same world.

Or at least, he might circa 1590. The line is different in the edition of 1596, and again in 1609: "And unto all that live in high degree, / Ensample be of mind *intemperate*, / To teach them how to use their present state."[56] There is no reform in this version; the example just consolidates the punishment. Tantalus may serve to teach others, but he is condemned to mean without intending, to teach without learning. His fate is the fate of a sign.

––––––––

In the first chapter, I described two large-scale models of an educational career that humanism cultivated in default of (or against) narrative. The first was the careful preservation of an original innocence; the second, the constant, corrective chastising of an original corruption. Guyon's progress through Book II looks a lot like the second, and it seems as though he learns something by the process: the rash boundary-breaking of the first cantos gives way to perfect abstemiousness.[57] His paralysis before Amavia is repeated with the bloody-handed babe Ruddymane, but after that it is transformed, and his escape from repetition is the kind of learning romance knows best. What he learns in particular—what springs him from that cycle of destructive sympathy—is how to recognize examples, how to frame and excerpt the world like a text, to recognize the natural boundaries around its lessons and treat them with the proper respect. Or perhaps, how to *make* examples, how to defuse the claims of moral commensurability by a particular attitude of study. This last account makes him something like an agent within the poem of what Gordon Teskey calls "allegorical capture": "the moments in which the materials of narrative are shown being actively subdued for the purpose of raising a structure of meaning."[58] The "ensample" is Spenser's way of examining that capture at the specifically

56. Italics mine; see the textual notes in Hamilton's edition of *The Faerie Queene*, 742.

57. Prominent accounts of Book II have evolved from Woodhouse's famous argument about its "order of nature," compared to Book I's "order of grace." Harry Berger is among the critics who finds both orders within Book II, with Guyon personifying a specifically Christian temperance after his faint and revival in canto viii. I am more inclined to see these patterns governed by a steady development of his skills as maker and reader of examples. See Woodhouse, "Nature and Grace in *The Faerie Queene*"; Berger, *The Allegorical Temper*, 62.

58. Teskey, *Allegory and Violence*, 23.

pedagogical point of its origin, when its mode is still unsettled, when the possibility of a middle way is open. These are all, again, scenes of teaching.

For Guyon it might be said that the boundary of the example is more important than anything it contains; one might even think of that boundary as drawn more surely around the student than around the object of study, a kind of quarantine expressed as a necessary condition of learning. It defines what it is to learn, the standing back, the pointing out. And perhaps this is what the reader of *The Faerie Queene* in turn is meant to do, treating the allegory as a *cordon sanitaire* (to return to Silberman's argument). But then again, there is another vantage from which the claim that this instruction in boundaries is learning—or that it is fashioning, institution, *education*—is much harder to defend. Many critics have remarked upon the infantile character of Guyon's final outburst in the Bower of Bliss, the intemperate "tempest of his wrathfulness" when he tears the place down.[59] At that moment of violent impulse one might be excused for thinking of Guyon as entirely *in*experienced, capable of no measured response, of nothing between self-surrendering desire (from which the Palmer must repeatedly restrain him) and destructive wrath. Perhaps—we might now speculate— the outcome of Guyon's instruction in example is paradoxically to have inexperienced him, uneducated him, by saving him again and again from exposure, involvement, entanglement. We are back to that first account of humanist training, as the preservation of original innocence. But original innocence and original corruption have become surprisingly hard to separate, or perhaps the difference just doesn't matter much. Now it looks as though Guyon's ultimate success as a student—his ability to complete his quest and bring down the bower—lies precisely in his failure to change, his failure to grow up.

What kind of teaching is this? And who should get credit for it? There have always been readers suspicious of the Palmer, how he steers Guyon toward the completion of a mission whose warrant is so much less clear than the apocalyptic stakes of the previous book's dragon fight.[60] The sophisticated back-and-forth between the two, Spenser's most concerted

59. Stephen Greenblatt's argument that Guyon's spasm of regenerative violence is both an act of desublimation and a restitution of civilizing norms has become a touchstone: see *Renaissance Self-Fashioning*, 173.

60. Paul Cefalu is the most recent and among the most severe of these skeptics: he sees Book II moving through orders of nature and grace but ending finally in an order of law: "Guyon's education in the Bower is not a step-wise progress in pagan or Christian virtue, but rather an 'education' in the virtue of obedience to the Palmer's unassailable commands" (*Moral Identity*, 75).

anatomy of instruction as an interpersonal project, suggests how a certain kind of training can unfit a young man for experience. Guyon in the last cantos is made perfectly manipulable. One might wonder, after the Palmer and the knight separate, why they are brought back together at all, given that Guyon has been shown to have learned so well his lesson of detachment: "Behold the ymage." Perhaps it is because, having learned restraint well and too well from that teacher, he also needs that teacher to let him loose.

Irrelevance

If we look back from this vantage to Redcrosse in the House of Pride, his tuition, or antituition, will appear as a kind of complement to the instruction Guyon has undergone over the course of Book II. Guyon's apprenticeship is in proper respect for examples. He has learned to frame and to point, to recognize and to make lessons out of what he encounters (part of his new art being the blurring of the distinction between recognizing and making, the case of the natural example). He perfects the humanist deference to example into a perfectly studious abstemiousness. Redcrosse gives us the same problem from the other side, the inside. He is himself the example around whom the boundary has been drawn, and that boundary seems to forbid his understanding the object lesson (in a strong sense of that phrase) that he has become. The transaction of the example is under scrutiny from both points of view. At the heart of that double critique is the idea that such instruction interrupts ordinary moral commensurability, suspending the moral claims that might otherwise obtain between the two parties: in Guyon's case, between the knight and another character like Amavia or Tantalus, and in Redcrosse's case, more weirdly and unsettlingly, between the knight and the reader of the poem. Example makes a boundary that care cannot cross. To speak of such an interruption may seem peculiar in the context of a poem whose allegorical poetics enforces the incommensurability of its agents as a condition of its meaning. (To say nothing of an incommensurability between character and reader.) But as I have already suggested, there are pressures of narrative, even of what we might call psychological realism, that resist this atomism, and those pressures mount against the example's boundary.[61] What Spenser's treatment of the figure suggests in the largest

61. I adopt here the sense of "realism" developed by Alastair Fowler in *Renaissance Realism*, where he treats early fiction not as incapable of what he calls "observational realism" (63), but as combining such mimesis with a variety of other modes, including allegory. "The origins of novelistic mimesis seem to lie in a slow succession of distinct narrative modes, until gradually non-realistic features were eliminated. This fluctuating process occupied more than three

sense is that this atomism itself is a side effect, or even an objective, of a certain kind of instruction.

And indeed, of course it is. Example works that way, by excerption and estrangement. And that is how the teaching machine of an allegory works too: analysis, separating things out, is its opening move. But again, my chief objective here is to suggest how Spenser finds ways of expressing both the general costs and the more particular abuses to which such instruction is liable. This he does principally by the fantastic modal flexibility of his poem, how it alternately flatters and rebukes any kind of reading at all that may be brought to it. Example itself is a hybrid of his modes, half experience, half precept, both narrative and not. That doubleness is its great service to its humanist champions—the classroom's self-justifying bridge to praxis—but it also makes example a kind of fault line in Spenser's project. His scrutiny of its workings is bound to make the reader feel a little queasy, above all for that uncanny question, must all of our lessons be borne as ignorant suffering by the characters that body them forth? Is that the only way for us to learn? And does the poem offer no alternatives to this vision of its own instruction? Is there no way to read it innocently, from the inside or the outside?[62]

The three books of 1596 brood upon this question again, and they will return us to it in chapter 6. There is, however, something of a provisional answer at the end of Book III, or at least a remedy for the uneasy reader. The hero of that book is the knight Britomart, and her virtue is chastity. Spenser's chastity is a flexible concept, and he is interested in it not least because its purity is contested in his culture between abstinence on the one hand, and continence (chastity in marriage) on the other. This is a problem of sexuality, but it is also a problem of knowledge. There is a kind of chastity of the understanding that comes in for particular scrutiny over the course of Britomart's career, and Book III poses the question of whether innocence is necessarily also a state of ignorance. Are we obliged to

---

centuries—too long for it to be regarded simply as transition from allegory to novel" (46). The most affecting case of the poem pressing back against the atomistic tendency of its allegory may be the exchange between Arthur and Una in canto vii of Book I, where the magnanimous knight is trying to persuade her to "disclose the breach" (1.7.42) that is the source of her sorrows. Traded stanzas become traded lines, an urgent stichomythia, and if *The Faerie Queene* were an opera they would end up singing the same words in duet. That pressing of their words nearer and nearer one another registers the poem's longing for unison. (On longing for unison as a structuring principle in the poem see Miller, *The Poem's Two Bodies*.)

62. Dennis Kezar makes a book—*Guilty Creatures*—of a similarly uncanny question, asking, do Renaissance writers ever conceive of themselves as responsible for the violence they represent, and should we as readers feel complicit in what he calls "killing poems" (7)?

understand evil in order better to resist it, or is any kind of understanding a concession, an apology, and a risk to our purity? Does understanding necessarily contaminate? Because it is Britomart's understanding that is at stake here, we are back to the question of allegorical agents as readers of the allegory, and as exemplars for the readers outside the poem. Her own powers as a reader come to the fore in the House of Busirane.

————

What is Britomart to the House of Busirane, or the House of Busirane to her? Houses (or what Angus Fletcher calls "temples") and the characters who transgress them pose another problem of insides and outsides in Spenser's poem.[63] Does the space diagnose the state of the visitor, as Redcrosse in the House of Pride, or is it a properly external challenge or temptation that the visitor must confront? In the most neutral, narrative terms, the Knight of Chastity ends up on Busirane's property because she pledges to help the hapless Scudamour recover his beloved Amoret from the wizard's inner sanctum. The house has three parts: a room lined with Ovidian tapestries, depicting mostly mortals raped by gods, at the far end of which stands an idol of Cupid; a room of "monstrous formes" (3.11.51) in metal frieze, festooned with the arms of warriors felled by Cupid; and finally the chamber where Busirane tortures Amoret, from which once a day Cupid's procession issues forth. Thomas Roche's reading of the episode has been generative for many subsequent critics; he takes the varieties of antierotic propaganda Britomart encounters to be "an objectification of Amoret's fear of sexual love in marriage," all seen "through the eyes" of the heroine.[64] Such anxieties are just the thing to derail the knight of chastity from a quest that can only be fulfilled by marriage and procreation. Harry Berger emphasizes Busirane's role as the spectacle's architect: "in showing Britomart what and how Amoret suffers, Busirane tries to dissuade both from their promised futures."[65] This sense of the house as a particularly apt test for the knight—or apt manifestation of her virtue—is an assumption that has become widespread, and indeed it is the assumption most native to the poem.[66] The two, house and guest, are made for each other.

63. Fletcher, *The Prophetic Moment*, 14–23.

64. Roche, *The Kindly Flame*, 77, 75. He departs from Lewis, *The Allegory of Love*, 343–45.

65. Berger, "Busirane and the War between the Sexes: An Interpretation of *The Faerie Queene* III.xi–xii," in *Revisionary Play*, 185.

66. See, for example, MacCaffrey, *Spenser's Allegory* (112), and Watkins, *The Specter of Dido* (171–74). For a nearly opposite reading see Lauren Silberman's *Transforming Desire*, where she treats the house as an interpretive contest between the authority of poet (Busirane) and reader

But it might at least give us pause to point out that Britomart seems to recognize nothing of this attunement. If we do in fact see the tapestries through her eyes, her reaction is not once described over nineteen stanzas: the mix of moralizing and delectation in the narrator's tone seems to be independent of the character whose progress from one tapestry to the next presumably strings the images together. This tacit disengagement becomes explicit when she comes to the idol of Cupid at the chamber's far end. She pays attention, but to no obvious effect:

> That wondrous sight faire *Britomart* amazd,
> Ne seeing could her wonder satisfie,
> But evermore and more upon it gazd,
> The whiles the passing brightnes her fraile sences dazd. (3.11.49)

This combination of avid spectatorship and incomprehension is repeated several times, with the "be bold" legends ("she oft and oft it over-red, / Yet could not find what sence it figured" [3.11.50]; "That much she muz'd, yet could not construe it"; "whereto though she did bend / Her earnest minde, yet wist not what it might intend" [3.11.54]) and again with the spectacle of the next room ("beholding earnestly" she "Did greatly wonder, ne could satisfy / Her greedy eyes with gazing a long space" [3.11.53]). There is not a little Virgil in these lines, the famous scene of Aeneas before the Carthaginians' murals of Troy.[67] Spenser's metaphors of feeding and his language of wonder both originate with Aeneas "feast[ing] his soul on the unsubstantial picture [*animum pictura pascit inani*]" and its "wonderful things [*miranda*]."[68] *The Faerie Queene* recombines the two to define the kind of reading taking place, or not taking place, in Busirane's house.

Wonder, as Aristotle's *Rhetoric* tells us, is the beginning of understanding.[69] It is the open-mouthed, exhilarating blankness of confronting something for which we have no categories. It becomes understanding (and ceases to be marvelous) as we assimilate its novelty to our existing, and ideally adapting, structures of knowledge—when we figure out, that is, where

---

(Britomart): "By imprisoning Amoret in the Masque of Cupid, Busirane attempts to assert the power of the poet to be supreme arbiter of meaning. By thwarting his attempt, Britomart reaffirms the view of allegory as a shared enterprise figured by the hermaphroditic embrace" (66). I am more inclined to think of Britomart as opting out of the enterprise.

67. See Watkins, *The Specter of Dido*, 170–74.

68. Virgil, *Aeneid*, 1.464, 1.494.

69. Aristotle, *Rhetoric*, 1371a31–b10. On Renaissance ideas of wonder and the Aristotelian tradition see Biester, *Lyric Wonder*, 1–66, and Platt, *Reason Diminished*, 1–18.

it fits in our commonplace books. In the meantime, it is an affective sign of *failure* to learn something, or to have learned something yet, even if its very intensity may suggest that an unexpected understanding awaits when it is overcome. The problem for Britomart is that she seems to idle at that threshold, feeding herself continuously without digesting anything. There is something of Guyon's respect for boundaries here, but now its occasion is a kind of spectatorial self-pleasuring (rather than study or moral-making). She is a hedonist of what ought to be a merely propaedeutic thrill. This posture may be exhibited as a mode of misreading the poem: wonder is among the terms most argued over by the Italian theorists of romance, and its critics disparage the idle self-sufficiency of its marvelous pleasures.[70]

Then again, perhaps it is an ideal mode of reading the poem; certainly it is one that subsequent generations of readers have recommended. (For example, Hazlitt's famous remark, "If they do not meddle with the allegory, the allegory will not meddle with them."[71]) That is a possibility I want to take seriously—but one more observation about Britomart's mis- (or non-) understanding first. The tapestries she may or may not scrutinize depict the monstrous, painful, and debasing shapes the gods take in their pursuit of mortal women. There is some attention to the subjectivity of these women early on, especially an enigmatic Leda, who seems to share a smile with the onrushing swan.[72] But the emphasis in everything that follows falls on Cupid's triumphs over the gods, all of them male (save Venus—"Ne did he spare . . . His owne deare mother" [3.11.45]—with whom no particular story is associated). The second chamber's bearing on Britomart is even more tenuous, filled as it is with the spoils of Cupid's victories over "mightie Conquerours and Captaines strong" (3.11.52). One might argue that insofar as she has adopted masculine armor for her quest—a metamorphosis of sorts—she is the proper audience for an ekphrastic lecture on the violence and humiliations of male desire. But the rhetorical focus seems misplaced, for the room's ironies are pointed at leaders of men and conquerors of land rather than at solitary questers like the Knight of Chastity.[73]

70. See Biester; on the debate over wonder in Italian criticism of the *romanzo* (much better developed than in England), see Weinberg, *A History of Literary Criticism in the Italian Renaissance*, 2:1050–55.

71. Hazlitt, "Chaucer and Spenser," *Works*, 5:38.

72. "Shee slept, yet twixt her eielids closely spyde, / How towards her he rusht, and smiled at his pryde" (3.11.32). Does Jove smile? Does Leda? Do both, in a conspiracy of unrefused ravishment?

73. This argument is developed at somewhat greater length in my article, "How to Stop Reading *The Faerie Queene*," which goes on to treat the procession that emerges from the third

There is, that is to say, a kind of mis-fit between this knight and the space where she finds herself: she cannot read it, and what is more, it doesn't seem spoken to her. They are mutually irrelevant. "Irrelevance" is a strange word to use in speaking of *The Faerie Queene*, for we tend to assume the overdetermined mattering of each of the poem's parts to all the others. Angus Fletcher describes this assumption as general to allegory, its construction of a *kosmos* or "total figure."[74] Harry Berger's "conspicuous irrelevance" neatly converts passages of apparent ornament to "nodal points of meaning, moments in which the larger significance of the narrative is compressed, illuminated, altered."[75] Almost all contemporary criticism inherits these assumptions: nothing about the poem, in short, is really irrelevant; where it seems most distracted, it is often thinking hardest. But Britomart may show us a place for an unreconstructed indifference—a moment when the habits of reading that allow us to fulfill the poem's ambitions for totality and wholeness might properly be suspended. The chaste knight's blankness is a caution to the reader that the contract of allegory is being broken, or at least that the poem is staging such a break, provoking us with the possibility. For a time it is as though the agent and the place mean nothing to each other.

In spite of this, Britomart is successful, however inarticulate and unarticulated with her surroundings she may be. Or might we even say, because of this? She accomplishes the immediate goal of liberating Amoret with uncommon dispatch and efficiency, and with none of the repeated self-overcomings that mark the last cantos of the previous two books (Redcrosse falling and rising again, Guyon resisting temptation after temptation). Her failure to understand is also a failure to be distracted or deterred. The barrier between her and the house is no longer a piece of didactic technology, and she is no longer a student; her wonder is a tendentious alternative to learning of any kind, an exemption from the persuasive machinery that is working with such hectic energy all around her (whether one considers it to be Busirane's machinery, or the poem's, or the first as a microcosm of the second). She has become the epitome of Wofford's "heroic ignorance," an ignorance that now almost seems to be a necessary condition of heroism. But it is essential to observe that her ignorance is meaningful because the poem holds out the stubborn possibility that she *might* become a reader of the allegory, a reader like us, as Guyon in his way was trained to be. It is not that characters can never be readers from the inside. It is rather that

chamber and to speculate that the intended audience for the spectacle is not Britomart but potential rivals to Busirane like Scudamour.

74. Fletcher, *Allegory*, 85.   75. Berger, *The Allegorical Temper*, 133.

it might be better for all parties not to read at all. *The Faerie Queene* momentarily figures itself as a bad teacher, an elaborate, often contradictory didactic engine, corrupt, entangling, a web of temptation and rebuke that forever undermines its own supposed work of fashioning.[76] Faced with these designs, our own virtue, as readers, may be safest if we do not try to understand. For to read is to risk being taught.

––––––––––

Such a reading brings *The Faerie Queene* to the point of discrediting its own fundamental procedure, and warning us off. The unnerving relation of readerly learning to the suffering or humiliation of characters is canceled by Britomart's exemplary detachment; she achieves Guyon's distance without troubling to make an example of anyone. (That is, Guyon's remove depends on assuming a posture either of teacher or student; wondering Britomart is neither, and cuts herself more radically free from the narrator, from Spenser, and from the teaching poem that hosts her.) But this solution comes at the cost of the poem's authority. Such self-skepticism brings *The Faerie Queene* around to something like the predicament that concludes both *Euphues and His England* and the old *Arcadia*, books that likewise cast systematic doubt upon their own didactic purposes. All three of course make a great show of teaching. They are elaborated out of the materials of a didactic poetics; they could not be what they are, could not move on from page to page, without the assumption that poetry instructs and without the host of conventions that give that assumption substance. And yet they do not believe in the project, or are fantastically sensitive to its costs. The result is a group of fictions that by different means sacrifice themselves to their own pedagogical misgivings. It is hard to say in each case whether that sacrifice is strategic and polemical, or whether it is a kind of bitter, private irony, without particular hope for an audience. Both Sidney and Spenser, however, returned to the problem (as did Lyly, in his way, sending his hero to England). Sidney revised the *Arcadia*, Spenser added three books to *The Faerie Queene* in 1596, and both poets use their sequels to explore alternatives to the nearly private jokes they had told against their teachers and their teacherly selves. The next two chapters take up these second thoughts, and with them, the possibility of escaping teaching altogether.

76. In this the House of Busirane (like many of the other temples in Spenser's labyrinth) is like Atlante's house in *Orlando Furioso*, where knights wander though an incomplete but telling microcosm of the poem, an interpretation of its structure embedded in the fiction. Citing Attilio Momigliano, Albert Ascoli draws out this analogy, comparing "the poem to the labyrinthine palaces of Atlante" (*Bitter Harmony*, 7, 37–38).

CHAPTER FIVE

Method

The new *Arcadia* is in almost every way more extravagant than its predecessor. The old *Arcadia*, written when Sidney had retreated to his sister's home at Penshurst, is a chamber opera. Its action is confined to the forest court of Duke Basilius, and the actors double or even triple up their roles: judge and father, prosecutor and counselor, Cleophila and Daiphantus and Pyrocles. The new *Arcadia*, which Sidney wrote in years of bettering prospects, is grand opera by comparison, or better, epic—played out on battlefields and calling for a cast of thousands. Had it been finished, it might have done much credit to a scholar-soldier-prince. For all its epic ambitions, however, its action begins very much inside the head. Two shepherds, Strephon and Claius, are standing together by the seashore, lamenting the departure of their beloved Urania. "[H]ither we are now come to pay the rent for which we are so called unto by over-busy remembrance—remembrance, restless remembrance, which claims not only this duty of us but for it will have us forget ourselves."[1] As they survey the scene, these two are reminded of "where she walked, where she turned, where she spoke" (63); "as our remembrance came ever clothed unto us in the form of this place," says Strephon, "so this place gives new heat to the fever of our languishing remembrance" (62). The rhetorical topography of trained memory is as real to the fiction as the contours of the shoreline, probably more so. The reader begins by looking round the places of a lovestruck, grieving mind.

If this topography is a sign of the shepherds' good education—their learning in the doctrine of the places—thanks for that learning go to love itself. Strephon continues: "Hath not the only love of her made us, being silly

---

1. Sidney, *The Countess of Pembroke's Arcadia*, ed. Evans, 61. Subsequent citations in this chapter are given by page number in parentheses in the text.

ignorant shepherds, raise up our thoughts above the ordinary level of the world, so as great clerks do not disdain our conference?" (63). The two rustics have clambered up Diotima's ladder from the love of an individual toward the love of ideas, and their conversation invites the reader into their neoplatonic pastoral. Within a few pages, however, we have another view of the matter: the Arcadian nobleman Kalender observes with mild condescension that "it is a sport to hear" (83–84) how the shepherds impute their erected wit to love. Moreover, their sweet discourse is cut short by the floating ashore of a mysterious "thing" (64), a brute, material interruption that turns out to be the body of Prince Musidorus. With its arrival the narrative shrugs off its shepherds' weeds to take up the heroic careers of the princes themselves, and Strephon and Claius are left to assume the status of minor characters whose unrivalrous, sublimated love for the same woman becomes a matter of gentle comedy. (Shortly after, they both receive a letter from Urania and hurry away together, leading the reader to wonder what practical configuration, exactly, would count as a realization of their amorous hopes.) The effect is to open the book with a brief exhibit of the sort of story *Arcadia* will *not* become, and the sort of characters whose fortunes it will *not* follow. It is almost as though the shepherds stand for something that must be pointedly left behind, a quintessence, perhaps, of the unworldliness that sometimes afflicted the hero-princes in Sidney's first attempt at the story. With them out of the way, his new epic romance can get started.

Two aspects of this transient scene, however, will abide. The first is its internality. The particular, melancholy inscape of the Arcadian shoreline may be banished when a body washes up, but the book will go on to be defined by maps of knowledge as much as maps of forests, castles, or countries. (As in *The Faerie Queene*, there is a constant problem of insides and outsides, mind and world, though it is put to very different uses here and driven by very different motives.) The second abiding aspect of the scene is that principle of refinement or analysis that leads Sidney to concentrate the book's adolescent idealism in the two shepherds. The fiction as a whole will show a tendency to separate out such qualities and distribute them among different characters. As the cast expands, each member becomes somewhat simpler, or at least purer—including, in important ways, the hero princes.

I take both of these developments to reflect the new *Arcadia*'s new commitment to method, and I take method to be Sidney's new answer to the problem of how to make a book that teaches. The old *Arcadia* defied the didactic imperative by dismantling its own authority: it is full of teacherly flourish, and it ultimately refuses to teach. The revision follows a different course. Its most obvious innovation is its turn to epic, and it gains the requisite girth by digesting a mess of new episode and experience, a welter of new knowledge. But the lineaments of that knowledge, and its impact both on character and plot, define an ambition deeper than merely superimposing a new generic identity on its mixed mode.[2] Out of this new stuff—and by means of principles of method, particularly Ramist method, that were the intellectual fashion of his circle—Sidney builds what amounts to an encyclopedia inside his fiction. The work that results is a strange hybrid of its ancient sources and the most up-to-date learning, a great experiment in how fiction and method might coexist. Most importantly, for Sidney, it is a work that can teach without a teacher. Method holds out the promise of escape into (or perhaps growth into) a didactic bearing toward the reader that we might now call objectivity.

Method and Epic

"Method" is a slippery word, probably even more so circa 1580 than it is today. It was not new then, but it had recently taken new shapes, and assumed a new centrality and volatility in academic debate.[3] However various the procedures that fell under its rubric—there will be more to say about one of its specific forms shortly—its promise was clear enough. By the application of method, by its regular steps, an intelligible order could be brought to disparate and unfamiliar materials. Method was a way of understanding, and teaching, anything. Examples abound in the 1580s of its use to rationalize instruction in the arts, or to make plain the meaning of a Ciceronian oration; for the moment, however, I will scout it in the thicket of fiction, since that is ultimately where this chapter will locate its influence. There is a passage particularly good for the purpose near the beginning of the new *Arcadia*: the tournament proclaimed by Phalantus to defend the supremacy of his lady Artesia's beauty. Knights come to challenge him from all quarters, bearing portraits of their ladies, and Sidney constructs an elaborate pageant of painting and armor quite unlike anything in the old *Arcadia*. Its

2. "Mixed mode" is Stephen Greenblatt's phrase for the generically polyglot character of the old *Arcadia*, which is only amplified in the new. He treats that mixture as a means of resisting resolution: "in the mixed mode, to resolve is to lie" ("Sidney's *Arcadia* and the Mixed Mode," 278). Method might be thought of as another ingredient in this generic soup, but one with particular ambitions to govern the whole. For a survey of the scholarship on generic mixture in *Arcadia*, see Mentz, "The Thigh and the Sword," 77–80.

3. Neal Gilbert offers the most comprehensive survey of the word's history in *Renaissance Concepts of Method*, 40–49.

lineage lies in the catalogues of epic, which are synecdoches of that form's ambitions to completeness; also in the pageant or triumph imported to romance by Ariosto and Spenser.[4] It is the first of many dazzling ekphrastic spectacles in the revision. What I am most interested in, however, is the way the episode is structured.

The portraits are borne to the field of combat in a processional order, Queen Andromana, the princess of Elis, Queen Artaxia, Queen Erona, Baccha, Leucippe, the queen of Laconia, Queen Helen of Corinth, Parthenia, Urania, and Zelmane. As that order unfolds, it becomes clear that it is defined by significant local oppositions: the ladies come two by two, and each pair parses a subquestion of the large problem, What is beauty? Neither Andromana nor Elis, at the procession's head, has a native claim to being called beautiful. The first is defended by a knight grateful for a favor she did him, the second by a knight whose liking is outwardly unaccountable, as liking will sometimes be. Between them they are the occasions when an unbeautiful woman might be celebrated for her beauty. Artaxia, next in line, is somewhat too "mannish" in countenance, and Erona—"Of a far contrary consideration"—too delicate and pitiful. Baccha is "of a fatness rather to allure than to mislike, yet her breasts overfamiliarly laid open" (158), and she is practiced in sophisticated, dissimulating glances; Leucippe is "of a fine daintiness of beauty, her face carrying in it a sober simplicity," a simplicity that makes her alas "apt to believe" (159). Helen and Parthenia are yet another tendentious pair: Helen's beauty is an intricate conversation between art and nature, her attire "costly and curious," while Parthenia's simplicity needs "no adorning but cleanliness" (160). Urania and Zelmane bring up the rear, near-paragons whose charms are qualified only by the need to leave room for the supernal beauty of the book's two heroines. Taken all together they make an anatomy of beauty as a system of binary oppositions.

What is this interlude for? What kind of knowledge is it meant to offer? Most of the portraits are occasions for *sententiae*, which are as plentiful here as in the old *Arcadia*. (The queen of Laconia, the only unpaired figure, provokes a particularly terse maxim: "she was a queen and therefore beautiful" [159]). But what is distinctive about their presentation is the way the group provides a systematic analysis, one that could be imagined

---

4. By the time Sidney was working on his revision, Spenser's *Faerie Queene* had evidently begun to circulate in manuscript (see the article on "Spenser, Edmund" in *The Spenser Encyclopedia*, 669–70, for a summary of the evidence); the new *Arcadia* seems to bear the stamp of new attention to Ariosto, and perhaps to Spenser's poem of pageants too.

as map or even diagram. This analysis—this partitioning of the topic—is different from the workings of such Spenserian processions as the House of Pride's seven deadly sins. Spenser's triumphal allegory explores an antecedent structure of ideas, accepting the traditional terms as his starting point and attaching them to vivid emblems. Sidney, by contrast, carves up his topic according to a scheme that is neither traditional nor ad hoc, but rather portable from case to case. The resulting dichotomies make a map of the conceptual territory. The passage might be thought of as an instance of *inventio*, as though Sidney had taken "beauty" through the places of causation, opposition, and so on. But the result has a structure more specific than the mere accumulations of Erasmian *copia*. To know beauty is to know these parts and know their systematic interrelation, holding them together in the mind in a structure that is itself a form of understanding.

I have used the visual analogy of a diagram advisedly, and I will continue to argue that the disposition of knowledge in the book courts description in visual terms.[5] To abstract a true diagram from this particular scene would not ultimately be a very satisfying undertaking. Above the level of its first-order distinctions, the architecture gets much blurrier. Nonetheless I want to register the intimations of system, even of a comprehensive, ramifying order, because there are other episodes, and larger coordinating structures, where the project can be carried further. For the moment, the point is only to suggest that the new *Arcadia* makes newly assertive solicitations to the reader inclined to see some method in its narrative profusion.

———

What, then, was Sidney's method? He used the word freely enough. To cite just two examples: a letter to his brother Robert about commonplace book keeping concludes, "Thus write I to you in great haste, of method, without method"; when Dametas instructs Musidorus, the clown "began with a wild method to run over all the art of husbandry, especially employing his tongue about well dunging of a field" (235).[6] The range and offhandedness of these uses is typical of the period. The intellectual historian Neal Gilbert, who traces the history of "method" (*methodus*) and companion words like *via*, *ordo*, and *modus*, writes that they flourished "not as standing for clear

5. Forrest G. Robinson, in *The Shape of Things Known*, also argues that Sidney thinks about knowledge visually, with a debt to Walter Ong: "Sidney proceeds from the assumption that the objects of artistic imitation are not the individual impressions derived from sensation but concepts both formed and viewed within the mind" (106–7). He is more interested in Sidney's ekphrasis, less concerned with demonstrating a methodical organization of the whole.

6. The letter to Robert is reproduced in Duncan-Jones, ed., *Sir Philip Sidney*, 293.

and well-defined concepts, but simply as neutral names used both for the content of a discipline and for any manner of investigating or teaching it." Particularly for teaching, as in the case of Dametas's fertilizer. "The number of school subjects 'brought into order' or 'reduced to art' during the late Renaissance," Gilbert continues, "is almost unbelievable."[7]

"Method" can be used for any sort of orderly instruction, and I will sometimes loosen, sometimes tighten the definition as I proceed. Over time, however—certainly after his death, and by compelling circumstantial evidence as early as 1572—Sidney came to be identified with one method in particular, that of the Protestant curricular reformer Petrus Ramus. Ramus's name was one to conjure with when Sidney was making his revision in the early 1580s, and mostly to conjure controversy.[8] His program, first set out in the *Dialecticae Partitiones* (1543) and amplified in the *Dialecticae Libri Duo* (1556), was essentially a reform of the trivium, intended to eliminate redundancy and make a strict separation between the arts of logic and rhetoric. Teaching in Paris, he had made a wide reputation for himself on the Continent, and his prestige in England was magnified by his conversion to Protestantism and subsequent martyrdom in the St. Bartholomew's Day massacre.

The controversy stemmed partly from Ramus's polemical attack on the influence of Aristotle, but the three laws by which he proposed to reorganize the curricular *artes* had a more lasting and divisive impact. In the traditional divisions of *inventio, dispositio,* and *eloquentia,* he saw redundancy and confusion. He decreed first that the principles of an art should include only what is true and necessary; second, that all and only things belonging properly to the art in question should be included in it; and third, that general things must be dealt with in a general way.[9] The first two laws mandated that all the rhetoric be purged from logic, and vice versa: in practice this meant that invention and judgment both became properties of logic, and to rhetoric was left the ornamenting of language, the schemes and tropes and the graces of *pronunciatio.* (The certainties of logic obtained thereby a much wider franchise; rhetoric was the loser.) From the third law followed the famous procedure of moving from generals to

---

7. Gilbert, *Concepts of Method,* 69.

8. Mordechai Feingold endorses Walter Ong's sense that the popularity of Ramist thinking in the 1570s and 1580s was driven not least by its suitability to an academic culture of sometimes "juvenile" dispute; "English readers of Ramus understood him to offer a facile tool for argumentation" ("English Ramism: A Reinterpretation," 127, 144).

9. See Ramus, *Scholae in Liberales Artes,* col. 31. I have closely paraphrased Peter Mack's summary of these laws in "Ramus Reading," 112 n.8.

particulars, attacking a complex problem by dividing and subdividing it until you reached its simple parts. This is the operation with which Ramus was above all identified. Dudley Fenner's adaptation of the *Dialecticae*, *The Artes of Logike and Rethorike* (1584), offers an appropriately stark statement of how it works:

> Methode is the judgement of more axiomes, whereby many and divers axioms . . . are so ordered as that the easiest and most generall bee set downe first, the harder and lesse generall next, untill the whole matter be so conveied, as all the partes may best agree with themselves, & be best kept in memorie. . . . Therfore according to this perfect way, the definition of that which is to be handled, must be first set downe, and then the division of the same into the members, & the generall properties of the same, and then the divers sortes of it, if there be anye: so proceeding untill by fit and apt passages or transitions, the whole be so farre handeled, that it can no more be devided.[10]

Method is a practice of analysis structured by rigorous dichotomy. Divide, divide, divide until you can divide no more. When you are done, you understand; or perhaps better, your subject is understood.

This procedure can be applied to any topic, and it advertised itself as the most efficient way not only of understanding that topic yourself but of teaching it to others. It implies that texts, even fields of knowledge, fall into parts, what Walter Ong—the most influential, and skeptical, of Ramus's latter-day students—calls "thought-corpuscles." "[T]he only kind of organization for discourse which Ramus imagines," writes Ong, "is the 'collocation' of thought-corpuscles or arguments, or of clusters of such corpuscles."[11] Ramus's method can be seen as a radicalization of more general assumptions guiding humanist teaching of logic and rhetoric, the learned habit of taking a text to pieces. It likewise radicalizes—which is to say, simplifies to its essentials—the reader's pursuit of the *sententia*. In the *Dialecticae Partitiones*, Ramus's analysis parses the Ciceronian oration *Pro Milo* into its constituent arguments; when it is disentangled (*retexere*) from its language, it resolves to the single maxim, "It is permissible to kill a criminal." As Ong writes, "We might say today that this is the 'meaning' of the oration *For Milo*, for everything beyond that summary statement, according to Ramus, is ornament."[12]

---

10. Fenner, "The Artes of Logike and Rhetorike," in *Four Tudor Books on Education*, ed. Pepper, 167.

11. Ong, *Ramus*, 186. 12. Ibid., 191.

Ramist method also takes on a signature visual form, which brings the discussion back around to the question of diagrams. His unfolding dichotomies were characteristically figured in schematic trees, sprouting from the seed of a single, complex concept and growing across the page by branching distinctions, until the concept's simplest parts line up against the right margin. Often the reception of the method was no deeper than this graphic format and its tell-tale brackets, which lent the appearance of dialectical rigor to any subject.[13] William Temple's edition of the *Dialecticae Libri Duo* offers one of thousands of interchangeable examples, this one laying out the kinds of arguments, divided first into simple and complex, and subdivided from there by strict dichotomies:

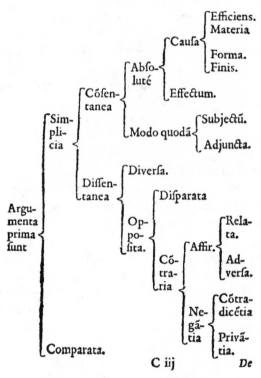

From Petrus Ramus, *Dialecticae* (Cambridge, 1584), fol. C3r. Reproduced by permission of The Huntington Library, San Marino, California, RB 22375 p. 37.

13. Feingold describes this broad but shallow influence: "Since English Ramism manifested itself almost exclusively in terms of format, I believe it would not be inappropriate to define this wide-spread diagrammatic predilection as 'low-grade Ramism'" ("English Ramism," 137).

For all the superficiality of most such diagrams, what Christopher Marlowe called their "flat dichotomies"—hardly intending the pun—betray deep currents in intellectual history.[14] It is Ong again who offered in 1958 the much-debated but durable claim that Ramist diagrams both capture and promote a change in the way knowledge was conceived in the new age of moveable type. He saw in Ramus a "movement away from a concept of knowledge as it had been enveloped in disputation and teaching (both forms of dialogue belonging to a personalist, existentialist world of sound) toward a concept of knowledge that associated it with a silent object world, conceived in visualist, diagrammatic terms."[15] Such knowledge is not unspooled in the time-bound operations of oratory, but rather is understood to be arranged as information in a neutral, visualized plane. No speaker is implied, and the time, needless to say, is taken out. It is this reorientation toward the nature of knowledge, and how knowledge is communicated, that I take to be the key to the methodizing impulse of the new *Arcadia*.

———————

Sidney moved in a milieu much occupied with this intellectual fashion. It may not be obvious that the methodizing project, so strenuously avant-garde, would be particularly useful to a poet bent on working in the ancient genre of epic. But in fact the two, epic and method, have strong filiations. Above all, both are totalizing constructions, ambitious to digest all the world. The epic side of this partnership—*Arcadia*'s conversion from an "idle toy" to what the *Defence of Poetry* would call an "absolute heroical poem"—has always been recognized.[16] (One way of thinking about the revision is as an attempt to transform a half-ludic, half-embittered antitext of the *Defence* into something more like an exemplar.) The largest structural changes from the old *Arcadia* are in overt imitation of Homer and Virgil: the revised second book, with its inset romance narratives, is an *Odyssey*; the third book is an *Iliad*, a long siege to redeem two captive women. These tributes fall in the order sanctioned by the romance and epic halves of the *Aeneid*, and even the book's famous incompletion—breaking off in the midst of battle—has been described as a Virgilian strategy.[17] Sidney's *Defence* says that poetry

14. "He that will be a flat decotamest [dichotomist], / And seen in nothing but Epetomies [epitomes], / Is in your judgment thought a learned man," says one of Ramus's murderers in *The Massacre at Paris*, 1.9.29–31.

15. Ong, *Ramus*, 151.

16. Sidney, *Old Arcadia*, 3; Sidney, *Miscellaneous Prose*, 81.

17. Thomas Roche draws the parallel with the end of the *Aeneid* in his article "Ending the *New Arcadia*: Virgil and Ariosto," 10–12.

gathers up the virtues of philosophy and history alike and "dealeth with *katholou*, that is to say, with the universal consideration"; the work of the poet is the fullest realization of "the mistress-knowledge, by the Greeks called *architectonike*."[18] Epic is the apotheosis of these qualities, a kind of poem that is supposed to make a place for everything, at once a fiction and an encyclopedia.[19]

The idea of an "encyclopedia," a term I will use with something like a sixteenth-century looseness to describe a total organization of learning, is associated with method, too, and method's capacity to bring all knowledge into a perspicuous and self-consistent order.[20] George Chapman—a great disciple of Sidney in his critical thinking—illuminates its convergence with epic in the dedication to his *Odyssey*:

> the Structure [of the *Odyssey* is] so elaborate and pompous that the poore plaine Groundworke (considered together) may seeme the naturally rich wombe to it and produce it needfully. . . . [The] worke so farre exceeds the Ocean, with all his Court and concourse, that all his Sea is onely a serviceable streame to it. Nor can it be compared to any One power to be named in nature, being an entirely wel-sorted and digested Confluence of all—where the most solide and grave is made as nimble and fluent as the most airie and firie, the nimble and fluent as firme and well-bounded as the most grave and solid.[21]

There is a Sidneian theory of composition at work here: the "Ground-worke" recalls the *Defence*'s "ground-plot of a profitable invention," that original idea or schema out of which the fiction is unfolded.[22] The resulting poem is oceanic in its totality, but also "wel-sorted" and structured by a set of antitheses, airy and fiery against solid and grave, nimble and fluent against firm and well-bounded, heaven against hell. The maker, continues

---

18. Sidney, *Miscellaneous Prose*, 88, 82.

19. This is a pervasive commonplace, as a claim both about the epic poem and the epic hero. For its history, see for example D. C. Allen, *Mysteriously Meant*, chaps. 4 and 6, and Weinberg, *A History of Literary Criticism in the Italian Renaissance* (see index under "magnitude").

20. For a summary of this association see Martin Elsky, "Reorganizing the Encyclopedia: Vives and Ramus on Aristotle and the Scholastics," in Norton, ed., *The Cambridge Encyclopedia of Literary Criticism*, 402–8. William West surveys the tradition of the encyclopedia, with particular attention to its spatial metaphors, in *Theatres and Encyclopedias in Early Modern Europe*, 14–42.

21. Chapman, *Chapman's Homer*, 2:5.

22. Chapman's general indebtedness to the *Defence* is apparent throughout the preface (e.g., "Nor is this all-comprising Poesie phantastique, or meere fictive, but the most material and doctrinall illations of Truth" [2:5], recalling Sidney's distinction between *eikastiké* and *phantastiké* in the *Defence* [*Miscellaneous Prose*, 104]).

Chapman, makes both "a Bodie and a Soule," and "if the Bodie (being the letter, or historie) seemes fictive and beyond Possibilitie to bring into Act"—if the fiction seems improbable, as a romance will—"the sence then and Allegorie (which is the Soule) is to be sought—which intends a more eminent expressure of Vertue."[23] There is an intellectual order implicit in the work, and it is by repairing to that order that the work may be justified.

It is not necessary to posit an allegiance to any method in particular to account for Chapman's antithetical construction of this order: habits of rhetorical balance and a helping of allegorical theory would suffice. But his preface allows us to see how a fiction poised between epic and romance might be conceived and defended in terms of a supervenient, systematic order of ideas. For the terms of such a defense, Chapman looks back to Philip Sidney.

———

The burden in what follows will therefore be to show how a concern with method gives shape to Sidney's polyglot fiction, its epic ambitions and its romance proliferation of episodes alike, which together are the generic means by which the book outgrows its pastoral origins.[24] The order of Phalantus's pageant is only a fractal glimpse of a much larger project. Before turning back to the new *Arcadia*, however, it will be useful to make one more observation about Sidney's Ramism. Namely, that he did not get it in school. In the 1580s Cambridge-educated William Kempe brought Ramus into the grammar curriculum, but in the 1560s, when Sidney was at Shrewsbury, Ramist influence was still limited. (His headmaster Thomas Ashton had been a don at Cambridge, which became over the course of that decade the center of Ramist activity in England—but he had been elected a fellow of St. Johns back in 1524 and took the helm at Shrewsbury in 1561.[25]) Sidney most likely got his first taste at Oxford, or even after,

23. Chapman, *Chapman's Homer*, 2:5.

24. Clare Kinney's "On the Margins of Romance" describes a counterpressure in the book, against the account of its method that I am developing in favor of an "over-arching history of never ending desire" (151) that keeps exfoliating episodes, often in the mouths of female storytellers. A good reader will keep accounts like hers in mind; I will err in the direction of the poem's effort to organize itself. See also Carey, "Structure and Rhetoric in Sidney's *Arcadia*."

25. On Ashton's career see Oldham, *History of Shrewsbury School*, 6. Louis A. Knalfa observes, "The introduction of Ramism into England dates from the early 1550s, but there appears to have been no decisive influence until the formation of an interest group at Cambridge in the 1560s" ("Ramism and the English Renaissance," 35). See also Jardine, "The Place of Dialectic Teaching in Sixteenth-Century Cambridge," 57–60.

on his Grand Tour, when he might well have met Ramus himself shortly before the massacre.[26] On returning to England, he kept company with men who would become important to the spread of Ramist influence, including his secretary William Temple and the lawyer Abraham Fraunce. Temple produced a Ramist analysis of the *Defence of Poetry*, and Fraunce filled his Ramist *Arcadian Rhetorike* (1588) with Sidneian examples.[27]

That is to say: I want to identify method, in Sidney's case, with growing up—another way in which it might keep company with epic, the genre of the poet's maturity. Method offers him a means of teaching that is not tangled up with his own career in the classroom, brilliant as it had been. And more than that: it offers a way out of the discomforts of adopting the role of teacher himself. Ramus's followers, writes Ong, were

> uncalculatingly but relentlessly reducing the personalist, dialoguing element in knowledge to a minimum in favor of an element which made knowledge . . . a-personal and abstract (almost as though it were something which existed outside a mind, as though one could have knowledge without anybody to do the knowing—as Ramists were eventually to maintain one could).[28]

This transformation is another version of the dream of teaching without a teacher. I associated that dream in chapter 2 with the promise of unmediated experience, learning by being in the world. Here, getting rid of the teacher—his personal authority, his voice, his point of view—could be a matter not of dismantling, but of perfecting the mediation, offering up the world as a diagram. Sidney certainly would not have formulated either the problem or his own motives in the way Ong has done. But the idea that the sort of teaching achieved by method is depersonalizing *while still being teaching* explains a great deal of what happens to *Arcadia*. Method allows Sidney to fulfill his didactic obligation, while at the same time transforming, even effacing, his own role and authority as the instructor.

---

26. Alan Stewart suggests that the two became friends, on the testimony of Ramus's posthumous editor Théophile de Banos (*Philip Sidney*, 78). See also Duncan-Jones, *Sir Philip Sidney*, 58, 60, 81.

27. See *William Temple's Analysis of Sir Philip Sidney's Apology for Poetry*. Temple dedicated his edition of Ramus's *Dialecticae* to Sidney, and a copy sent in 1584 seems to have led to Temple's employment in 1585: Katherine Duncan-Jones suggests that his Ramist analysis of the *Defence* was "his first piece of work in Sidney's employ" (*Sir Philip Sidney*, 272). Robinson discusses Sidney's Ramist milieu in *The Shape of Things Known*, 110–22.

28. Ong, *Ramus*, 152.

The Arcadian Encyclopedia

Fulke Greville, who met Sidney when they were schoolboys at Shrewsbury, saw the methodical skeleton beneath *Arcadia*'s skin, and the biography he wrote of his friend provides an x-ray:

> his intent and scope was to turn the barren philosophy precepts into pregnant images of life, and in them, first on the monarch's part, lively to represent the growth, state, and declination of princes, change of government and laws, vicissitudes of sedition, faction, succession, confederacies, plantations, with all other errors or alterations in public affairs; then again, in the subject's case, the state of favour, disfavour, prosperity, adversity, emulation, quarrel, undertaking, retiring, hospitality, travel and all other moods of private fortunes or misfortunes. In which traverses I know his purpose was to limn out such exact pictures of every posture in the mind.[29.]

The language of the *Defence* infuses this account, coloring its pregnant images, but the "rich wombe" of those images (in Chapman's phrase) is unfolded with discriminating rigor. If we were to realize a diagram of Greville's account it would look like this:

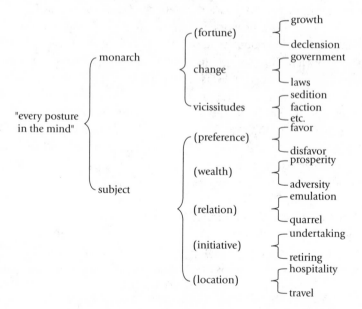

29. Greville, *Prose Works*, 10–11. John Hoskins's *Directions for Speech and Style*, his unpublished, *Arcadia*-based rhetoric handbook, offers a comparable typology of its characters, though

Greville begins from the assumption of the book's total ambition, its embrace of "every posture in the mind." The cardinal distinction—the distinction that first opens the problem to thought—is between the monarch and subject. (Nothing is more important to the mind's postures, evidently, than their relation to authority.) Subdividing the term "monarch," Greville makes a tripartite distinction among the conditions that affect a prince's career: (1) the inevitable shape given to experience by the wheel of fortune, (2) regulated change in laws and governmental forms, and (3) the illicit or unpredictable events that befall a reign ("errors or alterations"). In the case of the "subject," the division is fivefold, and the chart above supplies the implicit middle terms that Greville expands into binaries. Favor and disfavor, prosperity and adversity, and the rest are the species of fortune to which the ordinary man is heir (perhaps with a particular emphasis on his relation to the monarch: even hospitality and travel, for example, may be a question of nearness to power).

Greville's sense of the work's scope is echoed by modern critics: C. S. Lewis asserts that it "gathers up what a whole generation wanted to say"; Arthur Kinney writes admiringly that "[o]nly . . . a comprehensive vision could suggest such a massive anatomy of an entire culture as the *Arcadia*."[30] Nancy Lindheim's study *The Structures of Sidney's Arcadia* is the most systematically attentive to the way Sidney achieves this *copia*. She is particularly interested in how the work digests bodies of knowledge outside itself: the new *Arcadia* grows out of the old, she argues, by "extrinsically guided amplification; it realizes some antecedent or absolute idea of subject matter that has as it were a doctrinal existence apart from the particular action of the fable. . . . Any one of a hundred schemes can determine the material to be selected. The only quality they share is that each arises from some impulse extrinsic to the plot itself."[31] These "hundred schemes"—which might derive from nearly as many philosophical or rhetorical sources—I take to be expressions of an underlying methodical impulse. The subject matter may come from outside, from the political and ethical thought of Plato, Aristotle, or Cicero, as well as the newer influence of Protestant resistance theory. But the methodical order by which it is introduced is written deeply enough into the work that it might be considered to be native, a large-scale approach, dividing and subdividing, to the new knowledge the book adopts as its own. This is how *Arcadia* understands the world, and it

---

one without notable methodical structure: "unfortunate valor in Plangus; courteous valor in Amphialus; proud valor in Anaxius" (41) and so on.

30. Lewis, *English Literature*, 339; Kinney, *Humanist Poetics*, 277.

31. Lindheim, *Structures*, 148.

is how it proposes to its readers that it may be read. (Even, how it is already read before the first page is turned.)

The kind of order that Greville claims to see—what I will speak of as the *Arcadia*'s encyclopedia—is most visible in the second book, which is the most episodic, a copious elaboration of the intermittent storytelling that sketches the princes' histories in the old *Arcadia*. The methodical impulse emerges particularly in the handling of two topics, tyranny and love. Tyranny first. The princes' adventures begin in the kingdom of Phrygia, where shipwreck casts Pyrocles into the hands of the local despot, a man "of melancholy constitution both of body and mind; wickedly sad, ever musing of horrible matters; suspecting, or rather condemning all men of evil" (265). His descent through paranoia into tyranny is sketched in a vivid paragraph, and the next few pages describe how the princes spark a rebellion and his overthrow. Next, they pass into the kingdom of Pontus, whose monarch has captured their servants and put them to death. Pontus's characteristic vices are "delight . . . to be flattered" (271) and rapacious envy of others' fortunes; another brief anatomy of his character is followed swiftly by his defeat and execution. Each of these portraits is a set-piece of political and psychological analysis, and the sureness of judgment is borne out by the princes' success. As Musidorus observes, Pontus is "a tyrant also, not through suspicion, greediness or revengefulness, as he of Phrygia, but, as I may term it, of a wanton cruelty: inconstant in his choice of friends . . . giving sometimes prodigally, not because he loved them to whom he gave but because he lusted to give" (271). Phrygia's tyranny is driven by fear, Pontus's by appetite and social need.

Here at the threshold of a complex of adventures, then, a cardinal distinction is drawn, sponsored by these two bad monarchs.[32] A notional diagram of the ensuing action would divide Pontus into two aspects, masculine and feminine. The first is Tiridates, with his unquenchable and singular love for Erona: "love had kindled his cruel heart—indeed cruel and tyrannous" (302–3). Queen Andromana is his feminine counterpart, whose vacillating desires lead her to usurp her husband's authority, contrive the exile of

32. At least one early seventeenth-century reader observed that the 1593 *Arcadia* "would make as good a book of Characters as is yet extant" (Hamilton, *Sidney*, 149). A book of characters might be a serious ethical project in the period: the edition of the *Nicomachean Ethics* introduced into the Sidney library in 1582 was bound together with an edition of Theophrastus, Theophrastus presumably serving as a body of example illustrating Aristotle's theory. See Germaine Warkentin's survey of the contents of the Sidney library, "Sidney's Authors," in *Sir Philip Sidney's Achievements*, 85. The volume's printer was the Ramist André Wéchel. Behind such assemblies was the implication of a common method, by definition underlying any good thinking about ethics or politics.

his son, and eventually imprison the princes. That is: two types of desire afflict the appetitive tyrant, constant and obsessive (a masculine type), and violently inconstant (feminine). Into the category headed by Phrygia, the tyrant by fear, one might place the miser Chremes, who barely consents to admit Pyrocles to his castle "for fear, belike, lest I should have proved a young borrower" (343). Many storytellers contribute to elaborating this taxonomy in what follows, and once it has been introduced the scheme can be seen to ramify well beyond the retrospective romance of the second book. The princesses' two captors, for example, fall into these kinds. Basilius the domestic tyrant sequesters his family out of fear of the oracle's prophecy. Amphialus's desire forbids him to release the princesses: "that tyrant love (which now possesseth the hold of all my life and reason) will no way suffer it" (450–51). The Pontus/Phrygia dyad becomes a tool for analyzing a whole range of subsequent events.

The beginnings of a diagram on Ramist lines would look something like this:

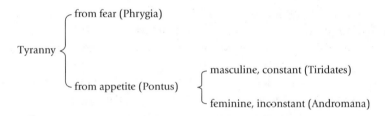

The categories defined here could be populated with more instances, as we will see. The structure does not get so very far, and will not remain so neat; there is in fact no final map on Ramist principles that would do justice to the fiction. The encyclopedia could never be cut whole and integral from the narrative. But the propaedeutic character of the portraits of Pontus and Phrygia makes clear the extent to which an analytic project both undergirds and generates important aspects of the fiction. The book is often thinking through concepts in a methodical way, and its plot adds episodes to further that analysis. A few more pages into the princes' Asian adventures, Sidney annexes a third term to the Phrygia-and-Pontus dyad. (Its thirdness is less typically Ramist.) At the head of this new branch are two giants, former servants of Pontus who have been "discarded . . . after many notable deserts" (273) and have embarked on a blindly vengeful rampage. The princes decide they are incorrigible and kill them both, but not before they have added to *Arcadia*'s conceptual map the idea of misrule born of resentment. Plexirtus (the bastard son of the king of Paphlagonia and the original

of Shakespeare's Edmund) and Cecropia (whose malevolence feeds on her son's displacement as heir to the Arcadian throne) are their heirs. Three, then, are the sources of tyranny: fear, appetite, and injured merit.

————————

The array of archetypical lovers that the fiction offers up is if anything more patently analytical than the system of its tyrants, though there is a less developed sense of division and subdivision in their ranks: the couples introduced to the new *Arcadia* offer something more like a spectrum. Strephon and Claius open the action with their almost comically pious yearning for Urania, giving the book its type of Platonic love. Shortly thereafter comes the tournament in which Phalantus defends Artesia's beauty against all comers, where love is reduced to its chivalric conceits. As Phrygia and Pontus divided tyranny between them, so these loves map extremes of idealism and worldliness, and set terms for thinking about everything that follows. Pamphilus later offers a variation on the tournament by representing love as a sport: women compete for his favor "like them I have seen play at the ball grow extremely earnest who should have the ball, and yet every one knew it was but a ball" (336). And then there are Argalus and Parthenia, who body forth a perfect, mutual love, "each making one life double, because they made a double life one" (501). These two enjoy the perfect union to which the others, in their different respects, are antithetical.

None of these couples has much more than an incidental relation to the main plot; they serve rather to mark out a field of concepts within which that plot can unfold: love as pure idea, pure convention, pure sport, pure devotion. The Argalus and Parthenia story in particular enjoyed an afterlife that suggests something about the self-contained character of such episodes. It was frequently adapted by later writers as a freestanding fiction, retold, for example, by Francis Quarles in the next century, and later mounted on the stage. (Still another imitator in the eighteenth century looked back over its history of adaptation and declared that it "may well be stil'd, The Lovers Common Place Book."[33]) Sidney braids some of the characters from these

33. Quarles' *Argalus and Parthenia* was printed in 1629; Henry Glapthorne's version for the stage, "As it hath been Acted at the Court before their Majesties: And at the Private-House in Drury-Lane, By Their Majesties Servants" (title page), came out a decade later. The anonymous eighteenth-century prose adaptation (which draws freely on Sidney's language) is called *The Unfortunate Lovers*, and the author comments further, "I Need not tell thee how Universally the History of Argalus and Parthenia has obtain'd in the World; the many Impressions that have been done of it in Verse sufficiently evince it: Nor cou'd any thing less be expected from the

exemplary digressions back into the main narrative in intricate ways. Artesia returns in the third book as a member of Cecropia's court, Pamphilus
poses a difficult choice for Pyrocles in his fight with Anaxius, and so on.
But there is all the same a modularity to their construction as exemplars
of love. If they were removed, their absence would change the intellectual
topography of the new *Arcadia*, but not its main story.

There is a parallel array of unrequited loves, more closely tangled with
the princes' fates. Basilius's love for Pyrocles-as-Zelmane, as a man of four
score years, is a defiance of death; Gynecia, as a woman whose prime is
being wasted in a stale bed, chooses life in falling in love with the prince.
The true Zelmane's unrequited love for Pyrocles has the purity, and im-
practicality, of his perfect innocence and her perfect reticence. Amphialus's
for Philoclea is corrupted by his self-deceptions. There are elaborate chains
of failed reciprocation too, such as Plangus's love for Erona, who loves
Antiphilus, who loves Artaxia. The point of all these types is to create an
analytic framework. In their midst—in the middle of the whole system of
love in *Arcadia*—stand the princes and the princesses. Their loves are deferred, unconsummated, the one held in check by Philoclea's innocent
instinct and the other by Pamela's strong reason—a narrative delay that
is at once a source of suspense and an interval of contemplation. In this
state of suspension the heroes are vulnerable to the full range of corruption
and dreamy error that is elaborated in their orbit. All of what happens to
the other characters could happen to them, and that relatively static map
expresses the potentials of the dynamic relations that define the main plot.
In the old *Arcadia* some of those darker possibilities are realized when
the princes give rein to their desires. In the new *Arcadia*—at least, in what
we have of it—that threat remains external to the princes, displaced into
a scheme that anatomizes the perils of love while keeping them at a safe
remove. That safe, analytic remove may be exactly what the scheme is for.

————————

It should now be clear that Sidney embarked on his revisions with a very
different book in mind: different from the old *Arcadia*, but from any of its
literary sources too. A comparison with *The Faerie Queene* is illuminating,
not least because the new *Arcadia* in many ways seems to draw nearer to
Spenser's poem as it becomes more episodic in design. But Spenser's hall
of mirrors—in which every episode is an uncanny double of others just

————————

Product of so celebrated an Author as the Immortal Sir Philip Sidney, whose Original Thought
it was" (A3r).

transpired or yet to come—is wired together on what turn out to be quite different principles. Angus Fletcher has adapted the word "parody" to describe its dynamics: how the House of Busirane, for example, asks to be read alongside the House of Holiness (each tripartite in structure, located at the end of a book, and exerting palpable didactic designs on the characters who transgress it). It is important to Fletcher's use of the concept, however, that a relation of parody does not necessarily privilege one or the other of its terms. It is always a potentially "symmetrical effect": the wasteland may be read as a demonic parody of the delightful maze, but circumstances may also favor the reverse interpretation, when the maze's pleasures turn out to be false comfort and the wasteland a severe truth. Hence decisions about which is theme and which is variation are crucial, but not necessarily stable: "the reader will have to look for the means of knowing the direction of parody."[34] A character's progress through a succession of episodes may follow or reverse the parodic vector, moving toward or away from the original, losing the thread or picking it up. All the while there is a pervasive sense that the episodes are derived from and even caused by one another. Disentangling the insidious intent of their argument is one of the things that keeps characters going and readers reading. (Isabel MacCaffrey calls this the poem's sense of ubiquitous "causal inexplicitness."[35])

Fletcher's kind of parody is not alien to the new *Arcadia*. The succession of island duels in the third book—Amphialus slaying Argalus, the combat of cowards, and the death of Parthenia—could be read as such a structure: which is the true form, the chivalric glory of the first, the bathos of the second, or the tragedy of the last?[36] But in the main the interrelationship of the episodes that fill out *Arcadia*'s new bulk is very different. They are aspects of a notionally comprehensive scheme, most useful when they are all held

34. Fletcher, *Prophetic Moment*, 36. See also Berger, in "The Spenserian Dynamics": "Spenser's world and its places are not actualized in advance like an obstacle course waiting to steer its assayers toward their preordained goal. They emerge out of the problems and actions of his characters. Spenserian landscape for the most part evolves from the projection of inscape. And where Dante's obstacle course is literally vertical, Spenser's, as it materializes, is for the most part 'horizontal': where Dante's cosmos is hierarchically organized in terms of *up* and *down*, the dominant Spenserian vectors are *in* and *out*, and these vectors control both the psychic, or allegorical, and the topographic (plains, forests, houses) elements of experience" (*Revisionary Play*, 23). Note that Berger finds an overall progress, an ever-higher dynamic integration, in these relations.

35. MacCaffrey, *Spenser's Allegory*, 47.

36. This question is raised by Alan Hager, who privileges the combat of cowards as ironizing the motives of single combat generally: "Honor is seen not as a proper ideal, but as a savage principle that forces one to reciprocate, even escalate, violence quite will-lessly in deadly rivalry. Love, of the Petrarchan type, is seen as a proper occasion for suicidal assaults" (*Images*, 169).

in the mind at once. Interpretive questions are not so much about *origins*, how episodes are derived from one another, as they are about *affinities*: what category does this character or this action occupy, define, divide? For this reason a map or a chart that lays its concepts side-by-side makes a useful heuristic for reading aspects of *Arcadia*, and a hopeless one for *The Faerie Queene*. Reading Spenser's poem as a storehouse of information or example travesties his poetics, insofar as the poem is built to rebuke our efforts to understand any part of it in isolation. (This is the super-relevance that the last chapter took Britomart to defy.) Great tracts of the new *Arcadia*, however, seem built to be read in just this way, as a variety of short studies primed for epitome or excerption in the commonplace book. In this there is more invitation than resistance to the well-trained reader.

That said: to grant the methodical scheme of *Arcadia's* knowledge of politics and love simple hegemony over its narrative would be a mistake. All of the episodes that make up the encyclopedia are told by particular characters at particular moments in the progress from the forest court of Basilius to the ramparts of Cecropia's castle. The recounting of the princes' adventures in particular follows a trajectory in mood and meaning to which the sequence of episodes is all-important. It begins auspiciously with the kings of Phrygia and Pontus: they are, as we have seen, not only the cardinal types in the unfolding of the concept of tyranny, but unproblematic occasions for the heroism of the princes, who defeat them handily and leave good government behind. From this point forward, however, nothing is so easy. The heroes' encounter with the *Lear* plot of Leonatus and Plexirtus appears to end with the reformation of the bastard son, but Musidorus, who tells the story, concedes his naïveté in hindsight. Other misjudgments follow: Pyrocles' freeing of Pamphilus, the death of Zelmane, and further doomed negotiations with Plexirtus. The intractability of the Erona story is a recurring frustration. Most critics recognize a pattern of increasing moral complexity and declining success over the course of the book, one in which the promise implicit in the princes' education that experience will consist in "the practice of those virtues which they before learned" (259) is increasingly mocked.[37]

---

37. Interpretations of this pattern differ. Richard McCoy sees the second book leading inexorably toward the nightmare of the shipwreck: "In this final episode, the intensity of the conflict renders mastery impossible, choice specious, and survival the sole heroic accomplishment" (*Rebellion*, 160). Nancy Lindheim notes the same deterioration but takes a more sanguine view of it: "Thus we find in Pyrocles' narrative a second phase of education where experience reflects the strong Sophistic and rhetoricist stress on factors of contingency or circumstance" (*Structures*, 95).

This general tendency might seem to disrupt the paradigm of analytic disaggregation that I have described as governing the book's intellectual map. Each episode is less easy to resolve than the last; the romance energies of the fiction seem steadily to erode the conceptual distinctiveness of its narrative materials. But the confusion the princes experience in responding to these new challenges should not be mistaken for ambiguity in the definition of those challenges. The new *Arcadia* uses romance to draw out, adventure by adventure, the intellectual counterplot that I am calling method.[38] And indeed, it may be possible to make an even stronger claim: that the integrity of the methodical counterplot is actually reinforced by the disintegration of the clean episodic structure of the narrative. For the princes' troubles begin when they attempt not just to dispatch or discipline, but to reform the malefactors they encounter. They act categorically against Phrygia and Pontus, slaying the first in battle and executing the second. The two giants are killed without compunction. Plexirtus, however, is an artist of apology, whose powers beggar Musidorus's formidable rhetoric: "how finely seeming to desire nothing but death as ashamed to live, he begged life in the refusing it, I am not cunning enough to be able to express" (282). By convincing the princes that he will mend his ways, he survives to plague them in a chain of ultimately unresolved treacheries. Mistaken optimism likewise drives the other major plotline of the second book. Erona's love for the lowborn Antiphilus cannot redeem his base qualities; a combination of sympathy and chivalric obligation makes the princes complicit in her blind hope for his improvement. As with Plexirtus's betrayals, the story spreads like a disease through succeeding episodes, contaminating a series that seemed at first to promise heroic closure at each stage. Finally Musidorus must concede, looking back at Plexirtus's career of deception: "so had Nature formed him" (281).

These parallel sequences project a profoundly conservative attitude toward the malleability, not to say educability, of human nature. But in this educational skepticism the second book simultaneously insists on the integrity of its own methodical curriculum: the types that constitute its encyclopedia are fixed, and we err principally in dreaming that we can change them. Even as the princes' humanist optimism mires them deeper and deeper in error and rash obligation, the encyclopedia that their errors

---

38. I borrow the term "counterplot" from Geoffrey Hartman's "Milton's Counterplot," where he uses it to describe the imperturbable, atemporal order of divine design that subtends all the hectic and apparently contingent action of the plot proper. It may be useful to think of this methodical counterplot as though it were another genre in the complex generic landscape, epic, romance, pastoral, lyric and so on, of *Arcadia*.

unfold intimates the possibility of conceptual mastery over a fixed field. To recognize all the kinds and accept their immutability would enable decisive and effective action: as Dudley Fenner puts it, the ability to calibrate one's actions "according to their matter, time, place, persons, and all such circumstances."[39] It is a model of knowledge, in a tacit didactic revolution, that is directed to a reader who can see through the story to the book's systematic lineaments, a methodical reader.

Method and Character

What I have so far described of the new *Arcadia*'s encyclopedia is populated by characters who are close to allegory in their simplicity. They translate readily into the concepts whose order is the mark of method on the book, and they provide a kind of grid of analysis that may be applied to the more complex characters at the center of the plot. Those more important characters, however, are also shaped by the lineaments of method. This chapter began with the shepherds Strephon and Claius: how their mooning in the memory places establishes a mental map under Arcadia's physical topography, but also how that Platonic devotion marks a limit for the princes, even annexes from them—from their prior, old-Arcadian selves—qualities unbecoming a newly robust heroism. And indeed, the princes are more pragmatical and worldly from the start. The evanescent, vanishing difference between them in the original, where they are separated by only a year, relaxes into "three or four" (259) years and a more workaday older-cousin, younger-cousin bond. Their education is also rendered more conventional. The original Pyrocles and Musidorus learn from each other in a schoolmasterless idyll of mutual fashioning, even as Strephon and Claius are raised up by love to converse with "great clerks" (63). In the new *Arcadia*, however, they seem to have gone to school, or at least to have been tutored:

> For almost before they could perfectly speak, they began to receive conceits not unworthy of the best speakers, excellent devices being used, to make even their sports profitable: images of battles and fortifications being then delivered to their memory, which after, their stronger judgments might dispense; the delight of tales being converted to the knowledge of all the stories of worthy princes, both to move them to do nobly and teach them how to do nobly; the beauty of virtue still being set before their eyes, and that taught them with far more diligent care than grammatical rules. (258)

39. Fenner, *Artes of Logike and Rhethoricke*, in *Four Tudor Books*, ed. Pepper, 167.

These students have teachers, and they are schooled in military practicalities as well as the images of virtue. Their training is an ideal, but it is not a fantasy. The fantasy has already been embodied and isolated in two shepherds, and purged when their fleeting candidacy for the role of heroes is dismissed.

Not purged altogether, it should be said. The princes' love for the princesses retains some of its Platonic coloring. Still that color is markedly diminished, and what I am trying to describe here is a tendency in the revision, a direction. If that tendency is toward the purifying of character, as I will argue that it is, then the greatest obstacle the original poses is the ungovernability of the princes' desires. The archetypical heroism championed by the *Defence*—the total virtue of an exemplary Aeneas or Cyrus—cannot abide such lapses as Pyrocles's night with Philoclea or Musidorus's interrupted kiss. In chapter 3 I described how those moments of desublimated desire make a kind of structural pivot of the old *Arcadia*, which ironically advances desire as the very *meaning* of the fiction. That structure is shattered by the new *Arcadia*'s ambitious expansion, and most critics concur that it is difficult to imagine the new story returning to revisit those moments of pastoral lapse. Certainly both scenes were bowdlerized from Mary Sidney's 1593 composite version of the story.[40]

What happens, then, to those lawless energies? The question might be a little peculiar: why should anything have to happen to them; why couldn't they simply be left out? But it turns out that there is an iron economy between the two versions, a law that insists on the conservation, one way or another, of even the most inconvenient aspects of the original. This means that when significant aspects of a character are pared away, they must be projected on another character in the course of revision—or even become another character. The most obvious product of this new law is Amphialus. In the old *Arcadia*, both princes, and especially Musidorus, get themselves into situations where seduction and coercion are uncomfortably crossed. When Amphialus takes the princesses captive, he takes that conflict onto himself, and away from the heroes. There is a little episode midway through the second book in which Sidney seems to nod ironically to this strategy. The princesses have gone to the river to bathe, accompanied by Pyrocles in his disguise as Zelmane, a delighted interloper in their sorority. While he

---

40. See for example Lindheim's comment: "For the princes, love is still a disordering force that drives them to assume shameful disguises and to turn aside from a life of heroic virtue. They remain flanked by the guilty passions of Basilius and Gynecia, though their own lust is now moderated, so that the act of preserving their mistresses' honour, keeping them 'still worthy to be loved,' becomes more a sign and less a test of their virtue" (*Structures*, 143).

watches, enraptured, a spaniel steals one of Philoclea's gloves, and taking up the chase he finds the dog's master Amphialus couched nearby in the grass. As soon as Zelmane realizes he is in the presence of a rival, he draws his sword and in a "witty fury" wounds the melancholy knight in the thigh. Afterward he is self-righteous: "Truly I am sorry for your hurt, but yourself gave the cause" (293). The comedy of the scene is that Amphialus's crime of voyeurism (if in fact he has been watching, which he denies) is shared by his punisher; Zelmane's fury displaces a proper shame at his own conduct, and spares him the sting of his own conscience.

Amphialus is a comical scapegoat. What makes the scene more than a joke about Pyrocles's double standard is a curious and unexpectedly charged transposition from the original. As he watches Philoclea disrobe, Zelmane sings to himself a blazon of his beloved's charms: "What tongue can her perfections tell, / In whose each part all pens may dwell?" The song—winkingly prurient in the manner of such exercises—comes to his lips as though it were dictated by Philoclea's beauty. Zelmane "(but as an organ) did only lend utterance" (287), and responsibility for his own appetites is once again gracefully shifted from the young prince's shoulders. But this song has a history. Sidney had last transcribed it in the manuscript of the old *Arcadia*, where it appears in the midst of the scene of Philoclea's seduction. There its relation to the hero's intentions is even more coyly oblique: as he "laid her on her bed . . . there came into his mind a song the shepherd Philisides had in his hearing sung," whereupon follow 122 lines of verse, and then the narrator's concession, "But do not think, sweet ladies, his thoughts had such leisure as to run over so long a ditty; the only general fancy of it came into his mind."[41] The song turns out to be a curtain hung decorously between the reader and the lovers' consummation, deflecting our gaze from the moral crux of the book. Its transposition into the little scene by the riverside suggests that the same dynamics of evasion and exculpation are at stake. Now, however—with this history in mind—Amphialus seems not only to draw off blame for an episode of playful

41. Sidney, *Old Arcadia*, 207, 211., ed. Duncan-Jones. The poem seems to have been generally overdetermined for Sidney: Ringler observes that he "worked over this poem more carefully than he did any of his other pieces, for the considerable variations among the 13 substantive texts show that he added to or revised it on at least four different occasions." Ringler also notes that it was "copied or quoted . . . more frequently than any of his other verses," appearing in many manuscript anthologies, in Puttenham, and so on (*The Poems of Sir Philip Sidney*, 410). Clare Kinney reads this whole episode in relation to the Actaeon myth in "The Masks of Love: Desire and Metamorphosis in Sidney's New Arcadia," concluding that "Sidney's revisionary Ovidianism proffers the reader a competing vision of the 'heroic' lover as a concupiscent and only partially redeemed Actaeon" (471).

voyeurism, but to protect the new Pyrocles against the gravest sins of the old. He exists so the original scene need not be replayed.

———————

Sidney's sister Mary was one of a very few sixteenth-century readers who could have reconstructed a story like this: the old *Arcadia* was not published until the twentieth century. She read the manuscripts of both old and new, and patched them together (minus the seduction scenes) for the edition of 1593. For the modern reader, with both texts to hand, my hypothesis about the motives of the revision is intended to demonstrate another way in which a methodical impulse shaped its text, as a scaffold of its new epic self-respect. Just as Strephon and Claius separate out idealism from the princes, so Amphialus takes over the threat of amorous coercion. The princes retain both traits in some degree, but they move in a narrower moral territory, now bounded on both sides, and their heroism is accordingly more sure. The same methodical distinction-making that creates an analytic field of political and amorous types around them—that gives the *Arcadia* its new scope and heft—constricts the range of their significance, refining them toward less problematic roles.

Amphialus helps define the princes' heroism in other ways, too. He provides Pyrocles and Musidorus with occasion to demonstrate their bravery by provoking the Iliadic siege in the third book: they can do battle with a daemon of the very impulses that tarnished their exemplarity in the first version. But this does not mean that internal conflict is altogether analyzed out of the moral landscape of the new *Arcadia*. Amphialus himself is represented as profoundly self-divided and un-self-knowing. Sidney puts the finest point on this problem when Cecropia, having engineered the kidnapping of Philoclea and the others, offers to release her captives. "No, good mother," he answers, "since she"—Philoclea—"is here, I would not for my life constrain presence, but rather would I die than consent to absence" (447). The specious balance of his reply smoothes the contradictions of his position: "presence" and "absence," "constrain" and "consent." The psychological phenomenon that a depth psychology would call repression or denial is in Sidney's hands a matter of rhetoric, and Amphialus hides himself from himself in the sophistry of his sentences.

This self-contradiction is writ large in his conduct at the siege itself. When he tourneys before the castle walls he is a paragon of chivalry: his conduct is faultlessly courteous, and his equipment is supremely elegant in conceit ("His armour was . . . of tawny and gold, but formed into the figure of flames darkened as when they newly break the prison of a smoky furnace" [496]). He lives in romantic hope, performing heroic feats at arms for the lady whose affections he would win. Behind these graceful performances, however, is a most unchivalric gift for realpolitik. His diplomatic overtures are unscrupulously sophistical, cynical distortions of resistance theory that "might hide indeed the foulness of his treason, and from true common-places fetch down most false applications" (452). There is a similar grim pragmatism in his treatment of his troops, "distributing each office as near as he could to the disposition of the person that should exercise it, knowing no love, danger nor discipline can suddenly alter an habit in nature" (455). This tension is made momentarily explicit when his old governor chastises him for his aristocratic self-indulgences in the tournament, pointing out "with persuasions mingled with reprehensions, that he would rather affect the glory of a private fighter than of a wise general" (495). The rift is exposed between the knight and the new man, the values of chivalry and of Machiavellian politics.[42] It is worth recalling how the Stoic ethos of the old *Arcadia* abhors self-division: "remember yourself" is its rallying cry. Amphialus can stand not only for unacceptable desires, but for the very divided self itself.

The new *Arcadia* can explain this self-division in terms of a contest between nature and nurture: Amphialus is the son of the arch-solipsist Cecropia, but he is raised by the good Timotheus, whose name (like that of Arthur's teacher Timon in *The Faerie Queene*) augurs honor. This is more of the quasi-allegorical thinking that enables the encyclopedia. But lest that scheme seem to govern the book altogether, let me tell a brief story. As a child, Amphialus forms a "friendship by education" (123) with Timotheus's son Philoxenus, who falls in love with Helen of Corinth. Philoxenus recruits Amphialus to woo Helen on his behalf, and of course Helen falls for the messenger, and Amphialus finds himself accused of treachery. In the duel that follows he wards the blows of his outraged friend, but a slip of the sword takes Philoxenus's life at just the unhappy moment that his father Timotheus arrives on the scene. Timotheus looks at his foster son and utters one broken sentence before he dies of grief: "Amphialus, Amphialus, have I—" (126). We are accustomed to thinking of Sidney's mastery in terms of his balanced periods and dazzling rhetorical structures. The psychological subtlety here, however, is all in the fracture of the question: Timotheus does not ask "did you," or "how could you," or "why," but instead, "have I." What could this mean?—if not that his

---

42. Sidney's correspondence with Languet testifies to his interest in Machiavelli; see *The Correspondence of Sir Philip Sidney and Hubert Languet*, 53, 60, 61–62, 78.

final thought is not anger or blame of Amphialus's *you*, but the question whether he himself had somehow failed the young man he was charged with bringing up. It is an extraordinary moment of paternal care, and an extraordinary usurpation, for with his dying breath Timotheus takes on himself responsibility for the scene. For a poet as concerned with the varieties of paternal tyranny as Sidney—not all of them by any means unkind—this usurpation cannot be unconsidered. He lodges in this story a little explanation of the Amphialus who cannot take responsibility for the circumstances in which he later finds himself, when his mother delivers to him his kidnapped beloved. His foster father Timotheus has preempted him.

I retell this story mostly in order to ease my own critical conscience: it is legible as a small, subtle cause, or at least contributing cause, of great events, and one must read backward from Amphialus's later exploits to understand the significance of that striking half-sentence. It is evidence, that is, of the subtlety of Sidney's narrative sensibility, and of how much more is going on in *Arcadia* than the encyclopedia can compass. The book works in many modes. But with that said, I hope that the construction of the character of Amphialus in his largest outlines—as a paragon of self-division—will still appear to be the function of a new distribution of virtues and vices among the central characters. As he stands for erotic coercion, so he stands for self-division itself, and the rest of the book and its characters are eased of those vices. He is a pillar of its method.

———

There is one more character central to the redrawing of the map of the old *Arcadia*, or better, to the way the old *Arcadia* is redrawn *as* a map. That is Cecropia herself. She is not to be found in the original, but she appears early in the revision when she writes a letter of apology to Basilius for the accidental release of the lion and bear who threaten the princesses in the first book—animals who were originally just part of the Arcadian surround. As the book continues, her baleful agency is more and more in evidence, as she orchestrates the kidnapping that sets in motion the events of the third book. Sidney finds her motives in the frustration of dynastic ambitions for her son, who was the heir apparent to aged Basilius before the King of Arcadia sired his two autumn daughters. She is full of Satanic sentence: "the fall is greater from the first to the second than from the second to the undermost" (446). Or perhaps Machiavellian: "what is done for your sake (how evil soever to others) to you is virtue" (444). Her posture in the book is pure solipsism, and she boasts that "there is no wisdom but in including both heaven and earth in oneself" (154). Her love for her son—she "confined all her love only unto him" (546)—threatens to swallow him up altogether into her inverted moral universe.

She is also a surprisingly frank apologist for sexual desire. She celebrates the joys of marriage when, trying to persuade Philoclea to grant her son's suit, she laments her own husband's death: "I . . . embrace the orphan-side of my bed which was imprinted by the body of my dear husband. . . . What shall I say of the free delight which the heart might embrace without the accusing of the inward conscience or fear of outward shame?" (460–61). Her candor takes a darker turn when she tells her son that women crave forcefulness, even violence, in a lover: "we think there wants fire, where we find no sparkles at least of fury" (533). She becomes, that is, a figure for erotic violence who can serve to uncomplicate even the ambivalent Amphialus. (Particularly important if Sidney planned, as seems likely, for her death to prepare the way for Amphialus's rebirth from his wounds and marriage to Helen.[43]) Not only does she take her place in the book's conceptual map as the apotheosis of unregulated desire, as both a female version of her son, and the root of her son's malefaction. She also becomes the *cause* of all the evil in the main plot. In the old *Arcadia* there is no central villain, only a cryptic providence that plays out the consequences of a series of mostly sympathetic errors. The revisionary analysis that the new *Arcadia* performs upon those older materials stipulates a single, radical origin. There is no single symptom more indicative of the book's methodical ambitions.[44]

As *radix malorum* Cecropia also illuminates aspects of the old design that the new *Arcadia* would stigmatize or purge from itself. She is, first of

---

43. The scene in which Cecropia tries to whet her son to ravishing Philoclea may even be a stillborn revolution for Amphialus. Her apology for rape—"'No' is no negative in a woman's mouth . . . we think there wants fire, where we find no sparkles at least of fury" (533); "show thyself a man; and believe me upon my word, a woman is a woman" (534)—is the equivalent of her speech on atheism to Pamela, an attack at the roots of his faith in courtly love. "Amphialus was about to answer her" (534), the narrator tells us, and who knows what that answer would have been? But he is interrupted by a last chivalric challenge, and goes off to his nearly fatal combat with Musidorus. The possibility of reform is left tantalizingly suspended.

44. Cause is the first of the topics of invention in Ramus's *Dialecticae Libri Duo*: see William Temple's 1584 edition, A8vff. Michael McCanles, in *The Text of Sidney's Arcadian World*, offers a different account of the origins of evil in the text: "Evil . . . is the consequence of attempts to escape the dialectical reciprocity that potentially informs all our actions, all our motivations and thoughts and judgments, regarding both ourselves and our relations with others" (40). His argument I think ignores the new *Arcadia*'s reductiveness, but attends to some countervailing complexities that my argument necessarily scants.

all, the character within the fiction most ambitious to organize the fiction. Not only does she loose the animals and arrange the kidnapping, but she stage-manages the elaborate horror shows that are designed to overcome the captives' resistance. In her directorial ambitions she is an unexpected heir of *The Lady of May*'s meddlesome schoolmaster Rombus. She is, moreover, also the book's most concerted teacher, the closest thing it has to a schoolmaster of its own. We first see her instructing the impressionable young Artesia, whom she "taught . . . to think that there is no wisdom but in including both heaven and earth in oneself; and that love, courtesy, gratefulness, friendship, and all other virtues are rather to be taken on than taken in oneself" (154). The language of pedagogy infuses her campaign in the castle, where her persuasions are twice called a "lesson" (465, 483) and her closely reasoned apology for atheism becomes the most protracted scene of instruction in the book. (Pamela turns the event into an unwelcome *disputatio* by taking up the other side with such righteous vigor.) When the princesses remain unswayed by these efforts, frustration finally drives her to corporal punishment: "matching violent gestures with mischievous threatenings, she having a rod in her hand . . . fell to scourge that most beautiful body" (551).[45] The rod is a classroom tool, and the whole sequence is a parody of humanist best intentions, devolving to the beatings so frequently deplored and so commonly practiced.

All of this is to say that the new *Arcadia* identifies schoolmasterly instruction—perhaps even personal instruction—with its arch-villain. At the same time, she is integral to the new way that the book teaches. One might ask of the old *Arcadia*, what is the root of evil? The answer, working backward through the story from the bleakness of the trial, would have to be something like Basilius's foolish abdication, or perhaps, on a more severe view, desire itself (Basilius's January lust for Gynecia's May, or even the princes' for the princesses, following the parodic structure I described in chapter 3). There is really no other way to get at the question than by trying to retrace patterns of causation, patterns that will not allow us to point an unwavering finger at any single character. The same question put to the main plot of the new *Arcadia* can be answered with a name: Cecropia. The cause of evil, the *radix malorum*, is one term in the synchronic encyclopedia that is

---

45. On the rod as an instrument of classroom punishment see Stewart, *Close Readers*, 93–94. As many humanists feared, this punishment comes to be a pleasure in itself for the sadistic schoolmaster: "Cecropia employing her time in using like cruelty upon Pamela, her heart growing not only to desire the fruit of punishing them but even to delight in the punishing them" (553). See Erasmus, *De Pueris Instituendis* (*Works*, 26:326–28), and chapter 6.

the book's cast of major and minor characters. (The new *Arcadia*, or at least this way of reading the new *Arcadia*, makes the strongest contrast with the "inexplicit causation" of *The Faerie Queene*.) In this double sense, then—by embodying personal instruction, and by providing a kind of anchor to the schema of the book's ethical and political knowledge—Cecropia is pivotal to the new method of encyclopedic instruction to which Sidney commits his story.

———

One could once again describe the difference at stake here as between narrative understanding and paradigmatic understanding, where method becomes a way of generating and organizing an elaborate, schematic paradigm. The new *Arcadia* seems to align personal instruction with the person of the storyteller when it turns its back on the structure of the old: certainly it jettisons them both together. We are now in a position to understand better the one significant character who is actually subtracted from the exfoliating revision, the narrator himself. In the old *Arcadia* he is a recurring presence, whether reflecting on his own storytelling ("alas, sweet Philoclea, how hath my pen forgotten thee") or rendering sudden judgment ("so evil a ground doth evil stand on").[46] There is no such voice in the new *Arcadia*. Some of the burden is assumed by the characters: Kalendar takes over the description of Arcadia that introduced the narrator in the original, and most of the second book is a thicket of quotation marks, stories within stories. The rest is told in a mostly neutral third person that dominates the last book in particular. The implications of the work's new polyvocality are locally inconsistent: sometimes the storyteller matters a great deal, sometimes not.[47] But the overall effect is that there is no longer a single, personal, not to say teacherly authority behind the whole. The new *Arcadia* has a new objectivity.

46. Sidney, *Old Arcadia*, 95, 230, ed. Duncan-Jones. The latter quotation comes from the narrator's wrathful invocation of "The everlasting justice" at the beginning of the fourth book.

47. Compare, for example, Pyrocles explaining why he had to leave off combat with Anaxius to succor Dido, with the princesses' largely uninflected narratives of Plangus and Erona. S. K. Heninger, in his book *Sidney and Spenser: The Poet as Maker*, studies the narration of the new *Arcadia* closely with an eye toward describing the disappearance of an "evident narrator" (490). See pp. 490–93 for his useful account of how the narrative burden is reassigned in the revision. His concern is primarily with Sidney as an image-maker, and he treats the disappearance of the narrator as an artistic triumph in the development of "a poetics of self-justifying images . . . by the end of the revised fragment of *Arcadia* the author has slain himself in order to license the reader" (497). My claim is in some ways similar: that the author has slain himself to escape the burden of teaching, giving over his book to the authority of its method.

The End of Teaching

Back in the old *Arcadia*, before the trial begins, the princes Pyrocles and Musidorus have an opportunity to reflect on the events that have brought them to their prison cell and on the fate that awaits them. The reckoning is notably abstract. Musidorus wonders what their adventures will amount to in an afterlife where they will be deprived of their senses: what if "memory likewise fails (which riseth out of them), and then is there left nothing but the intellectual part or intelligence which, void of all moral virtues (which stand in the mean of perturbations) doth only live in the contemplative virtue and power of the omnipotent God"? Will they remember what has happened to them, or even recognize each other? Pyrocles answers confidently:

> Neither do I think we shall have such a memory as now we have, which is but a relic of the senses, or rather a print the senses have left of things past in our thoughts; but it shall be a vital power of that very intelligence which, as while it was here it held the chief seat of our life, and was as it were the last resort to which of all our knowledges the highest appeal came, and so by that means was never ignorant of our actions . . . it cannot but be a right intelligence (which is both his name and being) of things both present and past, though void of imagining to itself anything, but even grown like to his creator, hath all things with a spiritual knowledge before it.[48]

This is a philosophical debate between a roughly Aristotelian account of memory (founded in the senses) and a Christianized Platonism. It is also a proleptic rinsing-clean of the young men's complicated and compromising history in Arcadia. When Pyrocles tries to commit suicide in Philoclea's chamber, it is in order to "escape from myself," and his account of the next world has some of the same promise of release from heteronymy.[49] There will be no more trouble from the senses. The princes will be reborn into the afterlife. The prison exchange—which never descends to consider their own conduct—is one of the best arguments that they don't learn much in the old *Arcadia*. In this weakness, however, lies one of the book's remarkable strengths: its heroes' deficit in self-knowledge is an ambitious provocation to the reader.

Arcadia is itself reborn. There is no indication that Sidney intended to leave any evidence of a prior version. (In the next chapter I will want to

---

48. Sidney, *Old Arcadia*, 322, ed. Duncan-Jones.
49. Ibid., 253.

contrast this strategy with the second part of *The Faerie Queene*, which continues where the first left off.) Still, as I have argued throughout, the book has a memory. The revision takes a peculiar kind of responsibility for its unconfessed original, conserving but redistributing its elements according to procedures I have identified with Sidney's interest in method, particularly Ramist method. The result is that *Arcadia* lays across its plot a far wider field of ethical and political knowledge, and simultaneously, that it straitens its characters so that they may better fit into that schema. In many ways this methodical expansion could be thought of as an extension, even a redemption, of Sidney's original preoccupation with sententiousness. There is an impersonality to *sententiae*: they can be spoken by anyone, anywhere, at any time, with equal verity. What I have described as the new *Arcadia*'s encyclopedia—the structure of knowledge that undergirds its narrative—is a new, more systematic way of organizing their wisdom, almost like a grand commonplace book. If Phrygia is tyranny born of fear, one can look to his pages to find that "accusing sycophants, of all men, did best sort" with the tyrant's nature, or that "there is no humour to which impudent poverty cannot make itself serviceable" (265). The new architecture of Sidney's epic romance makes a safer house for the maxim, according it a new respect as knowledge, a kind of knowledge that is beyond the contamination of such perjured and self-contradictory speakers as the old *Arcadia*'s narrator.

It is that objectivity—to import a word Sidney would never have used—that may be the most important effect of the methodical impulse. Ramus and his adherents aspired to an impersonality and schematization of knowledge that may not look quite like what we call "objective," but is well along the way. Ong's claim that this impersonality came specifically at the expense of the authority of oratory, and the person of the speaker, remains convincing. So much knowledge in *Arcadia* does not have a speaker; it is not a component of a persuasive argument so much as a place on a comprehensive map, where virtues and vices, their causes and effects, are laid out alongside one another so that the reader may see the matter whole. This laying-out is a kind of teaching, to be sure. In many ways the Ramist program is the perfection of the humanist idea that the natural form of knowledge is the form in which it is best taught. But it is a kind of teaching that does not demand a teacher. The old *Arcadia* betrays a Sidney profoundly ambivalent about assuming that role, a role to which he understands the very taking up of his pen to bind him: the book agonizes about its own instructive authority. In the revision he finds a way of escaping from himself.

It should be said again: when I insist in the authority of the methodical order of the work—the overall influence of the concept, and the instances where we can see in x-ray its very roots and branches—there is much in the intricacy of its plot and imagery that I fail to capture. (The little story of Amphialus's grief can stand for that abundant surplus.) My argument moves in a direction opposite that which most modern critics, myself included, generally prefer, insofar as I assert the authority of a coherent, ideological structure over the welter of detail that might call it into question. Critics of our moment love best to unsettle structures, and for this there are good reasons. But the availability of the text of the old *Arcadia* for comparison puts us in an unusual position, because we can see the direction in which Sidney himself was moving, the new order that he imposed over the materials of his original fiction. The methodizing of the text—its preparation to greet the reader who approaches it with methodical tools—may be far from complete. But I have tried to demonstrate that fundamental aspects of the new book, including aspects inseparable from its ambitions as epic, have a shape that is the shape of methodical thinking—and perhaps more to the point, of methodical reading. It greets the Ramist reader with open arms.

There is, however, some cost to this innovation. In chapter 3 I described an old *Arcadia* preoccupied with the way its readers had been trained. Everything turns there on the trope of *sententia*, a trope so woven into the texture of the book that to condemn it is to offer up the book itself as sacrifice. Sidney's ultimate discomfort with teaching—his refusal to do it, his bewilderment about what else a book could do—is expressed in a fiction that achieves its greatest power by the deliberate surrender of its didactic authority. With the new *Arcadia*, Sidney, a little older, a little more successful in the world, is looking to pay greater honor to an imperative that had previously seemed so irredeemable. Amidst the enthusiasms of his circle, he may have felt himself astride a transformation in how teaching works, the transformation promised by method. He brought its principles to bear in remaking his "idle toy," and the encyclopedia that results is in so many ways a success. The writing remains brilliant, the pictorial surface gleams even more brightly, and underneath it all is a new didactic skeleton for the new reader of his moment. But the book lacks that peculiar, self-dissecting courage of his first attempt. The new *Arcadia* figures out a new way to teach, a way its author could both endorse and from which he could absent himself. It extracts itself from the predicament he had shared with Lyly and Spenser, and it is somewhat poorer for it.

CHAPTER SIX

Punishment

I played my mayster a mery pranke or playe yesterdaye and therfore he
hathe thaught me to synge a newe songe to daye.... The more instantly that
I prayed hym to pardon me the faster he layed upon.... He hath thaught me
a lesson that I shall remembre whyles I lyve.[1]

The schoolboy speaker of these lines—a stock character in the especially
minor genre of the grammar exercise—hails us from Robert Whittington's
Vulgaria of 1520, and his real-life counterparts across England were put to
translating his complaint: *heri dolosum preceptori ludum lusi.*[2] They worked
on pain of like treatment. When Roger Ascham looks back at textbooks
like Whittington's, it is hard to say which he deplores more, the jocu-
lar violence of this little scene or its "butcherly" Latin.[3] He and his humanist fellow travelers sought to reform the two together. But the boy's
expression—"he hath thaught me a lesson"—is a good deal older than Whittington, and it long outlives the efforts of the reformers and their gospel of
"play and pleasure."[4] It points to an idea deep enough to call an intuition,
then and now: that punishment is not just an instrument of order in the
classroom, but is itself a mode of instruction; that beating is a kind of
teaching.

1. Stanbridge and Whittington, *The Vulgaria of John Stanbridge and the Vulgaria of Robert
Whittington,* ed. White, 89.
2. Note the transposition from "mery" to *dolosum*: in Latin, one sees things for what they
really are.
3. Ascham, *Schoolmaster,* 14. Mary Thomas Crane discusses the politics of the vulgaria by
Whittington and Stanbridge in *Framing Authority,* 81–86; see also Stewart, *Close Readers,* 95–98.
Cf. Ong's "Latin Language Study as a Renaissance Puberty Rite."
4. Ascham, *Schoolmaster,* 6.

The 1596 *Faerie Queene,* and particularly its last two books, wrestles with that equation. So will this chapter; for punishment fits all too well into the didactic problems that I have been unfolding, in a way that almost suggests it could be paradigmatic. Whittington's little scene, for example, has a familiar double aspect. First, there is the lesson it teaches to its victim, who actually suffers the blows. (Whittington doesn't spare details of the beating, any more than his schoolmaster spares the child.) Second, there is a lesson for the audience that watches the scene, whether in the imaginary schoolroom where the beating takes place or in the real schoolrooms where the sentences were read. This doubleness offers a particularly stark version of a problem to which this study has returned again and again, the relation between the representation of the scene of instruction inside a poem, among its characters, and the poem's didactic designs on its readers. It returns us as well to Spenser's dark suggestion that learning by example must come at the example's expense.

Here too is the question I have described as constitutive of the scene of instruction: *how do I know you understand?* And as urgent as it is in the classroom, it may be more so in the public square. When a criminal is punished in public, what is at stake in his understanding—or submission—is whether or not he will repeat his crime. It is not enough to rely on time to unfold the banal chronicle of his reformation. There is pressure to construct a scene that can give evidence then and there that he has learned his lesson, and this imperative makes punishment a great arena of symbol-making. A certain exhibition is presumably made of Whittington's schoolboy, humiliated in front of his classmates in the long hall. Public justice outside the schoolroom walls could be much more intricate and imaginative: take for example a pair of deceitful coal merchants, condemned in 1553 to ride through the streets of London facing backward on their horses, with bags of coal around their necks.[5] Continue along this spectrum and you will eventually reach Spenser's extortionate Munera, complicit in a bad tax levied on passing knights by her sarazin father. Her golden hands and silver feet are nailed up on a post "that all might them behold" (5.2.26).

As it moves from Justice to Courtesy, from Book V to Book VI, *The Faerie Queene* worries the question of how much of its teaching falls under this punitive shadow. A brief glimpse of Munera is enough to suggest how central allegory is to that problem: when Talus makes his quasi-crucifix of

---

5. This scene is described by Martin Ingram in "Shame and Pain: Themes and Variations in Tudor Punishments," in Devereaux and Griffiths, eds., *Penal Practice and Culture, 1500–1900: Punishing the English,* 42.

her gleaming members, the penalty and the emblem are one and the same. Book V's interest in public justice moves this interrogation of the poem's allegorical mode further away from the precincts of the schoolroom, and in general this chapter will follow it. But not without looking back; for such questions are never altogether distant from pedagogy in the Elizabethan imagination. Roger Ascham begins *The Schoolmaster* by recounting a memorable meal at Windsor in 1563, when the court was taking refuge from the plague in London. William Cecil, playing host at dinner to a most distinguished company, relates the "strange news brought me . . . this morning, that divers scholars of Eton be run away from the school for fear of beating." A debate is joined, with William Petre vouching that "the rod only was the sword that must keep the school in obedience and the scholar in good order." Nicholas Wotton, like Petre a member of the Privy Council, counters that "the schoolhouse should be indeed . . . the house of play and pleasure, and not of fear and bondage." The argument goes back and forth among the most powerful men in England, with Ascham deferentially opining that "children were sooner allured by love than driven by beating to attain good learning." But the old Etonian Walter Haddon sides with Petre in declaring that "the best schoolmaster of our time was the greatest beater."[6] Haddon's remark could be formulated as an axiom, and it is that axiom that Spenser sets out to test.

The Lessons of Poetic Justice

That test extends over the last two books of 1596; the stakes are not just the fate of instruction in various of its forms, but the possibility that a character can change, or that we fallen mortals can reform ourselves. It will all end with courtesy, and the equivocal triumph of Calidore, but it begins, unsurprisingly, with a crime. In canto i of Book V, Arthegal, the Knight of Justice, comes upon the headless body of a lady, beside whom kneels a weeping squire. The young man is the obvious suspect, but he maintains that the lady was slain by a passing knight—her own knight, in fact, who cast her off in favor of the squire's beloved and has ridden away with his new prize. Arthegal sends Talus in pursuit and the iron man returns shortly with the malefactor, whose name is Sanglier. Now that the two suspects face each other, it is a squire's word against a knight's, and Arthegal must resort to a bit of trickery to get to the truth: he offers to divide the surviving

---

6. Ascham, *Schoolmaster*, 6–7. There is some disagreement over who in particular is meant to be the "greatest beater": see Lawrence Ryan's note on p. 7.

lady in half, and when the horrified squire surrenders his claim, Sanglier's bloodthirstiness is made plain. Talionic justice—an eye for an eye—would cost the knight his own head. Arthegal, however, has something different in mind:

> And you, Sir Knight, that love so light esteeme,
> As that ye would for little leave the same,
> Take here your owne, that doth you best beseeme,
> And with it beare the burden of defame;
> Your owne dead Ladies head, to tell abrode your shame. (5.1.28)

For a year Sanglier is condemned to wear his lady's severed head about his neck. This bit of allegorical grotesquerie will make his shame known wherever he goes: the crime, and the responsibility for the crime, are now obvious.

Arthegal's Solomonic ingenuity is necessary because before the punishment was imposed, Sanglier looked like any other knight, in that damnably interchangeable armor that makes life so difficult in *The Faerie Queene*. Now, having been properly punished, he is *self-evidently* a murderer. His name may testify to his bloody nature, but it is not clear whether any of the characters know it, or can read it if they do; it is revealed only in an aside to the reader ("so cleeped was that Knight" [5.1.20]). What Arthegal has done in meting out his punishment is to produce an emblem legible in both registers, inside and outside the poem. That punitive action makes a useful contrast with the habits to which Guyon is trained up in Book II. There, the hero approaches experience as a set of discreet examples and learns to respect their boundaries, disciplined to a kind of study that forbids intervention. He is above all a reader. Arthegal, by contrast, gets involved, refashioning Sanglier as an emblem of his crime. The Knight of Justice is a full-blown allegory-maker. Chief among the principles of his making seems to be a kind of punitive decorum: the punishment fits the crime, both juridically and aesthetically, according to a law that later ages have come to call poetic justice. Such justice imposes an allegorical clarity where before there was only the moral ambiguity (or indifference) of armor, like the moral ambiguity (or indifference) of our natural bodies.

There are poets from whom Spenser could have learned about this kind of justice. We cannot be certain that he read Dante, but the *Inferno*, stocked as it is with spectacles of such suffering, is a *locus classicus* for the problem. The usurers make a good example: they are seated among the flames of the seventh circle, and "from the neck of each"—just like Sanglier—"hung a pouch, which had a certain color and a certain device, and thereon each seems to feast his eyes."[7] Dante the character does not recognize them, but the heraldic details of their devices have allowed scholars to place them in thirteenth-century Florence, as the poet surely intended: we would not otherwise remember Catello di Rosso Gianfigliazzi or Rinaldo Scrovegni. These usurers were once men, and the fact that they now mean only their crime—that they must mean, like Book II's Tantalus, without intending—is a part of their suffering. Ovid, too, tells such stories, and is a far more obvious influence on Spenser. Take Arachne, turned to a spider for daring to challenge Minerva at weaving. The goddess curses the upstart with the words, "Live on, indeed, wicked girl, but hang thou still; and let this same doom of punishment [*lexque eadem poenae*] . . . be declared upon thy race, even to remote posterity."[8] Poetic justice again, for the new arachnid is condemned forever to spin out testimony to the particular form of her hubris: Minerva interweaves the crime and the sentence of death by hanging.

But Spenser could just as well have learned this lesson on the streets of London. If the phrase "poetic justice" has no currency before the late seventeenth century, it may be because there was no thought yet that such spectacles might ever be relegated to poetry.[9] As an infant, in 1553, Spenser might well have been carried past those cheating coal merchants, who had the stuff of their crimes hung once again around their necks, and who faced the horse's tail to signify their recalcitrance to good order. Both the sacks and the posture—sometimes criminals were instructed to hold the horse's tail in their hands—were familiar tropes of penal practice. In those years, and especially in the early century, poisoners might be condemned to be boiled alive in water or in lead, inverting and exposing the secret operation of their poison. A slanderous pamphleteer might have his writing hand cut off. (John Stubbs, whose name seems to have condemned him to a

---

7. Dante, *Inferno*, 17.55–57. The identifications are suggested in Singleton's notes.

8. Ovid, *Metamorphoses*, 6.136–38.

9. Michel Foucault's *Discipline and Punish* takes as its chief problem how punishment "gradually ceased to be a spectacle" (9) as the Enlightenment penal program across Europe moved it out of the public eye. He quotes Giambattista Vico's observation that the early modern period featured an "entire poetics" (45) of punishment; his own account of the panoptic prison makes much of the contrast with that old regime. J. A. Sharpe is guarded about the applicability of Foucault's story to England, but ventures that "there does seem to have been a decline in officially ordered and enforced shaming punishments. In 1478, for example, one William Campion was found guilty in London of tapping a conduit and diverting the water into his own well. He was ordered to be paraded through the streets of the city on a horse, 'with a vessel like unto a conduit full of water upon his head. . . . ' It is a little difficult to imagine the London authorities ordering this sort of punishment in the eighteenth century" ("Civility, Civilising Processes, and the End of Public Punishment in England," 225–26).

life of allegory, was one such.[10]) And there was an arsenal of placards and costumes in regular use, written in a language that a Londoner would not have to be literate to read. Punishment—along with the old pageants and the spectacle of royal processions—was part of the city's education in allegory.

The general notion that such punishments carried lessons was a commonplace: trial records testify to the ambition to "stey, reforme or w[i]t[h]drawe" wrongdoers "from their detestable & devylysshe vice & synfull lyfe" by shame and pain.[11] There are also subtler effects—and, for the justicers, advantages—to parading the criminal as the image of his crime. They are held up for scrutiny in one of the period's emblem books, Geffrey Whitney's 1586 *Choice of Emblemes*:

From Geoffrey Whitney, *A Choice of Emblemes* (London, 1586), fol. F1r. Reproduced by permission of The Huntington Library, San Marino, California, RB 79714 p. 41.

10. Stubbs was punished for writing against Elizabeth's proposed French marriage in 1579; later the same year Spenser chose to publish his *Shepheardes Calendar* with Stubbs' printer, Hugh Singleton, a decision that has been interpreted as a show of sympathy. See Lane, *Shepheards Devises*, 59–60.

11. Ingram, "Shame and Pain," in *Penal Practice*, ed. Devereaux, 48. See also Briggs, ed., *Crime and Punishment in England*, esp. 73–80, and Sharpe, *Judicial Punishment in England*, 18–27. Susan Amussen discusses the meaning of violence generally, including its public didactic functions, in "Punishment, Discipline, and Power: The Social Meanings of Violence in Early Modern England": see especially her discussion of "the symbolic language of popular shaming rituals" (9).

The legend above Whitney's image is *poena sequens*, "punishment follow-ing," and the emblem (as some subsequent verses explain) portrays a thief who has stolen a sack of meat. He takes his rest outside a tavern with his ill-gotten gains slung, once again, around his neck, and he is strangled by the burden in his sleep. The revenging sack even looks something like a big plucked chicken. *Sequor* is an important verb here, carrying as it does a sense of logical necessity, the steps of a proof ("it follows that"). And indeed no contingent, human authority is involved in this punishment. It seems to arise naturally out of the crime itself, in a world where such retribution must be inevitable: there is a providence that shapes our ends, and shapes them with a certain macabre elegance. The aesthetic satisfaction of seeing a thief strangled by his loot—not the loftiest of such satisfactions, perhaps, but still artful—reinforces our satisfaction in the justice done. In fact, these two satisfactions can be a little hard to tell apart.

And so it is with the coal-cumbered colliers, or the boiled poisoners, or the spider-weaver Arachne. Poetic justice convinces us that we live in a world that has the power to regulate itself. Even where the apparatus of human justice must bring the punishment about, the punishment itself is fit, inevitable, natural. Its potent decorum affords another lesson, too. Any criminal punished in a manner that symbolically invokes the nature of his crime will look guilty; he has the evidence of his infraction around his neck. This may be the greatest benefit to the punisher, that the righ-teousness of the punishment is made self-evident by the act of punishing. The criminal is made to mean his crime. By what ought perhaps to be a troubling short-circuit, it is as though the *punishment* itself could now be entered into the *evidence* for the judgment, looping back to the beginning of the process to assure us, and assure any spectators, that we have the right man.

With this reversal in mind—the afterness of punishment becoming the be-foreness of evidence—let us loop back again to *The Faerie Queene*, and to the next of Arthegal's adventures, his encounter with Pollente and Munera. Along with Sanglier's, this episode sets the terms for the rest of the book's encounter with punishment. Pollente is a sarazin who exacts an unjust toll from all travelers who cross his bridge, and Arthegal impales his "blasphe-mous head" on a pole "Where many years it afterwards remayned, / To be a mirrour to all mighty men" (5.2.19). So far, so good; his daughter Munera is next. It is she who profits from her father's extortions, and her "golden hands and silver feete" (10) transform the "gift" promised by her name into graft. Arthegal finds her, appropriately enough, hiding under a heap of gold in her father's house, and he hands her over to Talus:

> Yet for no pitty would he change the course
> Of Justice, which in *Talus* hand did lye;
> Who rudely hayld her forth without remorse,
> Still holding up her suppliant hands on hye,
> And kneeling at his feete submissively.
> But he her suppliant hands, those hands of gold,
> And eke her feete, those feete of silver trye,
> Which sought unrighteousnesse, and justice sold,
> Chopt off, and nayld on high, that all might them behold.
>
> Her selfe then tooke he by the sclendar wast,
> In vaine loud crying, and into the flood
> Over the Castle wall adowne her cast,
> And there her drowned in the durty mud:
> But the streame washt away her guilty blood.
> Thereafter all that mucky pelfe he tooke,
> The spoile of peoples evill gotten good,
> The which her sire had scrap't by hooke and crooke,
> And burning all to ashes, powr'd it downe the brooke. (5.2.26–27)

On the face of it, this punishment too has the poetic fitness we are beginning to expect. Like all the "mucky pelfe" of her father's trade, Munera is consigned to the mud of the river, from which all those riches were presumably once dug. But this time, Spenser probes just a bit more thoroughly how Arthegal's justice works. There is, for example, the "sclendar wast" at the beginning of stanza 27: one had not had to think of what connected those golden hands and silver feet up to that moment, but she is given an unallegorical middle, a surprising and touching detail that might almost be felt in the crook of an arm before she is gone from the poem for good.[12] The allegory of justice struggles to contain this brief, humane rupture in its prosecutorial rigor. The rude mercy of the stream, which seems to be rinsing her clean rather than flushing her away, conspires in this reproach.

---

12. The phrase might be folded back into the parable of greed—a hoarder, she wastes little—but such a move seems weak against the phrase's visceral impression. Spenser remains interested in the trouble caused by touch: when Talus shoulders his next victim off a cliff, they stand for a strange moment "cheeke by cheeke" (5.2.49), like the song says.

In the pause such details give we can recognize Munera as an exhibition in poetic justice as a process: we get to watch, even half-feel, the new allegory being imposed upon her. As Danielle Allen argues, "any punishment is not a single final moment of execution but, and more important, an *unfolding drama about the attempt to establish a final moment as authoritative.*"[13] That drama or process is completed when an emblem is left behind, those hands and feet "Chopt off, and nayld on high" (5.2.26) to serve as a monument on the razed plain. The lesson of the emblem itself is ominously obscure: is it a threat of dismemberment? A précis and parody of a Catholic crucifix? We know only that it is the sole sign left of what has transpired: the castle has been leveled "That there mote be no hope of reparation, / Nor memory thereof to any nation" (28). The deeper lesson of the process, as the narrative has tracked it, may be that allegory itself can devolve so readily to a species of punishment. Gordon Teskey has written about the violence at allegory's origin: the idea that it is built to conceal the moment of "capture" "in which the materials of narrative are shown being actively subdued for the purpose of raising a structure of meaning."[14] It is the power of justice to render that capture orthodox. The allegorical agent is convicted of and sentenced to its nature, and its guilt is newly written all over its face.

Sanglier's punishment says "murderer." Munera's punishment touches what we might think of as the lower limit of allegory: pure resistance, utter darkness, meaning as a broken promise. If Pollente's severed head is a "mirrour" to all mighty men, his daughter's fate leaves that didactic trope behind, crossing over into mere threat. This is the danger that the Book of Justice obliges itself to explore: that such punishments leave out the middle—that slender waist—and fold the end into the beginning, proclaiming their justice self-evident and unquestionable. Poetic justice is a species of punishment that has evolved from instruction, from the teaching mission of public exhibitions, but that reaches its limit in a spectacle with no lesson but the power of the punisher. The question that is framed here in all but words goes beyond whether instruction must come at the expense of characters. It is whether all instruction—or whether the only truly effective instruction—is a kind of punishment.[15] Book V has other quarry to hunt as

13. D. S. Allen, *The World of Prometheus*, 34.

14. Teskey, *Allegory and Violence*, 23.

15. Ullrich Langer's "The Renaissance Novella as Justice" depicts the Renaissance novella—Ascham's Italian tales, another tributary of romance—as a kind of fiction with a knack for bringing about just outcomes: "What ends well is . . . what is *banal*: the exchanges in a novella reinforce sociability, reinforce what is normal or should be normal" (318). They describe societies, that is, with a knack for regulating themselves without or in spite of the impositions

it proceeds, but this reproach does not go away over the succeeding cantos, and it will find no concerted answer until Book VI.

Back to School

Spenser works out that answer by recourse to courtesy, and to a kind of pedagogical nostalgia that harkens back *before* both Irish politics and humanist schoolrooms to the chivalric traditions of aristocratic training. In those old ways he hopes to find a different kind of teaching. Before following his thinking into that idealized past, however, fairness demands one more consultation with the reformers of his own time. Their answer to that question—whether all teaching is punishment—is emphatically *no*. Roger Ascham is famous for insisting that the schoolroom should be a "sanctuary against fear," where students are drawn on to learning by "playing and pleasure."[16] In this he follows such ancient authorities as Quintilian and Plutarch, and he is in harmony with almost all of the theorists of his century: disapproval of teaching by beating is virtually constitutive of humanism as a pedagogical movement. There is a particular current of outrage at gratuitous punishment. Erasmus tells with disgust the story of visiting a schoolmaster who whipped a pupil to the point of fainting, then turned to his learned guest and said, "'He did not do anything to deserve this, but he simply had to be humbled'—yes, 'humbled' [*humiliandus*] was the word he used."[17] Mulcaster, who did not altogether spare his pupils, agrees: no child should ever fear "the rod, which he will not deserve."[18] This sort of thing, Erasmus says, will lead a boy "to harden himself [*indurescit*] to a state of utter wickedness."[19] In this idea of hardening there is perhaps a hint of the emblem-making, or at least example-making, that is such an undersong of suffering in allegory.

The reformers' fears about what would happen to boys who were subjected to excessive punishment had a characteristic name, and it was slavery—a refrain from the Classical rhetoricians forward. Quintilian warns of it (beating is "fit only for slaves and undoubtedly an insult"), as does Plutarch ("punishment is meter for villaynes and slaves than for them that

---

of official authority (like Jonson's *Bartholomew Fair*, after his *Volpone*). Spenser, Sidney, and Lyly all have some truck with this tradition, but do not share its self-confidence.

16. Ascham, *Schoolmaster*, 38, 32.

17. Erasmus, *De Pueris Instituendis*, in *Works*, 26:327.

18. Mulcaster, *Positions*, 39.   19. Erasmus, *Works*, 26:328.

be francke or of gentill bloud," in Elyot's translation).[20] Vives deplores the boy who "is of such a disposition that he has to be incited to his duty by blows, like a slave," and Mulcaster insists that "learners be no slaves" to punishing masters.[21] The curriculum taught in the schools and carried forward into the universities was after all widely known as the *artes liberales*, the liberal arts, the arts proper to a free man. The recurring warnings about enslaving the child tapped a general anxiety about the unfreedom of the schoolroom. Vives admits the necessity of beating "since the mind is misled by passions," but he tries to draw a distinction: "I should prefer this beating to be done as amongst free men, not harshly or as among slaves."[22] The reformers' interest in teaching boys Stoic self-mastery demanded that there be a difference.

What substitute did they offer for the mastery of the rod? The pedagogy unfolded over the last five chapters is one answer, but the most explicit alternative was love.[23] Ascham not only uses words like "lead," "draw," and "persuade" to describe good teaching, but explains that those boys will flourish in school who "love learning," and it is the schoolmaster's work to cultivate that delight.[24] As Mulcaster puts it: "we do the children wrong in those tender years to plant any hatred, when love should take roote, and learning grow by liking."[25] Love was a vital part of the reformers' vocabulary. It had to be distinguished, of course, from pederasty—a problem that receives a certain amount of ginger commentary in the literature—and from the eros of punishment itself.[26] Some rhetorical energy was likewise

---

20. Quintilian, *The Orator's Education*, 1.3.14; Elyot, *Education*, in *Four Tudor Books*, ed. Pepper, 30.

21. Vives, *Education*, 119; Mulcaster, *The First Part of the Elementarie*, 19.

22. Vives, *Education*, 119. This anxiety is also inevitably about the classroom as a microcosm of the nation, an autocracy where ancient republican texts were part of a promising young man's curriculum. William Harrison testifies to the importance to the English of their free commonwealth: "As for slaves and bondmen, we have none; nay, such is the privilege of our country by the especial grace of God and bounty of our princes that if any come hither from other realms, so soon as they set foot on land they become so free of condition as their masters" (*The Description of England*, 118). The problem of "the analogy . . . between the schoolroom and the state" (47) is surveyed by chapter 2 of Bushnell's *A Culture of Teaching*, "The Sovereign Master and the Scholar Prince"; on slavery in particular see 46–47.

23. Richard Halpern's *Poetics of Primitive Accumulation* makes the argument that the humanist rhetoric of play and pleasure is an attempt to "produce an active embrace of ideology rather than a passive acceptance" (28).

24. Ascham, *Schoolmaster*, 29.   25. Mulcaster, *Positions*, 36.

26. Lyly's rendering of Plutarch in the *Anatomy*'s "Euphues and His Ephebus" addresses the question of pederasty directly: "But the greatest thing is yet behind, whether that those are to be admitted as cockmates with children which love them entirely or whether they be to be

required to separate love of learning from the affection one might have for the wrong sort of book, say, a novella, or a romance, and from the feelings such a book might stir. Ascham praises Lady Jane Gray for taking up her Plato "with as much delight as some gentleman would read a merry tale in Boccaccio": she possesses what he calls, marvelously, a "deep knowledge of pleasure."[27] The eccentric Francis Clement, author of *The Petie Schole* (1587), seizes on the same problem: "literall erudition is as it were the key, that openeth the doore to the perfect viewe of vertue, and is chiefly obteined by a longing love, and lovyng longyng after it," he allows. But he means "bookelove . . . not lovebookes, which as they be the enemies of vertue, nources of vice, furtherers of ignorance, and hinderers of all good learnyng: so doe they expressly represent the ougly shape and disguised Image of that beastly, brutishe and furious love."[28]

All of which is to say that while the reformers may have scorned the carnal knowledges of romance, they were just as opposed to beating—or at least excessive beating—as a remedy for digressions from the curriculum's straight path. Here we will have to position Spenser a little differently than the poets in previous chapters. School was an undeniably violent place, but the men who wrote about it (as distinguished from the run of schoolmasters) offered as sharp a critique of punishment as any in *The Faerie Queene*. If their remedy has its own traces of nostalgia, insofar as they looked back to Rome to discover what to read, still they were pioneers of institutions that truly justified their association with what was called "the new learning": Tudor schools were different from anything England had seen before. Spenser shares their concern about brutality in instruction. He, however, looks more purely backward in the face of violence. Book VI is a

---

banished from them. . . . If any shall love the child for his comely countenance, him would I have to be banished as a most dangerous and infectious beast" (*Euphues*, 135). His "cockmates" and "the greatest thing is yet behind" temper his censure with an unexpected jocularity. When Elyot translates the same essay, however, as *The Education or Bringing Up of Children*, he omits this discussion altogether. See Stewart, *Close Readers*, esp. 98–109, as well as Ong, "Latin Language Study as a Renaissance Puberty Rite." Diagnosing the eros of punishment, Erasmus recounts some horrific abuses, and the pleasure taken in them, in his *De Pueris*: "So schools have become torture-chambers," he concludes: "you hear nothing but the thudding of the stick, the swishing of the rod, howling and moaning, and shouts of brutal abuse. Is it any wonder, then, that children come to hate learning?" (*Works*, 26:325).

27. Ascham, *Schoolmaster*, 36. A "deep knowledge of pleasure" has some of the same peculiarity as Wittgenstein's provocation, "I know I am in pain" (*Philosophical Investigations*, § 350).

28. Clement, *The Petie Schole*, in *Four Tudor Books*, ed. Pepper, 83–84. Note that once again, the trope of metamorphosis attaches itself to bad reading.

reactionary experiment, or an experiment in reaction, revolting against the brutality of Book V by harking back to the world of knights and squires, as though that old-style, prehumanist training could redeem the poem from the increasing depravity of its own allegorical instruction.

———————

The beginning of Book VI brings a sense of starting over: going back to an origin where fundamental errors in the course might be corrected, even as if they had never happened. Such a new beginning is not particularly the spirit in which the 1596 *Faerie Queene* as a whole sets out. Sidney may have revised his *Arcadia*, effacing the original, but Spenser pressed ahead, carrying the story of Britomart and Arthegal forward with all of its baggage. Book VI would seem to be the moment when he thinks better of that strategy. Its cardinal virtue, courtesy, is a flower "on a lowly stalke" (6.pr.4), the fairest blossom in the "sacred noursery / Of vertue" (6.pr.3). That renewed potential is repeatedly figured in the person of a squire who is just starting out on his road to knighthood. At the start of canto i, one of these promising figures is in trouble, just as in Book V—this time, tied to a tree after his beloved has been stolen away. The villain is a seneschal in the employ of the lady Briana, who has ordered him to shear the beards and locks of all passing travelers. (She is making a mantle with the spoils to win the knight Crudor, who "Refused hath to yeeld her love againe" [6.1.15].) The poor squire has been left behind because he has no beard to give, as he explains to Calidore when the Knight of Courtesy discovers him in his embarrassing predicament:

> My haplesse case
> Is not occasiond through my misdesert,
> But through misfortune, which did me abase
> Unto this shame, and my young hope subvert,
> Ere that I in her guilefull traines was well expert. (6.1.12)

This emphasis on the squire's youth—his "young hope," his inexperience with misfortune, his ready shame—is not an altogether new note in the poem, but it acquires new importance in the sixth book's waxing mood of nostalgia. Calidore is especially attuned to threatened promise, and he promptly and courteously unties the captive. In fact, he unties him twice, once before the squire tells his story ("for no demaunds he staide, / But first him losde" [11]) and once after ("Eftsoones he loosd that Squire" [18])—an oddity to which I will want shortly to return. This deed twice done, the knight rides off to track the bad custom to its discourteous source.

The confrontation with Crudor that ensues allows Calidore to demonstrate the wily, opportunistic style of fighting characteristic of his cardinal virtue, and it leads to an unexpected result—one that sets up an important problem for the book as a whole. Crudor begs mercy; Calidore delivers a sententious sermon, advising him that "All flesh is frayle" (6.1.41) and so on; then Crudor repents, "And promist to performe his precept well" (43). The episode ends with general feasting, and the squire returns at the end of the canto to take possession of the castle, which Calidore confers upon him. What is so striking here to any experienced reader of *The Faerie Queene*—a revolution, really, in its allegorical practice—is the reform of Crudor. Recall the episode of Sanglier, so conspicuously Crudor's double. (Both episodes are first in their respective books; both begin with a crime reported by a squire.) Arthegal's success with Sanglier is a matter of marking him with the sign of his own villainy, a symbolic punishment that aligns his visual aspect with his name by hanging a bloody head around his neck. Justice consolidates the allegorical framework. Courtesy, it would seem, accomplishes the opposite. Crudor has a name like Ignaro's, here from the Latin *crudus* meaning raw, undigested, rough, cruel—the very incorrigible opposite of courtesy. And yet Calidore's genteel mercy seems adequate to convert him to the host of a hospitable table. Briana too is "wondrously now chaung'd, from that she was afore" (46), and the squire's new title to the castle confirms the promise of these new beginnings.

Book VI, it would seem, is a great time to be young. Calidore's kindness exemplifies the best of the apprenticeship system that is one of the pillars of chivalric romance, where young men are tutored by brave knights until they prove themselves worthy of their armor. To be sent as a youth to another noble household and trained up there in feats of arms as well as (sometimes) letters had been the traditional education of a nobleman before the rise of humanist schooling. This training was symbiotic with literary romance, which celebrated and perpetuated it, and which could even be part of its loose curriculum.[29] Ascham was reacting against such

---

29. The stories of Tristram, including the French prose *Tristan* (1215–35), the English *Sir Tristem* (fourteenth century), and a version by Malory, pay particular attention to the education of their heroes, and were read for their models of training. Nicholas Orme writes of the chain of these stories: "Right from the start, the Tristan writers established the romantic hero as a well-educated man, whose tutor and curriculum were worth mentioning as part of his story" (*From Childhood to Chivalry*, 83–84). Orme describes this household education in the first chapter of *From Childhood to Chivalry*; he also discusses the role of romances in this training (82–84). On

training when he wrote his *Schoolmaster* in the 1560s; it is one of the targets of his diatribe against experience, along with the newer institution of the Grand Tour, and he had plenty of company in his critique.[30] School was part of a concerted Elizabethan program to get these well-born young men out of the countryside and into the court's sphere of influence, while equipping them to be of practical service to the government. So when Spenser looks nostalgically backward to this older order—or at least, summons such nostalgia into his poem for scrutiny—he is not only casting back before the punishing instruction of Book V, as though a better tuition were to be found in chivalry, the gentler predecessor of the beating master. He is also looking to a chivalric instruction before humanism, in an effort to reconstitute another version of that elusive education by experience.

Under these traditional auspices, the Knight of Courtesy is as promising a teacher as we have seen in the poem. The next canto begins in hope with another exhibit of the old ways, when Calidore comes upon a "goodly youth of amiable grace"—a "slender slip" of a lad, in his lincoln green jacket "belayd with silver lace" (6.2.5)—who is fighting with a mounted knight. As Calidore watches, the boy fells the knight with a dart. When Calidore questions him about this breach of the law of arms, he explains that he intervened to prevent the knight's abuse of his own lady, and she corroborates the story. Calidore is delighted by the youth's courage and eloquence—"I never saw in any greater hope appeare" (26)—and his delight is redoubled when he learns of his noble birth. Tristram, as the youth is known, is son of King Meliogras of Cornwall, and he was sent away from home at the age of ten to be trained up

> with many noble feres
> In gentle thewes, and such like seemely leres.
> Mongst which my most delight hath alwaies been,
> To hunt the salvage chase amongst my peres,
> Of all that raungeth in the forrest greene (6.2.31)

---

household training generally and its persistence see also Simon, *Education and Society in Tudor England*, 333–53. On the influence of medieval romance on *The Faerie Queene*, see A. King, *The Faerie Queene and Middle English Romance: The Matter of Just Memory*.

30. As J. H. Hexter observes in "The Education of the Aristocracy in the Renaissance," "there was a great deal of complaint about the education of the aristocracy, and . . . with a few exceptions the Jeremiahs of the time were all saying pretty much the same thing. The well-born were ignorant, they were indifferent to learning, and they preferred to stay that way"; they were addicted to "dress, dining, drinking, and gadding about . . . hunting and hawking" (*Reappraisals in History*, 46). See also Alexander, *Growth of English Education*, 30, 185–207; Simon, *Education and Society*, 353–68.

This upbringing recalls the childhoods of characters like Satyrane and Arthegal, who grew up practicing on animals, but it differs in substituting for the tuition of a satyr-father or a goddess the bonhomie of the rural court. Tristram has been raised as a young aristocrat.

The word "hope" recurs like a mantra in describing this well brought up young man: "I never saw in any greater hope appeare" (6.2.26), "For the rare hope which in his yeares appear'd" (34), "In hope he sure would prove a doughtie knight" (36). It is hope not just for youth itself but for an older, better way of training the young. Calidore honors that optimism by making Tristram his squire, and when the youth kneels and swears fealty before his benefactor, the ancient, storied progress to knighthood is begun again. So far, so good for the new old curriculum of Book VI. Perhaps it is part of that curriculum for Calidore to refuse the new squire's request to accompany him on his adventures, charging him instead with protecting the dead knight's lady. Left behind in the forest, Tristram arms himself:

> But *Tristram* then despoyling that dead knight
> Of all those goodly implements of prayse,
> Long fed his greedie eyes with the faire sight
> Of the bright mettall, shyning like Sunne rayes;
> Handling and turning them a thousand wayes (6.2.39)

Now Tristram is a proper squire, taking up the tools of his calling. What to make, then, of that word "despoyling," as though he were a scavenger on the battlefield? Are these weapons best thought of as implements of praise (as opposed to war, or better, justice)? Why his "greedie," narcissistic fascination with their glittering surfaces? This is the first real dissonance in the book, and there is a key to its meaning back at that peculiar moment when Tristram's predecessor, the youth tied to the tree, is untied twice.

That odd double untying—setting the youth free both before and after his interrogation—captures a problem with courtesy itself, courtesy which by its nature extends its credit in advance. The narrative stutters because it cannot quite commit itself to this new open-handedness. Instead of just letting him go, Calidore *both* trusts the boy unconditionally *and* waits to hear his story, and the glitch lights up an unresolved conflict between the counsels of courtesy and of justice. In Book V, justice marks the criminal once the evidence is given and the case is tried: justice is patient and comes after. But we have also seen how the symbolic character of some punishments short-circuits that order, and the punishment (properly last) becomes part of the evidence (properly first). An analogous problem now arises for courtesy. Courtesy goes before, acting as though the world were itself already courteous in order to call that world into being. But its programmatic faith in first impressions can be called into question by extending the narrative just an extra beat, lingering to watch what Tristram does after the ceremony is over. It may not be courteous to wait for proof, but wisdom (even justice?) may recommend it.

And the glimpse we catch of Tristram's greedy eyes might make us wonder in turn: what would have happened if the narrative had stayed an extra stanza or two in Briana's castle, after Calidore left? Again and again in *The Faerie Queene* an emblem that consolidates a lesson is unraveled by the story. Now, at the start of the Book of Courtesy, it is as though romance digressiveness or even inattentiveness has been enlisted by courtesy in the *hope* that these lessons can abide. *Entrelacement*, the interweaving of the multiple plot, has become a subtle art of looking away at just the right moment. It is simply impolite to inquire closely, *do you understand?* Book V was preoccupied with the demand for proof after the fact. It is—or ought to be—the book of *after*, and its corruptions arise from a temptation to make the punishment into evidence for the crime. Book VI is concerned with polite trust, the faith in others that allows courtesy its unguarded, optimistic latitudes. It is, or ought to be, the book of *before*, extending forgiveness in advance. Its creeping anxiety about proof diagnoses some mistakes we may have made in reacting against the juridical harshness of its predecessor; the costs, not least in bad faith, of committing ourselves to courteousness.

———

If Tristram's greedy gaze raises preliminary doubts about courtesy's credulity, still that virtue's promise of reform is by no means dead—and it is well to remember what a generous promise it is, even more radical than turning Ignaro into Sapiento. For if Crudor does become courteous, and his name is still Crudor, then evidently his name no longer matters much, or tells us anything. These fundamental markers of the poem's personifications would become as accidental as any Christian name. Like the idyll of chivalric training, however, the promise of such learning, or reform, or flexibility—learning as the overcoming of allegory—comes in for increasingly strenuous critique. Most critics of the poem have noted that the pattern of episodes in Books V and VI alike is of diminishing success, each less neatly resolved than the last. In Book VI that unsuccess is a function of lingering slightly longer each time: the poem definitively loses its gift for averting its eyes, and we learn more and more of what happens *after* courtesy does its reforming work. Calidore, the hero, manages to slip away during the middle cantos when this tendency becomes most dispiriting. (This escape act is crucial to the book's ultimate definition of courtesy.) Meanwhile, we—and his unfortunate, less nimble surrogate Calepine—are obliged to stay behind and follow the career of the base knight Turpine, whose name is the last word on the high hopes of the opening cantos.

Turpine is as close kin to Crudor as turpitude is to crudeness. If courtesy is a matter of bending down to tend a "flowre . . . on a lowly stalke" (6.pr.4), Turpine flouts it by repeatedly taking unearned high ground, a riverbank or horseback, to assail knights below him. He is a study in recidivism, shrugging off Calepine's shaming rebukes to commit ever-greater offenses against chivalry. It takes the arrival of Arthur to put him on the defensive; eventually the prince chases him into his bedchamber, where he takes cowardly refuge beneath the skirts of his lady Blandina. When she raises her hems to discover him, he "still did lie as dead," and only gradually "rising up at last in ghastly wize, / Like troubled ghost did dreadfully appeare" (6.6.32). This reluctant parturition is one of many parodies of rebirth in Book VI, rebirth that throughout the poem has been the favored mode of change where *Bildung* has either failed or been rejected.[31] Now, however, not even this little renaissance works: when Arthur and Turpine next meet, the shameless knight tries to kill the prince while he sleeps. Arthur finally strips the would-be assassin of his armor,

> And after all, for greater infamie,
> He by the heeles him hung upon a tree,
> And baffuld so, that all which passed by,
> The picture of his punishment might see,
> And by the like ensample warned bee (6.7.27)

We are back, in exasperation, to the punitive language of Book V. This punishment is not especially intricate: just hanging upside down, like being made to ride backward on a horse through town, a schematic representation of his incorrigible frowardness.

The progress from Crudor to Tristram to Turpine charts how the poem loses faith in the good faith of courtesy. Book VI began as an exploration

---

31. Humphrey Tonkin discusses this pattern in terms of its governing myth, the Proserpine story, in *Spenser's Courteous Pastoral*, 307–15.

of the presumptions of innocence that might be warranted in a new Eden. From the retrospect of Turpine's punishment, its successes seem to have depended on (politely) not inquiring, on not lingering past the happy ending, and the hope for reform—for learning, for redemption, for change—is dashed if we wait around for proof. I have suggested that this skepticism is applied particularly to the quasi-historical form of that hope, the chivalric instruction defined by the relationship between knight and squire. That critique receives its fullest and final elaboration in the story of Arthur and Timias. The two are first separated back at the beginning of Book III, when Arthur goes charging after Florimel, and Timias (full of "proud envy, and indignant yre" [3.4.47]) is left to pursue the foster who threatened her. They meet again in Book IV after Timias has been rebuked by Belphoebe, but Timias is unrecognizable in his sorrow and cannot identify himself. In Book VI they are finally brought together again. "My liefe, my lifes desire, / Why have ye me alone thus long yleft?" (6.5.23) cries Arthur, in language that seems better suited to a reunion with the Faerie Queene herself. Timias does not answer, "But shedding few soft teares from tender eyne, / His deare affect with silence did restraine" (24). The squire is ashamed, and shame is the final fate of instruction.

Shame and Shamelessness

Shame is already everywhere in Book VI: the word tolls through the cantos like a leper's bell. The squire tied to the tree in canto i is "captyved in this shamefull place" (6.1.12); Calidore proclaims Briana's custom a "shame-full use" (14), and she in turn subjects the Knight of Courtesy to an intense countercampaign of shaming before Crudor returns: "yet shame shal thee with shame requight" (25). Tristram testifies to the "shame" (6.2.10) in the conduct of the knight he kills. What does this shame do to the hopes for courtesy, and to the gentle influence of chivalric tuition? Can shame itself be a teacher where milder means have failed? An answer must begin with another question: what might Spenser have meant by shame?

To that question, there are two old answers, or perhaps two fundamental attitudes. The first is more optimistic, and a strong strain in humanist writing about politics and education alike. Aristotle bequeathed to the Renaissance an appreciation of the social value of shame, how for all its corrosions—and he appreciates keenly its special discomfort—it can function as a useful deterrent to bad behavior. (Perhaps importantly for Spenser, he also thinks it is appropriate and even becoming in youths, whereas adults should know better.)[32] Among his many heirs is Pierre de la Primaudaye, whose courtesy book *The French Academie* (1586) makes a particularly strong version of this case: "a good nature . . . is yet never without some shame. . . . Honest shame and shamefastnes (saith *Quintilian*) is the mother of all good counsaile, the right Gardian of dutie, the mistresse of innocencie."[33] This civilizing potential was by no means lost on educators: Erasmus declares that "there are two sharp spurs that will rouse a child's natural talents, shame and praise"; Elyot offers his own version of the commonplace in his *Governour*: "the most necessary thinges to be observed by a maister in his disciples or scholars . . . is shamefastnes and praise."[34] Vives puts it particularly starkly: "The feeling of shame was given to man as a tutor," and its instructive powers are such, indeed, that it "takes the place of education in children and women."[35] The idea that shame could actually substitute for formal instruction, for men or women, implies that education is not a matter of transformation, but of self-regulation and self-control.

Such teaching depends upon a notion of shame—shared by many Renaissance and modern theorists—as a consequence of public exposure. (Sidney distinguishes between "the accusing of the inward conscience" and "fear of outward shame."[36]) Shame's blush blooms in your cheeks because you have been revealed in the eyes of others to be something other than what you are supposed to be. You may feel guilty about what you *did*, but you are ashamed of what you *are*, and what you want to hide—shame's reflex of covering—is not so much your deed as yourself.[37] The humanist conviction that this affect can have a regulative and even

32. Aristotle, *Nicomachean Ethics*, in *Works*, 1128b 10–35. On Aristotle and other ancient thinkers about shame, e.g., Galen and Pliny, see Gundersheimer, "Renaissance Concepts of Shame and Pocaterra's *Dialoghi Della Vergogna*," 35–39. In analyzing Pocaterra's tract Gundersheimer argues for a resurgence of interest in shame generally in the period.

33. La Primaudaye, *The French Academie*, R8v–S1r.

34. Erasmus, *De Pueris*, in *Works*, 26:332; Elyot, *Governour*, 41. Elyot is adapting Erasmus: both cite Lycon, and Elyot picks up his predecessor's "sharpe spurre" in the next sentence.

35. Vives, *The Passions of the Soul*, 115.

36. Sidney, *New Arcadia*, ed. Evans, 461.

37. So Stanley Cavell, writing about *King Lear*: "For shame is the specific discomfort produced by the sense of being looked at; the avoidance of the sight of others is the reflex it produces. Guilt is different; there the reflex is to avoid discovery. As long as no one knows what you have done, you are safe; or your conscience will press you to confess it and accept punishment. Under shame, what must be covered up is not your deed, but yourself. It is a more primitive emotion than guilt, as inescapable as the possession of a body, the first object of shame" (*Disowning Knowledge*, 49). See more generally Ewan Fernie's excellent survey of Classical and Renaissance backgrounds as well as modern thought in *Shame in Shakespeare*. He makes a compelling argument about the redemptive power of passing through shame in Shakespeare's plays; but for Spenser there is no other side to shame, save shamelessness. As

instructive effect in human affairs has a kind of counterpart in the world of chivalric romance. The community of knights is structured by a code; shame, which is endemic there, marks the lapses from that code, as when Gawain flinches at the Green Knight's stroke. Theresa Krier explains why such a generic propensity might be redoubled in a personification allegory: "characters are vulnerable to shame because the romance fiction posits for them extraordinary ego ideals—ideals of true knighthood, glory, holiness, chivalry—toward which they continually strive."[38] When the Knight of Holiness acts in a manner less than holy, shame is the sign of the dissonance. It is a marker both of a social breakdown and of the allegory's failure to contain its materials.

In moving from the French Academy to the courts of Arthur or the Faerie Queene, the picture of shame darkens considerably; it is rarely a constructive force in romance, tending to pull social forms apart rather than to hold them together. This pessimism reflects the other old attitude to shame, shame as the irrevocable sign of our first disobedience. If humanist optimism descends from Aristotle, pessimism reaches the sixteenth century from Genesis via Augustine and the commentators' accounts of the ongoingly shameful disobedience of our bodies.[39] Such shame can be so bountiful, so cripplingly in excess of its occasion, that it spoils us for society altogether. We have already seen in Book VI the beginning of a story of the triumph of this darker shame over courtesy—over courtesy first as the prospect of reform, of a true return to beginnings; and as the book proceeds, over courtesy as a project of good manners, too, the latter-day, civilizing habits for which Calidore comes to stand, and which are so central to the optimism of the courtesy books. To that story there are

Sidney's Gynecia says, "In shame there is no comfort but to be beyond all bounds of shame" (*Old Arcadia*, ed. Duncan-Jones, 81).

38. Krier, "'All suddeinly abasht she chaunged hew': Abashedness in *The Faerie Queene*," 133. See also her *Gazing on Secret Sights*, 155–76. The phrase "ego ideal" is an early coinage of Freud's for the ego's image of itself: shame results when actual behavior is exposed as other or less than this ideal. He first uses the term in "On Narcissism: An Introduction" (*Standard Edition*, 14:93–94).

39. Gundersheimer, quoting Donald Nathanson, discusses the view that shame is a kind of "cognitive shock, a period of time during which we are unable to think clearly or plot effective action" ("Renaissance Concepts," 39). See Arnold Williams, *The Common Expositor*, for an account of commentaries on Genesis, emphasizing shame as a function of the disobedience of the sexual organs and lack of erotic self-control generally (126–27). Gail Kern Paster focuses on incontinent bodies and the regulative power of shame in *The Body Embarrassed: Drama and the Disciplines of Shame in Early Modern England*; her shame is somewhat leakier than Spenser's, but not altogether alien to his poem.

two endings. The first is the one played out between Arthur and Timias, Spenser's final reflection on the old school of chivalry. The second is a story of shamelessness, in the person of Calidore himself.

———————

Recall that outburst of baffled affect when Arthur and Timias meet again in canto v, "My liefe, my lifes desire" (6.5.23). I have already suggested that the overplus of this obscurely unconsummated reunion might provoke a look backward through the poem, pointing the reader to their first separation at the beginning of Book III. That scene is one of erotic renunciation for the squire, who must pursue the foster and leave the lady to his lord—he feels a "proud envy" (3.4.47) that can hardly be for his quarry, and the Adonis-like wound he sustains when the foster's boar spear "thrill[s]" (3.5.20) his thigh is a none-too-subtle return of the repressed. The idea that we are working in a territory of generational rivalry bordering on the Oedipal is underscored when they meet again after Timias's fall from grace with Belphoebe. Although he will not reveal himself—"Shame would be hid" (6.8.5), as the narrator will later say—the squire is poised between reverence and aggression when he takes up Arthur's "naked sword" to "try the edges keene" (4.7.45). This sword is double-edged, just as Timias's shame might be said to have a double source: first the lack of erotic self-control implicit in the rivalry, and second the ambition for a change of station.

This excruciatingly incomplete series of reunions undermines the pedagogical possibilities of the old tuition, and Spenser's point seems to be just how complicated the dynamics of such apprenticeships can be, how contaminated with the complexity of fathers and sons, and even displacements of erotic love. The succession of reunions between the two is a tangle of chivalric and erotic discourses that together eclipse the justifying aim of instruction. It is a peculiar angle of reproach, to go after the old modes of teaching because they are so beholden to the vicissitudes of personal bonds. But it does suggest a specific contrast with the legalism of Book V: how messy courtesy is, and how good law comes to look when you are mired in manners and affections. The poem has been preparing these confusions since 1590, and when Book VI, in its nostalgia, leans on the old customs as a prop for its waning faith in teaching, they turn out to be too corrupt to bear the weight. Timias's shame is what ultimately happens to the hope of Tristram. Its final act is his encounter with Mirabella, when he comes upon the ungainly pageant of her punishment and tries to set her free. That episode begins in shame: his foot slips, and he is bound and incorporated into the spectacle, led on a rope "like a dog" (6.8.5).

One might at first assume that the resulting parade—the lady, the squire, the dwarf Scorne and the giant Disdaine—is to be read as a parody of a mode of punishment that the poem has outgrown. It has elements of public justice, that shaming procession through the streets. It is also the most concerted exercise in high, emblematic allegory since the end of Book V, to an extent that verges on comedy. Mirabella carries a bottle and a bag, and duly explains, "Here in this bottle (sayd the sorry Mayd) / I put the teares of my contrition . . . And in this bag which I behinde me don, / I put repentaunce for things past and gon" (6.8.24). In case we missed the absurdity of this self-exegesis (which might not have seemed so absurd in Book I), Disdaine makes the comedy too broad to miss. He is the brother of Orgoglio, the giant who felled Redcrosse, and though he is "huge and hideous" (6.7.41) he somehow fails to menace this time around: "And stalking stately like a Crane, did stryde / At every step upon the tiptoes hie" (42). In his richly quilted jacket and linen turban he must look something like a big, finicky bird. The fastidious allegorical articulation and emblematic vividness of this spectacle make the whole contraption ludicrous, and it is no surprise that Timias is ashamed to be seen bound to it when Arthur arrives: he "did his head for bashfulnesse abase, / As loth to see, or to be seene at all" (6.8.5). To this shame Arthur is again oblivious when at last he recognizes his squire: "He thereat wext exceedingly astound, / And him did oft embrace, and oft admire, / Ne could with seeing satisfie his great desire" (27).

But more astounding even than this latest, overdetermined unconsummation is Mirabella's response to being set free. Cupid has charged her to abide her symbolic punishment until she has saved as many lives as once her Petrarchan cruelty spilled, and she chooses to "fulfill / This penaunce, which enjoyned is to me, / Least unto me betide a greater ill" (6.8.30). Refusing Arthur's help, she exits the scene as she entered, the central exhibit in a shameful procession whose motto she will read out to anyone who asks. She would seem to be one more case of instruction at the expense of the character, another painful example of the poem's cynicism about its own teaching. But there are two differences here: first, she is unequivocally guilty of the crime she represents; and second, when Timias is taken captive, she "Was touched with compassion entire, / And much lamented his calamity" (3). That is to say, the cruel-fair has somehow become compassionate, and she seems to have learned that new sympathy under the scourging of Scorn's whip. What are we to make of *this* reform, a reform under punishment? One throws up one's hands. Except perhaps—in the very largest sense—to say that *The Faerie Queene* is not finally interested in making final claims about anything, punishment or courtesy or shame. It can bring itself only to dramatize how such claims might work, where they come from, why we make them, and why we lose faith in them.[40] The severity of allegorical punishment in Book V engenders a longing for a more courteous alternative, for an old-time instruction free of punitive violence, full of fatherly love. But Book VI's travesties of reform leave the poem longing for punishment, hopeful for its powers all over again—and willing to resuscitate its own high allegory one more time, even in the creaky, ramshackle version that teaches Mirabella her lesson.

That is the fundamental story I want to tell about Books V and VI: Book V's anatomy of instruction by punishment; Book VI's nostalgia for the training up of chivalry, and its gradual loss of faith in that courteous alternative. Each is used against the other. Book VI's part of the story is played out in a mixed contest and collaboration between courtesy and shame. The dream of courtesy as a permission for change—whether the reform of the allegory, or even just the structured progression from squire to knight— gives way to courtesy as a conservative, straitening, hierarchical force. The difference between the two is the difference between an original, primitive instinct, and the latter-day or even belated codes and manners that are the mark not only of civility but of sophistication; between something given, and something taught. The blight of shame ultimately helps to enforce this second kind. It is a sobering story, which has Spenser opening in hope, then shutting in dismay a chapter in the generic history of his poem and the social history of his nation. And yet original, innocent courtesy—we might say, unknowing courtesy, the courtesy with the grace to look away—is not altogether lost after Mirabella makes her awkward exit. Very briefly, and very schematically, I want to follow its transformation through the rest of Book VI, as a way of suggesting what all this skepticism about instruction might ultimately mean for the reader of the poem.

---

40. Much of Harry Berger's more recent work emphasizes the poem's critical detachment from its every move: for example, in "Narrative as Rhetoric in *The Faerie Queene*," he asks what difference it makes "if, instead of merely reading the poem as a piece of storytelling, we approach it as a poem that *represents* storytelling" (3). There are of course dangers to granting the poem a kind of Socratic immunity from identification with the cultural materials it allows into itself; I want to emphasize how the poem registers *those* dangers too, in a despair about its teaching, even a kind of self-disgust.

To follow the career of this innocent courtesy is to pick up the trail of Calidore again.[41] He has the grace to slip out of the poem just as its problems are becoming intractable, and he is conveniently offstage through the bitter history of Turpine and through Calepine's declining fortunes. When he returns, it is to pursue the Blatant Beast to the limit of the book's nostalgia in pastoral, where he is smitten by a shepherd lass and forsakes his quest. Earlier episodes have already begun to explore the element of deception in his courtesy: there is, for example, the "counter-cast of slight" (6.3.16) by which he conceals Priscilla's love for Aledine from her father. Now courtesy is fully unfolded as an art of blandishment. Calidore's conversation with the aged Meliboe about *otium* and the golden age is a study in the rhetoric of half-attention, with one "hungry eye... alwayes bent" (6.9.26) on the old man's daughter. There is also his treatment of his rival Corydon, the shepherd whom he bests in all the shepherd games. After winning a garland for his dancing, Calidore courteously bestows it on the despondent rube: "Then *Coridon* woxe frollicke, that earst seemed dead" (42). The moment is another one of the book's travesties of the promise of rebirth. It is also an exemplary case of courtesy's power to help the shepherd misrecognize his inferiority, to say nothing of his class, and to forget his shame.

This revision of courtesy as a gift of not-knowing—a not-knowing that is beginning to seem strategic, rather than innocent—is completed on Mount Acidale, where *The Faerie Queene*'s final hero encounters a personification of its youthful poet. The Knight of Courtesy comes to a clearing and sees perhaps the most important visionary spectacle in the poem, certainly in its second half: two concentric circles of dancers, a hundred naked maidens and the three Graces, all whirling round a "countrey lasse" (6.10.25) crowned with a "rosie girlond" (14). Piping them in motion is Spenser's alter ego Colin Clout. Much has been made of the insertion at this visionary climax of Colin's old flame Rosalynd (hence the "rosie" garland), a "minime" of praise for a "poore handmayd" (28) that momentarily displaces the poem's notional focus on Queen Elizabeth in favor of a shepherd girl. Here *The Faerie Queene* makes contact again with the adolescent ambitions

---

41. This is a severe reading of courtesy, or of what it has become; for a sense of the potential Calidore betrays, see Gordon Teskey's subtle article "'And therefore as a stranger give it welcome': Courtesy and Thinking," in which he argues that, for a poem that represents ideas as persons, courtesy is a model of approaching new ideas that respects their strangeness: "Courtesy does not seize the object or dive into its center: it moves into nearness with the otherness of the stranger" (344).

of its creator, and hints that its great edifice may be founded not so much on political awe as on a youthful, rustic love, love that may still have the power to resolve the poem's materials into a reverential, dancing order.[42] If Book VI is a book of nostalgia, then this is nostalgia in its most potentially redemptive form. Calidore, ambassador from the main narrative to this lyric idyll, looks on from the margins, but he cannot just look ("he him selfe his eyes envyde" [11]). When he breaks into the clearing, the vision is dispersed.

Calidore should be ashamed of himself: this transgression is a paradigmatic failure of erotic self-control, and its costs are obvious. Instead, he engages the disconsolate Colin in his trademark courteous banter. Calidore inquires who the maidens were; Colin explains.[43] "But gentle Shepheard pardon thou my shame, / Who rashly sought that, which I mote not see," Calidore then apologizes: "Thus did the courteous Knight excuse his blame, / And to recomfort him, all comely meanes did frame" (6.10.29). When the narrator ratifies Colin's excuse, the poem turns away from Colin's grief and from whatever has just been lost.[44] The moment might be said to perform a final separation of courtesy from grace, as the Graces vanish and the Knight of Courtesy carries on with his quest. What is left of courtesy when the grace—*grazia*, courtly savvy, but also Christian grace—is taken out? Perhaps nothing more than that gift for turning away at the right moment, for not knowing what it is inconvenient to know, and convincing others not

---

42. James Nohrnberg surveys the mythography and the analogies within the poem in his *Analogy*, 720–23.

43. Harry Berger Jr., in "A Secret Discipline," describes the visionary stakes of the dance, and takes Colin's conversation with Calidore as a scene of instruction: "The episode as a whole circles through three familiar emphases: first, the vision of delight . . . second, the plaintive moment in which the vision is interrupted . . . third, the moral emphasis when Colin converts the vision into an emblem" (*Revisionary Play*, 239). Theresa Krier reads the episode as a successful scene of instruction, and answers her question "what Calidore learns" by specifying not only the mythographic information Colin gives him but also a new appreciation of "the elusiveness of bestowed presence" (*Gazing on Secret Sights*, 237–38).

44. The narrator's voice grows increasingly distinct, increasingly personal in Book VI. I can only gesture here at the complexity of that transformation, which can be glimpsed in the self-reflection of the proem to Book VI, and the defensive turn to georgic at the beginning of canto ix (an earnestly didactic mode that might cover or excuse a waning of seriousness). Harry Berger discusses the problem in "Narrative as Rhetoric," describing a narrator who is "the first reader of *The Faerie Queene*" (44), commenting on but incompletely transmuting materials he receives from the authority of old books. Stan Hinton, reading Books III–V, suggests that poet and narrator cannot be pried apart: "Because we cannot go so deep that we can avoid him, he is not distinct from the poet. He is Spenser's epic voice" ("The Poet and His Narrator," 180). Kathleen Williams sees them as analogous figures on Acidale in her "Vision and Rhetoric: The Poet's Voice in *The Faerie Queene*," 143–44. Paul Alpers offers the strongest rebuke to the idea of narrator as character in "Narration in *The Faerie Queene*."

to know it, too. The perfect opposite of learning and of teaching alike. At this fork, the poem has a choice: linger with Colin to count the costs to his visionary project, or ride away with Calidore? We ride, of course, with Calidore, and the separation his departure makes might even be said to be between the poet and the narrator whose job it will now be to smooth the knight's path forward.

The story that *The Faerie Queene* is at liberty to tell now that it has broken with Colin is the story of the loss and redemption of Pastorella, who is revived—without the skepticism that has dogged such rebirths throughout—after her season underground with the brigands, and restored to Calidore. And better than restored: she is revealed to be of noble birth after all, and with the "rosie marke" (6.12.15) that signifies her lineage, she enfolds and exalts the humble Rosalynd, granting her to the knight as a sublimed, aristocratic double of the poet's first love. There is nothing quite like this development elsewhere in *The Faerie Queene*. It is a perfect romance wish-fulfillment. The Calidore who is its beneficiary is the Calidore who goes on to bind the Blatant Beast; he can disarm that daemon of slander because his brand of courtesy has finally emerged as the perfect enemy of shame, the perfect shamelessness. Shamelessness is a condition of not-knowing before the fall, and also, as it turns out, afterward. One might say that the poem, by pretending to return to that original condition, has finally lost its sense of shame.

———————

Slander is bound at just the moment when it would be most useful to have it around, and for any reader who misses its teeth, the last stanzas' story of the Beast's escape in subsequent generations has some consolations.[45] What has happened to the poem at the end of Book VI is that it has capitulated to the enemies of romance by conforming to their critique, finally allowing itself to become the sort of idle, profitless toy that the schoolmasters deplored.[46] It has done this by making a show of separating out its visionary ambitions—invoking and exiling, if you like, an internal figure of its own highest lessons—in order that its courteous hero may be satisfied

45. Kenneth Gross discusses the debilitating effects of Slander in *Spenserian Poetics*, 224–34. He pursues questions of slander and shame further in *Shakespeare's Noise*. The fast-forward through the centuries to Spenser's own slanderous age is perhaps the most striking instance of how courtesy achieves its victories by bowing out at the right moment, and how it is undone if we look for proof of its achievements over time.

46. This is the romance that Margaret Doody describes as "a rather cloudy literary mode characterized by wishful thinking" (*The True Story of the Novel*, 15).

at last. It does so, perhaps, in exhaustion. The poem's endless work has finally worn its teller out, and he cuts his ties with a visionary conscience that he now identifies slightingly with his own idealistic adolescence. But I prefer to think that this is the poem's moment of most surprising, paradoxical strength. Over its six books it has relentlessly critiqued any mode by which a reader might constitute its didactic authority, tempting us again and again—and for all its sensualism, for all its ladies in fountains, this is perhaps the mode of temptation the poem knows best—tempting us with *lessons*. Now, there are no lessons left, and no rebukes, and the final temptation is just a story about a knight who gets everything he wants. If we have learned anything from *The Faerie Queene*'s refusal to teach us, we will have cultivated enough skepticism to kick the poem away as it falls. If not, it hardly matters.

Ordinariness

I have said that *The Faerie Queene* refuses to teach; I have said the same of Lyly's *Euphues*, and of Sidney's *Arcadia*. But in each of these cases, that refusal is a matter not of discovering an alternative, but of staging and sabotaging a wide variety of didactic protocols, many of them directly indebted to the poets' training. All these works are constructed as an extended series of teaching gestures. It is just that those gestures are relentlessly discredited; the stories they tell, meanwhile, are stories where instruction goes awry again and again. Is there, for Spenser, any way out of this predicament? If not a reform of teaching, then an escape?

Let us return to Arthur, sleeping under the tree just before the arrival of Turpine and the ugly scene of punishment that follows. He is "Loosely displayd upon the grassie ground, / Possessed of sweete sleepe, that luld him soft in swound" (6.7.18):

> Wearie of trauell in his former fight,
> He there in shade himselfe had layd to rest,
> Having his armes and warlike things undight,
> Fearelesse of foes that mote his peace molest;
> The whyles his salvage page, that wont be prest,
> Was wandred in the wood another way,
> To doe some thing, that seemed to him best,
> The whyles his Lord in silver slomber lay,
> Like to the Evening starre adorn'd with deawy ray. (6.7.19)

These are hard lines to know how to read. On the one hand, the sleeping prince is an image of millennial confidence, the Arthur of Tudor mythology who slumbers for centuries beneath the hills of Wales: *rex quondam rexque futurus*. The evening star is also the morning star, and the dews are purifying, renewing (like Crysogone's "wombe of Morning dew" [3.6.3], or the dews of the Garden of Adonis, or the balm that rescues Redcrosse from the dragon fire). On the other hand, the description is full of familiar warning signals. "Loosely displayd upon the grassie ground" recalls Redcrosse by the fountain, "Pourd out in loosnesse on the grassy grownd" (1.7.7), and Calepine's travails in the preceding cantos have made clear the perils of taking off your armor. Perhaps the relaxing of Arthur's vigilance is a kind of exhaustion. As the magnanimous knight, summary of the virtues, Arthur *is* the poem: is he greater now than any of its dangers, or too tired to fend them off?

In worrying about Arthur, and about Turpine's impending arrival, it would be easy to forget about the Salvage Man. After all, there is not so much to attend to: he has "wandred in the wood another way, / To doe some thing, that seemed to him best" (6.7.19). The lines are almost written to shrug off attention. They reward it, however, if peculiarly: that wandering "another way" is perfectly reticent, admitting only that his way is not the one marked out by the prince; "some thing, that seemed to him best" is equally incurious, with "seemed" gently drawing a curtain between the Salvage Man's desires and the poem's hierarchy of goods. He is no squire; he is no student. And are there any other lines in *The Faerie Queene* more genially offhanded? The Salvage Man has ambled off in the direction of something I would like to call ordinariness.

At the end of chapter 4, which considered the first three books of the poem, I introduced the concept of irrelevance, a kind of strategic rupture in the allegory, a staged breach of its promise to constitute a unified, interdependent, overdetermined *kosmos*. I read Britomart's odd independence from the circumstances of the House of Busirane as a question for the reader, whether heroic action—inside and outside the poem—might only be achieved by blocking your ears to its teaching. Such irrelevance is an affront to allegory, but it depends on allegory's authority for its own refractory power. Ordinariness works differently. While the allegory revolves its burning wheels above the head of the sleeping Arthur, the Salvage Man slips away, to do, well, whatever. For this indifferent activity—one wouldn't want to call it action—even the word "experience" seems too fraught, too charged. Nor would one want to say that there is any narrative character to it, for his amble seems to be altogether outside of the dialectic of paradigm and narrative that has preoccupied this study. There is no story here, and no emblem, just a glimpse of the everyday. And as muted as this brief interlude is, the counterpoint with Arthur is calculated and vital to an understanding of the poem's energies. The Salvage Man hints at the tantalizing possibility that one does not have to live a life of allegory after all.[47]

Does this ever happen elsewhere in *The Faerie Queene*, this brief intimation of ordinariness—not the rupture of its instruction, but its surcease? I will suggest another couple of instances, though I believe there are more to be found, if we learn to listen for them. One is that odd little scene after the dragon has been killed, when the mother worries that her son will cut himself playing near its talons. It is a brief access of the domestic, the un-eschatological, that in its touchingly practical concern for "his tender hand" (1.12.11) is a subtle rival of our investment in the high allegory of Revelation.[48] Another is the fate of Hellenore near the end of Book III. She bears all the cultural baggage of her name-fate through a travesty of the Troy story, but when she finally falls in with the satyrs, she seems to settle into a routine of domestic regularity and sexual satisfaction: happy "as housewife ever to abide, / To milk their gotes, and make them cheese and bredd, / And every one as commune good her handeled" (3.10.36). In a poem where punishment is so often the fixative of meaning, Spenser never gets around to making her pay for her licenses. Perhaps being handled as a common good is punishment in itself: there is plenty of purchase here

47. Stanley Cavell has put his stamp on the word "ordinariness," in his writing about Shakespeare and about ordinary language philosophy. Ordinariness on his account is to be understood over and against skepticism, as the acknowledgment of what skepticism denies: the accessibility of the world to knowing and feeling. Epistemology itself, arising from doubts about our ability to know, is accordingly regarded as a strategy for evading what otherwise we would have no excuse but to allow. As Cavell writes, "The power of this recognition of the ordinary for philosophy is bound up with the recognition that refusing or forcing the order of the ordinary"—turning either to skepticism or to metaphysics—"is a cause of philosophical emptiness (say avoidance) and violence" ("Declining Decline," 322). I want to position his term not against skepticism but against allegory, which is to say, I want to consider allegory as a species of skepticism, refusing the order of the ordinary, a mediating language intended not so much to access the truth as to keep the world at bay.

48. The stanza is not altogether generous to this mother and her "gossibs": it retracts its sympathy in the next line, to sneer at them in the by-now perhaps too easy idiom of duality: "So divlyersly them selves in vaine they fray" (1.12.11). Book I can register the claim of such concerns, but shrug them off, too, recollecting itself to its higher purposes. As the poem proceeds, the claims of such ordinariness become more and more powerful on a poem that is more and more disillusioned with its allegory.

for allegorical reading, and for condemnation.[49] But a tone of judgment is difficult to detect in the rhetoric, particularly when compared with the violent daemonizing of her husband Malbecco, who is turned to *Gelosy* and consigned to a most unenviable life in a cliff-side cave. Hellenore seems to be left—unreflectively, shamelessly—to her flourishing, and some part of the poem's cosmic ambition is momentarily diverted into her eddy of the everyday.

These glimpses are fleeting, ephemeral, and they are always in danger of being erased by an interpretation that will fold them back into the allegory's master plan. But I think the poem's attitude toward its own procedures—in particular its nostalgia for something before or outside allegory, and its weariness of its own reflexes of self-critique—cannot be understood without registering this subtle and recurrent longing. If what Spenser's poem cannot do is tell a story of education by experience, ordinariness is no solution to that problem, because it too eludes narrative. Ordinariness knows nothing of that sense of extrinsic purpose that drives all of our didactic projects. *The Faerie Queene* has to be the least hospitable of fictions to such a dream—if one can speak of ordinariness as a dream, as in this poem, perhaps one can—but that dream's sporadic tenacity may finally be the most powerful sign of its desire to be released from its great burden, the agon with its obligation to instruct.

49. James Nohrnberg, for example, reads her as a figure of natural love: "An intimation of this kind of fulfillment is present in the story of Hellenore and the satyrs. A relation of 'natural' love is not ordinarily accessible to waking experience, where sexuality does not remain morally neutral, like stimulus and response, but either degrades or elevates" (*Analogy*, 602; see also 642). I do not disagree, but I want to explore the consequences of this "fulfillment" for the allegory: in a poem underwritten by the quest of Arthur for the Faerie Queene it may be that any fulfillment will threaten (especially threaten to obviate) the mode.

The Sense of a Lesson

In the preceding chapters I have described the ways three poets sabotage their own didactic authority, dedicating and in some sense sacrificing their works to a protest against the training of their best educated readers. I have also tried to make the case that for all the virtuosity of their discontent, they are in some sense balked—that there is a story, a particular kind of story, that they particularly cannot tell. I have called that story an education by experience, the narrative accumulation of event as the fashioning of a virtuous self. It is a difficult thing to talk about, the pressure of an idea that never achieves direct expression. I have drawn some comfort, in puzzling over it, from Christopher Hill's account of the poets and writers of the years before the revolution of 1640. Deposing the king, or killing him, would have to be an obvious idea to anyone in the gathering opposition, indeed *the* obvious idea; but there was, Hill argues, a "stop in the mind" that made it unsayable, even unthinkable.[1] Something like this stop in the mind afflicts Lyly, Sidney, and Spenser, as a result (I have argued) of the training to which they owed so much of their virtuosity. They were taught to think, and particularly taught to think about learning, in ways antithetical to such storytelling. Their debt to that training was too profound and entangling for them to write their way altogether free of it.

Some time over the next century, of course, this stop in the mind wore away. By the eighteenth century the story that Sidney and Spenser cannot tell was on its way to becoming the signature plot of the newborn novel, the bildungsroman. Which is not to say that the bildungsroman learns to tell this story without a hitch: *Tom Jones* is full of miseducation, and there

1. Hill, *The Century of Revolution*, 54.

are critics who take his marriage with Sophia to be every bit as equivocal as Redcrosse's to Una. Still, Fielding and others like him depended on the idea that you could learn how to do good in the world by trial and error, and that the account of such a career could have the shape of a story, and, what is more, that the reader of such a story might learn something from it. A novel could teach without being a schoolmaster.

It is beyond the scope of this study to explain whatever historical forces made this change possible, except by the largest gestures. Among its tributaries, as I ventured in chapter 2, must have been the increasing imaginative purchase of experimental science, and the authority it granted to a certain kind of experience of the world over the book learning of the classics. The theory of education changed substantially as a result. The gradual elaboration of more liberal ideas about virtue and social mobility also opened the way for stories about making something of yourself. Perhaps most importantly, the idea, and the practice, of reading for pleasure—outside of the shadow of any particular institution—became more and more of a cultural commonplace. These developments and others are rehearsed in many recent histories of the novel.[2] What I want to do in this coda, more modestly, is just to point to a moment when this change is happening, in the works of John Milton—particularly in his masque *Comus*, and (much more briefly) in *Paradise Lost*. These poems will provide occasion for some remarks about lessons and endings, a final restatement of a book-long preoccupation with the relation between teaching and narrative.

Harmony

Comus—or *A Maske Presented at Ludlow Castle*, as it was titled when it was published in 1637—is the story of the Lady, the virgin wanderer-through-the-woods who is the object of Comus's temptations. The definition and preservation of her chastity is what the masque is most conspicuously about. The untouchable sanctity of that condition comes to a test in the middle of the masque, when she and her tempter dispute the power of her high virtue. The stakes are apocalyptic: "the uncontrolled worth / Of

---

2. Michael McKeon offers the most influential account of how the novel is shaped by changing accommodations between empiricism and romance: see *The Origins of the English Novel*, esp. chapter 3, "Histories of the Individual," 90–130. Margaret Anne Doody, *The True Story of the Novel*, resists the distinction between romance and novel, though she does so by placing great emphasis on the ancient romances, which have characteristics of the bildungsroman that the books I have considered cannot accommodate.

this pure cause would kindle my rapt spirits / To such a flame of sacred vehemence," she threatens,

> That dumb things would be moved to sympathize,
> And the brute earth would lend her nerves, and shake,
> Till all thy magic structures reared so high,
> Were shattered into heaps o'er thy false head.[3]

More than thirty years later, in *Paradise Lost*, Milton would write this scene to its conclusion, but in 1634 the test is interrupted. (Perhaps out of something like the reticence he proclaimed when he published his unfinished poem, "The Passion": "This subject the author finding to be above the years he had when he wrote it, and nothing satisfied with what was begun, left it unfinished."[4]) The great question of whether the Lady is fit to stand alone therefore goes unanswered, and in the void it leaves, questions of practical, worldly instruction become more important than we had reason to suspect they would be. It is this side of *Comus* that I want to consider: the masque as it is bound to the profession of its makers, the music teacher Henry Lawes and the teacher-to-be John Milton. Mindful of his literary predecessors, Milton does his thinking about teaching in the language of romance.

Of course, *Comus* is first of all a masque, and it inherits its generic decorums from the likes of Ben Jonson and Inigo Jones. Milton's experiment in the form was a collaboration with Lawes, who was sometime tutor to the Egerton children in Wales and by 1634 an increasingly busy court composer. It was commissioned by the family's patriarch, the Earl of Bridgewater, for performance by young Alice, John, and Thomas, with Lawes himself in the tutelary role of the Attendant Spirit. The fundamental masque structures are observed, its progress from the rout of the anti-masque to the ordered dances of the resolution, but the plot is more than usually tangled up with romance: the children are on a quest to join their father; they must pass through a treacherous wood; they are threatened along the way by a son of Circe. The masque's major literary debts are to a romance tradition, too. Spenser is a central influence, and so is Shakespeare, such works as *Midsummer Night's Dream* and *Measure for Measure*

---

3. Milton, *Comus*, in *Shorter Poems*, ed. Carey, ll.792–98. Subsequent citations to this and other shorter Milton poems are given by line number in parentheses in the text. Carey's text is based on the printed editions, not the likely acting version, the Bridgewater ms.

4. Milton, *Shorter Poems*, 125.

and still more significantly *The Tempest*. That last play's preoccupations with instructive authority charge its frequent recollections in Milton's lines, and it turns out to be crucial to how the masque manages its mixed feelings about teaching.[5]

The brothers are the focus of those mixed feelings. They have been told to protect their sister, but they split up to pick berries, and now they cannot find her. The trouble appears to be the darkness. The Elder Brother calls for the stars to "Unmuffle" (330), or for a candle that might show the way "With thy long levelled rule of streaming light" (339), and the Second Brother responds with unsettling questions about what might happen to their sister in such a stygian predicament. "Virtue could see to do what Virtue would, / By her own radiant light" (372–73) the Elder lectures, with precocious, didactic bravado: "He that has light within his own clear breast / May sit i' the centre, and enjoy bright day" (380–81). This rhetoric burns hottest and brightest when he praises the "sacred rays of chastity" (424), rays that have the power to protect their sister in whatever "grots, and caverns shagged with horrid shades" (428) she may pass through. Chastity, he argues, does not permit the transcendence of sight; the chaste do not take leave of their senses. Rather, it *perfects* our sight, by casting a light that allows our eyes to serve as true and certain guides.

This commitment to ocular proof first emerges in the masque when the Lady surveys the "blind mazes of this tangled wood" (180) some lines before. She has heard the tumult of Comus's revels, and in the darkness her imagination starts to get the better of her, "A thousand fantasies... Of calling shapes, and beckoning shadows dire, / And airy tongues, that syllable men's names" (204–7). This wood has many voices, but she pulls herself together and calls for aid:

> O welcome pure-eyed Faith, white-handed Hope,
> Thou hovering angel girt with golden wings,
> And thou unblemished form of Chastity,
> I see ye visibly (212–15)

5. In the first edition of Milton's *Complete Shorter Poems*, John Carey counts four echoes of the *Tempest* and *Measure for Measure*, and five of *A Midsummer Night's Dream* (171). In his edition of *The Tempest*, Frank Kermode observes that the play "is almost as important to Milton [in *Comus*] as *The Faerie Queene*" (xlviii). Studies of the relations between the two include John M. Major, "Comus and *The Tempest*" (1959), and Ethel Seaton, "*Comus* and Shakespeare" (1945). Mary Loeffelholz's "Two Masques of Ceres and Proserpine" (1988) describes the relation between Milton's entertainment and Prospero's masque in Act IV.

Not only does chastity redeem the sight, but it can *itself* be seen. Such vision is still seeing, the Lady strenuously insists—"I see ye visibly"—but we might be tempted to say that at this upper limit of clarity its proper objects are allegorical. Allegory is characteristically a visual mode, after all, and the Lady's comfort comes from being able to see Faith and Hope as surely as she sees the silver lining of a neighboring cloud ("Was I deceived, or did a sable cloud / Turn forth her silver lining on the night? / I did not err, there does a sable cloud / Turn forth her silver lining on the night" [220–23]).

Such adamantine certainty begins to emerge as a much greater concern for the masque than the smoke and stir that first dimmed its characters' eyes. What can we trust if not our incorruptible vision? Perhaps our ears: the first half of the masque often seems to be working out an antidote to visual idolatry via the power of hearing. This preference is Protestant enough, privileging the sense that hears the sermon over the sense besotted with the graven image. While the Elder Brother longs for the leveled rule of light, the younger's common sense is figured in his willingness to settle for the reassurance of the pastoral sounds of folded sheep. The Attendant Spirit's very name suggests that he relies particularly upon hearing; his refrain to Sabrina later in the masque is "listen and save" (865, 888). But Milton hints that hearing too is vulnerable to false certainties. After the Lady first hears the noise of Comus's antimasque, she muses, "even now the tumult of loud mirth / Was rife, and perfect in my listening ear" (201–2). The awkward transition from "rife" to "perfect" seems to be a kind of self-correction on the fly: she fends off an aural invasion—the threat that mere, accidental hearing contaminates—by crediting the ear with the power to perfect wanton sounds.[6] This is at least one way of taking the *list*, the desire, in *listen*, as though the ear too will hear what it wants to hear.

The trouble, in short, is epistemological: these young people put too much faith in their senses. (Or too much faith in their Senses, for they only see Ideas.) Enter the Attendant Spirit, as played by the music teacher. He comes to the boys with a remedy in the form of "haemony" (637), the prickly, much commented-upon herb that promises to protect them against Comus's charms. Haemony is a "small unsightly root" (628), which the Attendant Spirit has received, for a song, from a "certain shepherd lad / Of small regard to see to" (618–19). As these lines suggest, Milton takes pains

6. The Elder Brother believes the reverse is true, too: angels sing to the chaste "things that no gross ear can hear" (457).

to dissociate the plant from the power of sight: it seems to have much more to do with the musical currency for which it was traded. Scholars have proposed any number of sources for the name, from Odysseus's moly (to which the Attendant Spirit compares it), to the Hebrew word *amon* (knowledge or belief), to Haemonia, or Sicily, a great exporter of magic herbs.[7] I want to emphasize its own sound: in particular, its closeness to "harmony," the word that closes the Lady's echo song, "And give resounding grace to all heaven's harmonies" (242). That phonemic proximity has a special power to explain Milton's coinage in his echo chamber of a poem. In suggesting this identification, however, I want at the same time to pry harmony away from sound, in order to call attention to its properties of concord and even collaboration, heavenly and earthly.

Harmony in the heavens expresses the celestial concertedness that reconciles all our mortal plots: the music of the spheres, a favorite trope for Milton all his life. But what harmony stands for *here*, in the middest of the wood, is the more day-to-day business of working together: the little scene of amicable exchange by which the root was first obtained, and then the combined assault on Comus that it is supposed to enable.[8] This is what the Attendant Spirit has come to teach, practical harmony as an answer to the lonely belatedness of echo. (Not entirely unlike the ensemble playing in which Lawes would have schooled the children.) Haemony-as-harmony figures the synchrony of cooperation, and as such it anticipates the intricate harmony of dance and of music that provides the masque form with its closure. Such harmony may still be best figured by sound (or at least better by sound than by sight), but this little scene of instruction in fact offers a radical transformation of the central problem of the drama. Resisting evil in the wood is a job the senses will never be up to. Neither ear nor eye can ever be so keen that it could pierce every deception (and indeed, the keener we take them to be, the more likely it will turn out we are only studying our own clear and distinct ideas). What works is sticking together. Milton doesn't change his mind on this point so much over the next thirty years: even our unfallen senses may be deceived in Eden, but what dooms our first parents is the moment when they go their separate ways.

7. John Carey surveys these and other modern hypotheses in his note to line 637.

8. Celestial harmony is a favorite figure of Milton's: see, for example, the harmony that "Could hold all heaven and earth in happier union" (108) in "On the Morning of Christ's Nativity." As for harmony on earth: that shepherd lad is sometimes taken to be Milton himself, in which case the barter is between Milton and Lawes, the collaborating creators whose "mixed power" of "Voice, and Verse" has made the masque ("At a Solemn Music," 3, 2).

This is all to say that epistemology turns out to be a fool's errand.[9] Milton's imagery may provoke us to intricate comparisons of seeing and hearing, but finally the challenge is not about the conditions of knowing so much as about the collaborative circumstances of learning. We must resist the particular moral glamour of standing alone, with all it assures us we already know. We have to give ourselves instead to the company of our teachers and our fellow students. The Attendant Spirit appears to the boys as a teacher, but in some sense the problem of representing learning that has haunted this study is annulled at a stroke by his answer. Milton reposes his confidence not in problems of knowledge, nor in any possible solution to problems of knowledge, but in an educable sociability.[10] We secure ourselves and know our virtue in practical, cooperative action.

And yet: this scene of instruction fails; the brothers botch the job, and Comus escapes. Their failure to learn the Attendant Spirit's lesson is a central fact of the plot, and understanding its significance turns out to demand recognizing where it comes from, for it is the strangest of the masque's many borrowings. Critics are agreed that Spenser and Shakespeare are Milton's most important sources, and there has been a special interest in how allusions to these two poets play off against each other. The problem has been

9. Such a claim has obvious similarities with Stanley Fish's reading of Milton's work as a whole; his essay "Problem Solving in *Comus*" describes how the masque's *insolubilia* gradually wean us from the idea that we can know the world by our senses. He argues that such problems are there "not because we are to solve them, but because we are to be moved by them to engage in a certain kind of activity—the activity of discerning an inner truth beneath the surface of external representations" (*How Milton Works*, 148). My argument is that Milton points us not so much to such a truth as to a practical sociability—really, just consorting with others who can check our self-confidence. Stephen Orgel also wonders whether it is any good trying to tell good from evil in the forest ("The Case for Comus," 34).

10. Some recent scholarship has emphasized Milton's sense of education as a collaborative enterprise. Paul Festa studies the marginalia in Milton's Euripides, a volume likely shared with his students, and ponders the effect of circulating these revisions: "Milton . . . understood that education is essentially communal—not something that happens in isolation, but rather at the intersection of several minds" ("Repairing the Ruins," 35). Angelica Duran's unpublished dissertation emphasizes in its second chapter how single teachers in pastoral settings give way to the collective efforts of "new scientific instructors" over the course of Milton's career ("Milton, Education, and the Scientific Revolution," 15–66). Notwithstanding *Comus*'s interest in collaboration, I am inclined to think that Milton still thought of instruction primarily as an encounter between individuals; but then Barbara Lewalski's generalization may be safest: "Milton's deepest conviction . . . is that genuine education (and especially higher education) must be largely self-motivated and self-directed" ("Milton and the Hartlib Circle," 208).

developed by John Guillory and Maggie Kilgour, among others, but it was first formulated, in durable terms, by Angus Fletcher in *The Transcendental Masque*. Shakespeare, "fancy's child," is for Fletcher the great imaginative threat to Milton's didactic voice: "He could not afford the Shakespearian openness, even if he had been able to imagine it."[11] Spenserian chastity becomes a recourse for bringing doctrinal discipline to this unruly influence. "Spenser is interposed between Milton and the persistent *memory* of Shakespeare," writes John Guillory: "Spenser becomes the source of the counteractive magic, 'reversing' the continued and attractive temptation to regress into the Shakespearean plenitude."[12]

A Midsummer Night's Dream gives Milton its love potions and its haunted woods; *The Tempest* goes straight to problems of teaching. The principal teacher on Shakespeare's island is Prospero, who serves as Miranda's "schoolmaster" (1.2.171) for all their years of exile. He is schoolmaster to Caliban too, who learns to curse under his tutelage, a tuition parodied later when the abhorred slave meets Stephano and Trinculo. (The scoundrels ply him with sack—"here is that will give language to you, cat" [2.2.79]— and repeatedly urge him to "kiss the book" [2.2.124].) Even Caliban has pedagogical ambitions of a sort, telling his new masters, "I with my long nails will dig thee pig-nuts, / Show thee a jay's nest, and instruct thee how / To snare the nimble marmoset" (2.2.162–64). Throughout these scenes of instruction, the ideological assumptions of the Tudor and early Stuart schoolroom keep cropping up, played straight or slant: Prospero's pure absorption in his studies, Gonzalo's peculiar classicism, Ferdinand's schoolboy boast when he first meets Miranda—"My language! Heavens! / I am the best of them that speak this speech, / Were I but where 'tis spoken" (1.2.429–31)—as though his social rank were derived from his eloquence. A play so preoccupied with freedom and slavery inevitably discovers ironies when it looks into what Prospero calls the "liberal arts" (1.2.73).

Connections between *The Tempest* and *A Maske* proliferate with a little reflection: there is all that concern with knowing and drinking, Prospero's own masque, his worry about chastity, and on and on. What I want to

11. Fletcher, *Transcendental Masque*, 143. Milton calls Shakespeare "fancy's child" (133) in "L'Allegro."

12. Guillory, *Poetic Authority*, 90. Maggie Kilgour comments on the different ways that the two are invoked: "Shakespeare comes in mostly through verbal echoes that are often so slight and fleeting as to seem addressed to an extremely attentive reader who is saturated in the plays; Spenser is introduced, however, through thematic and formal parallels that would announce themselves more directly, even if one did not have the extratextual evidence of Milton's testimony to Spenser as the exemplar of temperance in *Areopagitica*" ("*Comus*'s Wood," 318).

concentrate on is how Milton moves his characters into and out of alignment with Shakespeare's teachers and students, for he does some of his
own deepest thinking about education by managing the allusive entrances
and exits of Prospero, Caliban, and Ariel. But wait—Ariel? Prospero's nimble sidekick is surely the least likely recruit among the island's *dramatis
personae*, at least for thinking about teaching. No one tries to teach Ariel
anything—except perhaps when Prospero is browbeating him to remember his imprisonment and his debt—nor does Ariel have anything much
he wants to teach. Still, it is he who is invoked first when the Attendant
Spirit describes his mansion among the "bright aerial spirits... In regions
mild of calm and serene air" (3–4). The two figures are linked both by their
airy nature and by their common reluctance to be bound to the troubles
of earth; a pattern of more-or-less close verbal echoes sustains the association over the length of the masque.[13] Of course, there is some of the
schoolmaster Prospero in the Attendant Spirit too: he is stage manager,
masque maker, and the speaker of the epilogue. This doubleness is crucial
to Milton's design.

Miranda, as that design unfolds, lines up readily enough with the Lady
as a specimen of threatened chastity; Caliban and Comus are the respective
threats to that chastity, each in his own wilderness. And while Comus is a
born rhetorician and Caliban an embittered student of Prospero's grammar school, the two share certain pedagogical ambitions. Both have local,
topographical knowledge that they at least pretend to be eager to impart:
"I'll show thee every fertile inch o' th' island" (2.2.142), says Caliban to
Stephano and Trinculo, and Comus offers himself as guide to "each land,
and every alley green" (310). Comus ultimately means to teach the Lady to
"Be wise, and taste" (812). And finally, Caliban wants to teach Stephano
and Trinculo at least enough about Prospero's powers that together they
can overthrow the island's sorcerer-tyrant.

It is this last scene—Caliban turned teacher against his old schoolmaster—that is the pivot of these associations, the crucial precedent for
the failure of instruction in Milton's masque. When Caliban whets his new
companions to their revolution, he is full of caution about Prospero's powers: "thou mayst brain him, / Having first seized his books... Or cut his
weasand with a knife. Remember / First to possess his books; for without
them / He's but a sot.... *Burn but his books*" (3.2.86–93, italics mine).

13. For example: "I drink the air before me" (5.1.102), says Ariel; "There I suck the liquid
air" (979), says the Attendant Spirit. Both dally with tetrameter in a largely pentameter context
(as, of course, does Comus himself).

The Attendant Spirit has similar counsel to offer. With the protection of haemony, he says,

> you may
> Boldly assault the necromancer's hall;
> Where if he be, with dauntless hardihood,
> And brandished blade rush on him, break his glass,
> And shed the luscious liquor on the ground,
> *But seize his wand*, though he and his cursed crew
> Fierce sign of battle make (647–53, italics mine)

It is Spenser who is most often invoked here by critics, in connection with the spilling of that luscious liquor: the gesture recalls Guyon casting down Excess's "sappy liquor" (2.12.56) on his way to raze the Bower of Bliss.[14] The allusion would seem to be a paradigmatic instance of Spenserian moralism imposed as discipline on Comus's Shakespearian liberties. But the script followed by the brothers is still more deeply indebted to a Shakespearian scene of rebellion against an arch-pedagogue. The larger system of identifications that had seemed to define the place of *The Tempest* in *Comus* is upended: the Attendant Spirit now is playing Caliban's part, and Comus has become Prospero. Constant between the two versions is only the fact that the assault fails. Stephano and Trinculo are distracted by the bright clothing Ariel spreads for them on the boughs outside the sorcerer's cell; the brothers fail for obscurer reasons, spilling Comus's cup and scaring him off but neglecting to disarm him. "What, have ye let the false enchanter scape?" asks the Attendant Spirit, with a schoolmasterly insistence on the painfully obvious: "O ye mistook, ye should have snatched his wand / And bound him fast" (813–15).

The result of all this confusion is not only the escape of the enchanter but, in his wake, the puzzle of a bewildering allusive dissonance. One thing at least is clear, that the brothers have not yet learned anything from their trials, or not enough: Milton goes out of his way to show them botching their instructions. Like the Lady trapped in her chair, they cannot help themselves, and they cannot help each other. The Attendant Spirit's careful lesson of harmonized collaboration has been betrayed in practice. And this is where the allusion makes things so peculiar: for by its logic, if the Spirit is a tutor, he is *also* a Caliban, a student rebelling against his own domineering teacher, perhaps against teaching altogether. What can we make of this

14. See Guillory, *Poetic Authority*, 89.

self-divided doubleness? The pedagogical stakes are only raised when we recall that this was the boys' real teacher, Lawes, in the role; and that the masque itself, for which the children would have had to rehearse, might have been conceived as part of their lessons. Milton's harmony is such a powerful resolution to that old problem, *how do we know they understand?* So why don't the boys get it; why yet one more scene of romance miseducation; and why is their teacher so turned against himself?

Lessons and Endings

The answer lies in the ending: in the masque's destiny in dance, and Milton's handling of that inevitable, ceremonial closure. But before the end there are a few last remarks to make about the relationship between endings and lessons generally.

There are a great many things that can give us the sense that a work of literature, narrative or not, has come to its conclusion: a death or a wedding, a motto or an epigram, an alexandrine or a couplet. Among the most powerful is the sense that we have been taught a lesson.[15] No kind of literature is more forthcoming with such closure than fable, which tells a little story about animals and then boils it down into a sententious moral. Once we have that lesson in hand, we know we have heard all we need to hear about the fox and the crow, and we can close the book. Fables were among the first texts read by Tudor schoolboys, and they underwrite the general expectation that any text is well understood by deriving from it an epitome, or finding the part—usually a *sententia*—that can stand for the whole.[16] That *standing for* is important: it is as though the lesson were the reason you read the book in the first place, and possession of it permission to stop, having gotten what the book had to give. The two, lesson and ending, can be so strongly associated as to seem identical. Not only is an obvious lesson a sign of closure, but conversely, the ending—whatever comes on the last page, or the last line—is to be read as a lesson,

15. Barbara Herrnstein Smith's *Poetic Closure* is still the most thorough survey of the devices by which poems end, though for the most part she avoids larger-scale narratives. See especially her pages on "Closure and the Sense of Truth" (151–58), and on epigrams (196–210). Frank Kermode's *The Sense of an Ending*, from which I borrow this chapter's title, considers mostly a contrary movement of the ending into the texture of the fiction, at the expense, over time, of expectations of strong closure.

16. Erasmus remarks: "As for the so-called [moral], that is, the interpretation of the fable, it does not matter much whether you put it at the beginning or the end. You can in fact both begin with it and end on it, provided you incorporate variety of language" (*De Copia*, in *Works*, 24:633).

as the moral or motto or meaning of what has gone before. It is the part of the story you can take with you, and reuse: the most important part.

This kind of thinking about endings—on the model of the fable, or perhaps of the oration, which achieves its closure by a pithy summing up— might lead to a curious speculation. Namely: that the ending is not properly part of the story at all. Such an idea runs counter to our oldest and most influential account of narrative, Aristotle's description of a unified action with a beginning, middle, and an end. But it has a certain power when you think about it. Is the moral, for example, really part of the fable? If so, how exactly—who speaks it, when does it happen, what are its motives? If those are the wrong questions, then isn't that because it is somehow outside the sorts of *whos*, *whens*, and *whys* proper to fiction? One might counter that the moral is more a supplement than an ending, and that the true ending is when the fox takes the cheese. But how about a trickier case: the closure offered by the multiple marriages at the end of a comic plot, an ending like that of *Euphues and His England*, where romance machinations give way to the consolidation of three ordered pairs and the exile of the extra piece. There is something static, schematic about this arrangement, which resolves what goes before but seems to be of a different order of experience. In effecting its closure it takes us outside of the story, or at least behaves in a way that the story has never behaved. (Recall how marriage is something like an epistemological horizon in *England*: "What Philautus doth they can imagine that are newly married."[17])

Perhaps the ending is different from the story in something like the way death is different from life; it marks life's limit, but is itself another country. Or, perhaps it is different from the story in the way criticism is different from the story. If the ending is the lesson, then it is a way of understanding what has gone before, a representation and therefore potentially a substitute. In the ending the story interprets itself—and that makes the ending something different from, alienated from the story.

Or if that formulation—this alienation of the ending—seems too strong, perhaps one could think of the ending-as-lesson as a different genre. Closure is achieved by a generic modulation into a more ostentatiously didactic form. Hence the comic resolution of a romance; or perhaps the lyric resolution of a comedy, where confusion is reconciled not only in the abstract pattern of the marriages but in song and dancing. On a very small scale we see this within the Spenserian stanza. It wanders through eight lines of chronically unbalanced iambic pentameter, then finishes with a six-foot

17. Lyly, *Euphues*, 462.

alexandrine, which is distinguished by the gravitas of its length and the even-handedness of the medial caesura. The lesson often falls there, primed for the commonplace book. Such mottos return us to the idea that learning may be figured by a shift in genre, that the genres of telling (could we even say, of experience?) are different from the genres of knowing, or understanding—and that we do not understand, therefore, until we have completed the crossing from one to the other. In the most general terms this is another claim about the competition between narrative and paradigmatic modes of understanding. Endings will favor the latter: they will be, therefore, different in kind, different in genre, from what they resolve.

This version of the argument, too, finally cannot survive as an unqualified generalization. There are effects of closure that are achieved within and by narrative, by, for example, what Tzvetan Todorov calls "transformation."[18] The story that begins with a separation ends with a reunion, or the story that begins with a crime ends with revenge. These events are transformations of one another, and in recognizing that (in each case) the second reverses the first, we feel that something has come to a close. Of course, even here we will be inclined to scrutinize the ending with particular care for a lesson. We don't really know what the lesson is until we see how things turn out, do we? and it is a small step to saying that the way things turn out *is* somehow the lesson. Even where there is not an obvious modulation of genre there is pressure for the ending both to solve the problems of the fiction and to understand them, to offer a form for our understanding, to take the time and the contingency out and lift us up from the middle in order to make clear not just what happened, but what what happened means.

What I want to insist upon, then, is not so much that all endings are not part of what they end as that there is a strong expectation for them to be different: to be not the story itself, but an understanding of the story. Modern fiction places more of that obligation for understanding on the reader, letting the narrative resolve or even trail off and outsourcing the burden of making it make sense. Early modern fictions characteristically assume more of that burden within themselves, providing closural forms that are intended as forms of understanding—that already have the shape of thinking *about* the story, of reflection. The point of meditating on such endings for current purposes is that the question of whether they are properly part of their fictions is so like the question of whether a lesson is part of our experience, or must be conceived of as outside or above that

18. See Todorov, "The Two Principles of Narrative," in *Genres in Discourse*, esp. 28–31.

experience. This study has taken its bearings from a pedagogical tradition that is dedicated to the second proposition, that offers concrete and immediate forms of proof for what we might think of as inescapably time-bound attainments, virtue first among them. The authority of that tradition has again and again provoked the question: is this the only way to show learning? Is this what learning is? Must a teaching fiction end—or punctuate its lessons—by stepping outside itself, betraying its narrative nature in the service of a pedagogically defined usefulness?

In asking these questions it is important not to lose sympathy with the sort of lesson that *is* estranged, one way or another, from whatever it is a lesson *about*. That would be ridiculous: such lessons are too useful; they are mostly what we mean by understanding, maxims and diagrams and perhaps books of criticism. Nor do I want to lament the lesson-character of endings, and the closural character of lessons, in fiction. The counterpoint of lesson and story is an old and rich resource for making and complicating meanings: Sidney's use of *sententiae* is a particularly self-conscious example, and if it is agonized, it is also often amusing and engrossing. What I want is to register the strain of longing within these fictions for an escape from that dialectic. This longing is in spite of the fact that it is no small part of their greatness to be trapped within it. Nonetheless, they have lost faith in their lesson-making, and particularly in the didactic forms in which they have received that obligation. This means that they have little faith in endings themselves (another reason why the dilatory romance serves such temperaments so well). As always, the question of an alternative is much less clear: it would have to be a story that is somehow sufficient to itself in its unfolding, that is known by the complicated cause-and-effect that holds it together and that holds our attention, and not otherwise. In this direction lies the activity of reading for pleasure, letting go of *docere* to let *placere* take care of itself. In that sense these texts are all a particularly conflicted part of the history of reading for its own sake. That, however, is not exactly where the problem leads for Milton.

One last time, then, I want to ask, what have the children learned at the end of *Comus*, and how do we know they understand? It might be argued that these questions are precisely not the point, that what is demonstrated when Sabrina releases the Lady from her frozen seat is the power of chastity as a conduit of grace. Problems of practical instruction are outgrown. But I will suggest again that Milton's decision to interrupt Comus's temptation, and interrupt it by a notably bungled rescue, implies that the children must continue to live their lives in a meantime during which the Lady's high prophecies are necessarily deferred.[19] So long as that meantime lasts, practical lessons about collaboration—lessons analogous to what Alice, John, and Thomas were learning by putting on the masque—matter a great deal.[20] Comus is still out there, and it seems unwise to count on Sabrina's intercession next time, so how do we know the children will be, as Spenser would put it, ware of like again? They will not tell us, for none of them speaks again after the brothers' fiasco. Instead, they dance, first with the "Country Dancers," and then in a formal presentation to their parents after the Attendant Spirit waves the shepherds off. He celebrates their achievement in a song:

> Heaven hath timely tried their youth,
> Their faith, their patience, and their truth,
> And sent them here through hard assays
> With a crown of deathless praise,
> To triumph in victorious dance
> O'er sensual folly, and intemperance. (969–74)

The last line relaxes the four-beat dance rhythms into pentameter again, easing the transition back to poetry. But the dance remains irreducibly different.

So here is another one of those alienated endings. In some sense, of course, dance is native to masque, constitutive of it: it is how such dramas always end, and it has a place in the middle of the action too, with the antimasque. (It is even shot through much of the masque's talk, in a punning pas de deux with Milton's metrical games.) Still, when the masque wants to show the outcome of the children's trials—when it wants to prove their virtue to their parents—it switches modes, and puts their bodies into emblematic motion. As proofs go, this must have been moving in every sense, as the children gave themselves over to learned habits of coordinated

---

19. Debora Shuger also emphasizes the masque's operation in a pragmatic meantime: see "'Gums of Glutinous Heat' and the Stream of Consciousness: The Theology of Milton's Maske."

20. Stephen Orgel observes that the children had danced in the masques *Tempe Restored* and *Coelum Brittanicum* at Whitehall ("Case," 34). His article also ponders what the children might have been meant to learn from the experience of acting, and his focus on Alice—whom he takes to be the object of a muted campaign to temper her adolescent moral rigidity, and get her thinking about marriage—complements mine on the brothers, as a lesson for the meantime. The gentle erotic teasing and cajolery of the Spirit's summoning of Sabrina, with its cinnamon and "alluring locks" (881) and its injunction to "bridle [bridal?] in thy headlong wave" (886), I think corroborates his view.

action. If it is practical harmony that the Attendant Spirit sought to teach the brothers, surely this is its epitome. It is a kind of knowing, too. In the midst of her wanderings, the Lady asks, "O where else / Shall I inform my unacquainted feet / In the blind mazes of this tangled wood" (178–80). Now her dancing feet are informed by the dance itself. This is the great power of such motion, to suggest knowing in the doing of it, the harmonic reconciliation that Yeats recognizes when he can no longer tell the dancer from the dance.

But you can still tell the dance from the poem, and it is in the larger context of the poem—the text, the words the actors were to speak—that the dance is supposed to mean not only knowing how to dance, but knowing how to be virtuous. Milton was sensitive to the magical properties of dance, and how, in the masque tradition, it can figure celestial order and political deference alike—ways that the dancers might be said to comprehend something larger than themselves by their activity.[21] But what about those practical challenges with which the masque began, recognizing evil, working together? The masque has raised questions of practical instruction, and taken some trouble to probe their difficulties. Is the sublimation of dance an answer? Do we now know that the children understand what to do in the tangled wood?

These are Spenserian questions. The best evidence that Milton is troubled by them too comes at the end of the masque, when the Attendant Spirit takes his leave: "To the ocean now I fly, / And those happy climes that lie / Where day never shuts his eye" (975–77). In its impulse to liberty his valediction is like Prospero's, "Let your indulgence set me free" (5.1.339), and it is Prospero's demanding role that he has been playing, orchestrating the harmonious last act—and yet now his energy, his diction, and his meter seem much more those of Ariel drinking the liquid air, the airy spirit liberated into his element. "But now my task is smoothly done, / I can fly, or I can run / Quickly to the green earth's end" (1011–13). It is just the moment for a Spenserian correction to counterbalance this Shakespearian extravagance, and that is just where Milton's imagination tends, to the gardens fair "Where young Adonis oft reposes, / Waxing well of his deep wound / In slumber soft" (998–1000). The lines that follow deliberately evoke the Garden of Adonis, moving just as Spenser does from

---

21. See Blair Hoxby, "The Meaning of Dance: Milton and the Stuart Masque." Hoxby argues for Milton's fundamental faith in the power of dance to "tutor, temper, and transform the soul, whether for good or ill" (forthcoming, n.p.). While I am interested in a shadow of doubt that falls on dance as a representation of tuition and as a kind of tuition both, that doubt means less if we cannot acknowledge the hope Hoxby describes.

Venus to Cupid and Psyche in their bower. But the Garden of Adonis is not the Bower of Bliss. It is the one space in Spenser's poem that is never transgressed by any of its characters; its recirculation of souls superintends the action, lifted above all the drama of instruction and ignorance. There is nothing for the characters to learn there; what it has to teach the reader is perhaps just how little the romance plot matters.

It is to such a garden that the Attendant Spirit hastens, and I want to listen, in his last speech, for the sound of abdication:

> Mortals that would follow me,
> Love virtue, she alone is free,
> She can teach ye how to climb
> Higher than the sphery chime;
> Or if Virtue feeble were,
> Heaven itself would stoop to her. (1017–22)

There is great consolation to be taken here: virtue will teach you to how to ascend to heaven, by due steps, presumably, or even by Raphael's gradual scale; should this instruction be insufficient, heaven will reach down to lift virtue up, and presumably lift you along with her. But the Spirit seems to be trying awfully hard to get himself out of the picture, to become as free of that burden of instructing and stooping as the unteaching and unteachable Ariel is from the schoolmastering in *The Tempest*. If the *Maske Performed at Ludlow Castle* is Milton's first school, the students there have more or less botched their lessons, then gone silent while the generic machinery celebrates their triumph over sin. When the dancing is done, the schoolmaster Lawes exits the schoolroom running. What the masque above all does not want to know, what it perhaps even finds in its heart to joke about not knowing, is what these children have really learned. And once again: who dares ask that? Better to leave them dancing, and let that be the end their parents remember.

The Milton of the text of *Comus* I have relied upon is the Milton of 1637, rethinking and revising the Milton of 1634: still well before he published "On Education" in 1644, and before his own run as a schoolmaster tutoring his nephews. At the time of the performance he was in the midst of a half-decade of study in his father's house in Hammersmith, a self-prescribed antidote to the academic disappointments of Cambridge. But he seems to have loved and honored his grammar-school teachers: why this current of doubt, this half-winking, but only half-winking exasperation with the burden of instruction?[22] What was it that turned him to *The Tempest*, with its corrosive skepticism about schoolmastering? It is just possible that Milton felt that year more like a Lyly or Spenser than at any other time in his life. Even if he was not actively pursuing favor at court, still, on the morning of September 10, 1634, after the performance had taken place in Ludlow, he might well have wondered if this was what his vocation as a poet would amount to. Ann Coiro makes such a suggestion: she wonders if he "stood at the threshold of a life of literary service and artistic collaboration that seems to us now to be utterly inimical to our sense of Milton's career, but that then must have been the life he could see himself beginning."[23] Perhaps, that is, there was reason to wonder whether all his learning might come down to this, writing masques on commission, seeking patronage and preferment. Was this to be the fruit of his high study?

In the event, no. Not only did his learning ultimately lead to government office, in the drastically changed circumstances of the interregnum, but his career as a teacher and educational theorist unfolded in a much more various and variously promising pedagogical landscape. Even in his Cambridge years, he took an interest in the new science, and later he would make the acquaintance of Boyle and Hartlib and others in London.[24] In the writing of these men and their fellow travelers a new version of learning from experience was emerging, one that founded knowledge on progressive observation of the real world, and there was born with it a view of pedagogy as a recapitulation of empirical knowledge-making. Milton was by no means the most forward of the thinkers pursuing these ideas: Charles Webster describes him as "perhaps the only leading writer to embody a compromise between the new and old pedagogies."[25] But one can hear the ring of the new in his "Of Education": "our understanding cannot in this body found it selfe but on sensible things," he writes, "nor arrive so clearly to the knowledge of God and things invisible, as by orderly conning over the visible and inferior creature."[26]

---

22. On Milton's fondness for his grammar teachers see the letters to Thomas Young and Alexander Gill collected in the *Complete Prose* (1:307–43). Arthur Barker follows their careers in "Milton's Schoolmasters."

23. Coiro, "Anonymous Milton," 610.

24. Lewalski, *The Life of John Milton: A Critical Biography*, 29–30. Angelica Duran surveys the range of Milton's acquaintance among London's natural philosophers and educational reformers in "Milton, Education, and the Scientific Revolution," 15–66.

25. Webster, *The Great Instauration*, 113.

26. Milton, *Complete Prose*, 2:367–69. He goes on, "the same method is necessarily to be followed in all discreet teaching," an idea of method—moving from sensible evidence to abstract

His most ambitious work of educational thinking, of course, is *Paradise Lost*, a poem that particularly does not end with dancing:

> The world was all before them, where to choose
> Their place of rest, and providence their guide:
> They hand in hand with wandering steps and slow
> Through Eden took their solitary way. (12.646–49)

Instead of practiced steps, we have wandering steps, the uncertain footing readers of *Comus* might remember from the middle of the masque. Adam and Eve's departure from Eden does not cancel or displace or redeem what has gone before. It is not the kind of ending that is easily pried away from the story; it is not a form of understanding we can apply backward to it. It is barely an ending at all. For all these reasons it is as good a moment as any to point to and say: now it is somehow possible to hope to learn by trial and error, to subscribe to an education by experience; now it is possible to begin to unfold learning in the form of a story. How else could it be told? For Adam and Eve this has already begun to happen, with their sequence of angelic tutors and the various sad discoveries of the Fall. More importantly, it is all that can happen next, as they begin our wandering. The landscape into which they walk is that of a genre neither Sidney nor Spenser nor any of their contemporaries could contemplate, the bildungsroman.

But that is another story.

---

ideas—contrary to his persistent interest in Ramist doctrine. William Riggs argues persuasively for the looseness of Milton's methodical convictions when it comes to poetry in "Poetry and Method in Milton's *Of Education*," 458. See also Duhamel, "Milton's Alleged Ramism."

ACKNOWLEDGMENTS

This is a book about the impossible profession, written even as I have been finding my feet in it: chalk up its perversities to that predicament. They should not, in any event, be blamed on my own teachers, in whom I have been extraordinarily lucky. Sage and serious John Hollander deserves first mention, for many years of counsel by turns steadying and startling. He will always sit in the front row of my imaginary audience. Lawrence Manley too, shrewd and patient codirector of the original dissertation. A few who have never seen this book sit nearby: Stephen Seybolt, Howard Stern, Jonathan Lear, Geoffrey Hartman. Among those who have befriended its pages and its ideas—and I fear I have forgotten more than one—are Dan Aaron, Oliver Arnold, Leonard Barkan, Emily Barton, Harry Berger, Larry Berger, Leslie Brisman, Ann Coiro, David Coleman, Larry Danson, Billy Flesch, Angus Fletcher, Ken Gross, Blair Hoxby, Heather James, Sean Keilen, Rebecca Lemon, Nancy Lindheim, Maureen McLane, David Lee Miller, Erika Naginski, Jeff Nunokawa, Stephen Orgel, Annabel Patterson, Joanna Picciotto, Anne Prescott, Chris Pye, Jim Richardson, David Quint, Elaine Scarry, Nigel Smith, Susan Stewart, Julie Tannenbaum, Michael Wood, and, last but not least, the anonymous reviewers for the University of Chicago Press. At the Press itself, Alan Thomas has been infallibly generous and helpful. Graham and Christina Burnett deserve special thanks, for hermeneutic genius and fast friendship. Blessings upon my overqualified eleventh-hour research assistants, J. K. Barrett, James Bickford, Abby Heald, Liz Melly, Dan Moss, and Leah Whittington. Finally, my greatest debt is to my parents, who taught me how to love what I do.

The project has also been fortunate in its sponsors. Its earliest version was written as a dissertation while I was a Junior Fellow at the Harvard Society of Fellows, under Diana Morse's watchful eye. Its dismemberment and reinvention were abetted by a short-term fellowship from the Folger Library, and by a year spent in California under the dual auspices of the Stanford Humanities Center and the American Council of Learned Societies. Princeton University has provided extraordinary practical and collegial support over the last five years. I owe a debt of a different kind to Boston High School and the English High School, where I spent a year teaching a big group of ninth graders who (often in spite of themselves) helped me recover my vocation at a moment of doubt.

I am grateful to the Beinecke Library for permission to use portions of "When to Stop Reading *The Faerie Queene*," which first appeared in *Never Again Would Birds' Song Be the Same: New Essays on Poetry and Poetics, Renaissance to Modern*, ed. Jennifer Lewin (New Haven, CT: Beinecke Library, Yale University, 2002).

BIBLIOGRAPHY

PRIMARY SOURCES

Anonymous. *The Poems of the Pearl Manuscript: Pearl, Cleanness, Patience, Sir Gawain and the Green Knight*. Edited by Malcolm Andrew and Ronald Waldron. Exeter: University of Exeter, 1987.

———. *The Unfortunate Lovers: The History of Argalus and Parthenia*. London, 1705.

Aphthonius. *Aphthonii Sophistae Progymnasmata*. London, 1575.

Ariosto, Ludovico. *Orlando Furioso. Translated into English Heroical Verse by Sir John Harington*. Edited by Robert McNulty. Oxford: Clarendon Press, 1972.

Aristotle. *The Complete Works of Aristotle: The Revised Oxford Translation*. Edited by Jonathan Barnes. 2 vols. Princeton, NJ: Princeton University Press, 1984.

Ascham, Roger. *Letters of Roger Ascham*. Translated by Maurice Hatch and Alvin Vos. New York: Peter Lang, 1989.

———. *The Schoolmaster (1570)*. Edited by Lawrence V. Ryan. Ithaca, NY: Cornell University Press, 1967.

Bacon, Francis. *Novum Organum, with Other Parts of the Great Instauration*. Translated and edited by Peter Urbach and John Gibson. Chicago: Open Court, 1994.

———. *The Works of Francis Bacon*. Edited by James Spedding, Robert Leslie Ellis, and Douglas Denon Heath. 14 vols. Stuttgart-Bad Cannstatt: F. Frommann Verl. G. Holzboog, 1963–86.

Baldwin, William. *A Treatice of Moral Philosophy Contaynynge the Sayinges of the Wise*. London, 1571.

———. *A Treatise of Morall Phylosophie Contaynyng the Sayinges of the Wyse*. London, 1547.

Berry, Lloyd E., ed. *The Geneva Bible, a Facsimile of the 1560 Edition*. Madison: University of Wisconsin Press, 1969.

Brinsley, John. *A Consolation for Our Grammar Schooles*. London, 1622.

———. *Ludus Literarius*. London, 1612.

Burton, Robert. *The Anatomy of Melancholy*. 3 vols. London: Dent, 1964.

Cato, Marcus Porcius. *Catonis Disticha*. London, 1553.

———. *Preceptes of Cato with Annotacions of D. Erasmus of Roterodame*. London, 1560.

Chapman, George. *Chapman's Homer: The Iliad, the Odyssey, and the Lesser Homerica*. Edited by Allardyce Nicoll. 2 vols. Princeton, NJ: Princeton University Press, 1967.

Chaucer, Geoffrey. *The Riverside Chaucer*. Edited by Larry Dean Benson. 3rd ed. Boston: Houghton Mifflin, 1987.

Chrétien de Troyes. *Lancelot: The Knight of the Cart*. Translated by Burton Raffel. New Haven, CT: Yale University Press, 1997.

Cicero, Marcus Tullius. *Cicero in Twenty-Eight Volumes*. The Loeb Classical Library. Cambridge, MA: Harvard University Press, 1972.

Coote, Edmund. *The English Schoole-Maister*. London, 1596.

Dante. *The Divine Comedy*. Edited by Charles Singleton. 3 vols. Princeton, NJ: Princeton University Press, 1977.

Elyot, Thomas. *A Critical Edition of Sir Thomas Elyot's the Boke Named the Governour*. Edited by Donald Warren Rude. New York: Garland, 1992.

Erasmus. *Apothegmes*. Translated by Nicholas Udall. London, 1542.

———. *Collected Works of Erasmus*. 86 vols. Toronto: University of Toronto Press, 1974–.

———. *Opera Omnia Desiderii Erasmi*. 9 vols. Amsterdam: North-Holland, 1969–.

Ford, Emanuel. *Parismus, the Renoumed Prince of Bohemia His Most Famous, Delectable, and Pleasant Historie*. London, 1598.

Fraunce, Abraham. *The Arcadian Rhetorike*. London, 1588.

———. *The Lawiers Logike*. London, 1588.

Fulwood, William. *The Enimie of Idlenesse Teaching the Maner and Stile How to Endite, Compose and Write All Sorts of Epistles and Letters*. London, 1568.

Gascoigne, George. *A Hundreth Sundrie Flowres*. Edited by G. W. Pigman. Oxford: Clarendon Press, 2000.

Glapthorne, Henry. *Argalus and Parthenia: As It Hath Been Acted at the Court before Their Maiesties: And at the Private-House in Drury-Lane, by Their Maiesties Servants*. London, 1639.

Gosson, Stephen. *The Schoole of Abuse*. Edited by Edward Arber. New York: AMS Press, 1966.

Greene, Robert. *Greenes Never Too Late; or, a Powder of Experience*. London, 1590.

———. *The Life and Complete Works in Prose and Verse of Robert Greene*. Edited by Alexander Grosart. 15 vols. London, 1881.

———. *Mamillia: A Mirrour or Looking-Glasse for the Ladies of Englande*. London, 1583.

———. *Morando the Tritameron of Love*. London, 1584.

Greville, Fulke. *The Prose Works of Fulke Greville, Lord Brooke*. Edited by John Gouws. Oxford: Clarendon Press, 1986.

Guevara, Antonio de. *The Diall of Princes*. Translated by Sir Thomas North. London, 1557.

———. *The Golden Boke of Marcus Aurelius Emperour and Eloquent Oratour*. Translated by John Bourchier. London, 1535.

Hall, Joseph. *The Art of Divine Meditation*. London, 1609.

Harrison, William. *The Description of England: The Classic Contemporary Account of Tudor Social Life*. Edited by Georges Edelen. Washington, DC: Folger Shakespeare Library, 1994.

Homer. *The Odyssey*. Translated by Robert Fagles. New York: Penguin, 1997.

Hoole, Charles. *A New Discovery of the Old Art of Teaching Schoole*. London, 1661.

Horace. *Satires, Epistles, and Ars Poetica*. Translated by H. Rushton Fairclough. The Loeb Classical Library. Cambridge, MA: Harvard University Press, 1991.

Hoskins, John. *Directions for Speech and Style*. Edited by Hoyt H. Hudson. Princeton, NJ: Princeton University Press, 1935.

Jonson, Ben. *Poetaster*. Edited by T. G. S. Cain. The Revels Plays. Manchester: Manchester University Press, 1995.

Leach, Arthur F. *Educational Charters and Documents 598 to 1909*. Cambridge: The University Press, 1911.

Lever, Ralph. *The Arte of Reason, Rightly Termed, Witcraft*. London, 1573.

Lily, William. *A Shorte Introduction of Grammar*. London, 1573.

Ling, Nicholas. *Politeuphuia, Wits Commonwealth*. London, 1612.

Lyly, John. *Euphues: The Anatomy of Wit; Euphues & His England*. Edited by Morris W. Croll and Harry Clemons. London: G. Routledge, 1916.

Malory, Sir Thomas. *Le Morte D'Arthur*. 2 vols. London: Penguin, 1986.

Marlowe, Christopher. *The Complete Works of Christopher Marlowe*. Edited by Roma Gill. 5 vols. Oxford: Clarendon Press, 1987–98.

Merchant-Taylors' School. *The Schools-Probation: Or, Rules and Orders for Certain Set-Exercises to Bee Performed by the Scholars on Probation-Daies*. London, 1661.

Meres, Francis. *Palladis Tamia Wits Treasury Being the Second Part of Wits Common Wealth*. London, 1598.

Milton, John. *Complete Prose Works of John Milton*. Edited by Don Marion Wolfe. 8 vols. New Haven, CT: Yale University Press, 1953–82.

———. *Complete Shorter Poems*. Edited by John Carey. 2nd ed. London: Longman, 1997.

———. *Paradise Lost*. Edited by Alastair Fowler. 2nd ed. London: Longman, 1998.

Moffett, Thomas. *Nobilis; or, a View of the Life and Death of a Sidney, and Lessus Lugubris*. Edited and translated by Virgil B. Heltzel and Hoyt H. Hudson. San Marino, CA: The Huntington Library, 1940.

Montaigne, Michel de. *The Complete Essays of Montaigne*. Translated by Donald M. Frame. Stanford, CA: Stanford University Press, 1965.

Mulcaster, Richard. *Mulcaster's Elementarie*. Edited by E. T. Campagnac. Oxford: Clarendon Press, 1925.

———. *Positions Concerning the Training Up of Children*. Edited by William Barker. Toronto: University of Toronto Press, 1994.

Northbrooke, John. *Spiritus Est Vicarius Christi in Terra. The Poore Mans Garden*. London, 1575.

Nowell, Alexander. *A Catechisme, or Institution of Christian Religion*. London, 1583.

Ovid. *Ovid in Six Volumes*. The Loeb Classical Library. 6 vols. Cambridge, MA: Harvard University Press, 1969.

Parry, Robert. *Moderatus, the Most Delectable & Famous Historie of the Blacke Knight*. London, 1595.

Peacham, Henry. *The Garden of Eloquence (1593)*. Gainesville, FL: Scholars' Facsimiles and Reprints, 1954.

Pepper, Robert D., ed. *Four Tudor Books on Education*. Gainesville, FL: Scholars' Facsimiles and Reprints, 1966.

Pettie, George. *A Petite Pallace of Pettie His Pleasure*. London, 1576.

Plato. *Euthyphro, Apology, Crito, Meno, Gorgias, Menexenus*. Translated by R. E. Allen. New Haven, CT: Yale University Press, 1984.

Pliny. *Natural History*. Translated by W. H. S. Jones. The Loeb Classical Library. Cambridge, MA: Harvard University Press, 1938.

Primaudaye, Pierre de la. *The French Academie Wherin Is Discoursed the Institution of Maners*. London, 1586.

Puttenham, George. *The Arte of English Poesie*. Edited by Alice Walker and Gladys Doidge Willcock. Cambridge: The University Press, 1936.

Quarles, Francis. *Argalus and Parthenia*. Washington, DC: Folger Shakespeare Library, 1986.

Quintilian. *The Orator's Education*. Translated by Donald A. Russell. The Loeb Classical Library. 5 vols. Cambridge, MA: Harvard University Press, 2001.

Ramus, Petrus. *Dialecticae Libri Duo*. London, 1584.

———. *Scholae in Liberales Artes*. Basel, 1569.

Rich, Barnabe. *The Straunge and Wonderfull Aduentures of Don Simonides*. London, 1581.

Roberts, Henry. *Honours Conquest Wherein Is Conteined the Famous Hystorie of Edward of Lancaster*. London, 1598.

Shakespeare, William. *The Complete Works*. Edited by Stanley Wells and Gary Taylor. Oxford: Oxford University Press, 1988.

Sherry, Richard. *A Treatise of Schemes and Tropes*. London, 1550.

Sidney, Sir Philip. *The Correspondence of Sir Philip Sidney and Hubert Languet*. Translated by Steuart A. Pears. London: W. Pickering, 1845.

———. *The Countess of Pembroke's Arcadia*. Edited by Maurice Evans. London: Penguin, 1987.

———. *The Countess of Pembroke's Arcadia: The New Arcadia*. Edited by Victor Skretkowicz. Oxford: Clarendon Press, 1987.

———. *The Countess of Pembroke's Arcadia: The Old Arcadia*. Edited by Jean Robertson. Oxford: Clarendon Press, 1973.

———. *The Countess of Pembroke's Arcadia: The Old Arcadia*. Edited by Katherine Duncan-Jones. Oxford: Oxford University Press, 1990.

———. *Miscellaneous Prose of Sir Philip Sidney*. Edited by Katherine Duncan-Jones. Oxford: Oxford University Press, 1973.

———. *The Poems of Sir Philip Sidney*. Edited by William Ringler. Oxford: Oxford University Press, 1962.

———. *Sir Philip Sidney*. Edited by Katherine Duncan-Jones. The Oxford Authors. Oxford: Oxford University Press, 1989.

———, and Robert Devereux, Earl of Essex. *Profitable Instructions Describing What Speciall Obseruations Are to Be Taken by Trauellers in All Nations, States and Countries*. London, 1633.

Smith, G. Gregory, ed. *Elizabethan Critical Essays*. 2 vols. London: Oxford University Press, 1967.

Smith, Sir Thomas. *De Republica Anglorum*. London, 1583.

Spenser, Edmund. *The Faerie Queene*. Edited by A. C. Hamilton. 2nd ed. New York: Longman, 2001.

Stanbridge, John, and Robert Whittington. *The Vulgaria of John Stanbridge and the Vulgaria of Robert Whittington*. Edited by Beatrice White. London: Published for the Early English Text Society by K. Paul Trench Trubner, 1932.

Stockwood, John. *The Treatise of the Figures*. London, 1674.

Sturm, Johann. *Johann Sturm on Education: The Reformation and Humanist Learning*. Edited by Lewis William Spitz and Barbara Sher Tinsley. St. Louis: Concordia, 1995.

Taverner, Richard. *The Garden of Wysdome Conteynynge Pleasaunte Floures*. London, 1550.

Temple, Sir William. *William Temple's Analysis of Sir Philip Sidney's Apology for Poetry: An Edition and Translation*. Edited and translated by John Webster. Binghamton: Center for Medieval and Early Renaissance Studies, State University of New York at Binghamton, 1984.

Virgil. *The Aeneid of Henry Howard, Earl of Surrey*. Edited by Florence H. Ridley. Berkeley: University of California Press, 1963.

———. *Eclogues, Georgics, Aeneid 1–6*. Transated by H. Rushton Fairclough. The Loeb Classical Library. Cambridge, MA: Harvard University Press, 1999.

Vives, Juan Luis. *The Passions of the Soul: The Third Book of De Anima Et Vita*. Translated by Carlos G. Norena. Lewiston: E. Mellen Press, 1990.

———. *Vives and the Renascence Education of Women*. Edited by Foster Watson. New York: Longmans, Green, 1912.

———. *Vives: On Education: A Translation of the De Tradendis Disciplinis of Juan Luis Vives.* Translated by Foster Watson. Cambridge: Cambridge University Press, 1913.

Whitney, Geffrey. *A Choice of Emblems.* London, 1586.

Yeats, W. B. *The Poems.* Edited by Richard J. Finneran. New York: Macmillan, 1983.

SECONDARY SOURCES

Alexander, Michael Van Cleave. *The Growth of English Education, 1348–1648: A Social and Cultural History.* University Park: Pennsylvania State University Press, 1990.

Allen, Danielle S. *The World of Prometheus: The Politics of Punishing in Democratic Athens.* Princeton, NJ: Princeton University Press, 2000.

Allen, Don Cameron. *Mysteriously Meant: The Rediscovery of Pagan Symbolism and Allegorical Interpretation in the Renaissance.* Baltimore, MD: Johns Hopkins Press, 1970.

Alpers, Paul. "Narration in *The Faerie Queene.*" *ELH* 44.1 (1977): 19–39.

Altman, Joel B. *The Tudor Play of Mind: Rhetorical Inquiry and the Development of Elizabethan Drama.* Berkeley: University of California Press, 1978.

Amussen, Susan D. "Punishment, Discipline, and Power: The Social Meanings of Violence in Early Modern England." *Journal of British Studies* 34 (1995): 1–34.

Anderson, Judith H. *Words That Matter: Linguistic Perception in Renaissance English.* Stanford, CA: Stanford University Press, 1996.

Ascoli, Albert. *Ariosto's Bitter Harmony: Crisis and Evasion in the Italian Renaissance.* Princeton, NJ: Princeton University Press, 1987.

Astell, Ann W. "Sidney's Didactic Method in *The Old Arcadia.*" *Studies in English Literature, 1500–1900* 24.1 (1984): 39–51.

Baldwin, Thomas Whitfield. *William Shakspere's Petty School.* Urbana: University of Illinois Press, 1943.

———. *William Shakspere's Small Latine & Lesse Greeke.* 2 vols. Urbana: University of Illinois Press, 1944.

Barkan, Leonard. *The Gods Made Flesh: Metamorphosis & the Pursuit of Paganism.* New Haven, CT: Yale University Press, 1986.

Barker, Arthur. "Milton's Schoolmasters." *Modern Language Review* 32.4 (1937): 1–20.

Bate, Jonathan. *Shakespeare and Ovid.* Oxford: Clarendon Press, 1993.

Bates, Catherine. "'A Large Occasion of Discourse': John Lyly and the Art of Civil Conversation." *Review of English Studies* 42.168 (1991): 469–86.

Bennington, Geoffrey. *Sententiousness and the Novel: Laying Down the Law in Eighteenth-Century French Fiction.* Cambridge: Cambridge University Press, 1985.

Berger, Harry, Jr. *The Allegorical Temper: Vision and Reality in Book II of Spenser's Faerie Queene.* New Haven, CT: Yale University Press, 1957.

———. "Narrative as Rhetoric in *The Faerie Queene.*" *English Literary Renaissance* 21.1 (1991): 3–48.

———. *Revisionary Play: Studies in the Spenserian Dynamics.* Berkeley: University of California Press, 1988.

Biester, James. *Lyric Wonder: Rhetoric and Wit in Renaissance English Poetry.* Rhetoric & Society. Ithaca, NY: Cornell University Press, 1997.

Bourdieu, Pierre. *The Logic of Practice.* Stanford, CA: Stanford University Press, 1990.

———, and Jean-Claude Passeron. *Reproduction in Education, Society and Culture.* Translated by Richard Nice. London: Sage, 1977.

Bouwsma, William J. "The Two Faces of Humanism: Stoicism and Augustinianism in Renaissance Thought." In *Itinerarium Italicum: The Profile of the Italian Renaissance in the Mirror of Its European Transformations*, edited by Heiko A. Oberman and Thomas A. Brady, 3–60. Leiden: Brill, 1975.

Bracken, C. W. "The Plymouth Grammar School." *Report and Transactions of the Devonshire Association for the Advancement of Science, Literature and Art* 76 (1944): 141–66.

Braden, Gordon. *Renaissance Tragedy and the Senecan Tradition: Anger's Privilege.* New Haven, CT: Yale University Press, 1985.

Briggs, John, et al. *Crime and Punishment in England: An Introductory History.* London: UCL Press, 1996.

Brown, J. Howard. *Elizabethan Schooldays.* Oxford: Basil Blackwell, 1933.

Bruner, Jerome. "Narrative and Paradigmatic Modes of Thought." In *Learning and Teaching: The Ways of Knowing,* edited by Elliot Eisner, 97–115. Yearbook of the National Society for the Study of Education. Chicago: University of Chicago Press, 1985.

Bushnell, Rebecca W. *A Culture of Teaching: Early Modern Humanism in Theory and Practice.* Ithaca, NY: Cornell University Press, 1996.

Carey, John. "Structure and Rhetoric in Philip Sidney's *Arcadia.*" In *Sir Philip Sidney: An Anthology of Modern Criticism,* edited by Dennis Kay, 245–64. Oxford: Clarendon Press, 1987.

Cartwright, Kent. *Theatre and Humanism: English Drama in the Sixteenth Century.* Cambridge: Cambridge University Press, 1999.

Caspari, Fritz. *Humanism and the Social Order in Tudor England.* Chicago: University of Chicago Press, 1954.

Cave, Terence C. *The Cornucopian Text: Problems of Writing in the French Renaissance.* Oxford: Clarendon Press, 1979.

Cavell, Stanley. "Declining Decline." In *The Cavell Reader,* edited by Stephen Mulhall, 321–52. Cambridge: Blackwell, 1996.

———. *Disowning Knowledge: In Six Plays of Shakespeare.* Cambridge: Cambridge University Press, 1987.

Cefalu, Paul. *Moral Identity in Early Modern English Literature.* Cambridge: Cambridge University Press, 2004.

Charlton, Kenneth. *Education in Renaissance England.* London: Routledge and Kegan Paul, 1965.

Cheney, Donald. *Spenser's Image of Nature: Wild Man and Shepherd in the Faerie Queene.* New Haven, CT: Yale University Press, 1966.

Clark, Donald Lemen. *John Milton at St. Paul's School: A Study of Ancient Rhetoric in English Renaissance Education.* New York: Columbia University Press, 1948.

Coiro, Ann B. "Anonymous Milton, or, a *Maske* Masked." *ELH* 71 (2004): 609–29.

Colie, Rosalie L. *The Resources of Kind: Genre-Theory in the Renaissance.* Berkeley: University of California Press, 1973.

Cornilliat, Francois. "Exemplarities: A Response to Timothy Hampton and Karlheinz Stierle." *Journal of the History of Ideas* 59.4 (1998): 613–24.

Crane, Mary Thomas. *Framing Authority: Sayings, Self, and Society in Sixteenth-Century England.* Princeton, NJ: Princeton University Press, 1993.

Croll, Morris W. *Style, Rhetoric, and Rhythm: Essays by Morris W. Croll.* Edited by J. Max Patrick et al. Princeton, NJ: Princeton University Press, 1966.

DeMolen, Richard L. "Richard Mulcaster and the Profession of Teaching in Sixteenth-Century England." *Journal of the History of Ideas* 35.1 (1974): 121–29.

———. *Richard Mulcaster and Educational Reform in the Renaissance.* Nieuwkoop, The Netherlands: De Graaf, 1991.

Devereaux, Simon, and Paul Griffiths, eds. *Penal Practice and Culture, 1500–1900: Punishing the English.* New York: Palgrave Macmillan, 2004.

Dolven, Jeff. "The Method of Spenser's Stanza." *Spenser Studies* 19 (2004): 17–25.

———. "Spenser and the Troubled Theaters." *English Literary Renaissance* 29.2 (1999): 179–200.

Doody, Margaret A. *The True Story of the Novel*. New Brunswick, NJ: Rutgers University Press, 1996.

Draper, F. W. M. *Four Centuries of Merchant Taylors' School, 1561–1961*. London: Oxford University Press, 1962.

Duhamel, P. Albert. "Milton's Alleged Ramism." *PMLA* 67.7 (1952): 1035–53.

Duncan-Jones, Katherine. "Sidney and Titian." In *English Renaissance Studies Presented to Dame Helen Gardner in Honour of Her Seventieth Birthday*, edited by John Carey and Helen Peters, 1–11. Oxford: Clarendon Press, 1980.

———. *Sir Philip Sidney, Courtier Poet*. New Haven, CT: Yale University Press, 1991.

Duran, Angelica. "Milton, Education, and the Scientific Revolution." Ph.D. diss., Stanford University, 2000.

DuRocher, Richard J. *Milton among the Romans: The Pedagogy and Influence of Milton's Latin Curriculum*. Pittsburgh: Duquesne University Press, 2001.

Eliot, T. S. *The Sacred Wood: Essays on Poetry and Criticism*. London: Methuen, 1950.

———. *Selected Essays*. New York: Harcourt Brace and World, 1964.

Feingold, Mordechai. "English Ramism: A Reinterpretation." In *The Influence of Petrus Ramus: Studies in Sixteenth and Seventeenth Century Philosophy and Sciences*, edited by Mordechai Feingold, Joseph S. Freedman, and Wolfgang Romer, 127–76. Basel: Schwabe, 2001.

Felman, Shoshana. "Psychoanalysis and Education: Teaching Terminable and Interminable." In *The Pedagogical Imperative: Teaching as a Literary Genre*, edited by Barbara Johnson, 411–29. Yale French Studies. New Haven, CT: Yale University Press, 1982.

Ferguson, Arthur B. *The Articulate Citizen and the English Renaissance*. Durham, NC: Duke University Press, 1965.

Ferguson, Margaret. "Teaching and/as Reproduction." *Yale Journal of Criticism* 1.2 (1988): 213–22.

Fernie, Ewan. *Shame in Shakespeare*. London: Routledge, 2002.

Festa, Thomas. "Repairing the Ruins: Milton as Reader and Educator." *Milton Studies* 43 (2004): 35–63.

Fish, Stanley Eugene. *How Milton Works*. Cambridge, MA: Harvard University Press, 2001.

Fletcher, Angus. *Allegory, the Theory of a Symbolic Mode*. Ithaca, NY: Cornell University Press, 1964.

———. *Colors of the Mind: Conjectures on Thinking in Literature*. Cambridge, MA: Harvard University Press, 1991.

———. *The Prophetic Moment: An Essay on Spenser*. Chicago: University of Chicago Press, 1971.

———. *The Transcendental Masque: An Essay on Milton's Comus*. Ithaca, NY: Cornell University Press, 1972.

Foucault, Michel. *Discipline and Punish: The Birth of the Prison*. Translated by Alan Sheridan. New York: Vintage, 1995.

Fowler, Alastair. *Kinds of Literature: An Introduction to the Theory of Genres and Modes*. Cambridge, MA: Harvard University Press, 1982.

———. *Renaissance Realism: Narrative Images in Literature and Art*. Oxford: Oxford University Press, 2003.

Fowler, Elizabeth. *Literary Character: The Human Figure in Early English Writing*. Ithaca, NY: Cornell University Press, 2003.

Freud, Sigmund. *The Standard Edition of the Complete Psychological Works of Sigmund Freud.* Edited by James Strachey. 24 vols. London: Hogarth Press, 1953–74.

Fuchs, Barbara. *Romance.* The New Critical Idiom. New York: Routledge, 2004.

Gelley, Alexander, ed. *Unruly Examples: On the Rhetoric of Exemplarity.* Stanford, CA: Stanford University Press, 1995.

Gerrish, B. A. *Continuing the Reformation: Essays on Modern Religious Thought.* Chicago: University of Chicago Press, 1993.

Gilbert, Neil W. *Renaissance Concepts of Method.* New York: Columbia University Press, 1960.

Gless, Darryl J. *Interpretation and Theology in Spenser.* Cambridge: Cambridge University Press, 1994.

Gohlke, Madelon. "Embattled Allegory: Book II of *The Faerie Queene.*" *English Literary Renaissance* 8 (1978): 123–40.

Goldberg, Jonathan. *Writing Matter: From the Hands of the English Renaissance.* Stanford, CA: Stanford University Press, 1990.

Grafton, Anthony, and Lisa Jardine. *From Humanism to the Humanities.* Cambridge, MA: Harvard University Press, 1986.

———. "'Studied for Action': How Gabriel Harvey Read His Livy." *Past and Present* 129 (1990): 30–78.

Green, Ian. *The Christian's ABC: Catechism and Catechizing in England c. 1530–1740.* Oxford: Clarendon Press, 1996.

Green, Lawrence D. "*Grammatica Movet*: Renaissance Grammar Books and *Elocutio.*" In *Rhetorica Movet: Studies in Historical and Modern Rhetoric in Honor of Heinrich F. Plett,* edited by Peter L. Osterreich and Thomas O. Sloane, 73–115. Leiden: Brill, 1999.

Greenblatt, Stephen J. *Renaissance Self-Fashioning: From More to Shakespeare.* Chicago: University of Chicago Press, 1980.

———. "Sidney's *Arcadia* and the Mixed Mode." *Studies in Philology* 70 (1973): 269–78.

Greene, Thomas M. *The Light in Troy: Imitation and Discovery in Renaissance Poetry.* New Haven, CT: Yale University Press, 1982.

———. *The Vulnerable Text.* New York: Columbia University Press, 1986.

Gross, Kenneth. *Shakespeare's Noise.* Chicago: University of Chicago Press, 2001.

———. *Spenserian Poetics: Idolatry, Iconoclasm, and Magic.* Ithaca, NY: Cornell University Press, 1985.

Guillory, John. *Poetic Authority: Spenser, Milton, and Literary History.* New York: Columbia University Press, 1983.

Gundersheimer, Werner L. "Renaissance Concepts of Shame and Pocaterra's *Dialoghi Della Vergogna.*" *Renaissance Quarterly* 47.1 (1994): 34–56.

Hadfield, Andrew, ed. *The Cambridge Companion to Spenser.* Cambridge: Cambridge University Press, 2001.

Hager, Alan. *Dazzling Images: The Masks of Sir Philip Sidney.* Newark: University of Delaware Press, 1991.

———. "Rhomboid Logic: Anti-Idealism and a Cure for Recusancy in Sidney's *Lady of May.*" *ELH* 57.3 (1990): 485–502.

Halpern, Richard. *The Poetics of Primitive Accumulation: English Renaissance Culture and the Genealogy of Capital.* Ithaca, NY: Cornell University Press, 1991.

Hamilton, A. C. *Sir Philip Sidney: A Study of His Life and Works.* Cambridge: Cambridge University Press, 1977.

———, ed. *The Spenser Encyclopedia.* Toronto: University of Toronto Press, 1990.

Hampton, Timothy. *Writing from History: The Rhetoric of Exemplarity in Renaissance Literature.* Ithaca, NY: Cornell University Press, 1990.

Hanson, Elizabeth. "Torture and Truth in Renaissance England." *Representations* 34 (1991): 53–84.

Hartman, Geoffrey. "Milton's Counterplot." *ELH* 25.1 (1958): 1–12.

Hazlitt, William. *The Complete Works of William Hazlitt.* Edited by P. P. Howe. 21 vols. London: J. M. Dent, 1930.

Helgerson, Richard. *The Elizabethan Prodigals.* Berkeley: University of California Press, 1976.

Henderson, Judith Rice. "Euphues and His Erasmus." *English Literary Renaissance* 12.2 (1982): 135–61.

Heninger, S. K. *Sidney and Spenser: The Poet as Maker.* University Park: Pennsylvania State University Press, 1989.

Hexter, J. H. "The Education of the Aristocracy in the Renaissance." In *Reappraisals in History.* New York: Harper and Row, 1961.

Hill, Christopher. *The Century of Revolution, 1603–1714.* Edinburgh: T. Nelson, 1961.

Hinton, Stan. "The Poet and His Narrator: Spenser's Epic Voice." *ELH* 41.2 (1974): 165–81.

Howell, Wilbur S. *Logic and Rhetoric in England, 1500–1700.* Princeton, NJ: Princeton University Press, 1956.

Hoxby, Blair. "The Meaning of Dance: Milton and the Stuart Masque." *English Literary Renaissance* 37 (forthcoming in 2007).

Hunter, G. K. *John Lyly: The Humanist as Courtier.* London: Routledge and Kegan Paul, 1962.

Jardine, Lisa. "Gabriel Harvey: Exemplary Ramist and Pragmatic Humanist." *Revue des Sciences Philosophiques et Théologiques* 70 (1986): 36–48.

———. "The Place of Dialectic Teaching in Sixteenth-Century Cambridge." *Studies in the Renaissance* 21 (1974): 31–62.

Javitch, Daniel. *Poetry and Courtliness in Renaissance England.* Princeton, NJ: Princeton University Press, 1978.

Jay, Martin. *Cultural Semantics: Keywords of Our Time.* Amherst: University of Massachusetts Press, 1998.

———. *Songs of Experience: Modern American and European Variations on a Universal Theme.* Berkeley: University of California Press, 2005.

Jeanneret, Michelle. "The Vagaries of Exemplarity: Distortion or Dismissal?" *Journal of the History of Ideas* 59.4 (1998): 565–79.

Jones, Richard F. *The Triumph of the English Language: A Survey of Opinions Concerning the Vernacular from the Introduction of Printing to the Restoration.* Stanford, CA: Stanford University Press, 1953.

Kahn, Victoria A. "Humanism and the Resistance to Theory." In *Rhetoric and Hermeneutics in Our Time: A Reader,* edited by Walter Jost and Michael Hyde, 149–70. New Haven, CT: Yale University Press, 1997.

———. *Rhetoric, Prudence, and Skepticism in the Renaissance.* Ithaca, NY: Cornell University Press, 1985.

Kay, Margaret M. A. *The History of Rivington and Blackrod Grammar School.* Manchester: Manchester University Press, 1966.

Kermode, Frank. *The Sense of an Ending: Studies in the Theory of Fiction.* New York: Oxford University Press, 1967.

Kezar, Dennis. *Guilty Creatures: Renaissance Poetry and the Ethics of Authorship*. Oxford and New York: Oxford University Press, 2001.

Kilgour, Maggie. "*Comus*'s Wood of Allusion." *University of Toronto Quarterly* 61.3 (1992): 316–33.

Kimbrough, Robert, and Philip Murphy. "The Helmingham Hall Manuscript of Sidney's *The Lady of May*: A Commentary and Transcription." *Renaissance Drama* 1 (1968): 103–19.

King, Andrew. *The Faerie Queene and Middle English Romance: The Matter of Just Memory*. Oxford: Clarendon, 2000.

King, John N. *Spenser's Poetry and the Reformation Tradition*. Princeton, NJ: Princeton University Press, 1990.

Kinney, Arthur F. *Humanist Poetics: Thought, Rhetoric, and Fiction in Sixteenth-Century England*. Amherst: University of Massachusetts Press, 1986.

Kinney, Clare R. "On the Margins of Romance, at the Heart of the Matter: Revisionary Fabulation in Sidney's *New Arcadia*." *Journal of Narrative Technique* 21.2 (1991): 143–52.

———. "The Masks of Love: Desire and Metamorphosis in Sidney's *New Arcadia*." *Criticism* 33.4 (1991): 461–90.

Kintgen, Eugene R. *Reading in Tudor England*. Pittsburgh: University of Pittsburgh Press, 1996.

Knalfa, Louis A. "Ramism and the English Renaissance." In *Science, Technology, and Culture in Historical Perspective*, edited by Louis A. Knalfa, Martin S. Staum, and T. H. E. Travers, 26–50. Calgary: University of Calgary Press, 1976.

Krier, Theresa M. "'All suddeinly sbasht she chaunged hew': Abashedness in *the Faerie Queene*." *Modern Philology* 84.2 (1986): 130–43.

———. *Gazing on Secret Sights: Spenser, Classical Imitation, and the Decorums of Vision*. Ithaca, NY: Cornell University Press, 1990.

Kristeller, Paul Oskar. *Renaissance Thought: The Classic, Scholastic, and Humanistic Strains*. New York: Harper, 1961.

Lane, Robert. *Shepheards Devises: Edmund Spenser's Shepheardes Calender and the Institutions of Elizabethan Society*. Athens: University of Georgia Press, 1993.

Langer, Ullrich. "The Renaissance Novella as Justice." *Renaissance Quarterly* 52.2 (1999): 311–41.

Lanham, Richard A. *A Handlist of Rhetorical Terms*. 2nd ed. Berkeley: University of California Press, 1991.

———. *The Motives of Eloquence: Literary Rhetoric in the Renaissance*. New Haven, CT: Yale University Press, 1976.

Lechner, Joan Marie. *Renaissance Concepts of the Commonplaces*. New York: Pageant Press, 1962.

Lees-Jeffries, Hester. "From the Fountain to the Well: Redcrosse Learns to Read." *Studies in Philology* 100.2 (2003): 135–76.

Lewalski, Barbara K. *The Life of John Milton: A Critical Biography*. Oxford: Blackwell, 2000.

———. "Milton and the Hartlib Circle: Educational Projects and Epic *Paideia*." In *Literary Milton: Text, Pretext, Context*, edited by David Treviño Benet and Michael Lieb, 202–19. Pittsburgh: Duquesne University Press, 1994.

———. *Protestant Poetics and the Seventeenth-Century Religious Lyric*. Princeton, NJ: Princeton University Press, 1979.

Lewis, C. S. *The Allegory of Love: A Study in Medieval Tradition*. London: Oxford University Press, 1938.

———. *English Literature in the Sixteenth Century, Excluding Drama*. Oxford: Oxford University Press, [1954] 1973.

Lindheim, Nancy. *The Structures of Sidney's Arcadia*. Toronto: University of Toronto Press, 1982.

Loeffelholz, Mary. "Two Masques of Ceres and Proserpine: *Comus* and *The Tempest*." In *Re-Membering Milton*, edited by Mary Nyquist and Margaret W. Ferguson, 25–42. New York: Methuen, 1987.

Lucas, Caroline. *Writing for Women: The Example of Woman as Reader in Elizabethan Romance*. Philadelphia: Open University Press, 1989.

MacCaffrey, Isabel. *Spenser's Allegory: The Anatomy of Imagination*. Princeton, NJ: Princeton University Press, 1976.

Mack, Peter. *Elizabethan Rhetoric: Theory and Practice*. Cambridge: Cambridge University Press, 2002.

———. "Ramus Reading: The Commentaries on Cicero's *Consular Orations* and Virgil's *Eclogues* and *Georgics*." *Journal of the Warburg and Courtauld Institutes* 61 (1998): 111–41.

———. "Renaissance Habits of Reading." In *Renaissance Essays for Kitty Scoular Datta*, edited by Sukanta Chaudhuri, 1–25. Calcutta: Oxford University Press, 1995.

Major, John M. "*Comus* and *The Tempest*." *Shakespeare Quarterly* 10.2 (1959): 177–83.

Manley, Lawrence. *Convention, 1500–1750*. Cambridge, MA: Harvard University Press, 1980.

Maslen, R. W. *Elizabethan Fictions: Espionage, Counter-Espionage, and the Duplicity of Fiction in Early Elizabethan Prose Narratives*. Oxford: Clarendon Press, 1997.

Maus, Katharine Eisaman. *Inwardness and Theater in the English Renaissance*. Chicago: University of Chicago Press, 1995.

McCabe, Richard A. "Wit, Eloquence, and Wisdom in Euphues: The Anatomy of Wit." *Studies in Philology* 81.3 (1984): 299–325.

McCanles, Michael. *The Text of Sidney's Arcadian World*. Durham, NC: Duke University Press, 1989.

McCoy, Richard C. *Sir Philip Sidney: Rebellion in Arcadia*. New Brunswick, NJ: Rutgers University Press, 1979.

McKeon, Michael. *The Origins of the English Novel, 1600–1740*. Baltimore, MD: Johns Hopkins University Press, 1987.

———. *Theory of the Novel: A Historical Approach*. Baltimore, MD: Johns Hopkins University Press, 2000.

Meerhof, Kees. "'Beauty and the Beast': Nature, Logic and Literature in Ramus." In *The Influence of Petrus Ramus: Studies in Sixteenth and Seventeenth Century Philosophy and Sciences*, edited by Mordechai Feingold, Joseph S. Freedman, and Wolfgang Romer, 200–214. Basel: Schwabe, 2001.

Mentz, Steve. "Escaping Italy: From Novella to Romance in Gascoigne and Lyly." *Studies in Philology* 101.2 (2004): 153–71.

———. "The Thigh and the Sword: Gender, Genre, and Sexy Dressing in Sidney's *New Arcadia*." In *Prose Fiction and Early Modern Sexualities in England, 1570–1640*, edited by Constance C. Relihan and Goran V. Stanivukovic, 77–91. New York: Palgrave Macmillan, 2004.

Miller, David L. *The Poem's Two Bodies: The Poetics of the 1590 Faerie Queene*. Princeton, NJ: Princeton University Press, 1988.

Miller, William E. "Double Translation in English Humanist Education." *Studies in the Renaissance* 10 (1963): 163–74.

Montrose, Louis. "Celebration and Insinuation: Sir Philip Sidney and the Motives of Elizabethan Courtship." *Renaissance Drama* 8 (1977): 3–35.

Moss, Ann. *Printed Commonplace-Books and the Structuring of Renaissance Thought*. Oxford: Clarendon Press, 1996.

Mulder, John R. *The Temple of the Mind: Education and Literary Taste in Seventeenth-Century England*. New York: Pegasus, 1969.

Nauert, Charles G., Jr. "Renaissance Humanism: An Emergent Consensus and Its Critics." *Indiana Social Studies Quarterly* 33 (1980): 5–20.

Nichols, Stephen G. "Example vs. *Historia*: Montaigne, Eriugena, and Dante." In *Unruly Examples: On the Rhetoric of Exemplarity*, edited by Alexander Gelley, 48–85. Stanford, CA: Stanford University Press, 1995.

Nohrnberg, James. *The Analogy of the Faerie Queene*. Princeton, NJ: Princeton University Press, 1976.

Norton, Glynn, ed. *The Cambridge History of Literary Criticism: Volume 3, The Renaissance*. Cambridge: Cambridge University Press, 1989.

Oldham, J. Basil. *A History of Shrewsbury School, 1552–1952*. Oxford: B. Blackwell, 1952.

Ong, Walter J., SJ. "Latin Language Study as a Renaissance Puberty Rite." *Studies in Philology* 56.2 (1959): 103–24.

———. *Ramus, Method, and the Decay of Dialogue: From the Art of Discourse to the Art of Reason*. Cambridge, MA: Harvard University Press, 1958.

Orgel, Stephen. "The Case for Comus." *Representations* 81 (2003): 31–45.

———. "Sidney's Experiment in Pastoral: *The Lady of May*." *Journal of the Warburg and Courtauld Institutes* 26 (1964): 198–203.

Orme, Nicholas. *Education and Society in Medieval and Renaissance England*. London: Hambledon Press, 1989.

———. *From Childhood to Chivalry: The Education of the English Kings and Aristocracy, 1066–1530*. London: Methuen, 1984.

Parker, Patricia A. *Inescapable Romance: Studies in the Poetics of a Mode*. Princeton, NJ: Princeton University Press, 1979.

Paster, Gail Kern. *The Body Embarrassed: Drama and the Disciplines of Shame in Early Modern England*. Ithaca, NY: Cornell University Press, 1993.

Patterson, Annabel. *Censorship and Interpretation: The Conditions of Writing and Reading in Early Modern England*. Madison: University of Wisconsin Press, 1984.

Pepper, Robert David. "The Education of Children in Learning (1588) by William Kempe of Plymouth: A Critical Edition." PhD diss., Stanford University, 1963.

Pigman, G. W. "Versions of Imitation in the Renaissance." *Renaissance Quarterly* 33 (1980): 1–32.

Pinker, Steven. *Words and Rules: The Ingredients of Language*. New York: Basic Books, 1999.

Platt, Peter. *Reason Diminished: Shakespeare and the Marvelous*. Lincoln: University of Nebraska Press, 1997.

Prescott, Anne Lake. "Spenser's Chivalric Restoration: From Bateman's *Travayled Pylgrime* to the Redcrosse Knight." *Studies in Philology* 86.2 (1989): 166–97.

Quilligan, Maureen. *Milton's Spenser: The Politics of Reading*. Ithaca, NY: Cornell University Press, 1983.

Riggs, David. *The World of Christopher Marlowe*. London: Faber and Faber, 2004.

Riggs, William G. "Poetry and Method in Milton's 'of Education.'" *Studies in Philology* 89.4 (1992): 445–70.

Robinson, Forrest G. *The Shape of Things Known: Sidney's Apology in Its Philosophical Tradition*. Cambridge, MA: Harvard University Press, 1972.

Roche, Thomas P. "Ending *The New Arcadia*: Virgil and Ariosto." *Sidney Newsletter and Journal* 10.1 (1989): 3–12.

———. *The Kindly Flame: A Study of the Third and Fourth Books of Spenser's Faerie Queene.* Princeton, NJ: Princeton University Press, 1964.

Rose, Mark. *Spenser's Art: A Companion to Book One of the Faerie Queene.* Cambridge, MA: Harvard University Press, 1975.

Ryan, Lawrence V. *Roger Ascham.* Stanford, CA: Stanford University Press, 1963.

Schmitt, Charles B. "Experience and Experiment: A Comparison of Zabarella's View with Galileo's in *De Motu.*" *Studies in the Renaissance* 16 (1969): 80–138.

———, et al. *The Cambridge History of Renaissance Philosophy.* Cambridge and New York: Cambridge University Press, 1987.

Seaton, Ethel. "*Comus* and Shakespeare." *Essays and Studies by Members of the English Association* 31 (1945): 68–80.

Sharpe, J. A. "Civility, Civilising Processes and the End of Public Punishment in England." In *Civil Histories: Essays Presented to Sir Keith Thomas,* edited by Peter Burke, Brian Harrison, and Paul Slack, 215–30. Oxford: Oxford University Press, 2000.

———. *Judicial Punishment in England.* London: Faber and Faber, 1990.

Shuger, Debora. "'Gums of Glutinous Heat' and the Stream of Consciousness: The Theology of Milton's Maske." *Representations* 60 (1997): 1–21.

Sidney, Philip. *The Countess of Pembroke's Arcadia: The Old Arcadia.* Edited by Jean Robertson. Oxford: Clarendon Press, 1973.

Silberman, Lauren. "*The Faerie Queene*, Book II and the Limitations of Temperance." *Modern Language Studies* 17.4 (1987): 9–22.

———. *Transforming Desire: Erotic Knowledge in Books III and IV of* The Faerie Queene. Berkeley: University of California Press, 1995.

Simon, Joan. *Education and Society in Tudor England.* Cambridge: Cambridge University Press, 1966.

Smith, Barbara Herrnstein. *Poetic Closure: A Study of How Poems End.* Chicago: University of Chicago Press, 1968.

Steinberg, Theodore L. "The Anatomy of *Euphues.*" *SEL: Studies in English Literature, 1500–1900* 17 (1977): 27–38.

Stephanson, Raymond. "John Lyly's Prose Fiction: Irony, Humor and Anti-Humanism." *English Literary Renaissance* 11.1 (1981): 3–21.

Stewart, Alan. *Close Readers: Humanism and Sodomy in Early Modern England.* Princeton, NJ: Princeton University Press, 1997.

———. *Philip Sidney: A Double Life.* London: Chatto and Windus, 2000.

Stierle, Karlheinz. "Story as Exemplum—Exemplum as Story: On the Pragmatics and Poetics of Narrative Texts." In *New Perspectives in German Literary Criticism,* edited by Richard E. Amacher and Victor Lange, 389–417. Princeton, NJ: Princeton University Press, 1979.

Stone, Lawrence. *The Crisis of the Aristocracy, 1558–1641.* Oxford: Clarendon Press, 1965.

———. "The Educational Revolution in England, 1560–1640." *Past and Present* 28 (1964): 41–80.

Strauss, Gerald. *Luther's House of Learning: Indoctrination of the Young in the German Reformation.* Baltimore, MD: Johns Hopkins University Press, 1978.

Teskey, Gordon. *Allegory and Violence.* Ithaca, NY: Cornell University Press, 1996.

———. "'And therefore as a stranger give it welcome': Courtesy and Thinking." *Spenser Studies* 18 (2003): 343–59.

Todorov, Tzvetan. *Genres in Discourse.* Cambridge: Cambridge University Press, 1990.

Tonkin, Humphrey. *Spenser's Courteous Pastoral: Book Six of the Faerie Queene*. Oxford: Clarendon Press, 1972.

Warkentin, Germaine. "Sidney's Authors." In *Sir Philip Sidney's Achievements*, edited by M. J. B. Allen,. et al., 68–89. New York: AMS Press, 1990.

Watkins, John. *The Specter of Dido: Spenser and Virgilian Epic*. New Haven, CT: Yale University Press, 1995.

Watson, Foster. *The English Grammar Schools to 1660: Their Curriculum and Practice*. Cambridge: University Press, 1908.

Webster, Charles. *The Great Instauration: Science, Medicine and Reform, 1626–1660*. London: Duckworth, 1975.

Weinberg, Bernard. *A History of Literary Criticism in the Italian Renaissance*. Chicago: University of Chicago Press, 1974.

West, William. *Theatres and Encyclopedias in Early Modern Europe*. Cambridge: Cambridge University Press, 2002.

Williams, Arnold. *The Common Expositor: An Account of the Commentaries on Genesis, 1527–1633*. Chapel Hill: University of North Carolina Press, 1948.

Williams, Kathleen. "Vision and Rhetoric: The Poet's Voice in *The Faerie Queene*." *ELH* 36.1 (1969): 131–44.

Williams, Raymond. *Keywords: A Vocabulary of Culture and Society*. New York: Oxford University Press, 1985.

Wilson, K. J. *Incomplete Fictions: The Formation of English Renaissance Dialogue*. Washington, DC: Catholic University of America Press, 1985.

Wittgenstein, Ludwig. *Philosophical Investigations: The English Text of the Third Edition*. Translated by G. E. M. Anscombe. New York: Macmillan, 1973.

Wofford, Susanne. *The Choice of Achilles*. Stanford, CA: Stanford University Press, 1992.

Wolfe, Jessica. *Humanism, Machinery, and Renaissance Literature*. Cambridge: Cambridge University Press, 2004.

Woodhouse, A. S. P. "Nature and Grace in *the Faerie Queene*." *ELH* 16.3 (1949): 194–228.

Worden, Blair. *The Sound of Virtue: Philip Sidney's Arcadia and Elizabethan Politics*. New Haven, CT: Yale University Press, 1996.